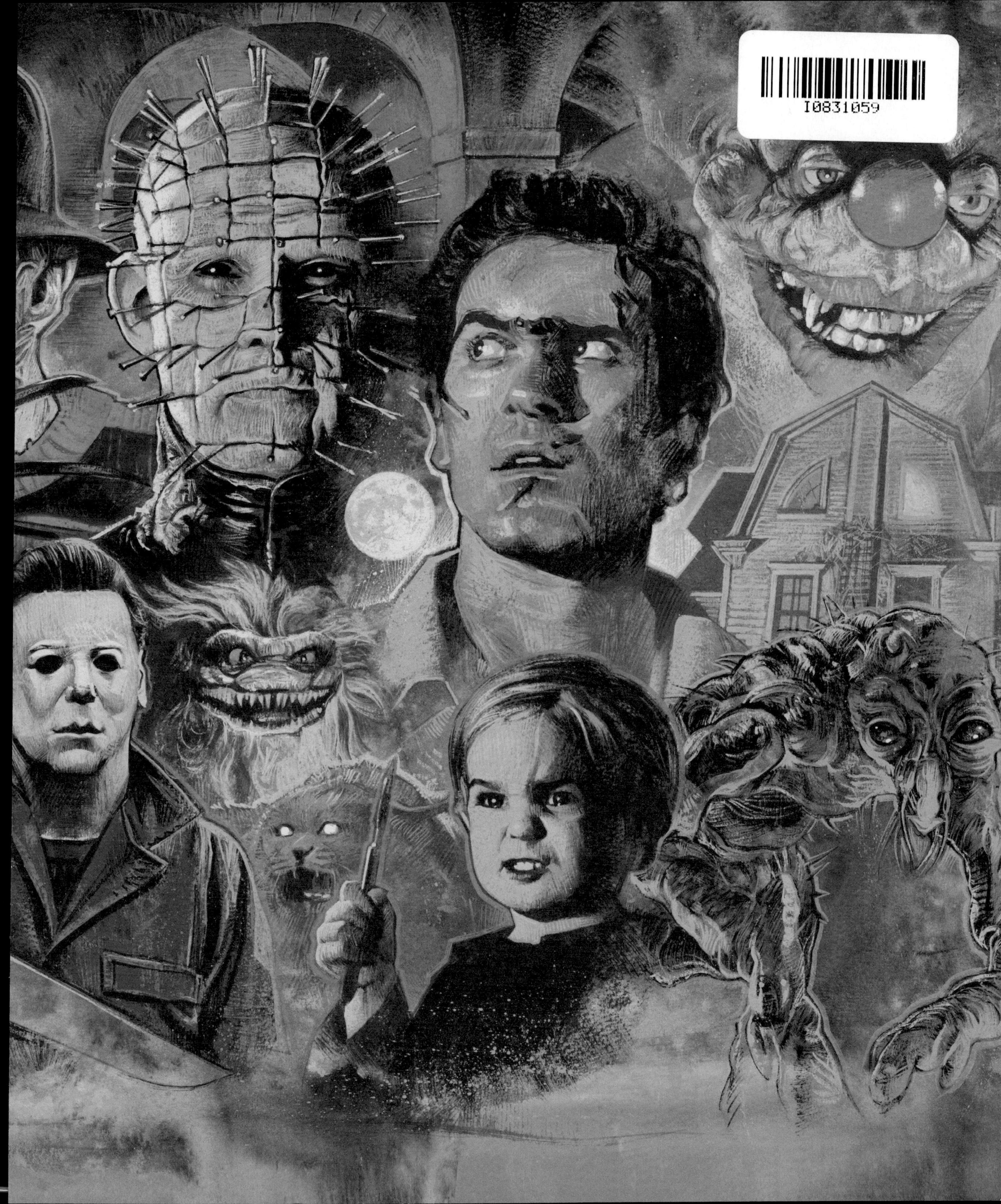
I0831059

CLASSIC MONSTERS MODERN ART

ANTHONY TAYLOR

preface by David Dastmalchian

foreword by Jonathan Maberry

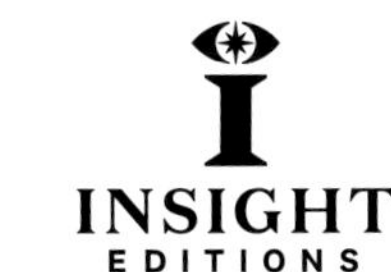

SAN RAFAEL • LOS ANGELES • LONDON

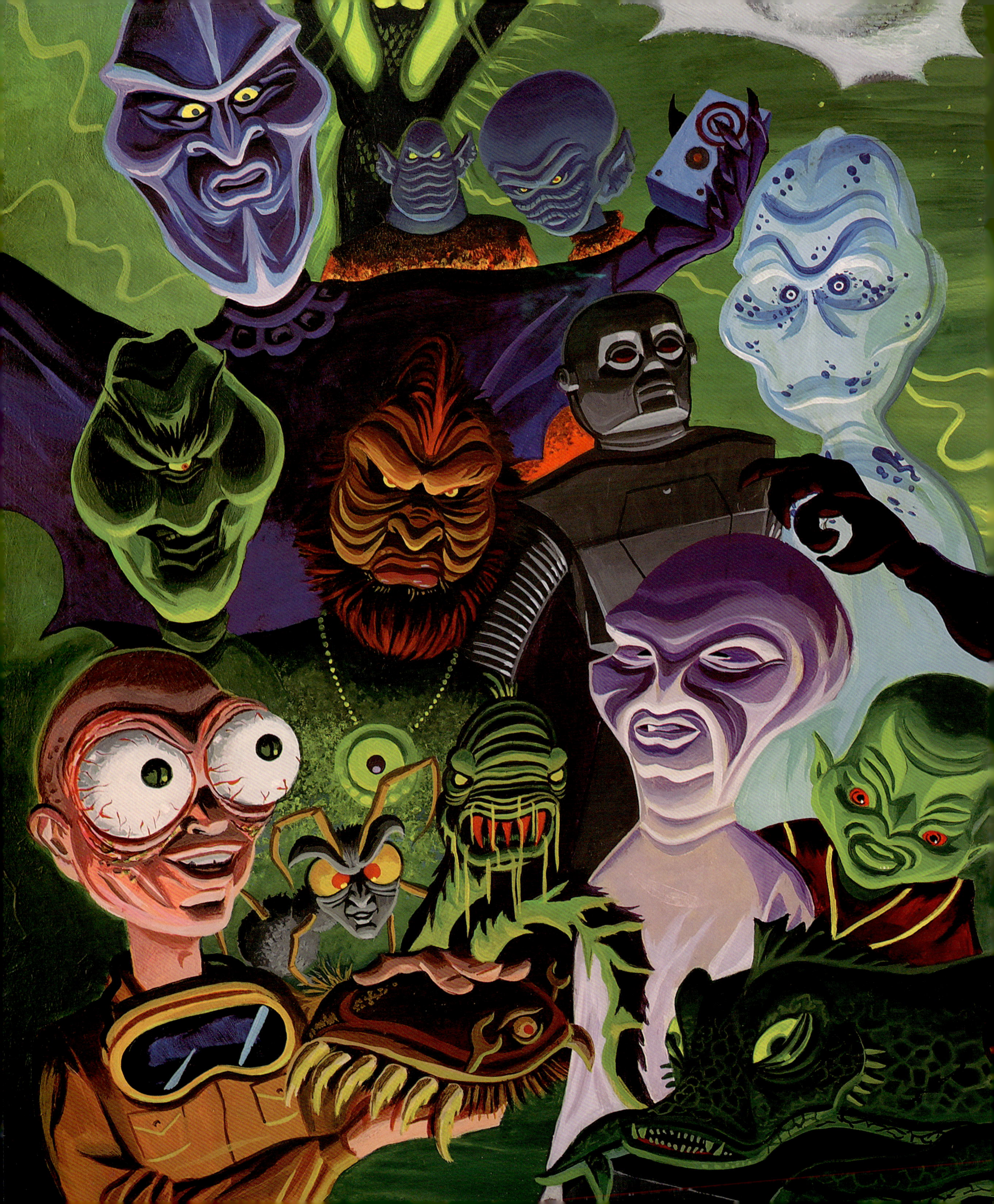

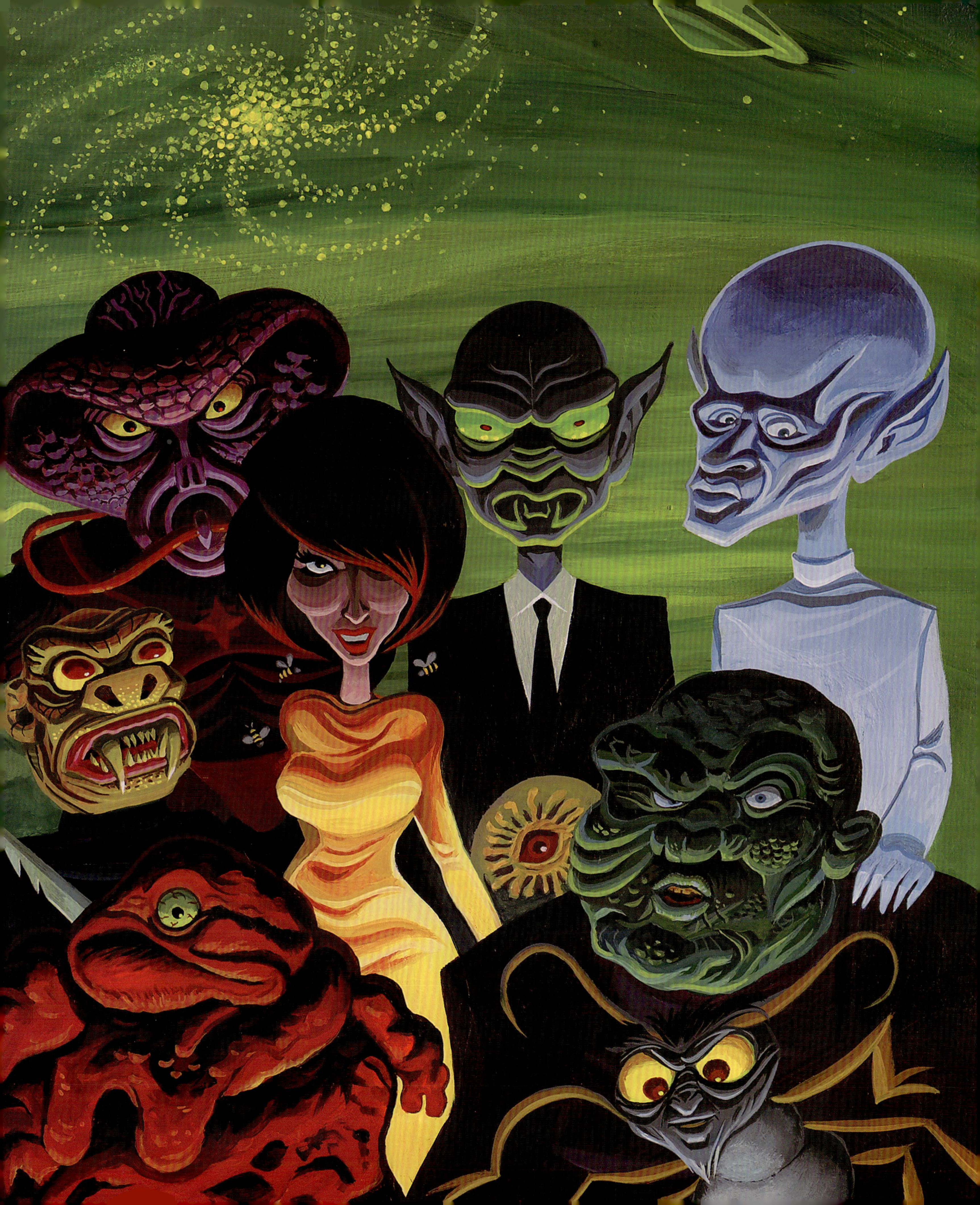

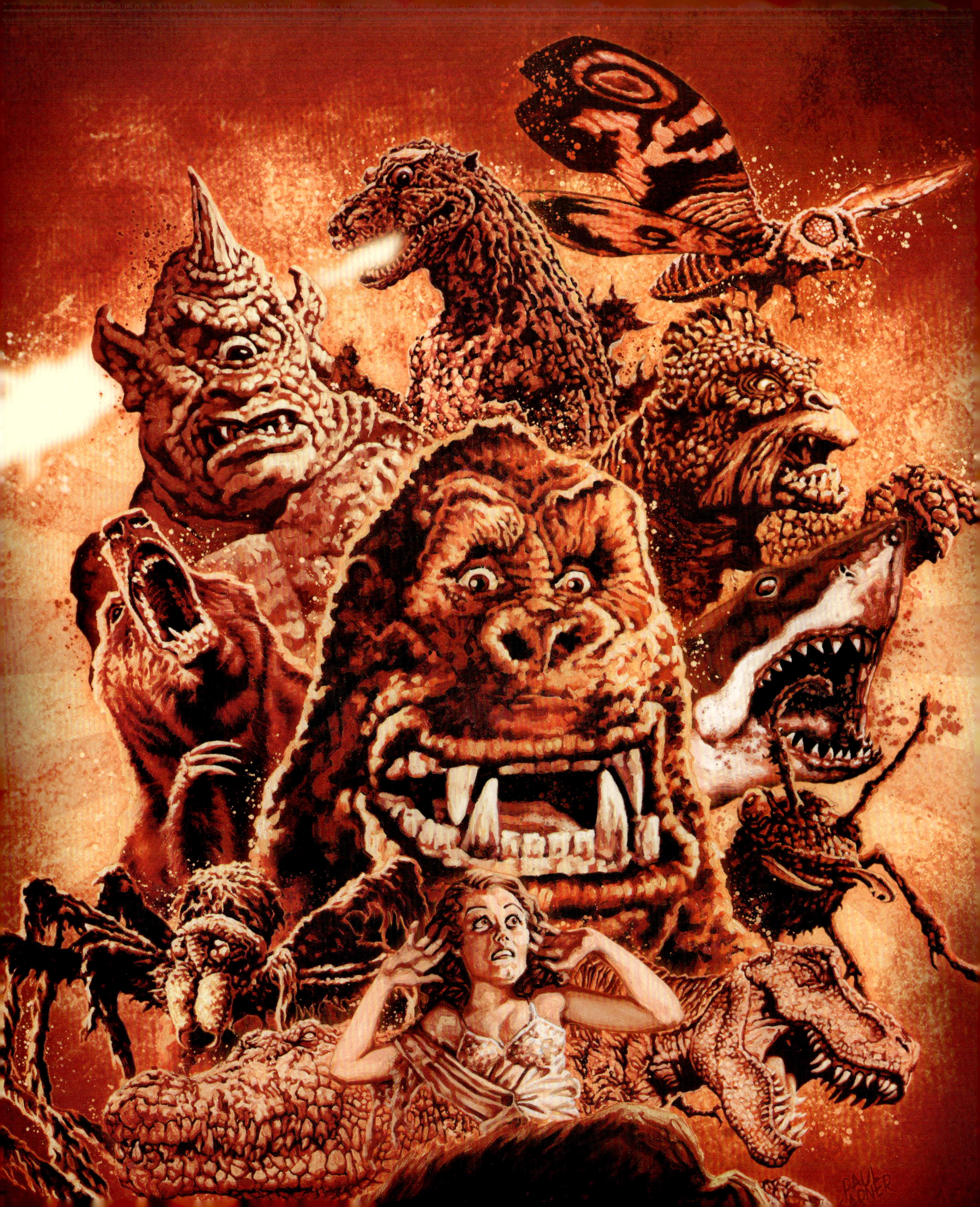

Table of Contents

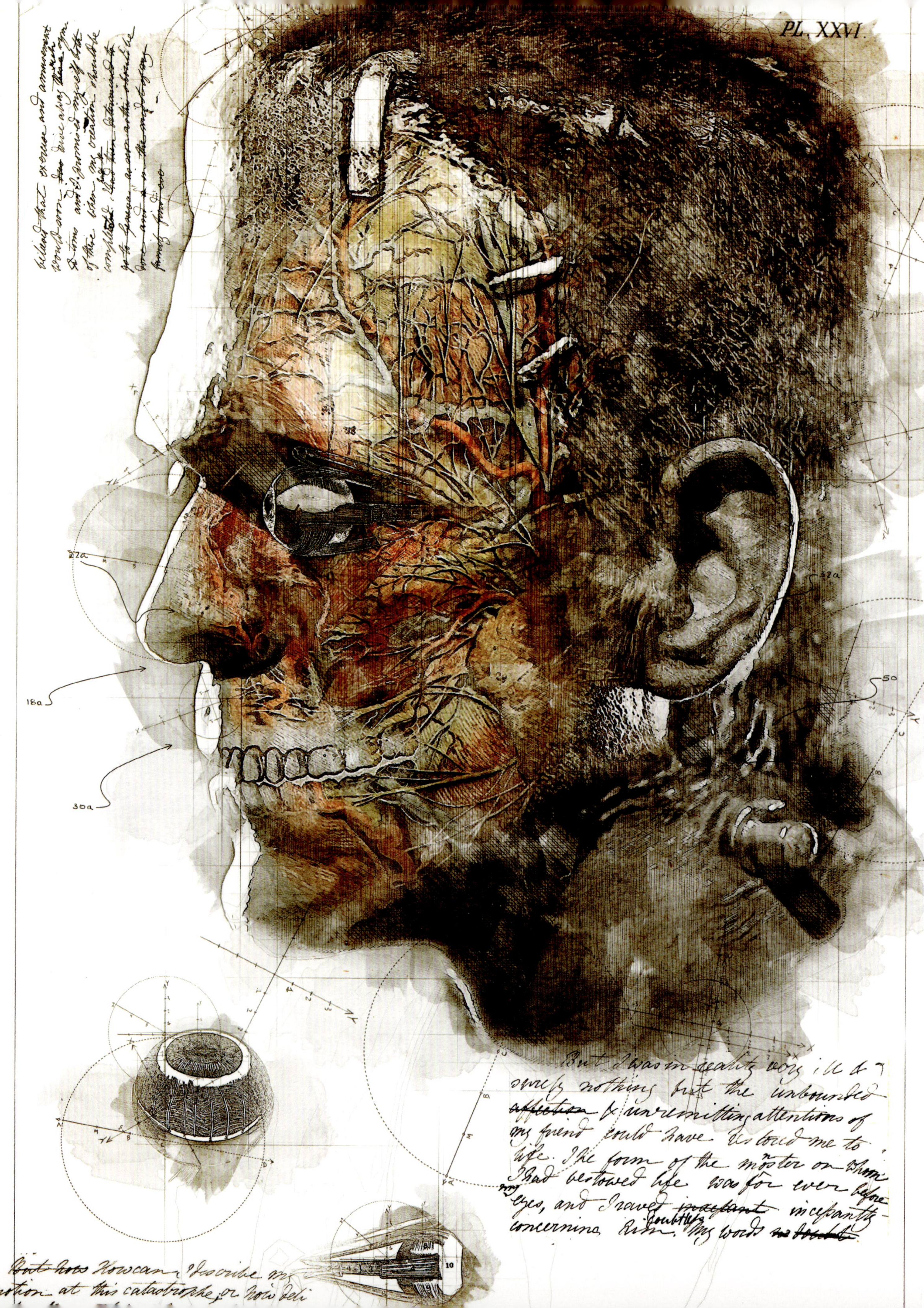
PL. XXVI.
22a
18a
30a
52a
50
10
But I was in reality very ill &
surely nothing but the unbounded
affection & unremitting attentions of
my friend could have restored me to
life. The form of the monster on whom
I had bestowed life was for ever before
my eyes, and I raved incessantly
concerning him. Doubtless my words
How can I describe my
emotion at this catastrophe, or how deli

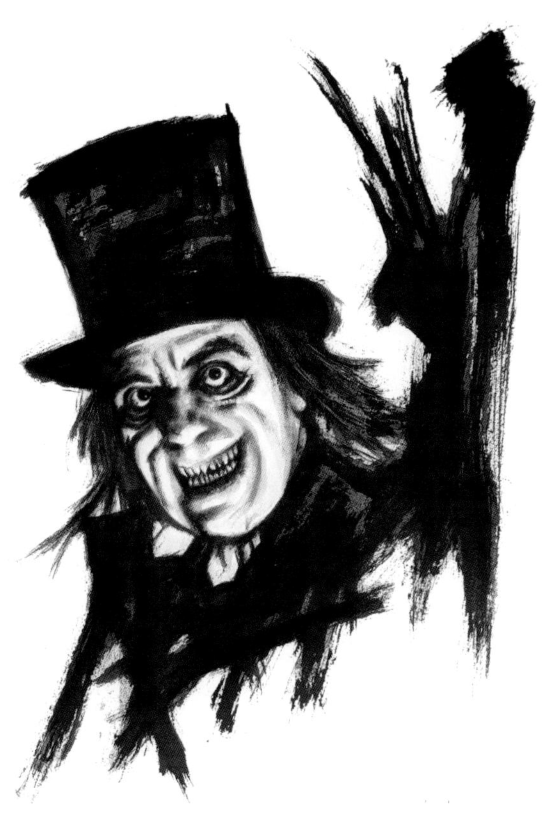

Preface

What was the first horror cinema image that knocked you sideways as a kid?

Did it grab your eyeballs and attention from the flashes of a TV advertisement, an image in a magazine perhaps? Were you, like me, wandering through your local library in search of anything that included the words "monsters" or "horror" in the title? Perhaps you were on a safe family outing to the cinema and happened upon some horrific lobby card framed up near the concession stand? I can't quite put my finger on that very first image, but they were all certainly lasting and haunting impressions that led my little mind into untold and imagined stories. My fear and fascination inspired countless fancied narratives that were all instigated by an image, a poster, an illustration. Art. A single frightening image.

Wandering through the aisles of our local video rental shop back in Kansas was one of the many ways I stumbled upon the key art from classic and contemporary monster movies. I remember the revulsion, dread, and insatiable curiosity I felt as I passed a copy of *The Texas Chainsaw Massacre*, *I Spit on Your Grave*, *The Exorcist*, or *Bordello of Blood* in those rows of plastic VHS boxes. As I turned the pages of a classic horror cinema book at my local library, I recall staring into the face of Frankenstein's monster in a still image from the 1910 Thomas Edison film. That twisted face. That ghastly gasp. I was terrified. And I was hooked.

One of the most significant ways I was introduced to much of my favorite horror cinema imagery was during the weekly broadcast of my local horror host, Crematia Mortem, during the *Friday Night Nightmare Theater* show, which she presented each week in Kansas City back in the 1980s. Crematia would play films from the 1930s all the way through the 1970s, and each time a new movie was introduced I was captivated by the old artwork that had been used to advertise it. Films like *The Black Cat*, *White Zombie*, *The Old Dark House*, and more were represented by an old piece of advertising art that always evoked the tone and intrigue of the coming movie. As time passed, I found myself drawn to that artwork and the ways I could collect it, frame it, and display it, much in the same way another person may be compelled to display a print of their favorite Monet or an old poster from their favorite concert.

As my adoration for the genre expanded, I came to admire the aesthetic of the German masters. All the artwork and imagery inspired by the Expressionists looked and felt like the world of my dreams. Once the bright, vibrant colors of the Italian masters started to appear in my movie books and magazines, I was equally enamored with the astonishing and innovative styles.

PAGES 2–3 *The Outer Limits* by Bob Lizarraga. Cover of *Famous Monsters of Filmland* magazine #261. 2012.

PAGE 4 *Giant Monsters of Filmland* by Paul Garner. Book cover for We Belong Dead Publications. 2020.

ABOVE *Lon Chaney Sr. as the Man in the Beaver Hat from Tod Browning's "London After Midnight"* by Gustavo Rapela. Gouache, 2020.

OPPOSITE *How to Make a Monster—Frankenstein* by Unlovely Frankenstein. Digital, 2020.

BELOW *Late Night with the Devil "TV Guide" Cover* by Unlovely Frankenstein. Digital, 2024.

OPPOSITE *The Bride* by Mike Hoffman. Acrylic on board, 2014.

At a certain point, I found myself afloat in a sea of images and ideas that swam into my consciousness from around the world and across the twentieth century. Similar themes and concepts began to emerge as I studied the work of so many filmmakers who had dedicated themselves to telling tales of monsters—both the "good" and "bad" kinds.

It was in the era of 1950s sci-fi filmmaking and horror expansion that so many of my favorite films went on to inspire the kind of art that captivated both my childhood imagination and the bigger thoughts that were challenged through themes of exploration, xenophobia, mutation, and the consequences of nuclear energy and environmental exploitation. To some, a painting or poster of a mammoth insect or a giant woman is a silly symbol of a bygone era. To others (like me) it's the intersection of pop art expeditions married to psychological and philosophical ideas about humanity's potential and the powers that dominate us. I can stare at these images, stills, paintings, and collages for hours. It's hypnotic and beautiful. It's as innocent and earnest as it appears. And yet it's more subversive and layered than we ever imagined.

All this brings me back to my fondness for the marvelous subculture that is The Horror Host. I hold a kind of reverence for the men and women who adorned their (often) goofy caricatures of horror figures and utilized humor and low-budget scenery to introduce their audience each week to classic horror films. The horror hosts over the past century have been great shepherds for the magnificent fun and entertainment that we seek when watching horror films. They hold no intellectual irony or attempt to employ overanalysis of what makes films like *The Invisible Man*, *The Satanic Rites of Dracula*, or even *Two Thousand Maniacs* so spectacular. They stand before the camera, makeup adorned, costume mildly dry cleaned, and invite us into the magical world of monster movies.

This is what I love the very most about staring at the artwork and advertisements that have come from horror cinema over time. My mind can wander, inspired just as it was when I was a kid, to memories of the film or wonderment over what I've forgotten, what stories lay within the images. Hours and hours I could spend just turning the pages, sipping my coffee, and getting lost in the marvelous imagery that has sprung from so many of the creatures and features that have stolen our hearts. My wish for you is that you may have just such an experience as you crack open these pages and behold what lies within!

David Dastmalchian

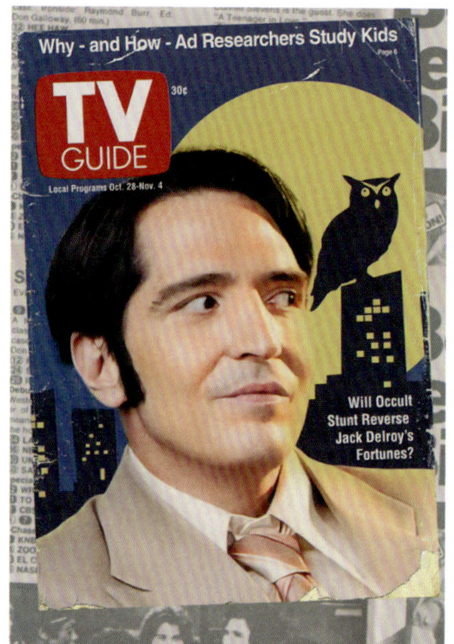

David Dastmalchian is an award-winning actor, writer, and producer who got his big break in Christopher Nolan's *The Dark Knight* (2008) and reunited with the director in 2023's *Oppenheimer*. His indie debut *Animals* (2014) was followed by *All Creatures Here Below* (2018), both starring and written by Dastmalchian. He made his mark in the DC Universe as the iconic Polka-Dot Man in James Gunn's *The Suicide Squad*. He was seen on the big screen as Jack Delroy in IFC's *Late Night with the Devil*, the first feature under his production company, Good Fiend Films. Previous screen credits include *Prisoners*, *Dune: Part One*, all three *Ant-Man* films, *Blade Runner 2049*, *Birdbox*, *Boston Strangler*, *Twin Peaks*, *Gotham*, and *The Flash*. Other appearances include *Dust Bunny* with Mads Mikkelsen and Sigourney Weaver, Mike Flanagan's *The Life of Chuck*, Netflix's live-action adaptation *One Piece*, and Apple TV+'s *Murderbot*. He authors a handful of comic book series, *Count Crowley: Mediocre Midnight Monster Hunter* and *Headless Horseman Annual* (Dark Horse Comics), *Knights vs Samurai* (Image comics), and *Creature Commandos* and *DC Horror Presents: Dollhouse* (DC Comics).

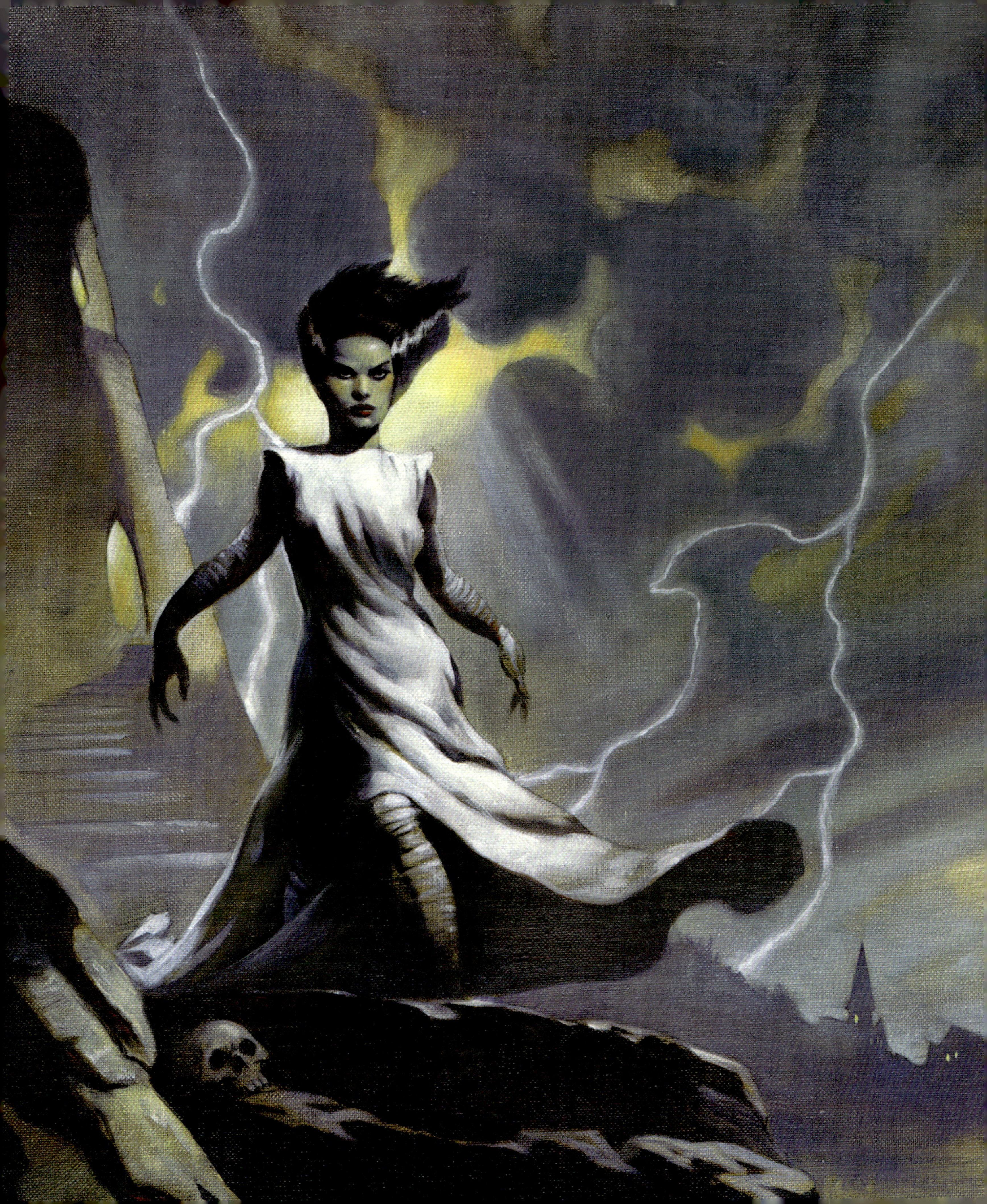

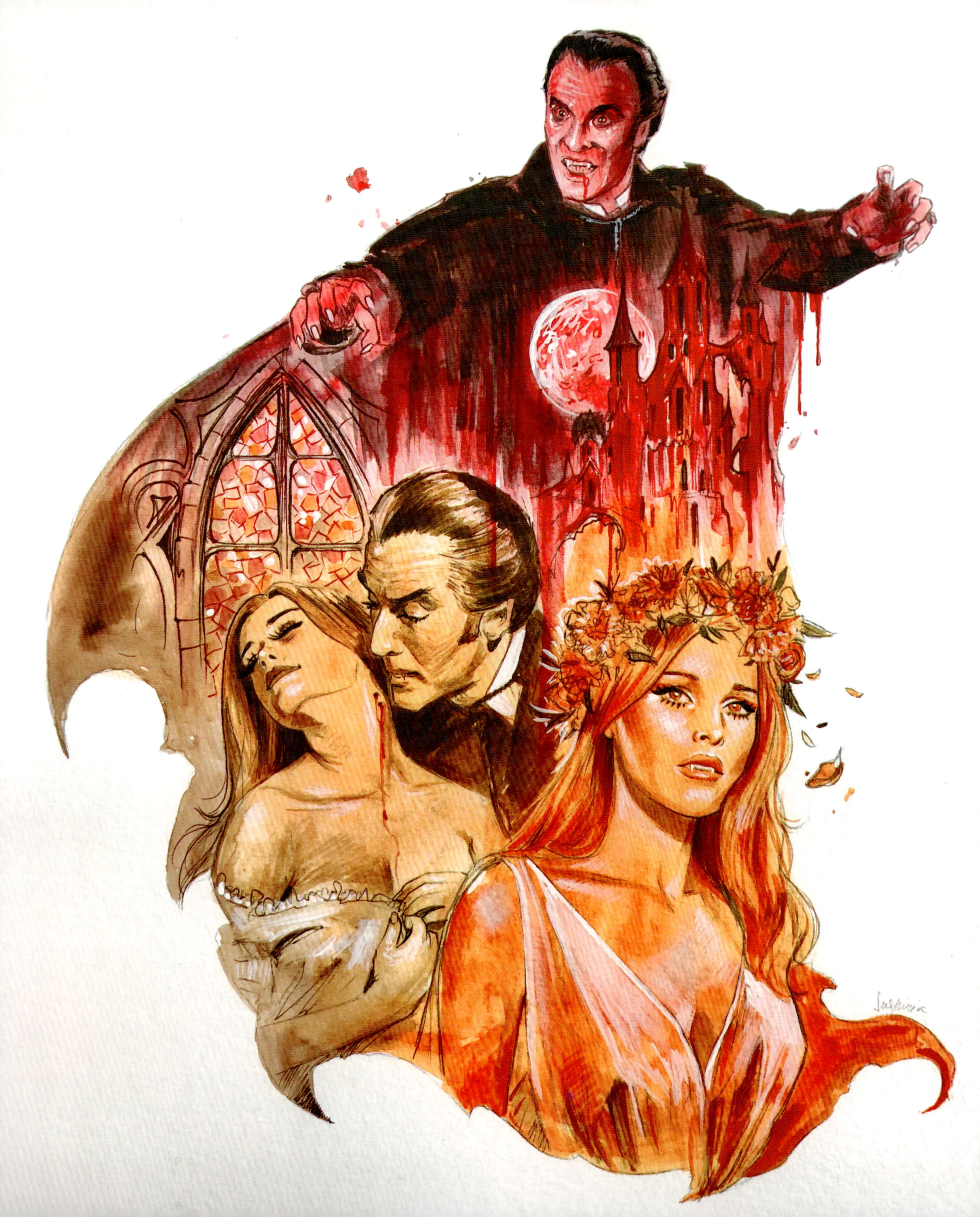

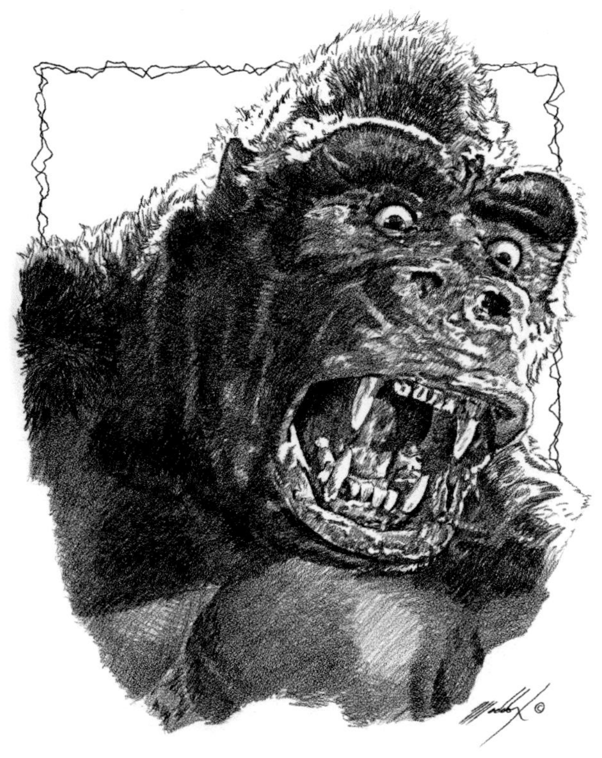

FOREWORD

The Monsters in My Head

One picture is worth a thousand words.

That's true enough, though I often felt it was a gross understatement. Certain kinds of images take root in the mind and grow into all kinds of strange shapes. The things we see in artwork tend to inspire the mind to wonder what happened in the moment before that image was captured by the artist—and what might happen next.

When I was a kid, my first love was comic books—EC mainly—handed down to me by my older brother, who left his childhood behind and went off to Vietnam. Then it was Marvel Comics, which I bought at the staggeringly expensive cover price of twelve cents.

We were poor as dirt and living in the low-income and crime-riddled Kensington neighborhood in Philadelphia. None of my friends read anything not assigned in school, and rarely even that. Few of them liked TV or movies. They mostly watched Roller Derby, or stock car races on TV. That made me different from the crowd. I was considered weird because I read. My teachers frowned with concern because I drew monsters in my school notebooks.

Whenever my parents were out or upstairs asleep, I'd turn on the TV to watch reruns of *The Twilight Zone* or first-run episodes of *The Outer Limits* and *Star Trek*. If my old man was working night shift, I'd sneak downstairs to watch *Double Chiller Theater*. Later, when I was twelve, Dr. Shock debuted, hosting classic monster movies ranging from actual classics like Bela Lugosi's *Dracula* to complete dreck like *The Robot vs. the Aztec Mummy*, *The Killer Shrews*, and *The Manster*. Personally, I loved them all. The only problem was that I was rarely allowed to watch such stuff, and frequently punished when caught.

It was worth it.

Mostly, though, my introduction to Dracula, Frankenstein's monster, King Kong, Gorgo, Godzilla, and all the other magnificent monsters was not through moving images on our little nineteen-inch TV screen. And at the time, I was too young to read any novels that might have been the source material. No. For me, 90 percent of the time, I saw them as static images, in the pages of *Famous Monsters of Filmland*. That was pretty much scripture for a weird little kid like me.

And movie posters. I loved movie posters. And back then—we're talking the 1960s—they still had lobby cards, which ranged between stills from the films and painted exaggerations in which the heroes were more stalwart, the ingenues more curvy, and the monsters far scarier.

We had one movie theater in my neighborhood, the Midway—a massive, reputedly haunted, visibly crumbling art deco monstrosity that began life in the vaudeville era and was later retrofitted as a movie house. For a while I wasn't old enough to enter, so I stood outside in front of the big posters framed on either side of the ticket booth and tried to imagine the story the artwork promised.

My earliest specific memory was in 1966. There was a double bill of *Queen of Outer Space* and *Dracula: Prince of Darkness*. Even if I could have afforded the tickets, I was eight and they wouldn't let me buy one.

OPPOSITE *Hammer Dracula Montage* by Susana "Suspiria" Vilchez. Acrylic, 2021.

ABOVE *Kong* by Mark Maddox. Colored pencil on coquille board, 2020.

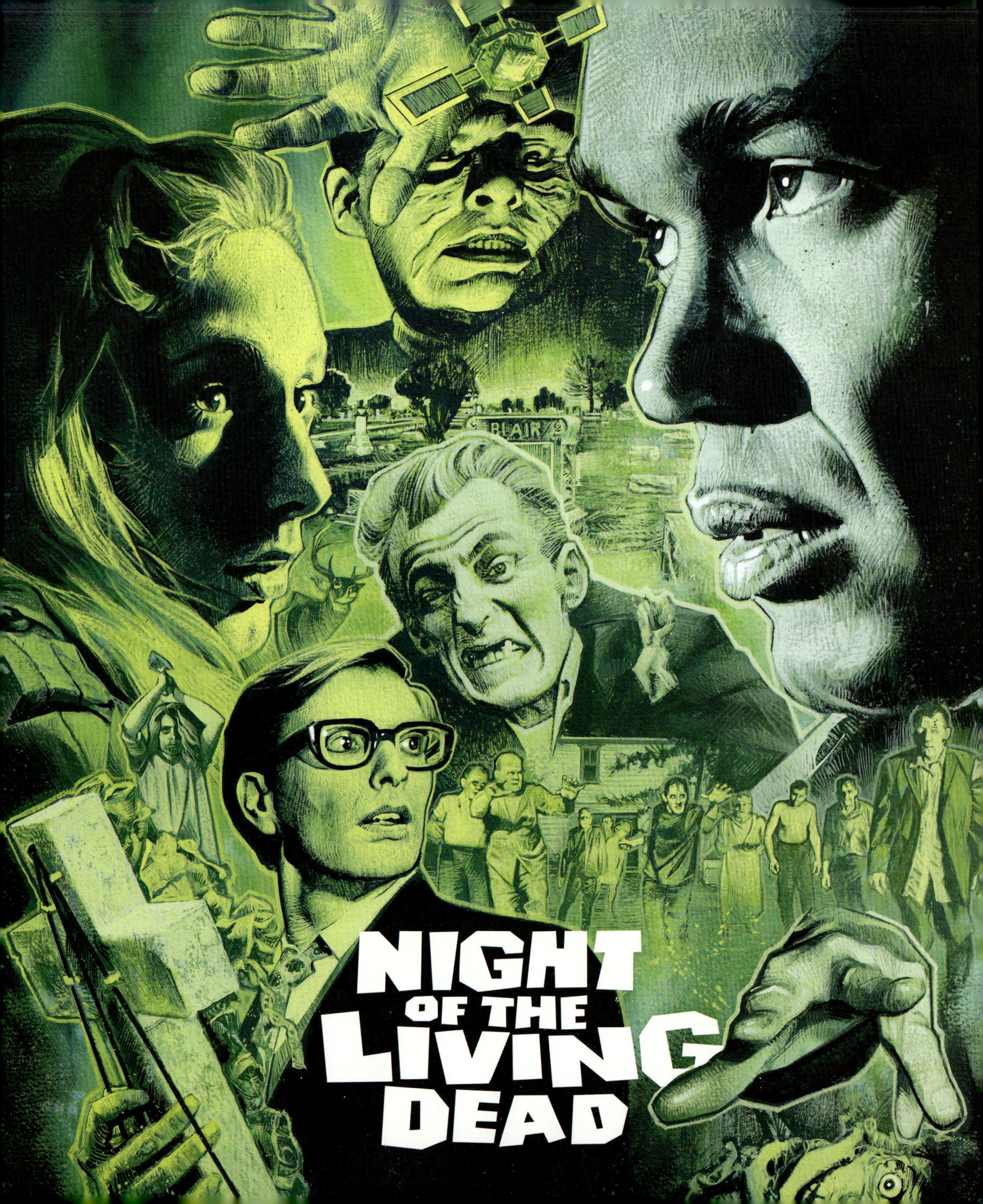
BLAIR
NIGHT
OF THE
LIVING
DEAD

Over the following weeks, they played relatively new films like *Island of Terror*, *The Deadly Bees*, *The Diabolical Dr. Z*, *Billy the Kid vs. Dracula*, *The She Beast*, *The Reptile*, *The Navy vs. the Night Monsters*, and *Manos: The Hands of Fate*. Most of these—I later learned—were not exactly cornerstones of any temple to cinematic excellence. But those posters!

I was there every Saturday when the films changed. They ran adult stuff—grown-up, I mean, not porn—during the week, but on weekends they shifted to what I suppose was intended as "date films." Always two horror or science fiction films, always with dynamic or lurid posters. As soon as my Saturday chores were done, I'd haul my butt down to the Midway to see that week's posters.

In 1968, a few months after my tenth birthday, I was stopped in my tracks by the poster for a brand-new movie that was set to debut at the beginning of October. The tagline screamed "More Terrifying Than Hitchcock's *Psycho*." I had not yet seen *Psycho*, but I knew how it had traumatized my older sister. The movie that poster advertised was *Night of the Living Dead*, and the poster was a collage of images—likely painted over photographs, mostly of people screaming, brandishing weapons, eating what looked like a beef bone (not so, I later found out)—and a naked woman with an overlapping image covering the naughty bits. The poster text claimed that the monsters—whatever they were—feasted on human flesh.

I was intrigued.

I was also scared.

And I was determined to see this one. That poster? Yeah, it didn't just feed my imagination, it made a feast of speculation.

So, being a poor kid with maybe a thin veneer of the criminality that defined my neighborhood, I snuck in the back door. An older teen had bragged about how easy that was, and my best friend and I tried it. We got in easily and hid in the balcony—which, no joke, was officially condemned as unsafe. We brought our own sodas and candy and hunkered down to see if the movie could live up to the promise of that art.

My friend bagged out about halfway through, and had bed-wetting issues well into his twenties. Not joking about that, either.

I stayed to see it twice.

That movie poster—an original that was later signed by the film's director, George Romero, and most of the cast—hangs in my office. George became a friend and collaborator, and I'm still friends with Judith O'Dea, who played Barbra.

The following week, the Midway ran a Saturday double feature of two movies that are, inarguably, classics: *Godzilla, King of the Monsters!* and *Creature from the Black Lagoon*.

The week after that it was *The Bride of Frankenstein* and *King Kong*.

I later learned that the new projectionist at the Midway—who also chose the movies—was a film student at Temple University, and an absolute nut for monster and sci-fi flicks. She switched the vibe from cheap old Z-rated movies to the good stuff. Around that same time, I had a growth spurt so that at eleven I looked like I was sixteen. Hell, I had a beard by the time I was thirteen. And I picked up a bunch of part-time jobs. This gave me movie money—tickets were thirty-five cents at the time—and I dropped most of that coin at the theater.

I even made friends with the projectionist, and she often gave me lobby cards and posters. I papered my room with them. Lots of RKO and early Universal stuff. Then Hammer films, complete with bright red blood and heaving bosoms. (Remember, I was going through puberty at the time.) Sometimes, my projectionist friend would give me posters from first-run films like *Fantastic Voyage*, *Planet of the Apes*, *Phantom of the Paradise*, *Barbarella*, *The Time Machine*, *Young Frankenstein*, *The Abominable Dr. Phibes*, and so many others.

This was pure gold for someone who wanted to become a writer. I would look at those posters, and at the art and stills from *Famous Monsters* magazine, and then write stories that expanded the implied stories. It was fan fiction before "fan fiction" was even a phrase.

My love of the art of horror and science fiction never diminished. In fact, it expanded as my understanding of those genres grew and deepened. At twelve, my middle school librarian literally introduced me to some of the kings of the fantastic. She served as a kind of secretary for two groups of professional authors. One group was the Hyborian Legion, which met in Philly and focused on sword-and-sorcery fiction. L. Sprague de Camp was a member, and he later became a mentor and lifelong friend. He introduced me to the fantastic artwork of Roy G. Krenkel and Frank Frazetta. At the time, Frazetta was doing horror covers for *Eerie* and *Creepy* magazines, the 1960s and '70s reincarnation of what EC had been decades before. The other group she took me to was in New York and was really more of a semiregular cocktail party and networking event where a publisher invited genre writers to hang out. Up there,

OPPOSITE *Night of the Living Dead* by Graham Humphreys. Mondo movie poster design. Mixed media, 2020.

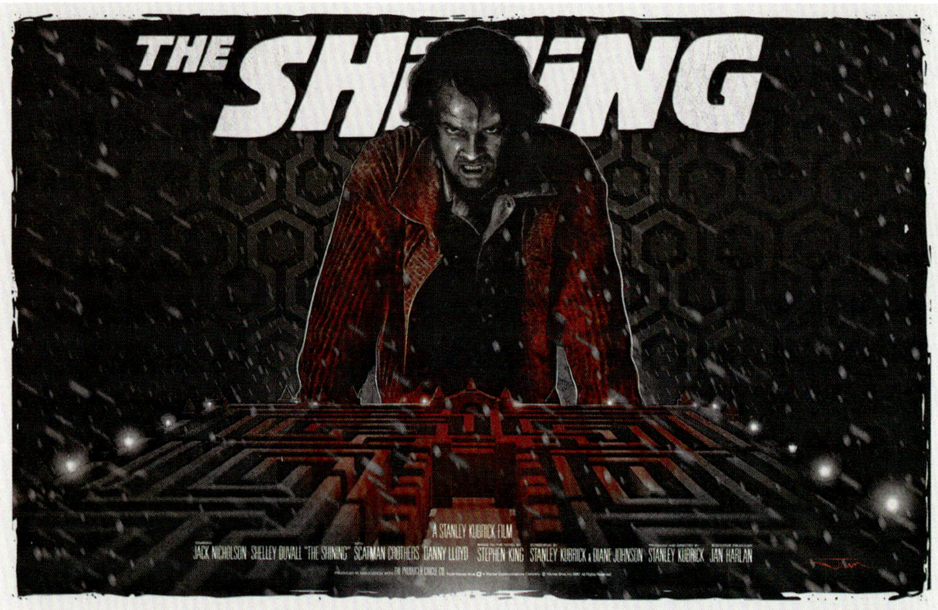

I met Ray Bradbury, Richard Matheson, Robert Bloch, Harlan Ellison, and others.

Yes. There I was, a poor kid from a bad neighborhood, talking with—and being mentored by—the giants of fantastic fiction. More than that, they each had TV shows or movies adapted from their works. I had posters for Matheson's *The Incredible Shrinking Man*, *The Last Man on Earth*—the first adaptation of his novel *I Am Legend*—and Bloch's *Psycho* (yes, I got around to seeing it), and more. And I had promotional posters from TV episodes like "Soldier" from *The Outer Limits* and "The City on the Edge of Forever" from classic *Star Trek*, both written by Ellison.

The publisher's penthouse was decorated with framed book covers—*Fahrenheit 451*, among others—and posters for movies based on books he had published. Sometimes, Bradbury and Matheson would bring me shopping bags filled with novels and other books, including some amazing books that collected movie poster art.

There was also a great horror TV show in the '70s called *Night Gallery*, hosted by Rod Serling, where a piece of artwork—classic or created for the episode—would be used to set the tone for a vignette.

I still collect art from movies, both classics and new ones. I have signed collections of artwork by Frank Frazetta. I have several high-quality books of movie posters.

But not all the art I collect, either to frame or in bound form, consists of images from years past. I've also been building a library of new artwork in which contemporary artists reimagine those classic monsters. Books like this one. New takes on Frankenstein's monster, the Wolf Man, Godzilla, the Creature, the Blob, and countless others. And I sometimes hire those artists to do covers for anthologies I edit, or for the cover of *Weird Tales* magazine, which I also edit.

Quite often, it is a piece of artwork that inspires me to write a story, poem, or novel. As someone who also works in comics, I get to work directly with artists, and, more often than not, we share a love of artistic interpretations of classic monsters.

One bit of fun trivia: Back in the days of pulp magazines, editors often contracted artwork for covers and *then* hired writers to build a story based on it. Many, many cover stories for *Thrilling Wonder Stories*, *Startling Stories*, *Argosy*, and the rest began as artwork, conjured by the sorcery of an artist looking beyond the obvious and beholding the amazing. Because of this, I recently began a new section in *Weird Tales* I call "Nightmare Gallery," in which I obtain a piece of new fantastical artwork and pick a writer to write a new tale based upon it.

Monsters should be seen. Monsters, no matter how familiar, can become fresh and new when any given artist infuses a rendering with their own imagination, their own unique interpretation. Their own magic.

It is a delight—both for the middle-aged man I am and the ten-year-old kid living inside my head—that new artists bring their talents to the task of reimagining those creatures who were better friends to me than my family or neighborhood kids. These new works of art showcase the evolution of fantastic horror, and that gives me both comfort and hope. Every single time I see a new painting or sketch of a classic monster, or a classically rendered painting of a new monster, it excites me. It galvanizes my imagination and makes me want to tell a new tale that contributes to each creature's legacy.

This book has its own kind of magic.

Apart from presenting new works of science fiction, fantasy, and horror artwork that draw on classic influences, it's also a deep dive into the history of this kind of storytelling. Anthony Taylor shares many fascinating bits of film and literary history that provide both context and insight. He brings a scholar's chops to pop culture, and makes it fun to read. It's impossible to get through any chapter without checking to see which streaming service has any given movie he references. My own to-watch list pretty much quadrupled while reading this book.

The artists whose work appears here are the modern masters of the strange and bizarre. Each has a unique

ABOVE *The Shining* by Juan Ramos. Movie poster design. Colored pencils and digital, 2020.

OPPOSITE *Creature Sexy Monster* by Erika Deoudes. Ink and watercolor, 2014.

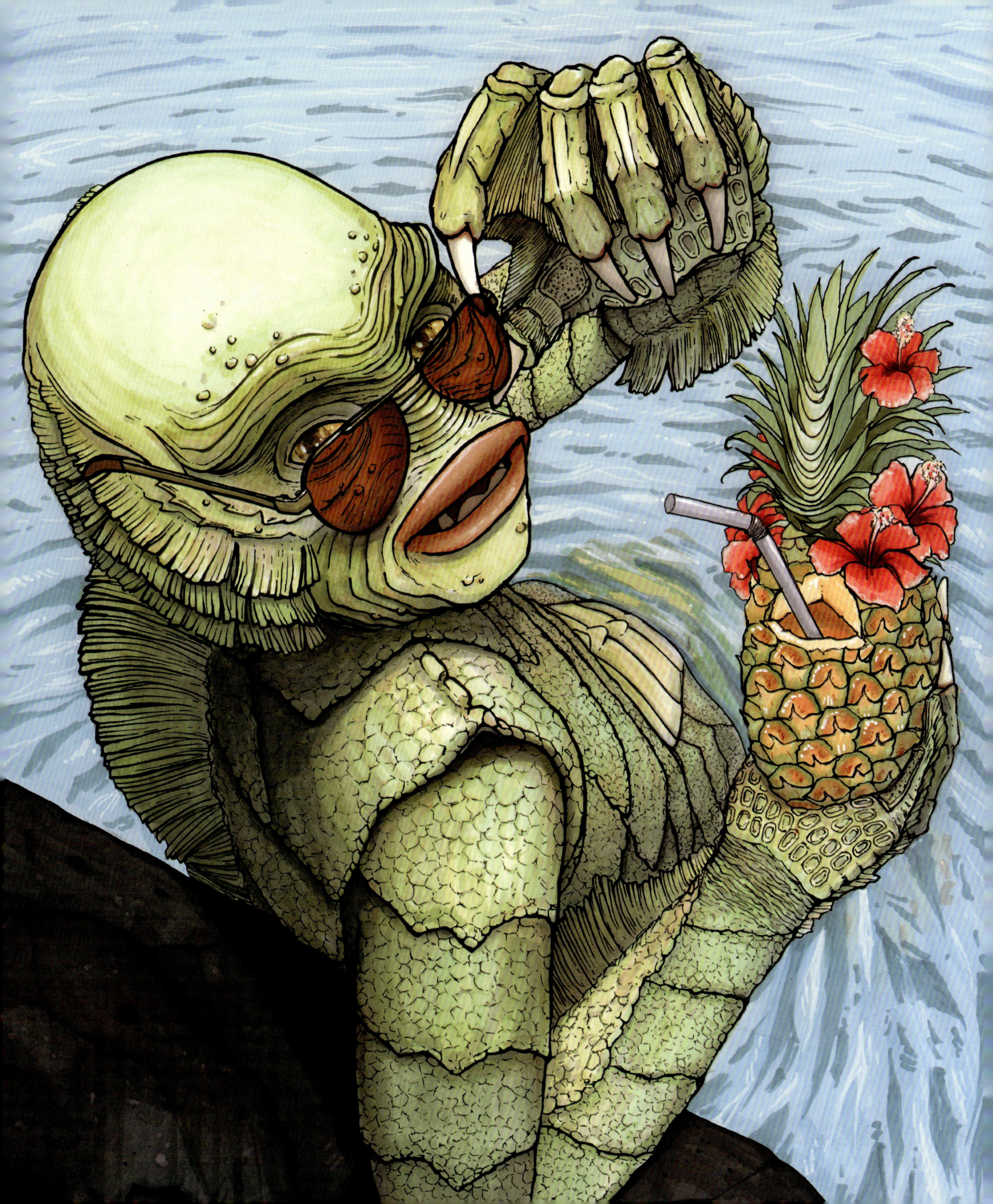

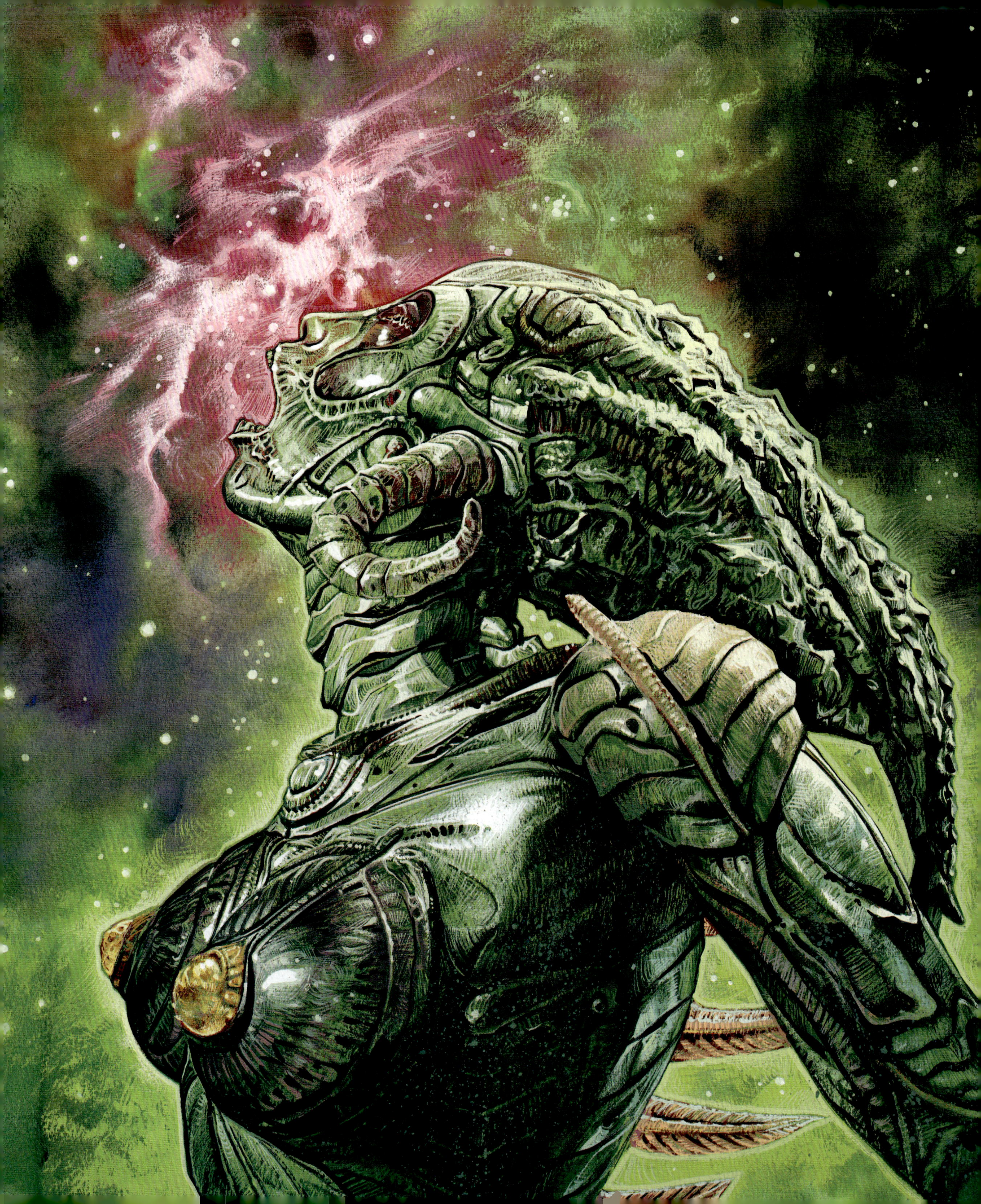

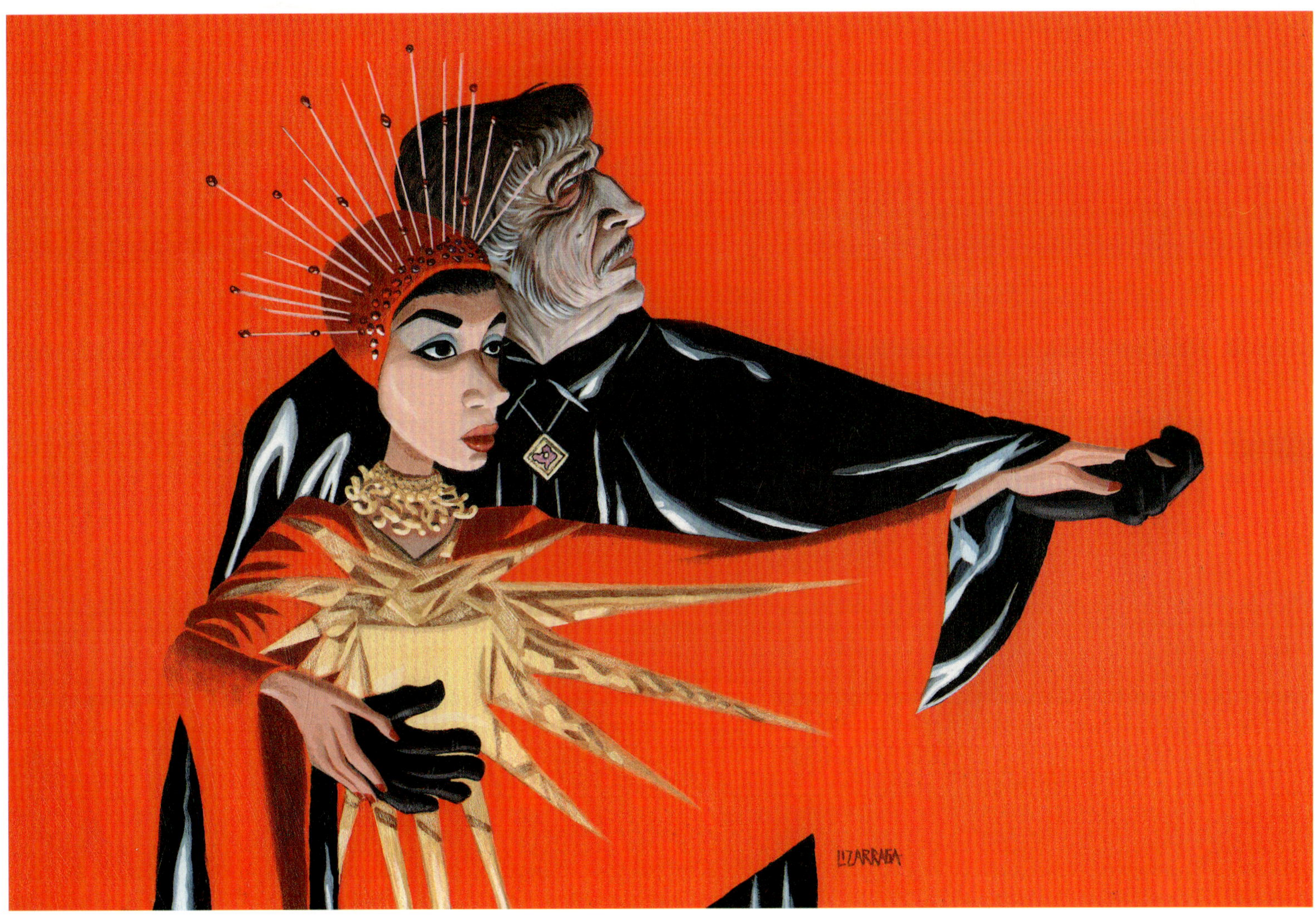

style; each has a back catalog showing their range and viewpoint. And each breathes new life into the monsters I grew up with.

The book is a treasure. It's creepy and fascinating, weird and insightful, strange and compelling. And it will both satisfy the hunger for those cinematic creatures and introduce new generations to film and TV fantasies that are foundational for much of what is filmed today.

I have no doubt you'll enjoy it as much as I have. And I know it's the kind of book I will return to over and over again. Some of my most precious memories are given new life in these pages. No doubt that will be true of everyone lucky enough to read it.

Sit back, turn the page, and experience the magic . . .

Jonathan Maberry

OPPOSITE *Sil from Species* by Graham Humphreys. 4K UHD disc cover design. Mixed media, 2025.

ABOVE *Dr. Phibes and Vulnavia* by Bob Lizarraga. Piece for *Folie à Deux* exhibition at SugarMynt Gallery. Acrylic on board, 2022.

JONATHAN MABERRY is a *New York Times* best-selling author, #1 Audible best seller, five-time Bram Stoker Award winner, four-time Scribe Award winner, Inkpot Award winner, comic book writer, and producer. He is the author of 52 novels, 16 short story collections, 28 graphic novels, 170 short stories, and 14 nonfiction books and has edited 26 anthologies. He has written comics for Marvel, IDW, Dark Horse, and others, and *Black Panther: Wakanda Forever* is partly based on his 2009–10 run in the comic. His Joe Ledger thrillers are being developed for TV by the director of the John Wick films. He is the president of the International Association of Media Tie-in Writers, and editor of *Weird Tales* magazine.

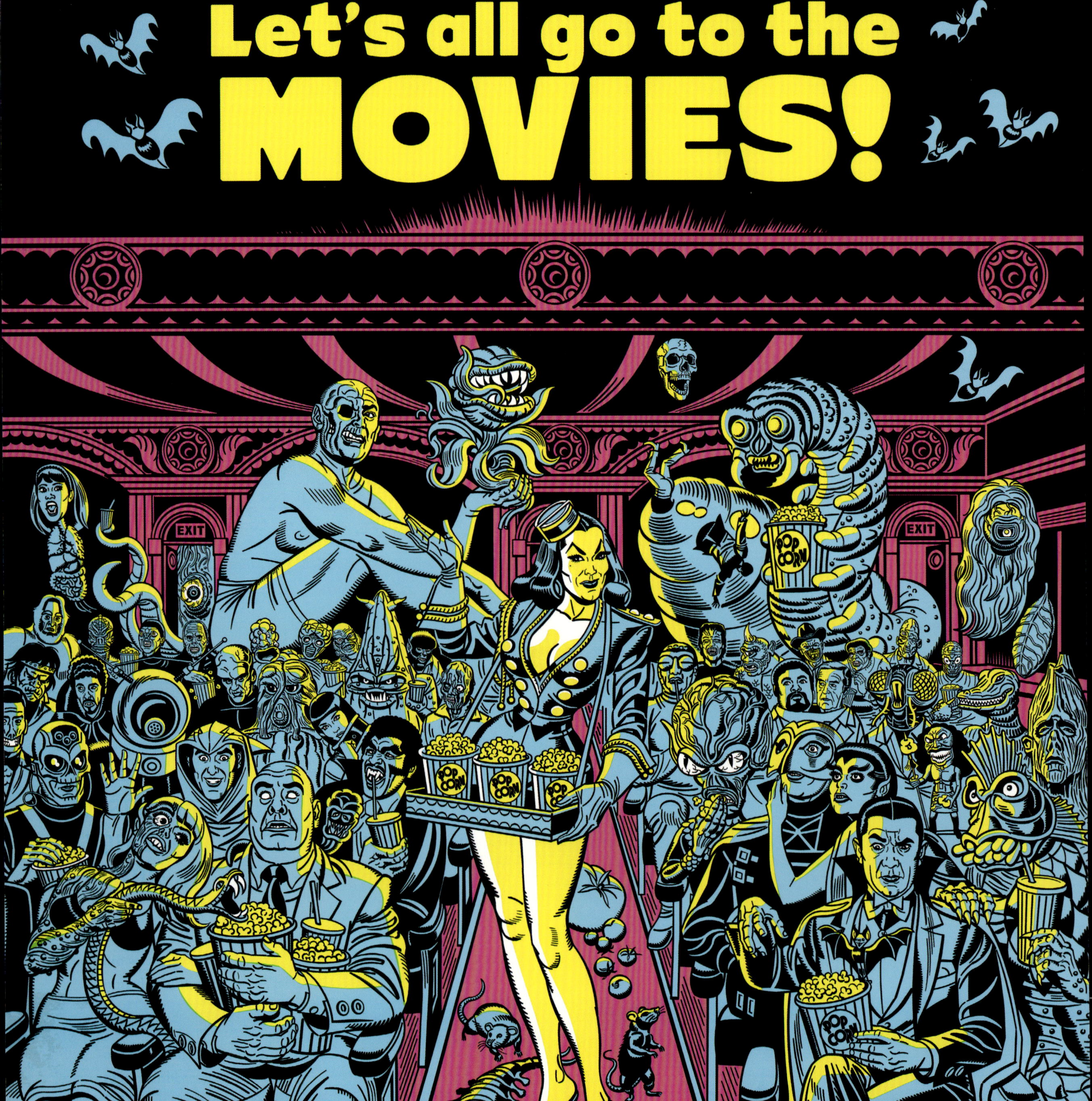
Let's all go to the
MOVIES!
EXIT
EXIT
POP CORN
POP CORN
POP CORN
POP CORN
POP CORN
POP CORN

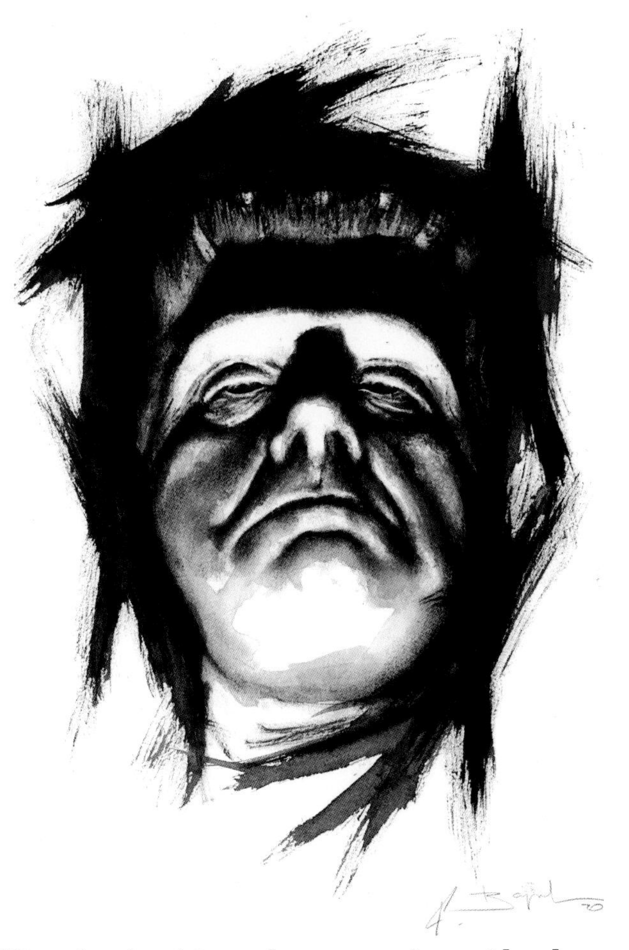

Introduction

When I set out to make a monster art book gathering together work with modern origins, I looked for a way to wrap them into a package that would be appealing to horror, science fiction, and fantasy fans of all ages. My solution was to only include characters and stories created *before* December 31, 1999, as represented in art created *after* January 1, 2000.

As we admire the gorgeous art in this volume, it's important to understand how we perceive art to enhance our appreciation of it. There are three components relevant to experiencing any creative work, be it literature, music, film, dramatic performance, or visual art: the work itself, the context surrounding the work, and observer bias.

The work the creator makes and releases into the wild is an unchangeable artifact confined in the amber of time, even if the creator later revises and reissues it.

Context is the aggregation of earmarks of the environment into which the work is released—the era, the place, the conterminous developmental events and works upon which it impacts—and the cultural temperature surrounding and enveloping it.

Observer bias is what the person who experiences art brings to the event, and is unique to each person and viewing. What the observer brings to the examination of a work is directly proportionate to what they take away from it, the unique personal impact. This impact may have no effect at all, it may inspire the observer to create a work in response, or it may lodge itself deeply into an emotional niche, never to be forgotten and always to be considered. Later reexaminations of the same work will be forever contextually updated and may create a different response.

Film historian and author Tim Lucas considers the effect in more depth relating to monster artworks in any media: "Before it can offer [therapeutic relief], the art must be channeled through the artist and perform some service of process and expression through them. To see a horror or monster image turned into a form of art is an invitation to study its appearance and meaning more deeply, and to thus welcome that image more deeply into ourselves. By adapting these things into art, the flinch, the refusal to see, is taken away from us and we are tempted by technique into deeper consideration and appreciation of them."

Chris Walas, an Academy Award–winning special effects artist (for 1986's *The Fly*), believes that the personal narrative can be profoundly affected by exposure to genre films, in a positive way. "Monster movies act as morality plays, especially when we are younger and more impressionable and uncertain. They show us that while fear is unavoidable and we will encounter difficulties

OPPOSITE *Let's All Go to the Movies!* by Mitch O'Connell. Screen printed poster for B-Fest. Pen and ink with digital color, 2024.

ABOVE Lon Chaney Jr. as Frankenstein's monster from *The Ghost of Frankenstein* by Gustavo Rapela. Gouache and ink wash, 2020.

in life, we can be reassured that things will eventually return to some form of normalcy." To him, "monster movies are a way of life. If you're a monster lover, they're your friends in a way. Some of them speak to you more than others. You don't get to pick your monsters; they pick you."

As a designer and illustrator, I've been privileged to know many of the artists in this book for years, some for decades. As much as I admire the work of Basil Gogos, James Bama, Mort Kunstler, and many of the other great horror artists of the twentieth century, I truly believe that the best work in this genre is being done right here, right now. The proliferation of art available on Blu-ray, toy, and consumer-goods packaging, magazines, book covers, online publications, poster designs, prints, and more has created a groundswell of illustrators who share a love of this frightening—yet appealing—subject matter. These artists return to monsters not only because it's financially profitable but also because it feeds their inner child; it makes them happy to create that which helped create them, in a spiritual sense. It's been a privilege to document the joy they and I have for these characters and stories, as well as the visions they've shared.

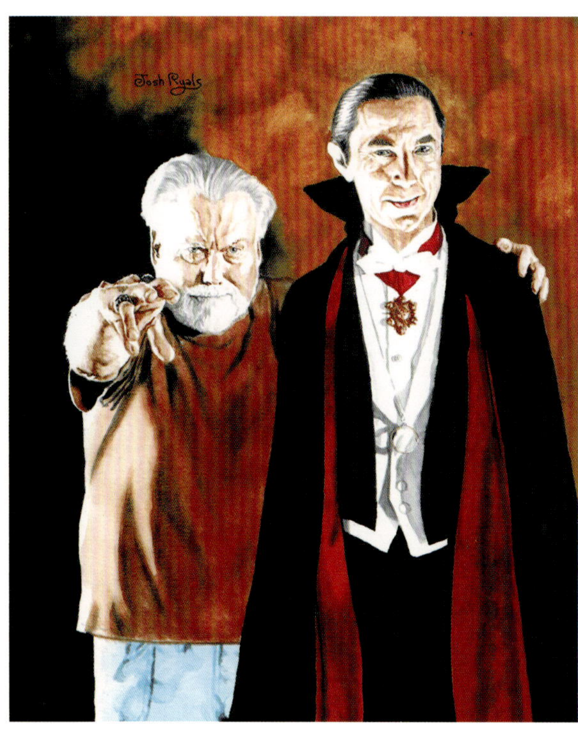

ABOVE This book is dedicated to the memory of David J. Skal, writer, friend, and inspiration. Without his work and encouragement, this book would not exist. *Portrait with Dracula* by Josh Ryals, 2024.

RIGHT *The Night Merchants* by Doug P'Gosh. Acrylic on illustration board, 2021.

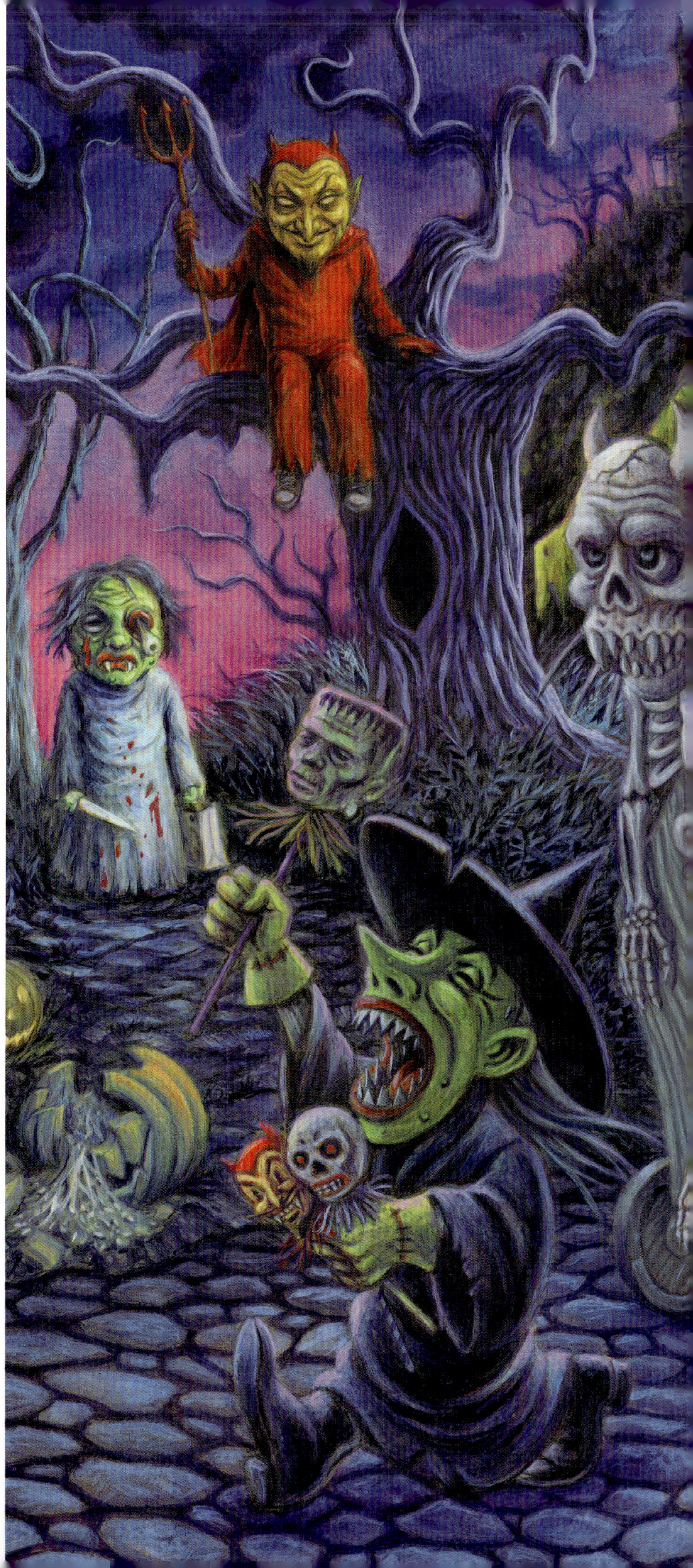

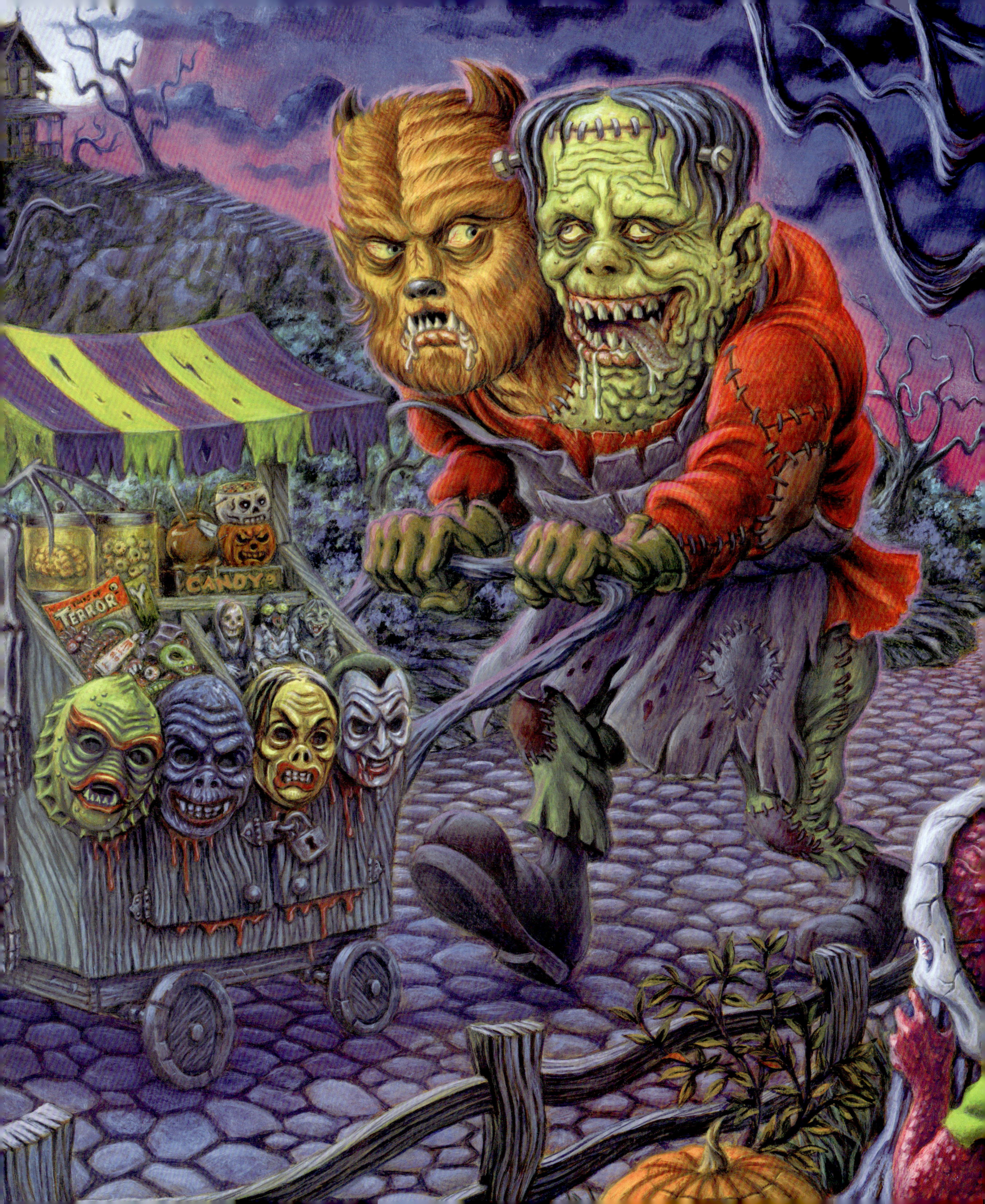
CANDY
TERROR

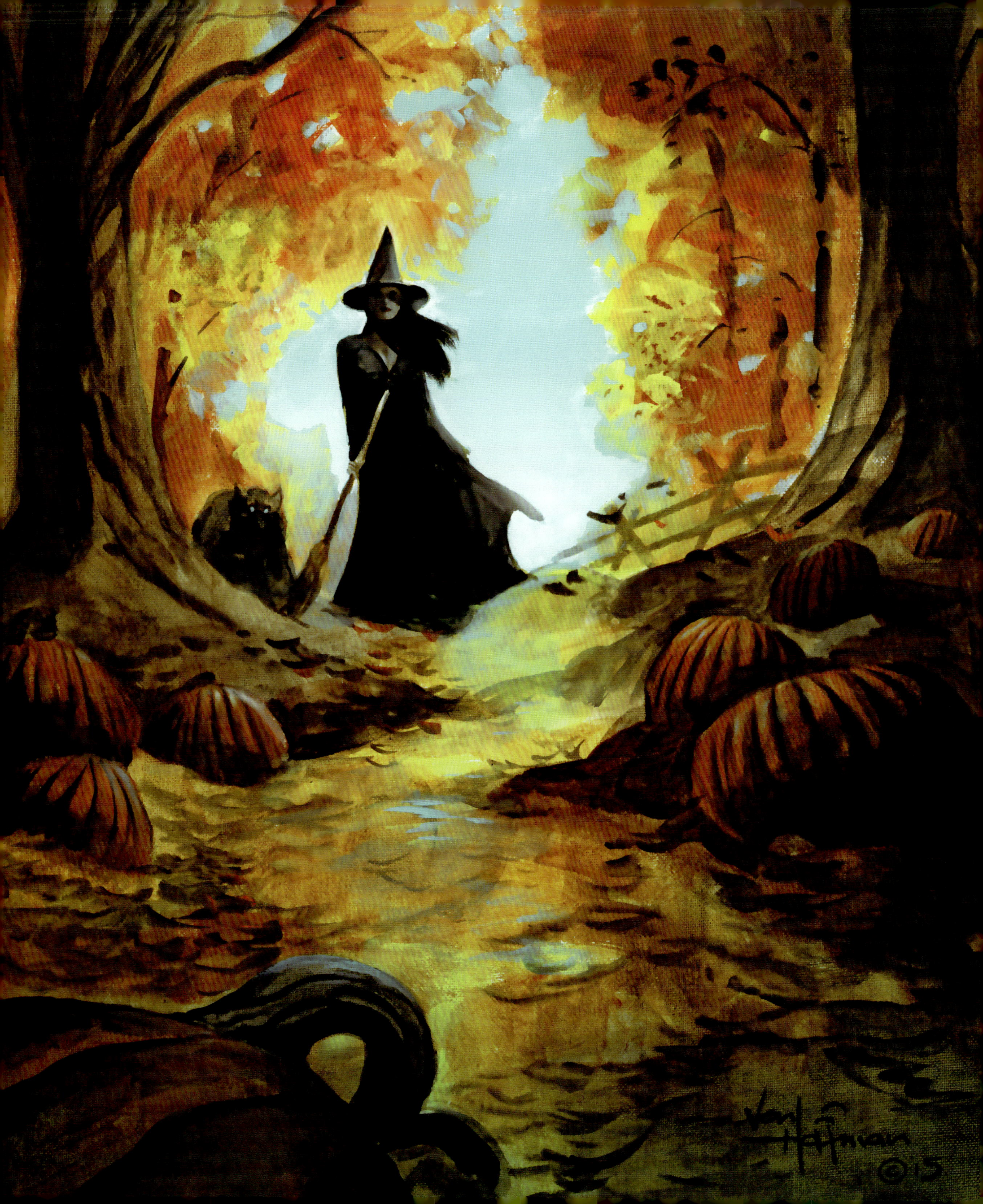

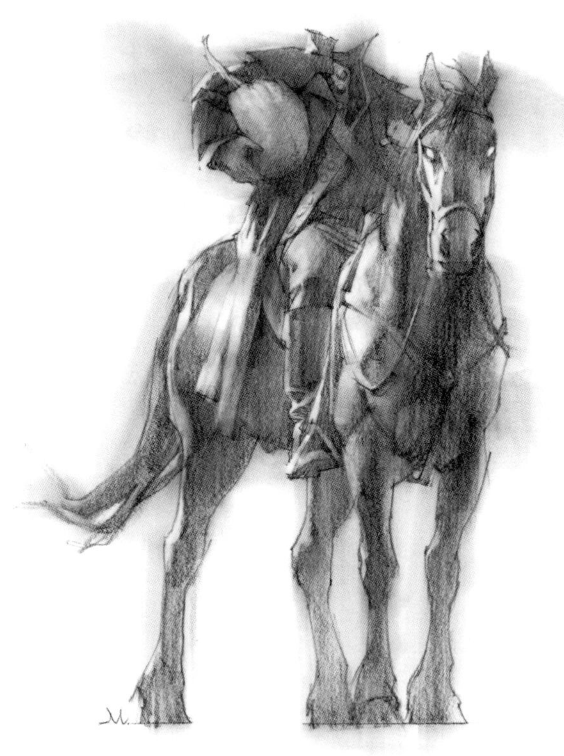

CHAPTER 1

From Darkness Borne (Prehistory–1917)

Since the dawn of humanity, illustration has been an essential communication tool. Artist Doug Pagacz (professionally known as Doug P'Gosh) says, "A good scary story has been engaging mankind since we were cavemen sitting around the campfire telling each other stories. It's a primal act to scare and be scared. One is no longer thinking about the mundane or the stressful in one's life."

Those scared cave dwellers painted their fears onto the walls that sheltered them from lightning, predators, and the unknown things that went "bump" in their nights. Artists have depicted common fears ever since, sharing them through whatever media was available. In pictures, words, songs, or performance, humankind has always peeled back the layers of menace through self-interpretation and shared these perceptions to allay fear in those who may be unable to interpret and process it for themselves.

Mary Wollstonecraft Shelley is most often heralded as the mother of science fiction for writing *Frankenstein; or, The Modern Prometheus* in 1818. Similarly, Bram Stoker is thought of as the father of modern horror fiction for his novel *Dracula*, published in 1897. The truth is, most people would never have heard of these writers or their books if not for Johannes Gutenberg, the father of mass media.

Famously, Gutenberg invented the movable-type printing press around 1450 in order to print Bibles in mass production so that anyone who could read might be able to afford a copy. Before his process, all books—Bibles or not—were handwritten, each copy an original artwork unto itself, which was obviously very expensive and time-consuming. Only the Catholic Church could afford these books, especially the manuscripts illuminated by monks and other clergy who were housed and fed specifically for the purpose of creating them. The Greeks invented theater, and while this was another form of mass communication, it was also hobbled by its dependence on the availability of writers who could create plays and actors who could read and perform them. Though well documented for their time, these plays were woefully unavailable to the great unwashed masses.

Before Gutenberg, the only thing approaching mass media besides public performances of Greek tragedies was art, and the only entity wealthy enough to commission art to display to the general public was the Church. When Martin Luther nailed his Ninety-five Theses to the door of All Saints' Church in Wittenberg, Germany, a mere sixty-two years after Gutenberg's first Bible (and on Halloween, no less), the power of mass communication became manifest, and the power of excommunication was manifested to try to silence the Reformationist.

OPPOSITE *October Fire* by Mike Hoffman. Acrylic, 2015.

ABOVE *The Headless Horseman* by Gregory Manchess. Pencil study for color painting, 2013.

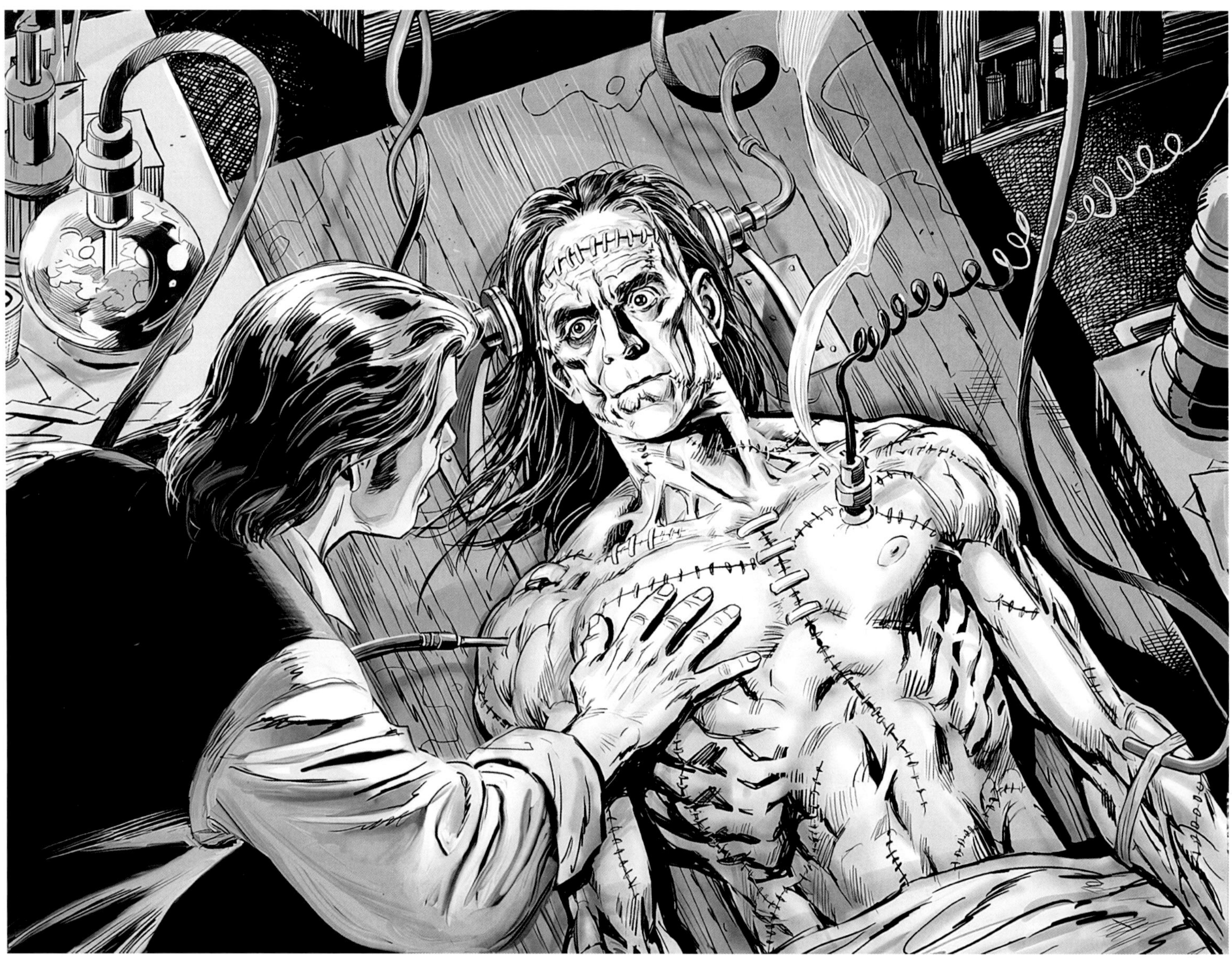

By then, the pope and the Church had begun to lose control of the narrative surrounding their religion, as well as society, and they've struggled to regain it ever since.

Without Gutenberg, society would still live in that figural pre-Reformation "Stone Age," each individual simmering alone in a pot of ignorance and belief. Without movable type, there could not have been any true scientific, creative, or ideological conversations on a societal level. Gutenberg not only created the format for our culture, he also begat pop culture, as fiction made its way into the public consciousness almost as quickly as his affordable Bibles. Suddenly, all the folklore and tales that had been dispensed by troubadours and wandering storytellers could be disseminated to the public in a handy, portable volume, and this information sank into other cultures and embedded itself.

Mary Shelley was challenged to write a ghost story on an 1816 vacation with her husband, Percy Bysshe Shelley, and friends Lord Byron and Dr. John Polidori. Mrs. Shelley and Polidori were the only two writers to see fruit from the challenge at Villa Diodati in Geneva that summer, which took form as her novel *Frankenstein* and Polidori's short story "The Vampyre," the first modern vampire tale published in English. Why did *Frankenstein* become a modern classic, while Polidori's tale is largely unremembered? Mary Shelley took a part of an existential conversation from the evening, married it to the reports about the intermittent reanimation of dead flesh using an electrical current by Luigi Galvani some thirty years earlier, and applied them to the most-asked questions in the history of humanity: Who am I, and why do I exist? Polidori cobbled together some folktales and wedded them with the tropes of the

ABOVE *Mary Shelley's Frankenstein Starring Boris Karloff* by Kerry Gammill and El Garing. Interior illustration for Legendary Comics graphic novel. Pen and ink washes, 2024.

OPPOSITE *Bram Stoker* by "Ghoulish" Gary Pullin. Pen and ink, digital, 2024.

Romantics, the poetic movement to which his employer, Byron, and Percy Bysshe Shelley belonged.

His story was a spark; Mary Shelley's was a bonfire.

Though it took a while to blaze brightly, *Frankenstein* inspired the likes of Jules Verne and H. G. Wells, igniting the science fiction genre before genres were even delineated properly. Polidori's spark was fanned into flame by a pair of Irish writers: Sheridan Le Fanu, whose lesbian-tinged vampire novella *Carmilla* would shake the dust off fellow Dubliner and Trinity College man Bram Stoker and inspire him to write his undisputed masterwork, *Dracula*. Considered by many to be the blueprint for modern horror fiction, *Dracula* has been examined, deconstructed, disseminated, and outright plundered by writers since its publication in 1897. It has become the firmament for thousands of stories and remains relevant more than 128 years later. Why? Because it fundamentally underlines the difference between human, humane, and inhuman, between the living and the dead, and outlines a path to remain sane in the face of undeniable insanity. It resonates at a level so deep within us as a species that it refuses to be denied as essential information to be stored within the collective unconscious. Stoker biographer David J. Skal noted that "Bram Stoker, working in a largely intuitive manner, and no doubt propelled by more than a few personal demons, managed to tap a well of archetypal motifs so deep and persistent that they can assume the shape of almost any critical container."

Stoker shockingly relegated humanity to a lower rung on the food chain and created the ultimate apex predator with a familiar face. The set of laws he collated to govern his monster—he can only come out at night, he must sleep in the earth of his homeland, he has no reflection in a mirror, holy water or sunlight might vanquish him—have defined vampire fiction ever since. Le Fanu's work also inspired American author Henry James, whose seminal ghost story *The Turn of the Screw* is itself a reservoir of influence in the groundwater of genre fiction.

At the turn of the twentieth century, publishing for the mass market was just getting its steady legs, and publishers were beginning to understand that the delineation of genres within fiction allowed them to market books, periodicals, and other printed matter more effectively to the readers. Penny dreadfuls and dime novels had begun appearing in the latter half of the nineteenth century, doling out horror, crime, and adventures of the American Wild West—both fictional and true (though often highly embellished). As they proved successful, publishers realized that speculative fiction à la Wells and Verne—as well as romantic fiction, children's stories, and other genres—had specific editing and marketing similarities and needs, and shared tropes and conventions that, with a bit of nudging, could be streamlined and consolidated, as much of the manufacturing and printing of the era had recently become. The assembly line process was still in the future with Henry Ford, but grouping similar publications together realized certain economies of scale in creation and publishing that became advantageous financially and allowed for greater capacity of product.

As publishing proliferated ideas via words to an ever-growing audience, it also lifted up images and brought them along for the ride. The initial application of illustration in the printing process involved the use of woodcuts, pioneered in Germany in the 1400s by Michael Wolgemut and elevated by his protégé Albrecht Dürer. It was Dürer who brought forward the use of copperplate engraving for printing, the metal providing a much more durable medium than wood and capable of finer detail. That practice was superseded in the seventeenth century by etching, a process involving an image being carved into wax that has been applied to a copperplate, after which acid is applied and

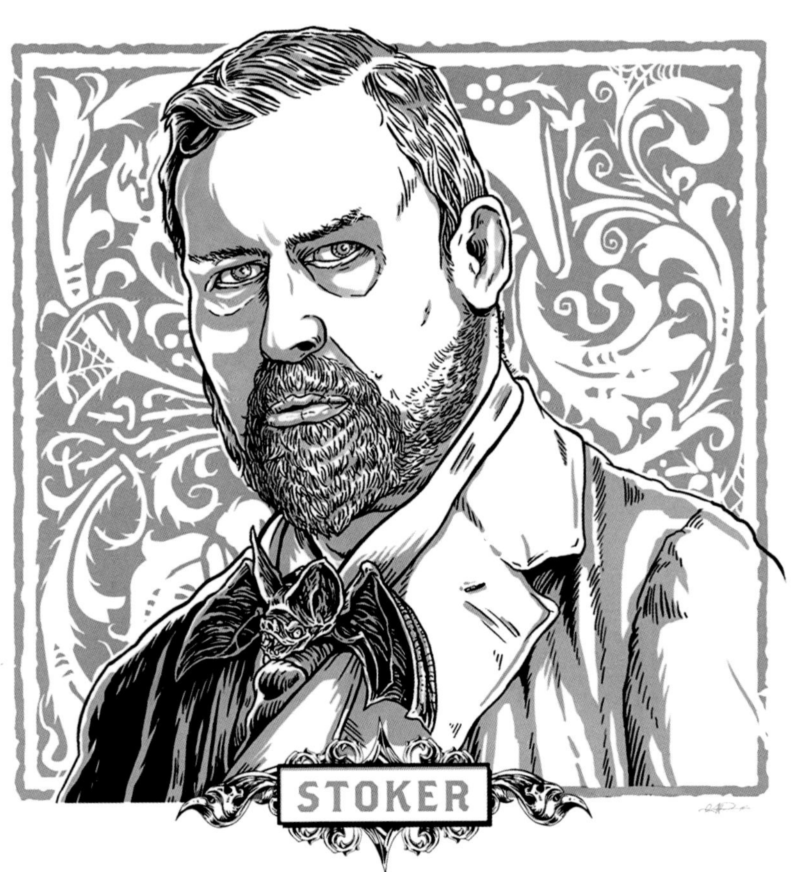

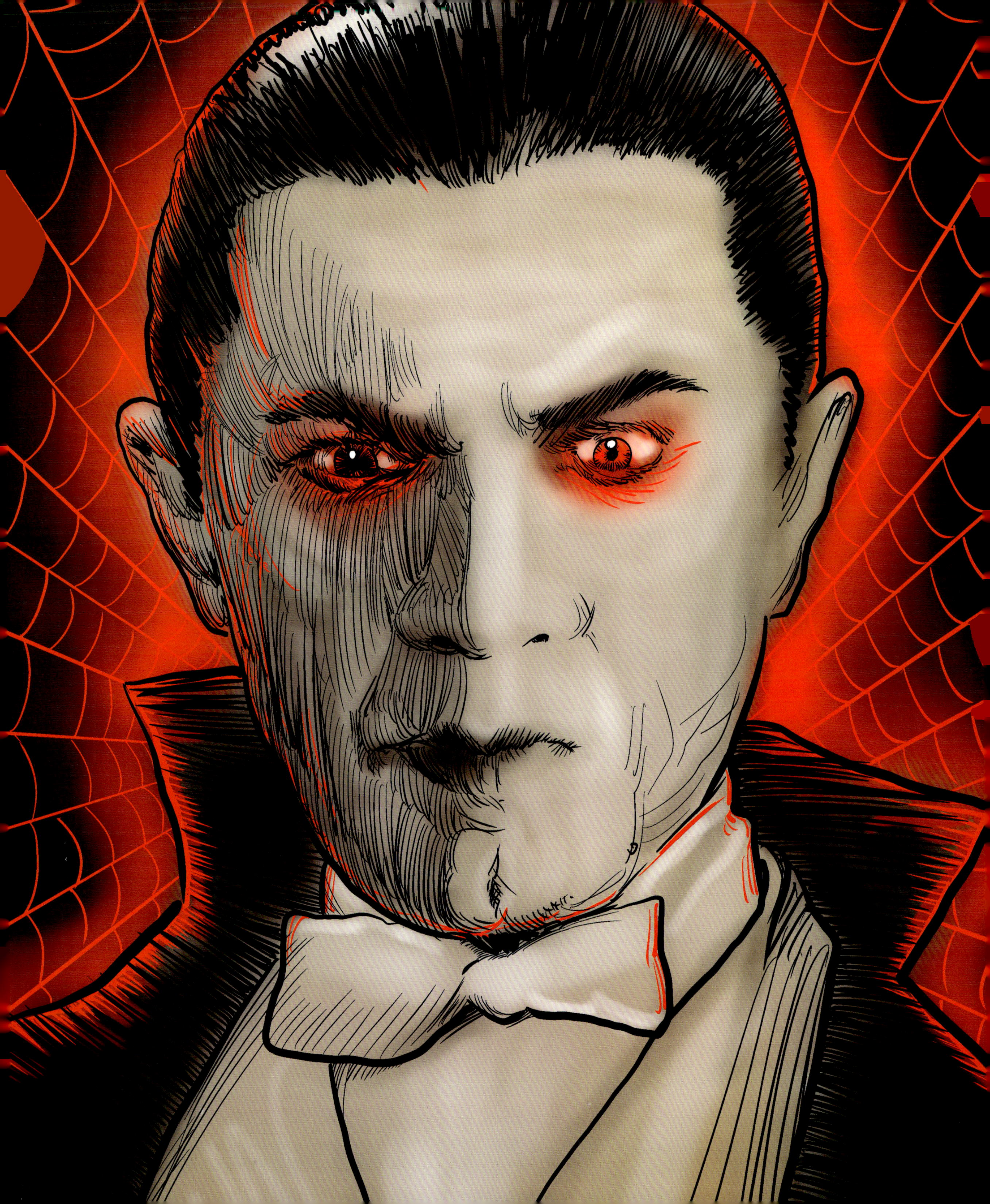

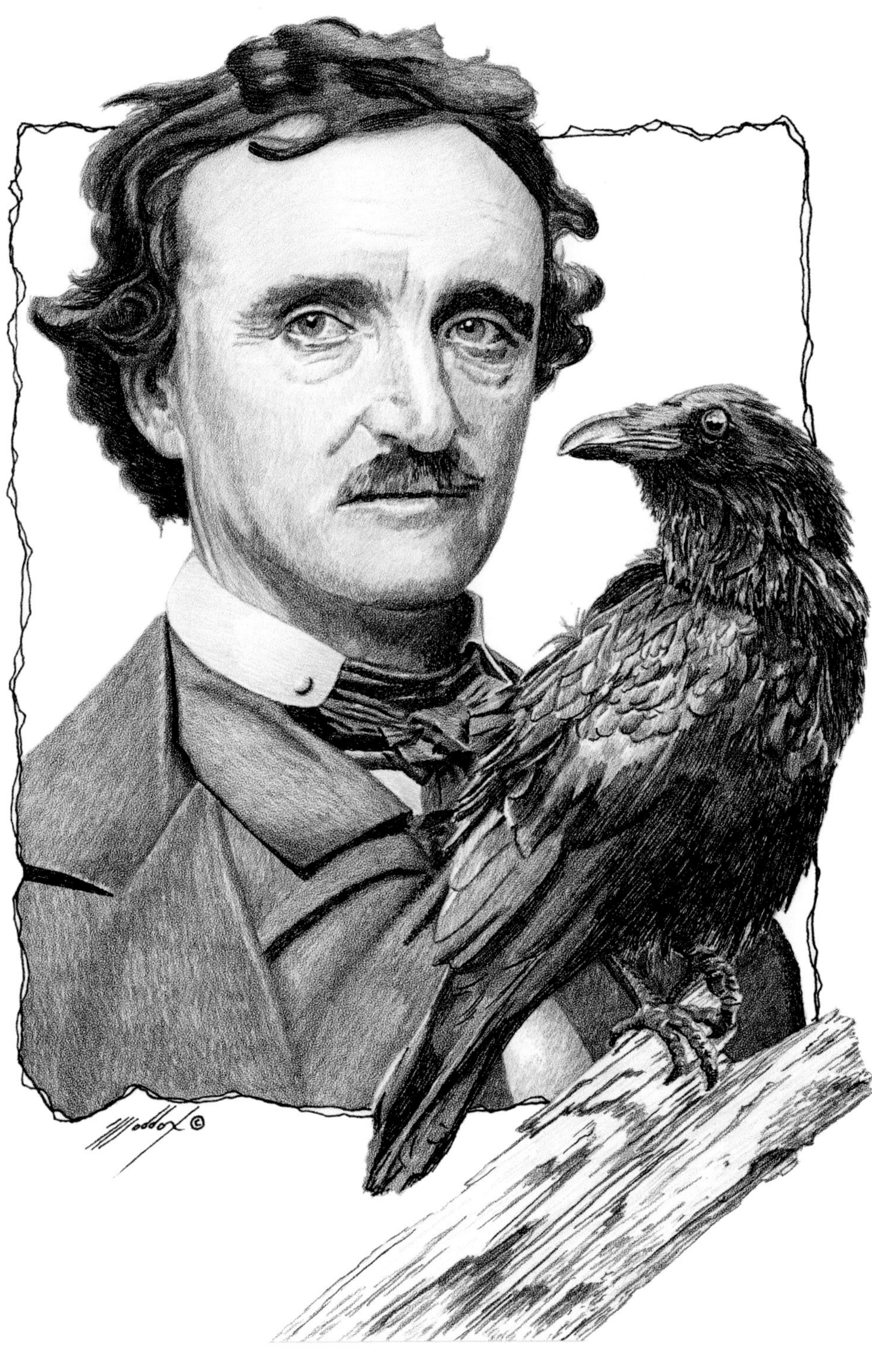

OPPOSITE *Bela Lugosi as Dracula* by Shane Morton. Digital, 2024.

ABOVE *Edgar Allan Poe* by Mark Maddox. Ink and colored pencil on coquille board, 2024.

etches the image into the plate where the wax has been removed.

By 1800, the lithography process became available and widely used. It allowed multiple color inks to be applied to the same print via chromolithography using multiple stone plates. Prior to this, any color other than black was applied by hand to each individual print, a painstaking and uneconomical procedure for mass media.

The invention of photography in 1826 revolutionized image-based communication, but it wasn't possible to print photographs for publication in a reliable form until the halftone process came about in the late 1850s. Halftones convert a photographic image into a series of dots through the application of filters, making them suitable for printing mediums. Halftone dots can be just about any size or shape but are most often round or elliptical, the latter of which is the preferred shape for process color printing. In this method, four colors—cyan, magenta, yellow, and black—are used to create a full gamut of color via tones and overlays, an innovation that became popular in the first decade of the twentieth century and is still the prevalent printing method in use today.

A series of pictures by early photographic pioneer Eadweard Muybridge of a horse at full gallop were published in an 1878 issue of *Scientific American* magazine, an event which led to the development of the first moving picture systems. These included a twelve-frames-per-second system called chronophotography and Thomas Edison's Kinetograph—a rudimentary movie camera—and Kinetoscope, for projecting films shot with it.

The true breakthrough for naturalistic motion pictures came with the Cinématographe projector, developed by France's Auguste and Louis Lumière, which projected sixteen frames per second, approximating realistic motion. The first films shown at public exhibition captured decidedly prosaic events, like a train arriving at a station and people dancing, but they caused a public sensation, and a new art form was born and adopted quickly by creatives and businessmen alike. The sped-up versions of these films we see today are so frenetically paced only because they are being projected at twenty-four frames per second, the standard adopted worldwide in the late 1920s as sound synchronization became widespread.

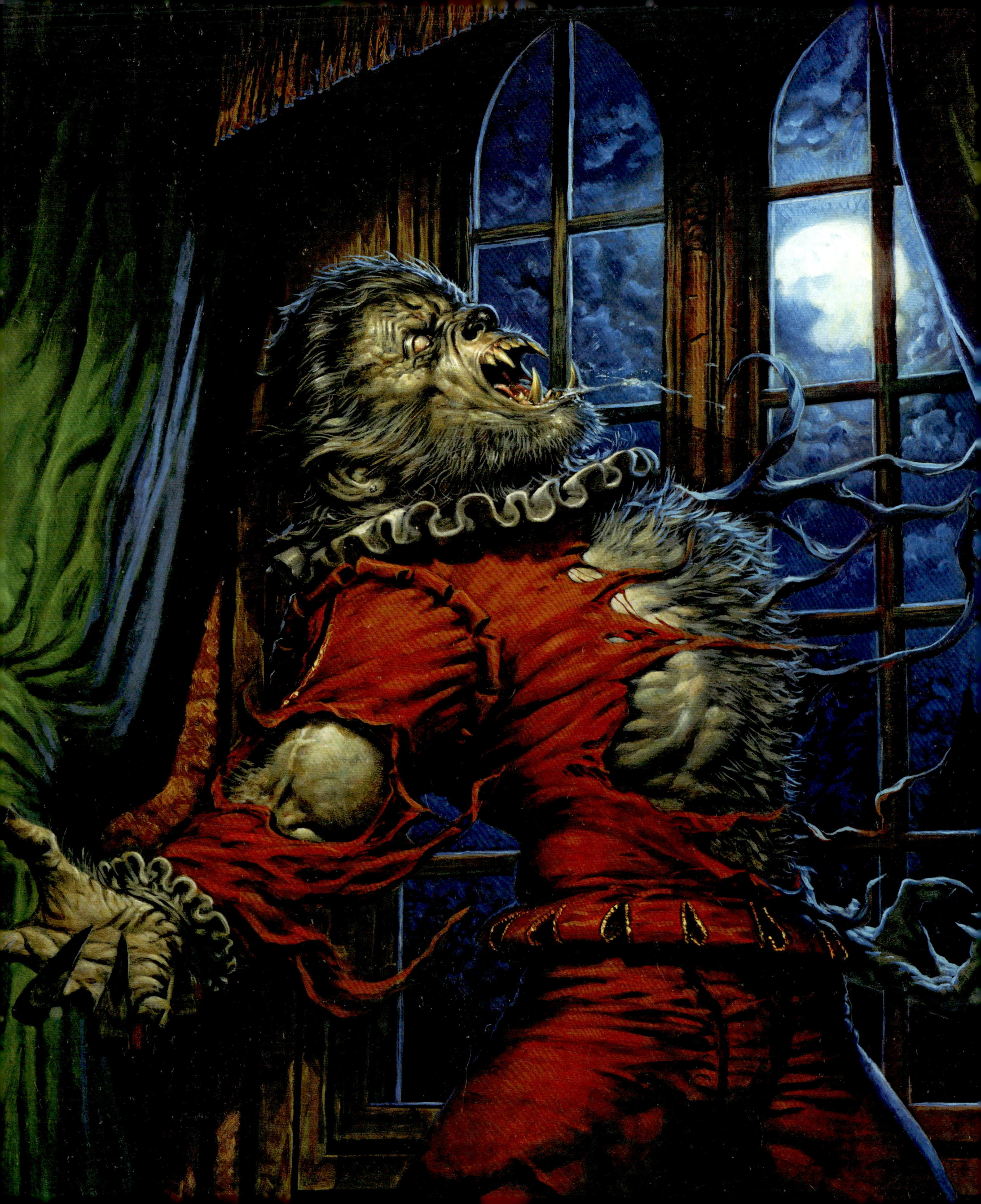

The French embraced the new medium with verve, creating countless short films. Leading the new form into the realms of the fantastic was stage magician Georges Méliès, most notable for his unforgettable *Le Voyage dans la Lune* (1902), the first science fiction film, based loosely on fellow countryman Jules Verne's novel *From the Earth to the Moon*. Within a few years, the first monster movies hit the screen and again changed the landscape of visual storytelling. *Frankenstein* (1910), produced by Edison and starring Charles Ogle as Frankenstein's monster, ran for only sixteen minutes, but it lit a pathway forward that is still followed today. Horror and monster films are now consistently among the most popular genres worldwide.

The first visual artwork created to represent these bold new films consisted of production drawings and poster images. In an era when illustrators were still the ruling class among publishers and editors—photography was only just beginning to grab a foothold, mostly in journalism—draftsmen and painters were commissioned to market these new visions of the fantastic told in glorious cinematography. Often, the illustrations were more fantastical and creative than the films themselves.

Lisa Morton, the author of *Trick or Treat: A History of Halloween* and winner of six Bram Stoker Awards, has a soft spot for monster and horror movie poster art. "My favorite recent development is the rise of the artist-created alternative movie poster, which reflects the increasing shift toward DIY projects and acknowledges the collectors' market that has exploded since *Star Wars* (1977) made movie memorabilia collecting hip. Mondo (the Austin, Texas–based company) was probably the first to really explore that whole market, but it's become a wide cottage industry since," she says. The market for such posters has indeed become very popular, with limited-edition screen prints selling on the secondary market for multiple times their original price soon after selling out from the publisher. "Alternative movie posters help keep classic movies constantly reinvigorated," Morton adds, "introducing them to younger viewers via the art and leading to alternative marketing of these films."

By the first decade of the twentieth century, world cinema was a bustling, growing concern and became a new frontier for anyone who could save enough coins to purchase a camera and film, cover development costs, and pay for editing equipment. The signal-to-noise ratio was high—for every true narrative feature, there were so many glorified home movies released that it became hard for potential audiences to sort out which was which.

As filmmaking began to evolve into an artistic and commercial landscape, the world plunged into war, disrupting channels of production and distribution. Cameras, previously focused on the fictional, now turned to the unbelievable reality of war, a spectacle that had previously been documented only with still cameras.

Out of this Wild West–like environment, genre legends were forged in Germany by directors Fritz Lang, F. W. Murnau, Paul Wegener, and Robert Wiene.

As the world waded through the aftermath of World War I, these directors picked up the pieces of the art and film scene in Germany and, through the metaphorical lenses of horror and speculation, tried to make sense of what had happened, what was going on around them, and what the future might bring.

OPPOSITE *The Horror Stories of Robert E. Howard—Wolfhead* by Greg Staples. Acrylic on cardboard, 2009.

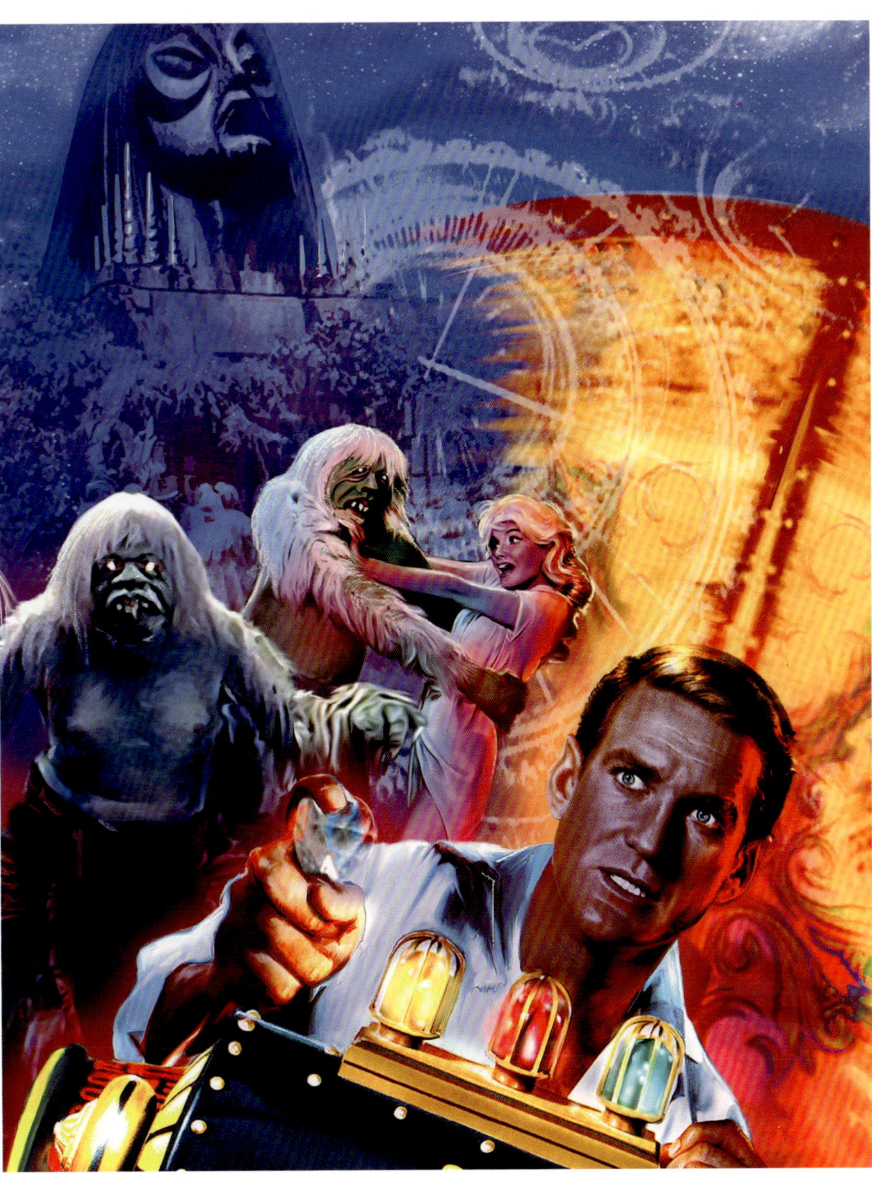

BELOW *The Time Machine* by Scott Jackson. Cover art for *Scary Monsters* magazine #111. Mixed media, 2019.

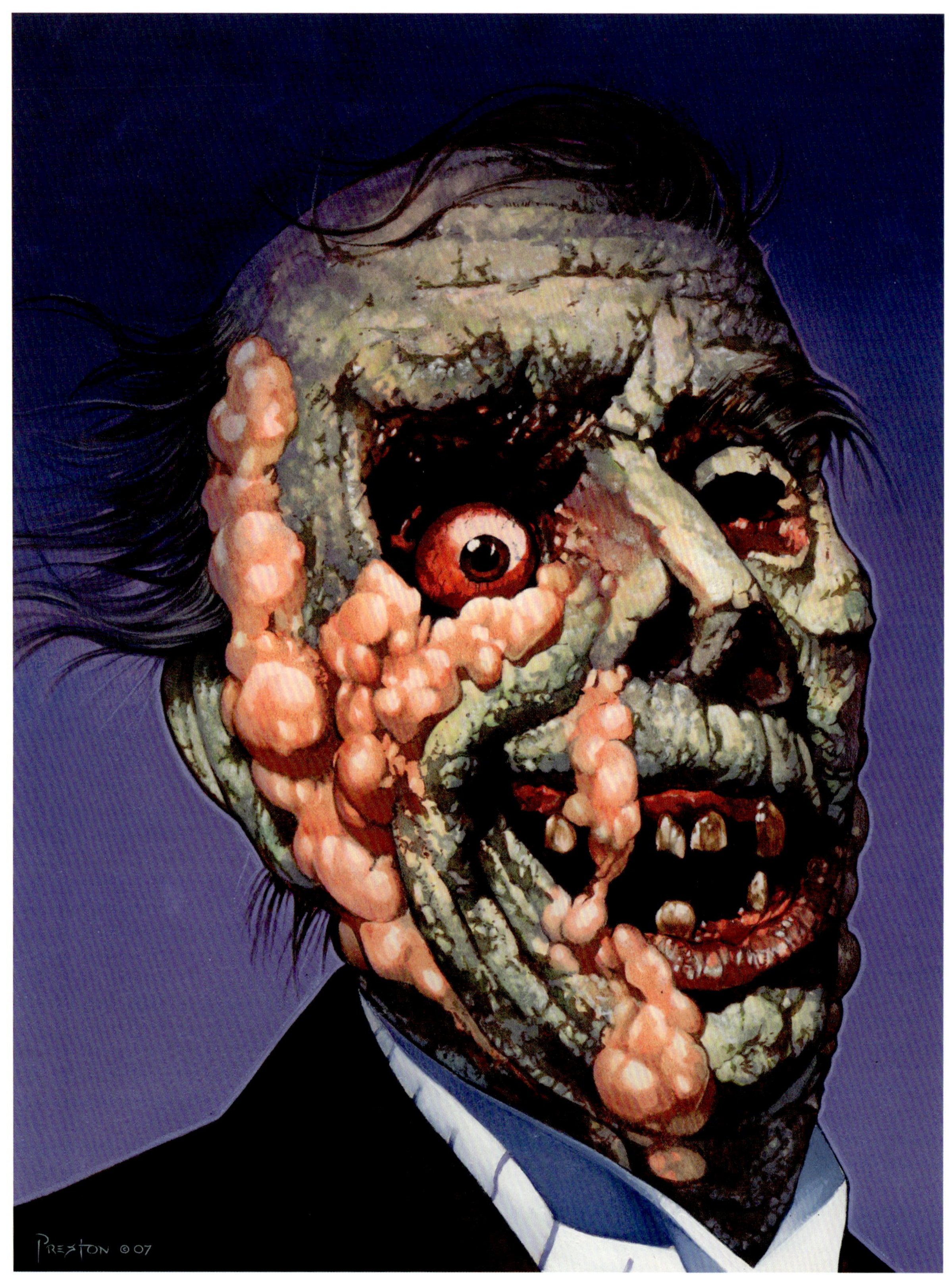

ABOVE *The Picture of Dorian Gray* by Jeff Preston. Magic Marker on paper, 2007.

OPPOSITE *The Horror Stories of Robert E. Howard—Out of the Deep* by Greg Staples. Acrylic on cardboard, 2009.

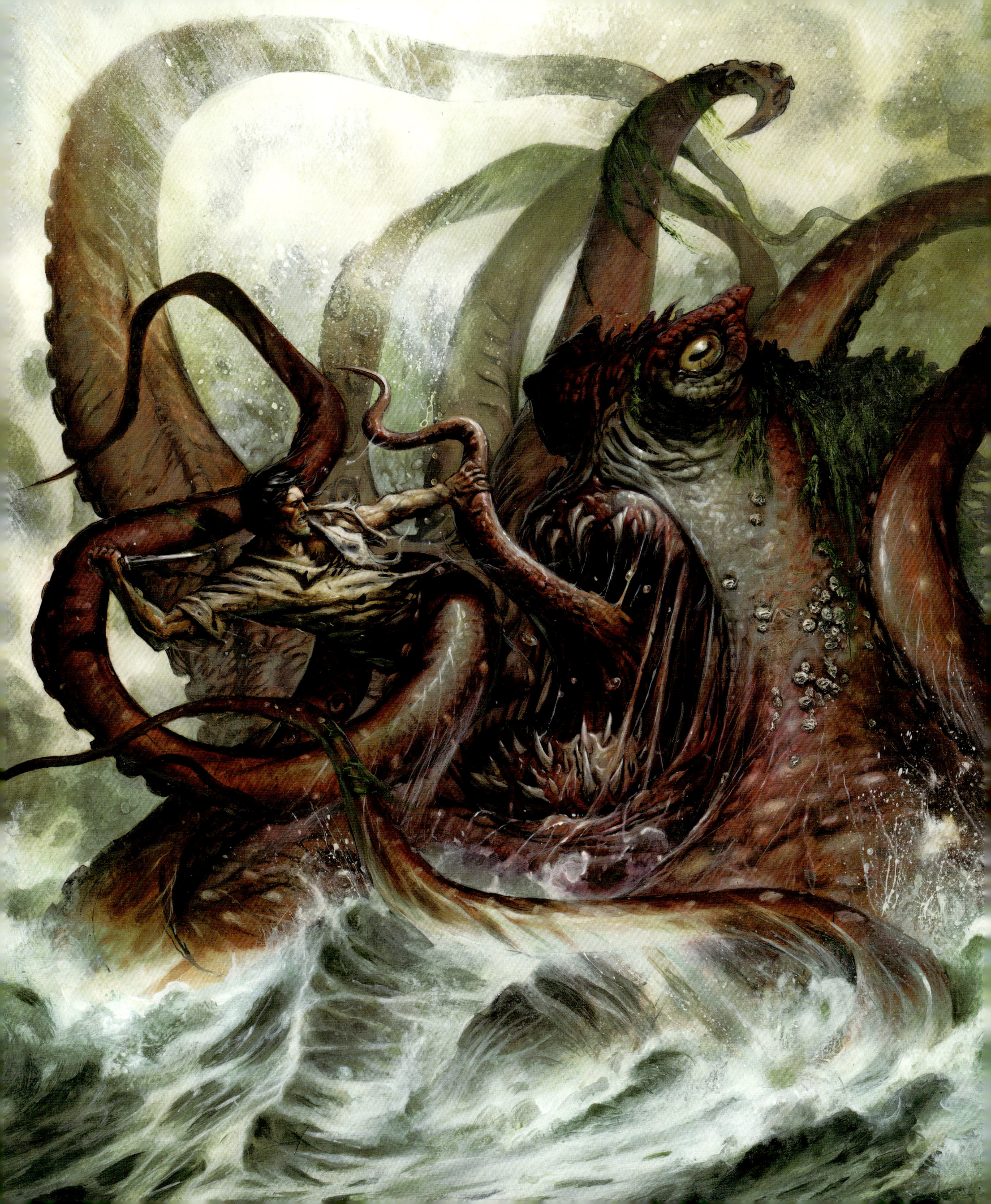

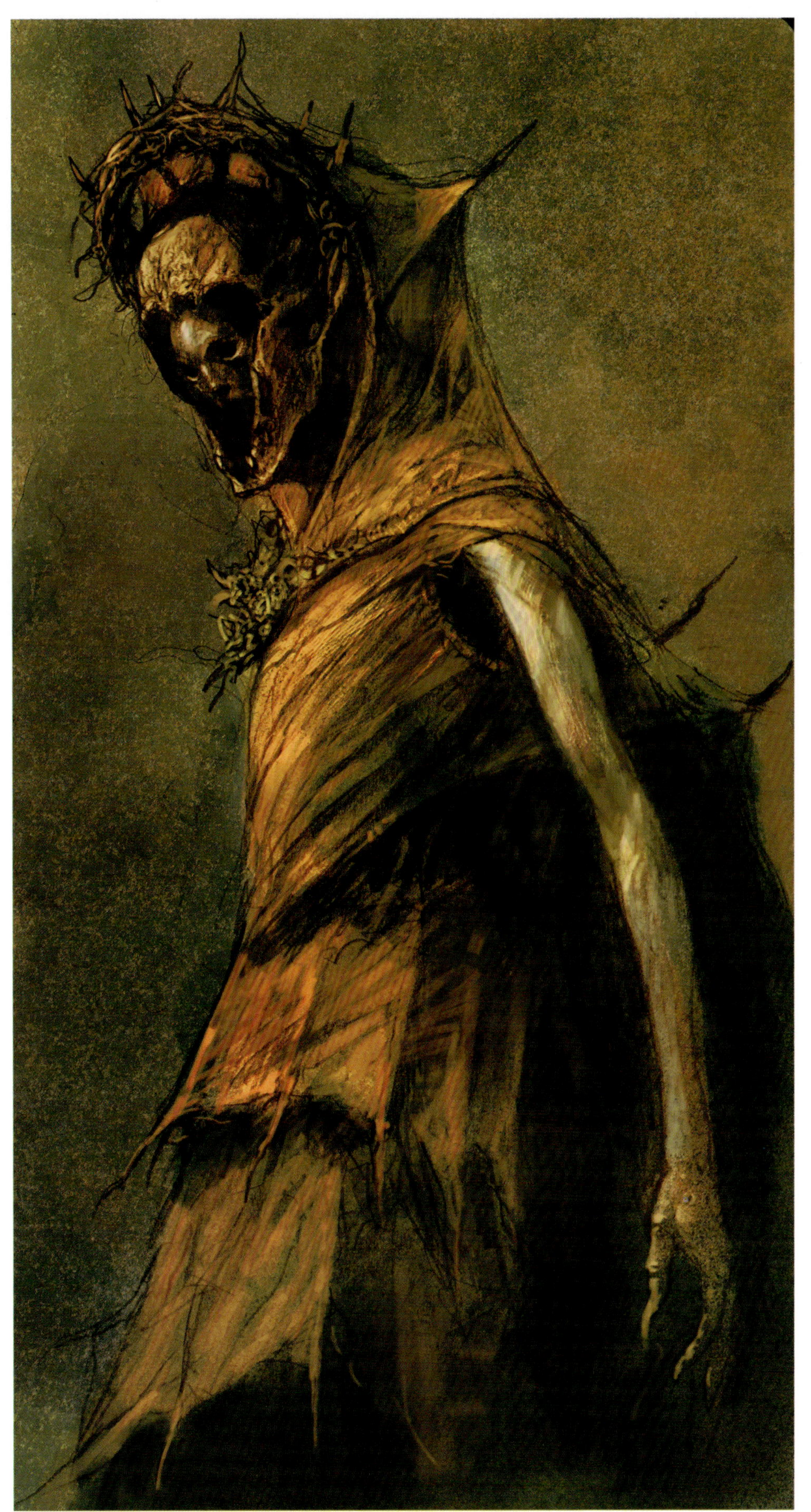

OPPOSITE *Abdul Alhazred Writing the Necronomicon* by Krent Able. Mixed media, 2023.

LEFT *The King in Yellow* by Dave Kendall. Mixed media, 2014.

Edison's Frankenstein

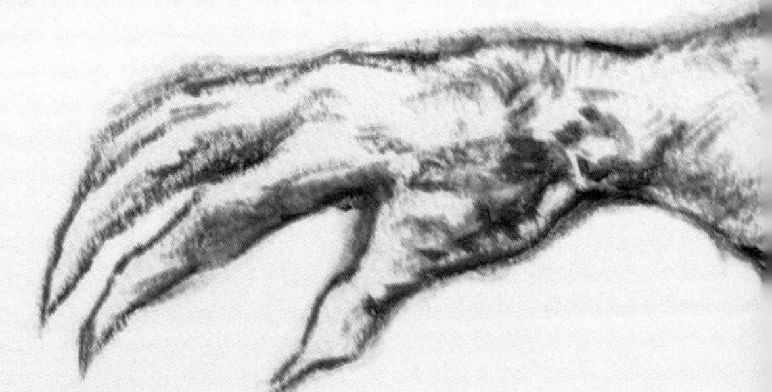

Author John Michlig (*It Came from Bob's Basement*) has a long personal history with the first monster movie and is preparing an in-depth book on it. He provides some context about this almost-lost film:

"Ah, the nearly lost treasure that is Edison's *Frankenstein*. No, Thomas Edison did not—in addition to inventing the light bulb—create a film based on Mary Shelley's classic story. His name is invariably attached to this 1910 gem because his namesake studio was responsible for what remains a pretty stunning depiction of the tale. Its existence was rediscovered in 1963 via a copy of the March 15, 1910, issue of *The Edison Kinetogram*, which advertised the release of a film that no one in the cinematic world seemed to remember.

"Frankenstein (the monster), portrayed by Charles Ogle, is truly a beast."

"Bits of the 'lost classic' were eventually recovered, and every now and then a clip would be shown on TV. In 1980, the American Film Institute named it one of the top ten most culturally and historically significant lost films.

"This version of the beast is, of course, unaffected by the decades-later Whale–Karloff–Pierce interpretation that immortalized the physical persona of the Frankenstein monster. The familiar flat head, neck bolts, and jacket are seen in multiple classic film depictions (as well as a comedic television series), so they've become canon Frankenstein to the world.

"I first stumbled upon the startling image of the Edison Studios Frankenstein in my hometown library at the tender age of twelve, and it shook me to my core. This wild-haired demon with claw-like appendages and shredded clothing was nothing like the Boris Karloff, Bela Lugosi, or even Fred Gwynne depictions I'd grown up with. Still, it's hard not to note that the top of the creature's forehead is very high and somewhat squared off, as if eerily prescient of the eventual Jack Pierce–designed monster makeup in Universal's 1931 *Frankenstein*.

"Frankenstein (the monster), portrayed by Charles Ogle, is truly a beast. That first image—a studio publicity shot—is also enormously nuanced. Cover his left eye, and the beast looks bewildered; cover his right eye

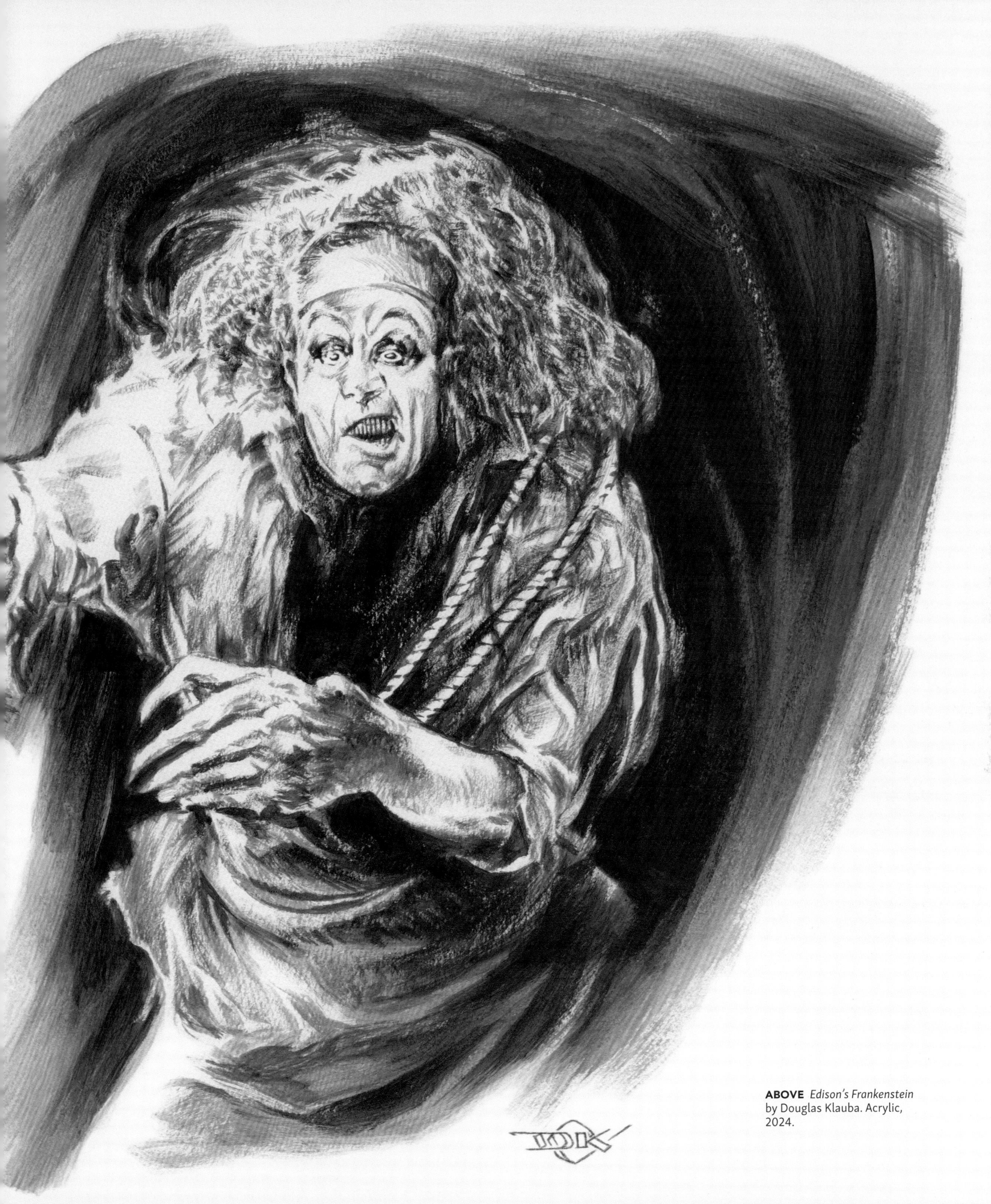

ABOVE *Edison's Frankenstein* by Douglas Klauba. Acrylic, 2024.

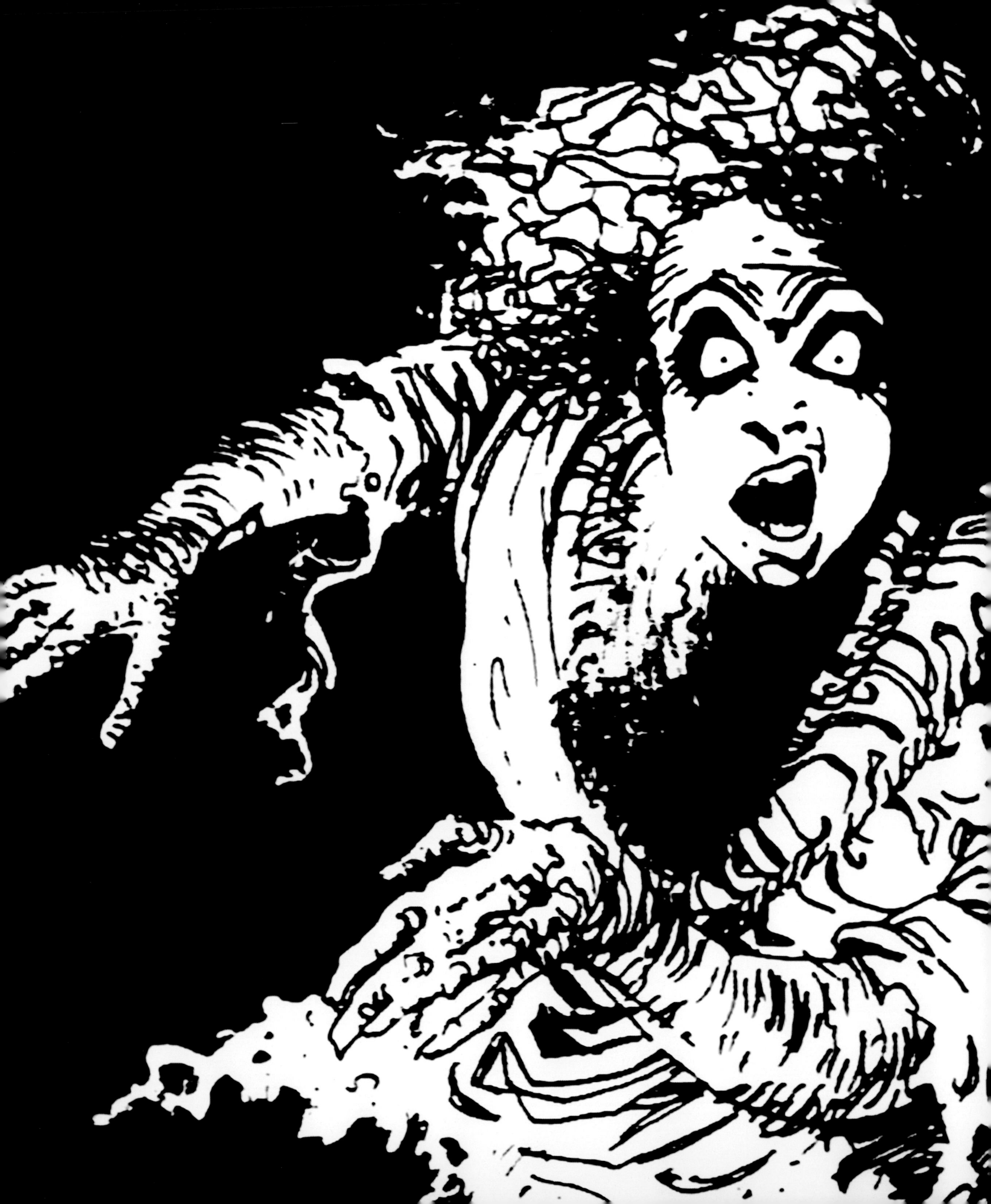

and you see anger. This is no surprise, as the monster's appearance was far from clearly defined in the book from which it sprang.

"Shelley's description of the being—whom [Victor] Frankenstein often calls a fiend or daemon—is decidedly sparse. He is enormous; he has long, black hair; is frightful to behold and stares at his creator with a 'dull yellow eye,' noted William Egginton, a professor of the humanities at Johns Hopkins University, in a *New York Times* article.

"Indeed, Shelley described Frankenstein's monster as an eight-foot-tall, hideously ugly creation with translucent yellowish skin pulled so taut over the body that it 'barely disguised the workings of the arteries and muscles underneath"; watery, glowing eyes; flowing black hair; black lips; and prominent white teeth. Not an incredibly detailed portrait, and definitely no flat-top skull, neck bolts, or badly tailored dinner jackets.

"With the exception of a few stills and a very short clip or two, Edison's *Frankenstein* was long thought lost or misplaced in a Hollywood vault or basement waiting to be rediscovered. Edison Studios generally printed forty copies or fewer of their films, which were leased to film exchanges for seven months. If they weren't returned to Edison Studios, the films were sold or salvaged for their silver content. In 1914, both the Edison film studio in the Bronx and the Edison laboratory in West Orange, New Jersey, were damaged by fire, further depleting the archive.

"In 1993, a few years after I'd relocated to Milwaukee, Wisconsin, I came across a poster advertising a Halloween and Halloween eve showing at the local Avalon Theater of 'Thomas Edison's *Frankenstein*.' No hyperbole, no 'first time ever!' Just a simple xeroxed poster stapled to a telephone pole.

"That was, alas, the year I was homebound with the flu for Halloween. Then, exactly a year later, another poster, this time advertising a showing at the local Paradise Theatre, with a live original score by area musician Sigmund Snopek III.

"That was the year I was out of town for Halloween. To fend off extreme disappointment, I convinced myself that the exhibitions consisted of merely a couple of clips from the film. It would be national news if a lost film of that stature were suddenly found.

"Eventually, through a piece in the local newspaper, I learned about an eccentric local character named Alois Felix Dettlaff Sr., who lived no more than a stone's throw away from me in the nearby suburb of Cudahy, Wisconsin. In the article, Dettlaff claimed to possess a virtually complete print of the Edison Studios production of *Frankenstein*, the only one known to be in existence. As I would learn over the course of many years, he wasn't lying, but at that particular point he wasn't letting it out of his sight.

"Fortunately, Dettlaff eventually released various versions of the film on DVD and, before his death in 2005, made arrangements for the print to be properly archived. You can watch a wonderfully restored print of *Frankenstein: A Liberal Adaptation from Mrs. Shelley's Famous Story for Edison Production* on, for instance, the Internet Archive."

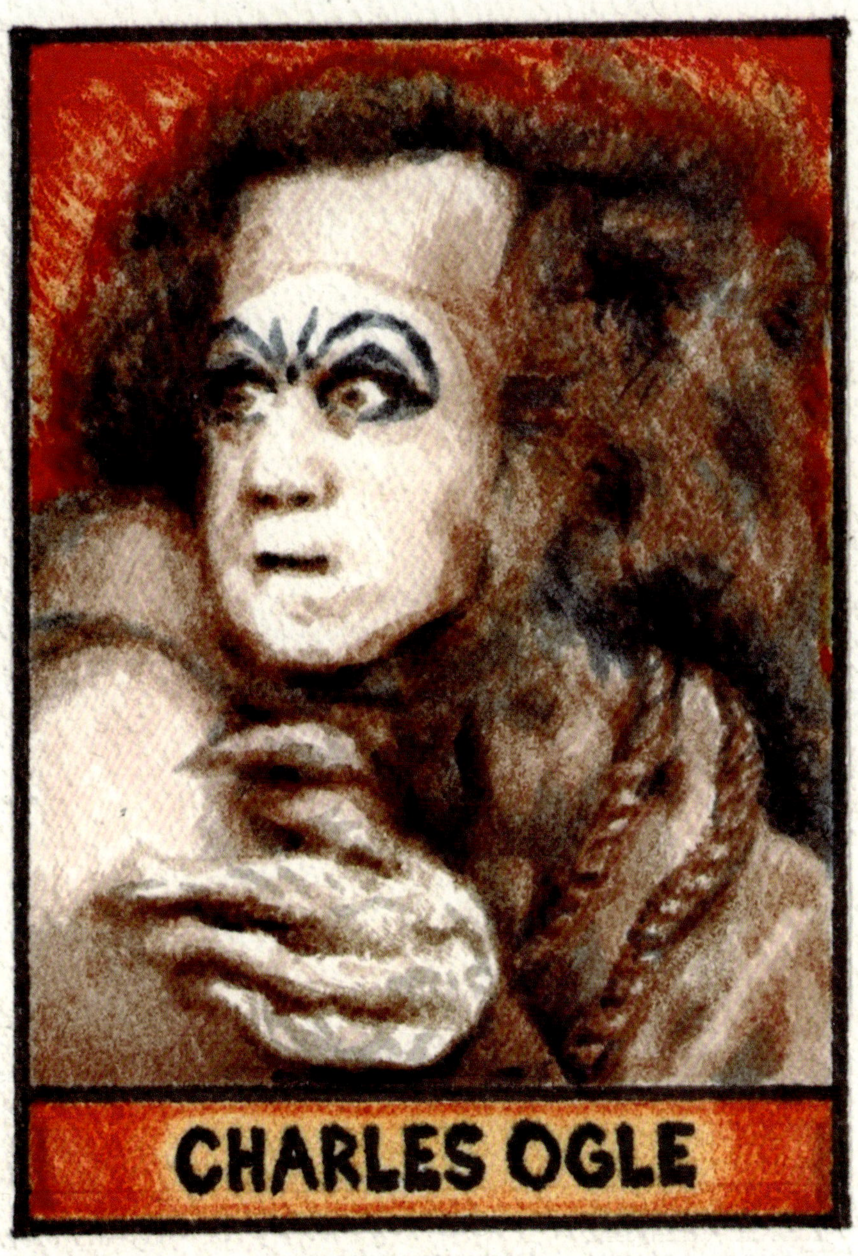

OPPOSITE *Charles Ogle as Frankenstein's Monster* by Neil D. Vokes. Pen and ink, 2019.

BELOW *Edison's Frankenstein Fantasy Cigarette Card* by Josh Ryals. Mixed media, 2017.

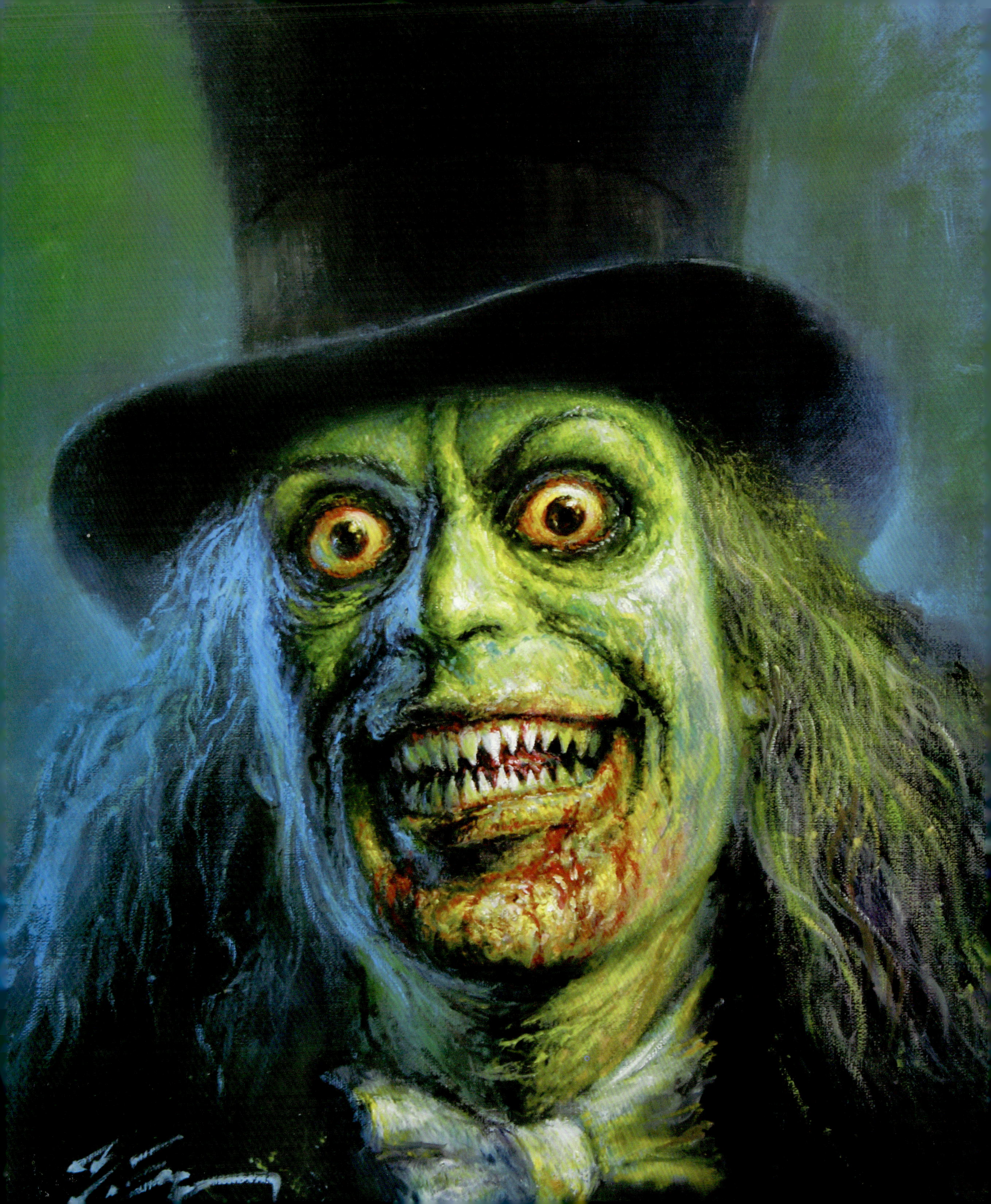

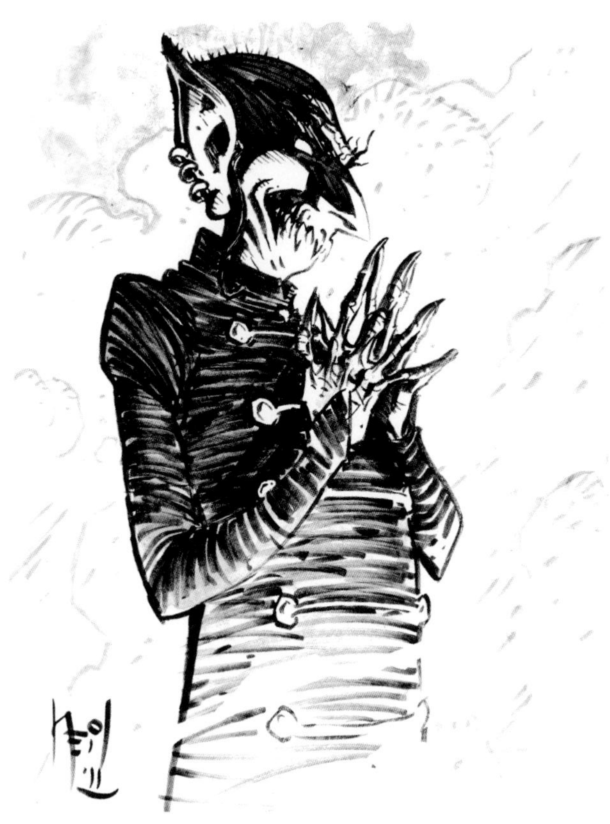

CHAPTER 2

Fiat Luxurious (1918–1929)

After World War I, Germany was relegated to reconstruction and a future of uncertain economic means. Social change occurred on a profound level, and the arts and cinema communities were in disarray. Film production (other than propaganda) had radically decreased during the war, allowing distribution and production systems to falter. This opened the door for films from other European countries to dominate the postwar film market in Germany, an unsustainable situation the government remedied by ordering the merger of all film production, distribution, and exhibition companies into the government-subsidized conglomerate Universum Film Aktiengesellschaft, or UFA. The company was later transferred to private control, and sparked a renaissance in the *deutsche* film industry, becoming the largest film studio in Europe and launching the country's entry into the international film market.

After the war, the zeitgeist in Germany was filled with expression of the fear and loathing of the encroachment of "the others"—people who look and sound like us, but mean us harm. The gestalt of art and cinema in the country depicting this subject was born of that "spirit of an era" and created an indelible mark on the culture not only in Europe, but everywhere these images and films were exhibited.

The period between 1918–1933 in Germany, known as the Weimar Republic, ushered in an era of artistic and creative propagation the country has never known since. During this great leap forward, the country would arguably become known best for its architectural advancements spurred by the Bauhaus school and the brilliant films created and embraced worldwide as masterpieces.

Paul Wegener's 1920 film *The Golem* (an expanded remake of his 1915 film) kicked off a streak of what are now classics, releases that included Robert Wiene's *The Cabinet of Dr. Caligari* (1920) and F. W. Murnau's *Nosferatu* (1922), as well as Wiene's *The Hands of Orlac* (1924), Murnau's *Faust* (1926), Henrik Galeen's *The Student of Prague* (1926)—another remake, this time of Stellan Rye's 1913 film—Fritz Lang's *M* (1931), and Carl Theodor Dreyer's *Vampyr* (1932). These films defined a narrative pattern for horror movies that would be globally adopted by filmmakers and carries on today in modified forms to great success. The directors embraced design motifs in which to envelop their works that reflected the aesthetics that were under development and being refined by the architectural and graphic arts movements adjacent to them—expressionism, in the case of *Caligari*, gothicism, in *Nosferatu*, and so on.

OPPOSITE *London After Midnight* by Bob Eggleton. Oil on canvas, 2018.

ABOVE *Count Orlok, Nosferatu* by Neil D. Vokes. Pen and ink, 2011.

"*The Cabinet of Dr. Caligari* is so influential and continues to be, that to see it for the first time now presents nothing 'new'," says film historian and critic Lucas Hardwick. "Its tropes and imagery have been referenced for over a century in films. And whether filmmakers realize they're cribbing this movie or borrowing from some other influence, the truth is that all roads lead to *Caligari*. Expressionism, impressionism, post-punk, goth, Lynchian, whatever you want to call it, this film is more than the result of an art movement, it is a movement in and of itself, inspiring multiple genres across generations. It is ground zero for filmmakers like Christopher Nolan and David Lynch, and punk rock would be remiss to not acknowledge appropriating elements of its disjointed, gloomy aesthetic."

As cinema entered its adolescent years, the sophistication of visual art to reinforce underlying themes began to be applied more distinctly and to greater success—especially enhancing powerful, visceral genres like horror. When synchronized sound entered the film lexicon in 1927, it added new elements to the subtextual emotional response palette available to filmmakers, as color would within a few years.

The best remembered of these films is almost certainly Murnau's *Nosferatu*, a blatant plagiarism of Bram Stoker's *Dracula* that Stoker's widow summarily shut down with a lawsuit that was meant to see all existing copies of the film destroyed. Luckily, at least a few slipped out and the film not only survived but thrived, becoming an iconic part of vampire-film lore.

Mark Dawidziak, author of *The Night Stalker Companion* and *The Bedside, Bathtub & Armchair Companion to Dracula*, believes that "horror stories always reflect what's going on in the culture and in society, whether consciously or subconsciously. Was it an accident that the rodent-like vampire of *Nosferatu* symbolized plague, pestilence, and death in a movie right after World War I and the influenza pandemic?"

Very little information survives about the first generation of movie poster artists, but *Nosferatu*'s look was designed for the film by Albin Grau, who also created the promotional and poster art. An artist and architect, Grau produced the film with Murnau—but his greatest contribution was as its production designer. Himself a soldier in the Great War, Grau created a grim, lean, and gothic visual palette that was familiar territory in the aftermath of the conflict, and applied his own arcane touches based on his experience as an avid occultist. Though he contributed to only four films, his work continues to inspire artists and writers today.

In America, at the same time, Universal Studios' Boy Wonder, Irving Thalberg, was busy making a star of Lon Chaney in *The Hunchback of Notre Dame* (1923), Thalberg's fourth film as a producer.

As Lucas Hardwick relates, "*The Hunchback* was a passion project of Chaney's that he'd sought to get off the ground for several years. His performance as the cathedral chimera evokes a tangible grotesqueness that is as visually off-putting to the audience as it is to the people who seek to abuse him for his deformities." And yet Quasimodo, the titular hunchbacked monster, is the only hero in the film and clearly the protagonist with which the audience identifies.

Chaney had been making his living in films as a day player since 1912, and was famously known to show up carrying his own makeup kit to tailor his look to

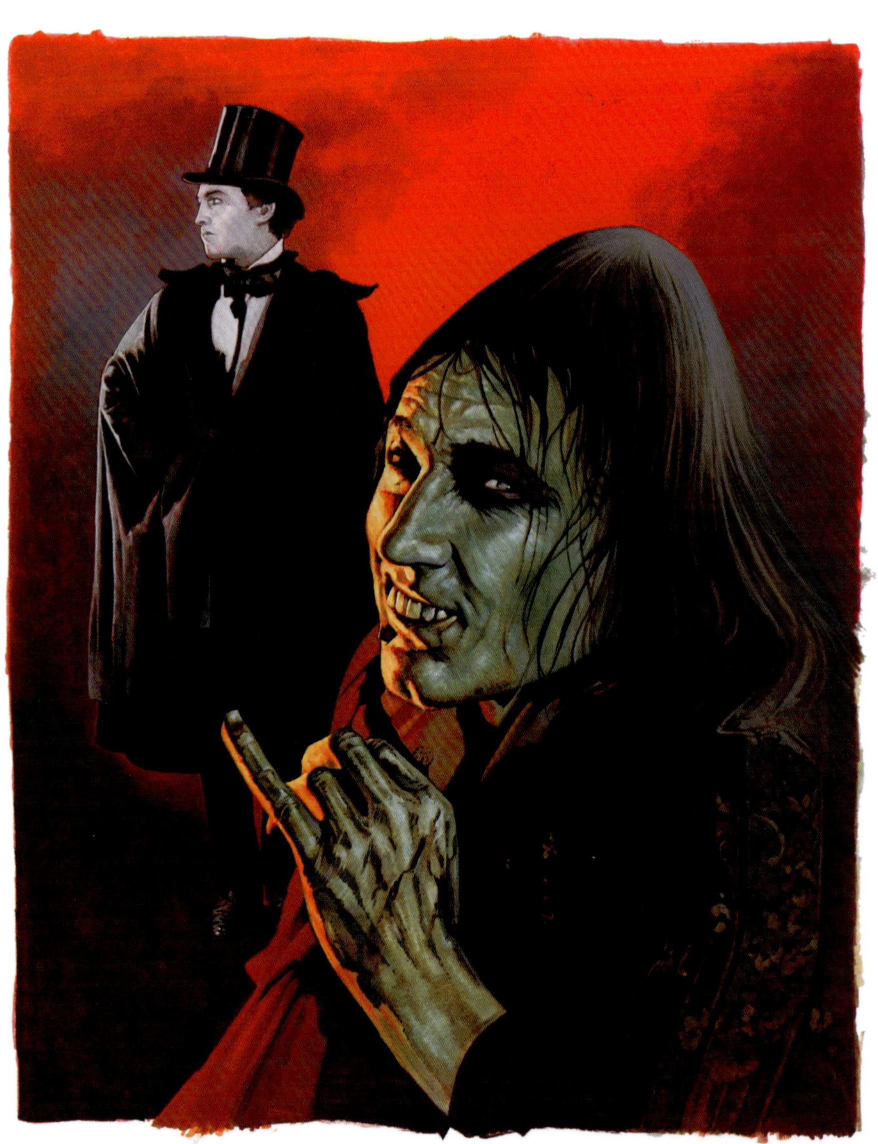

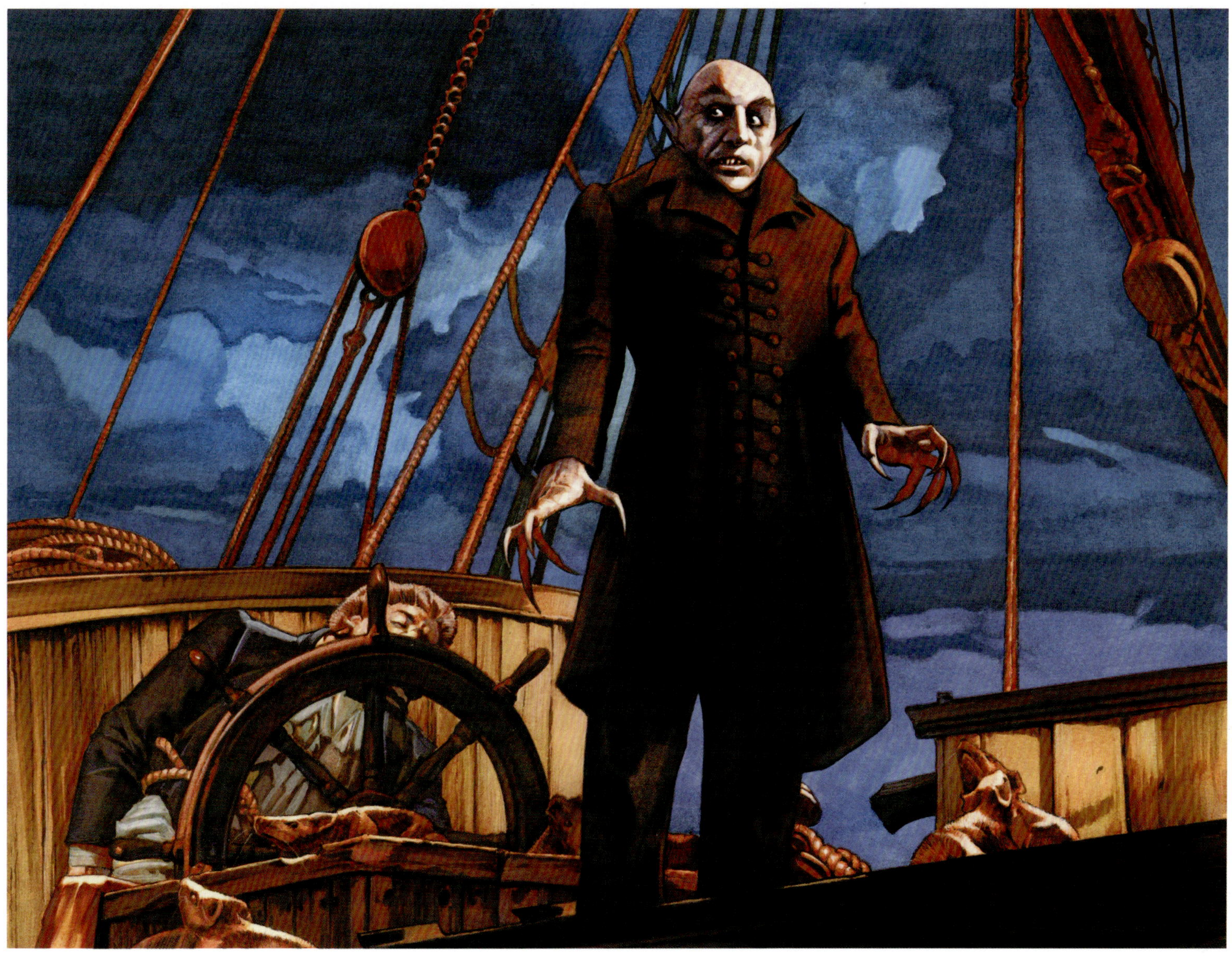

whatever physical type was needed on set on any particular day. Need a pirate? Chaney had an eye patch and swarthy makeup. An Asian? Chaney taped his temples back to narrow his eyes and added a mandarin mustache. How about a tattooed sailor? Chaney was your man.

He had made a splash in several films as a character actor, including *Riddle Gawne* (1918), *The Miracle Man* (1919), and *The Penalty* (1920), but *Hunchback* cemented him as a star. When Thalberg made the move to Louis B. Mayer Productions, eventually becoming head of production at Metro-Goldwyn-Mayer Studios in 1925, Chaney followed. Chaney's turn as Erik in 1925's *The Phantom of the Opera* put him at the top of the heap in Hollywood, and that same year he teamed up with director Tod Browning for *The Unholy Three* (1925), the first of ten films the duo would make together, including *The Road to Mandalay* (1926), *The Unknown* (1927), and the most elusively famous lost film of all time, *London After Midnight* (1927). Though the film is lost, powerful images of Chaney as a beaver-hatted faux vampire have survived and become iconic to legions of monster-film fans.

"He was someone who acted out our psyches. He somehow got into the shadows inside our bodies; he was able to nail down some of our secret fears and put them on-screen," said author Ray Bradbury of the actor. "The history of Lon Chaney is the history of unrequited loves. He brings that part of you out into the open, because you fear that you are not loved, you fear that you never will be loved, you fear there is some part of you that's grotesque, that the world will turn away from."

In several of his films, Chaney portrayed men without limbs or who were disfigured facially. This type of disability was sadly apparent in many of the soldiers

OPPOSITE *Dr. Jekyll and Mr. Hyde (1920) John Barrymore* by Jeff Preston. Markers on Bienfang bristol board/vellum finish paper, 2015.

ABOVE *Orlok Aboard the Empusa* by Jeff Preston. Illustration for unreleased collectible tin tote. Markers on paper, 2009.

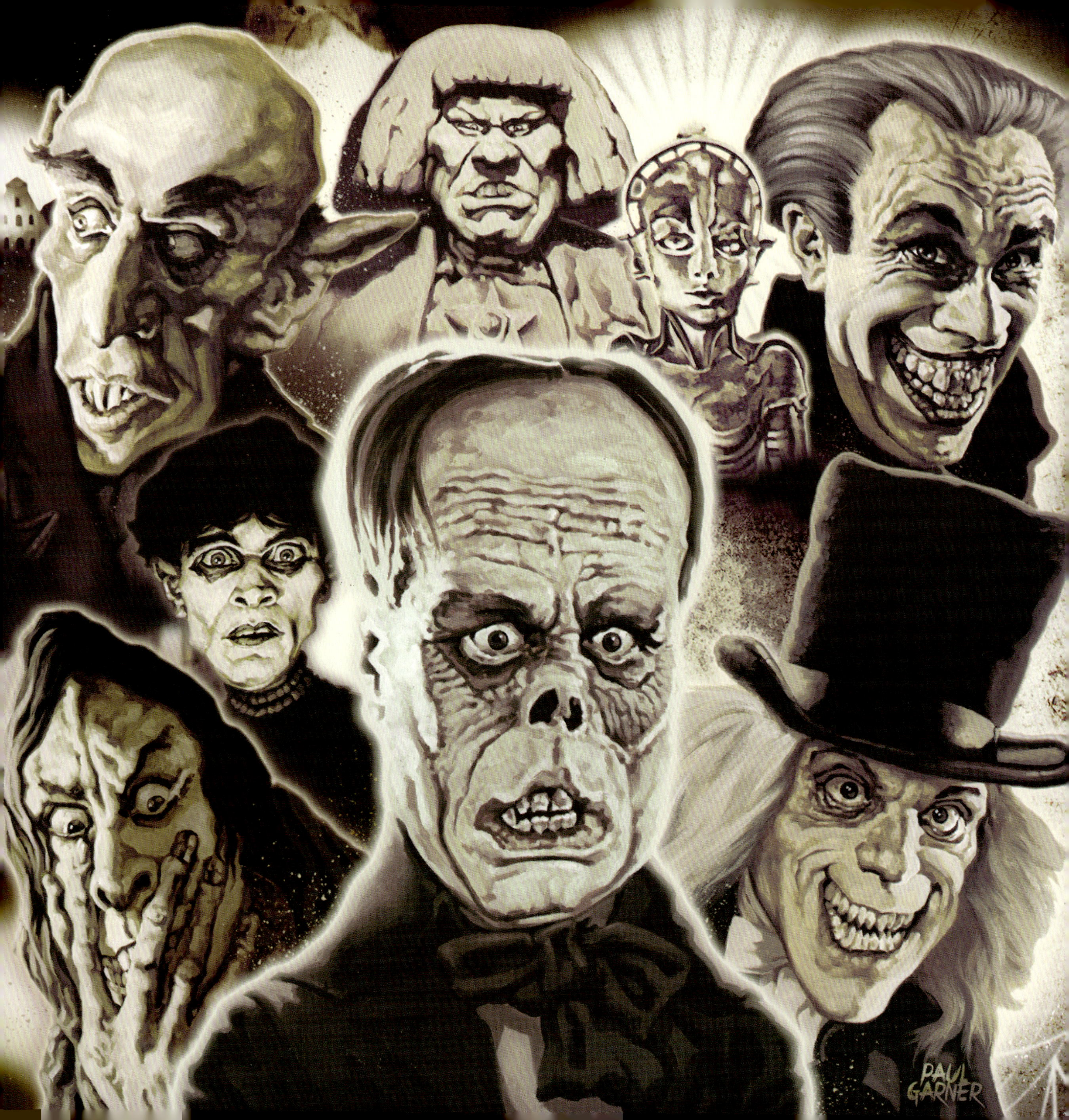
PAUL
GARNER

who survived the Great War, and depicting these real-life combat consequences on film helped viewers process their feelings, fears, and horror at what they viewed (sometimes unexpectedly) in reality. Chaney's portrayals of this type of character—whether a hero or a villain—allowed people to stare without fear of offense so that they could truly see beyond the scars and amputations and embrace the humans who bore them. In the darkened theater, one could observe and quietly express horror, rage, and disgust privately without fear of repercussions. For a society scarred by war—whether on the inside or the outside—and one that hadn't previously seen such ugliness up close and in person, the cathartic value of these characters and stories cannot be overemphasized.

"A work doesn't even have to have this effect as a conscious goal to cause considered reflection in a reader or viewer," says film historian and podcaster Rod Barnett. "By presenting scenarios with plausible extrapolations from the present day's realities, horror tales can bring an awareness of actions that can be made to stave off the worst things warned about. Just being able to lose ourselves in these stories makes thinking about terrible events in our own lives easier to manage. Think of watching horror movies as an inoculation against real-world trauma."

In 1930, Browning and Chaney began preparing a film version of *Dracula*—based on Hamilton Deane and John Balderston's popular stage play of the novel—when Chaney contracted pneumonia and was later diagnosed with throat cancer. He died of a hemorrhage that August.

Chaney, the fabled Man of a Thousand Faces, was gone—but *Dracula* would live on and start a wave of films depicting monsters from folklore and classic stories that would open a floodgate that has never closed.

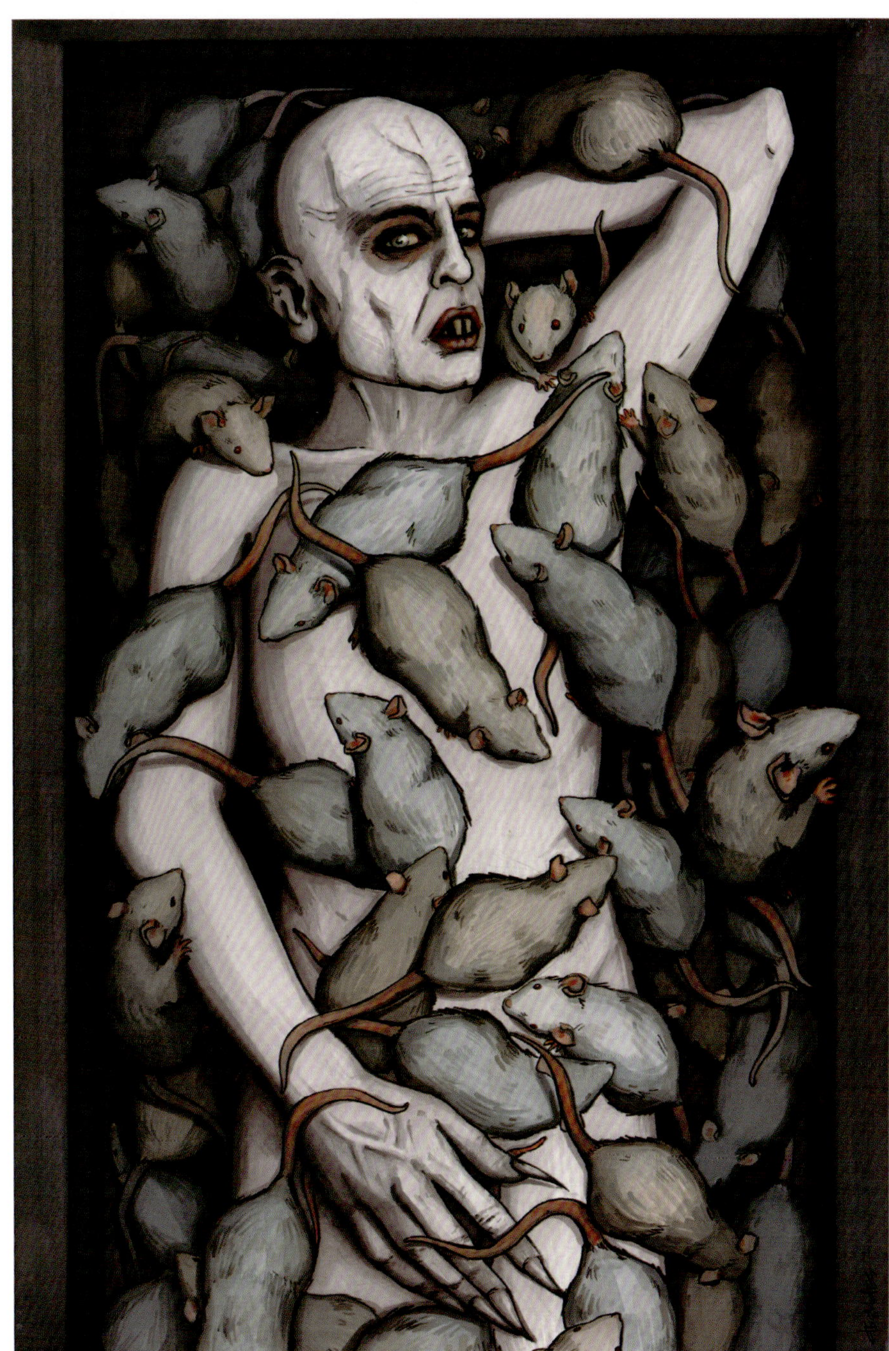

OPPOSITE *A Century of Horror* by Paul Garner. Book cover for We Belong Dead Publications. Mixed media, 2018.

LEFT *The Somnambulist Cesare* by Frederick Cooper. Mixed-media sketch, 2019.

ABOVE *Nosfember* by Erika Deoudes. Sexy Monsters Calendar. Ink, colored pencil, watercolors, 2012.

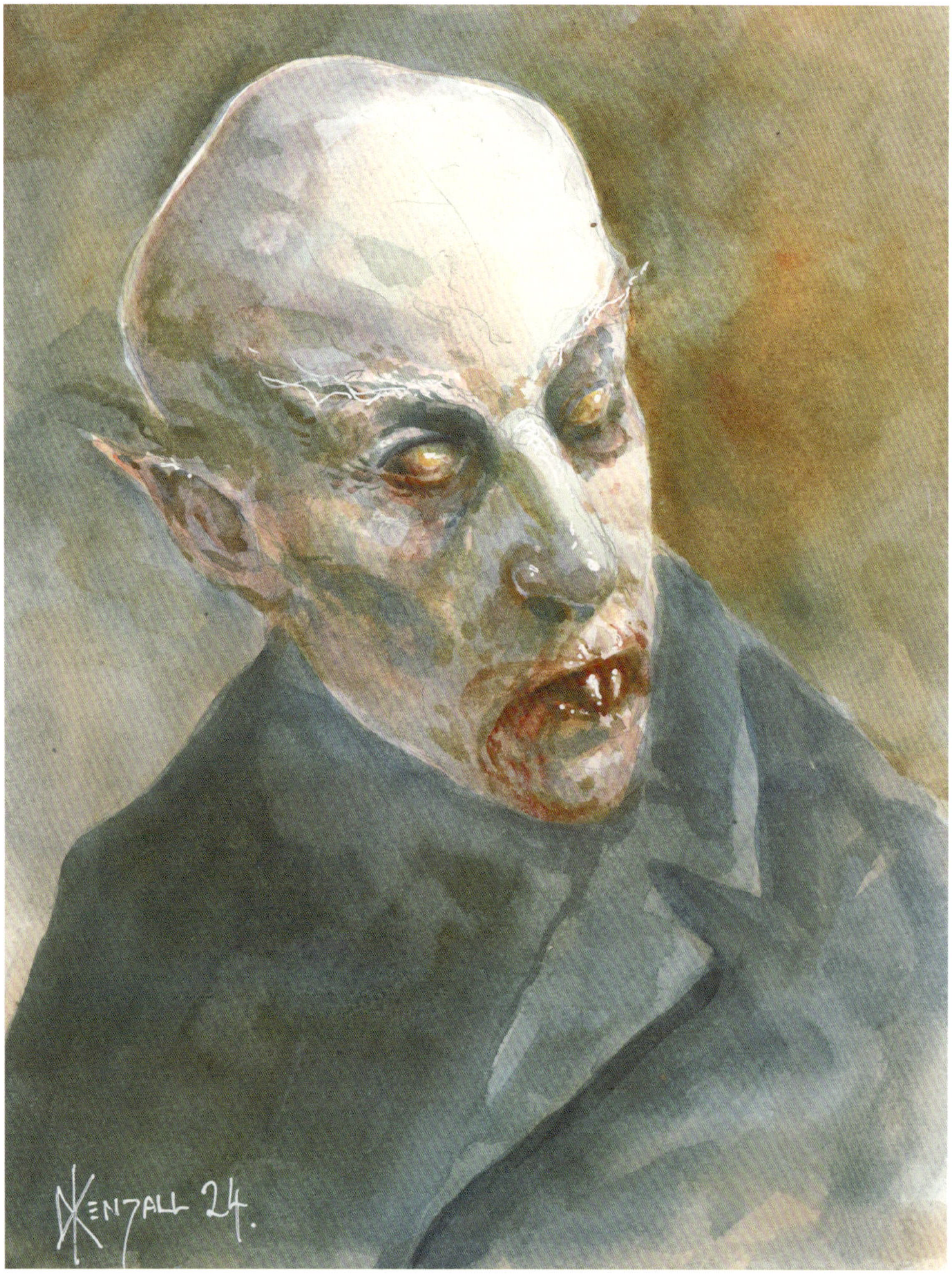

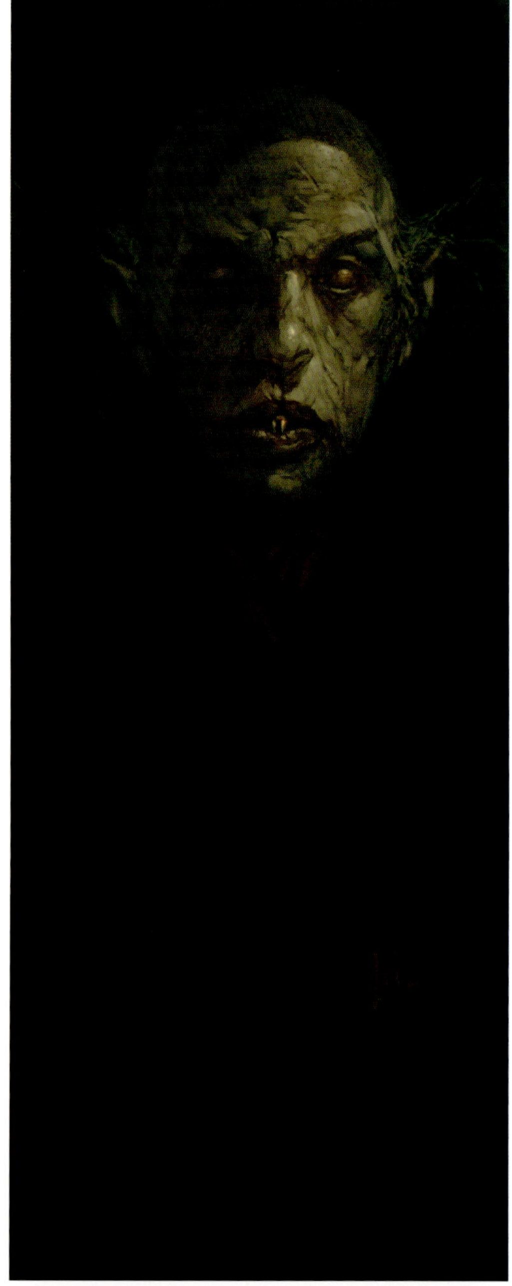

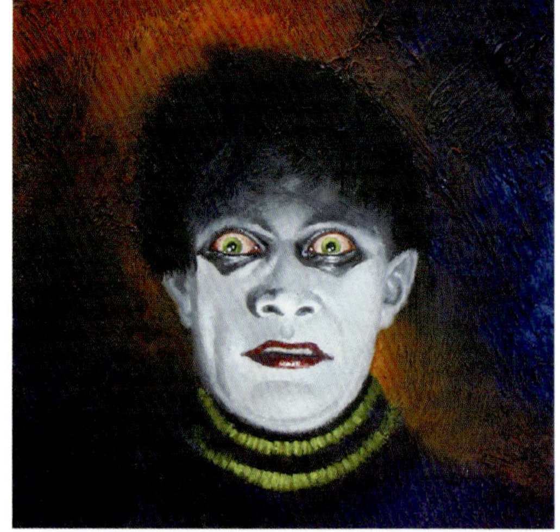

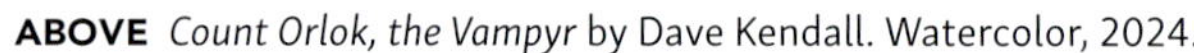

ABOVE *Count Orlok, the Vampyr* by Dave Kendall. Watercolor, 2024.

TOP RIGHT *Nosferatu* by Dave Kendall. Digital, 2014.

BOTTOM RIGHT *Cesare from "The Cabinet of Dr. Caligari"* by Jeff Busch. Oil on wood panel, 2017.

OPPOSITE *Nosferatu the Vampyr* by Greg Staples. Acrylic on paper, 2022.

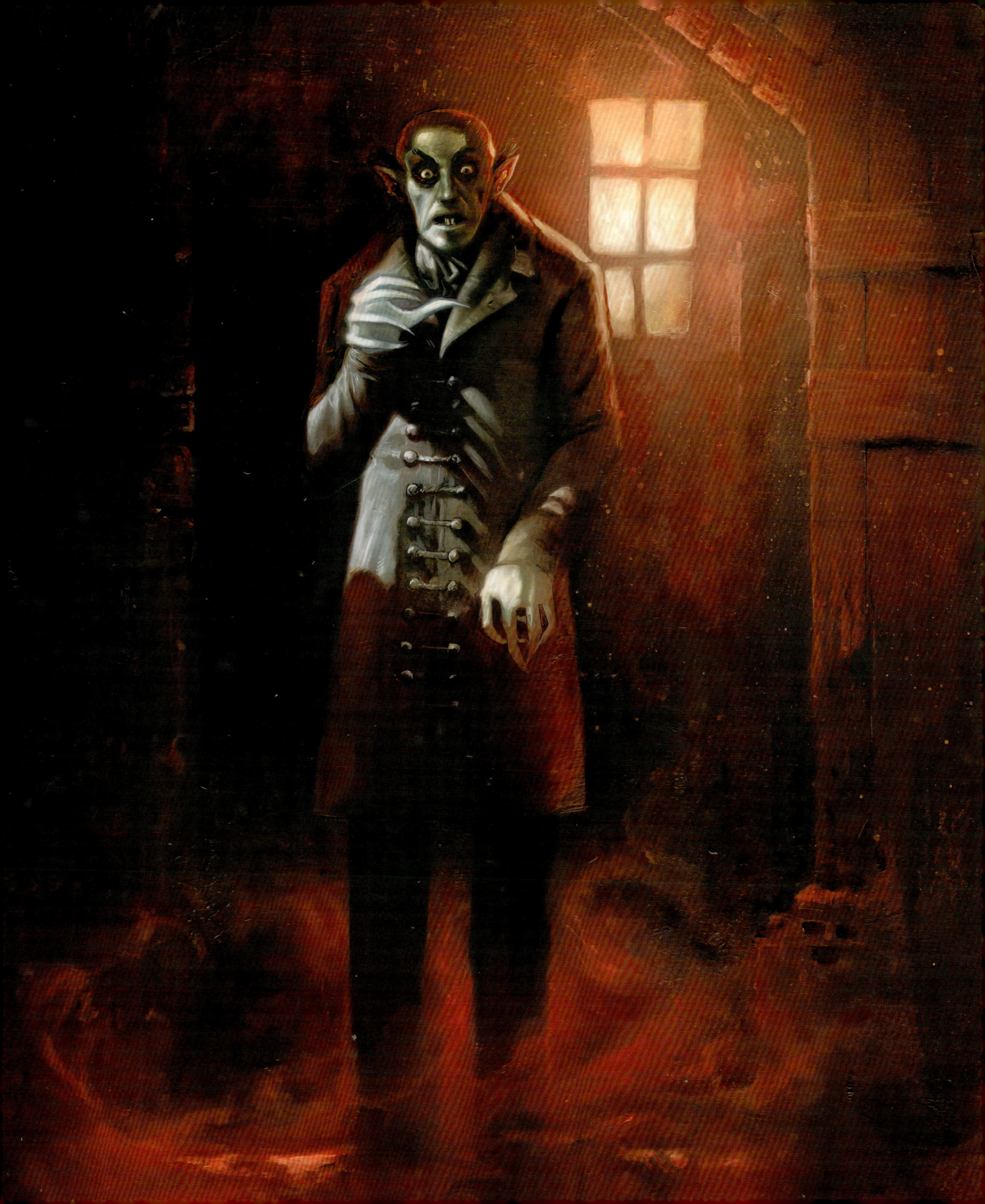

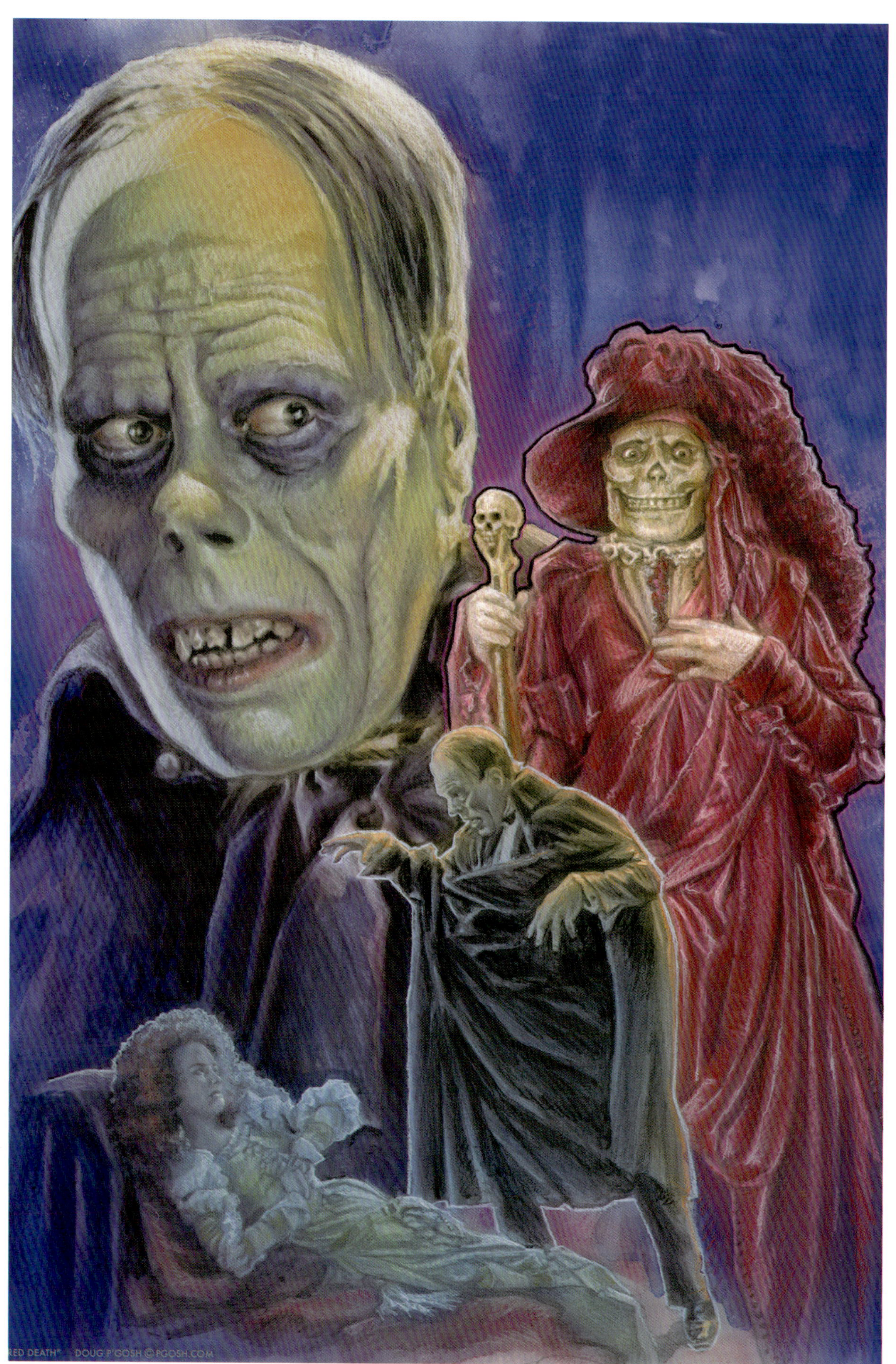

RIGHT *The Phantom of the Opera* by Doug P'Gosh. Acrylics and pastes on board, 2019.

OPPOSITE *The Man Who Laughs* by Frederick Cooper. Mixed media, 2023.

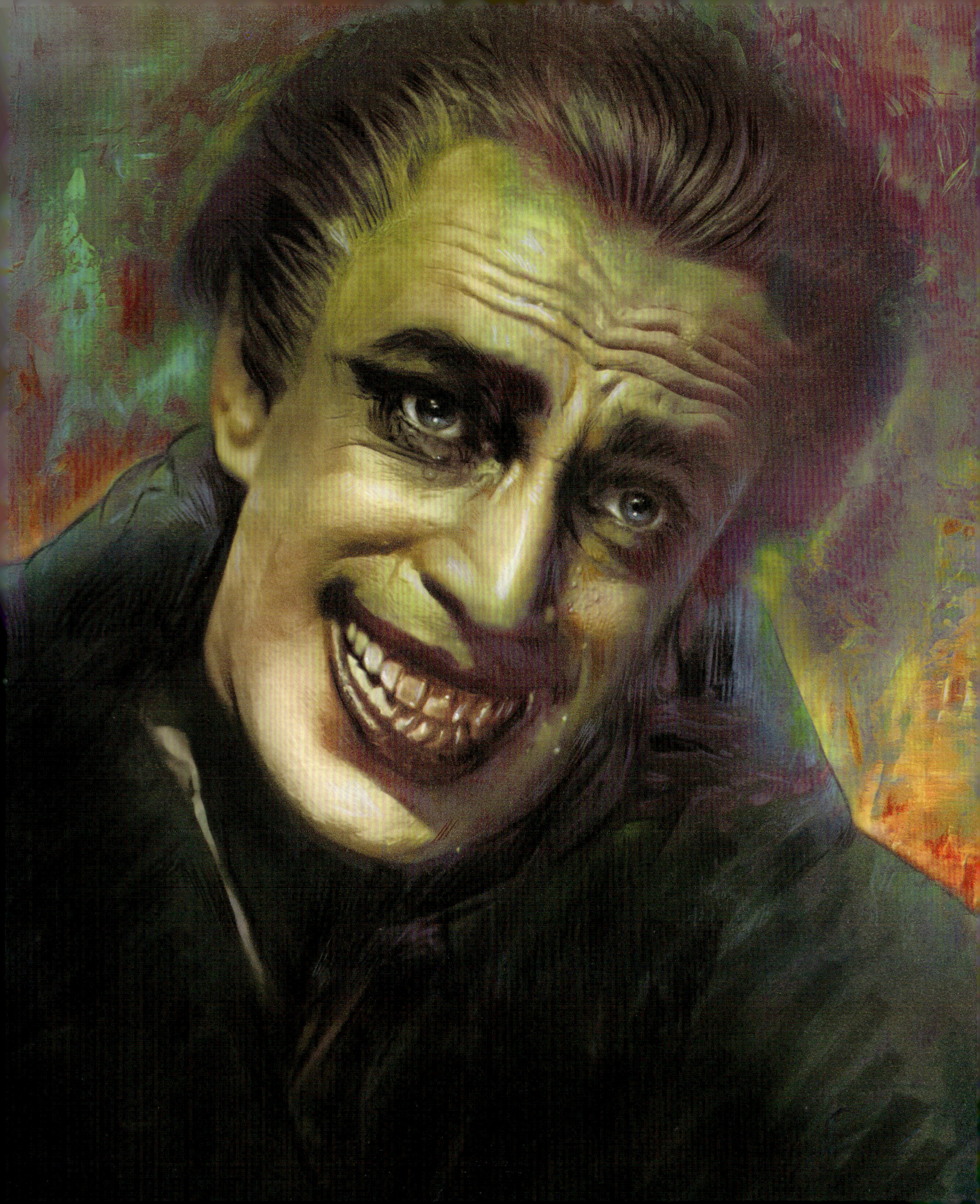

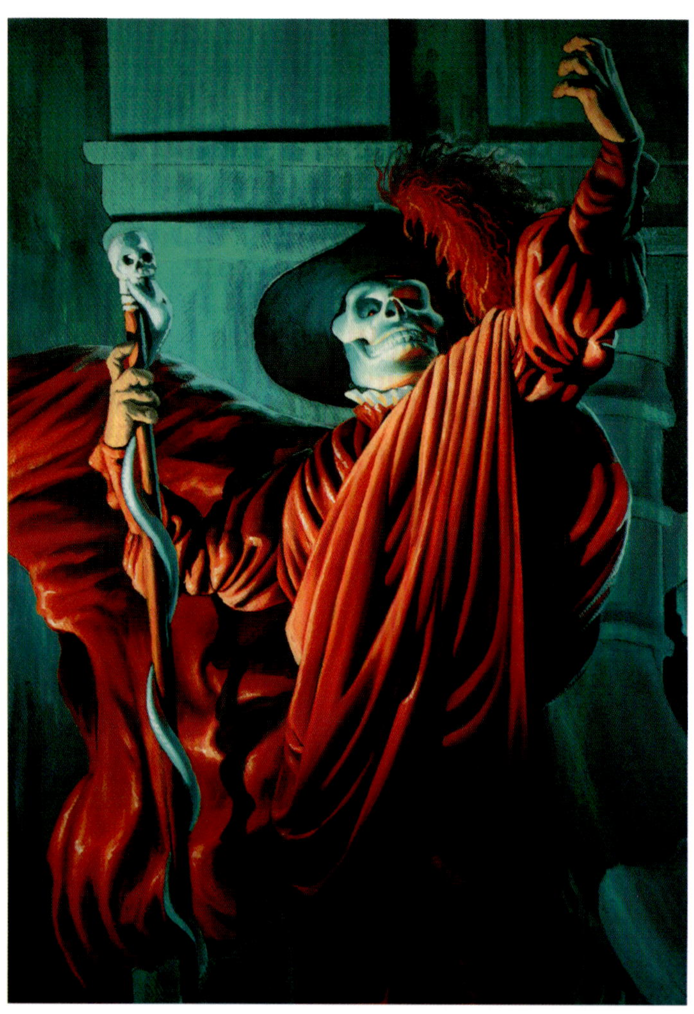

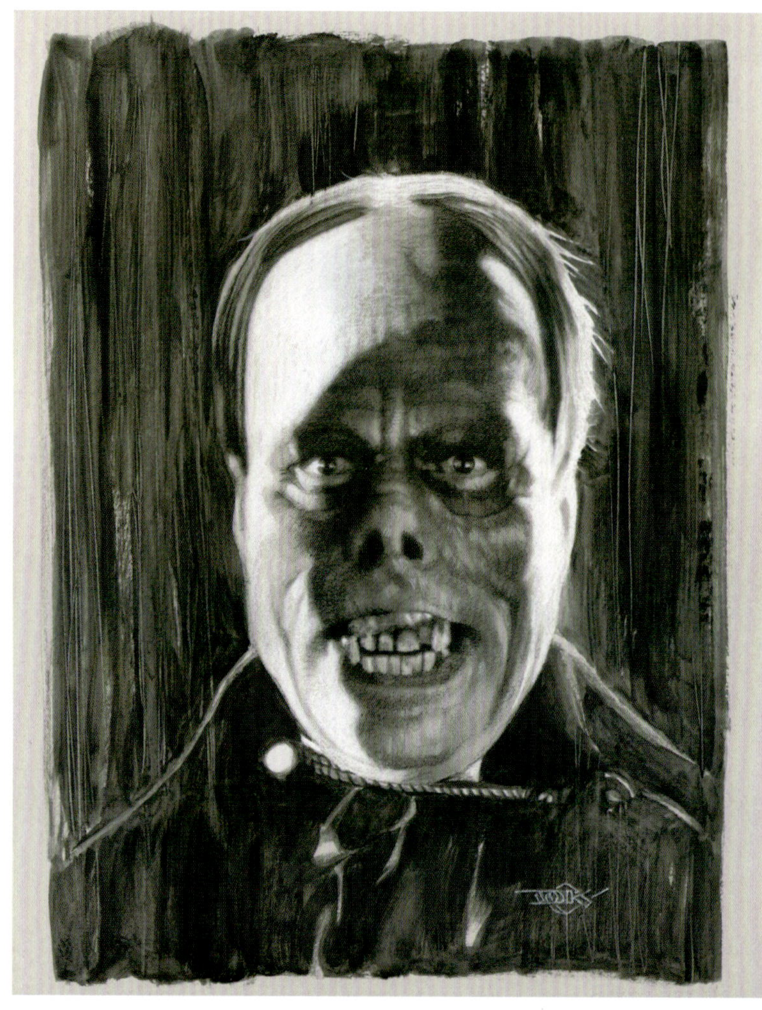

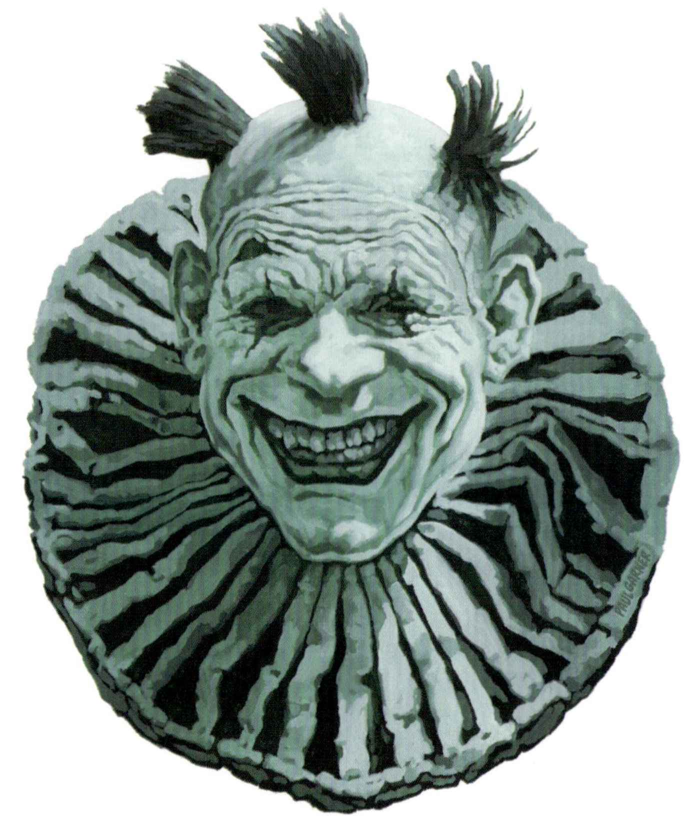

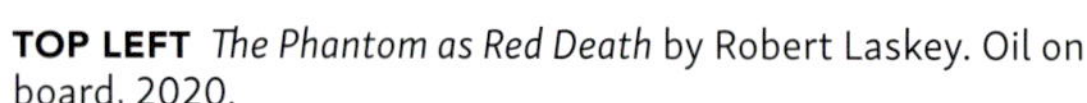

TOP LEFT *The Phantom as Red Death* by Robert Laskey. Oil on board, 2020.

TOP RIGHT *The Phantom* by Douglas Klauba. Charcoal and acrylic paint on gray Crescent board, 2022.

RIGHT *He Who Gets Slapped* by Paul Garner. Acrylic on canvas, 2018.

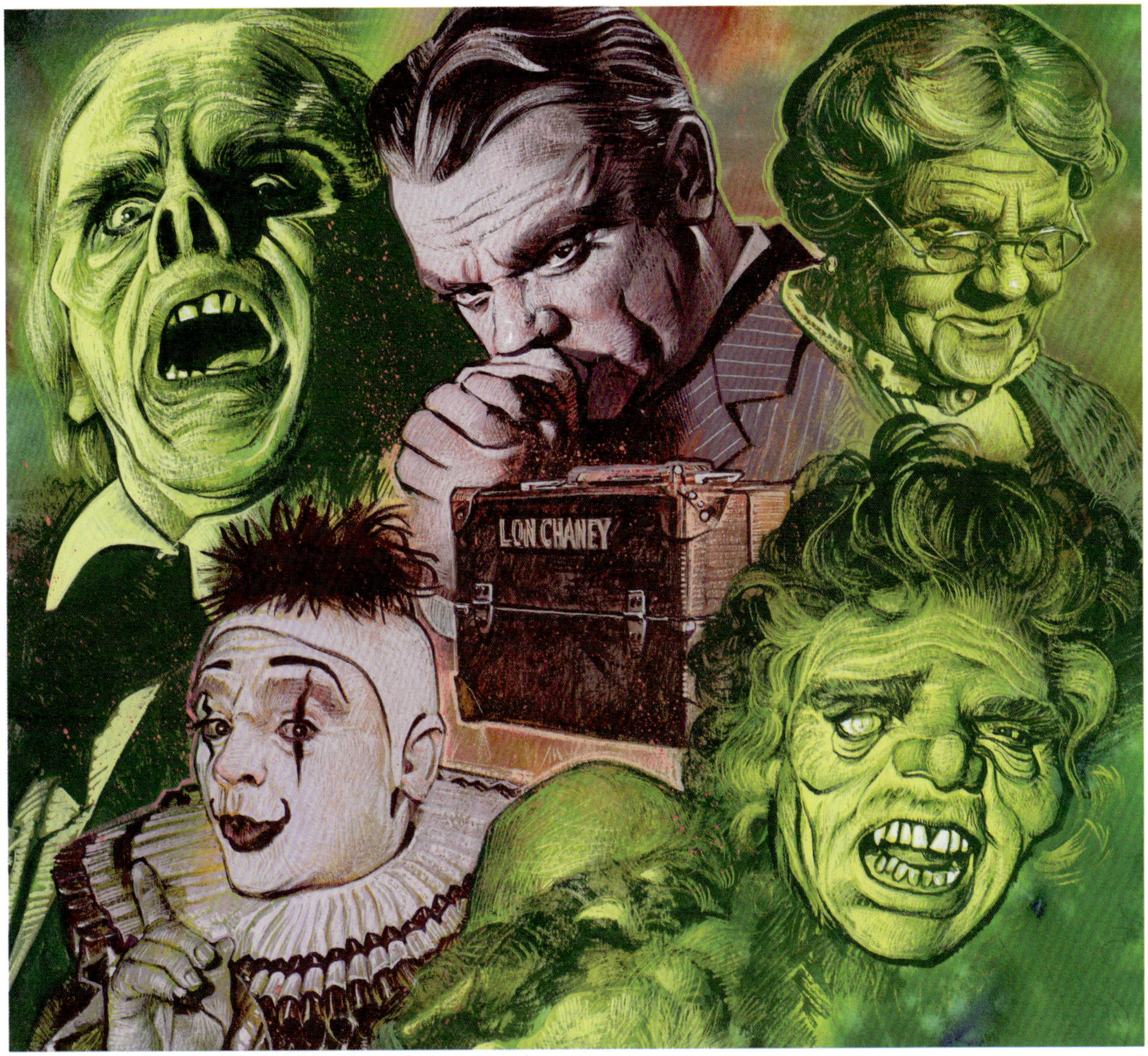

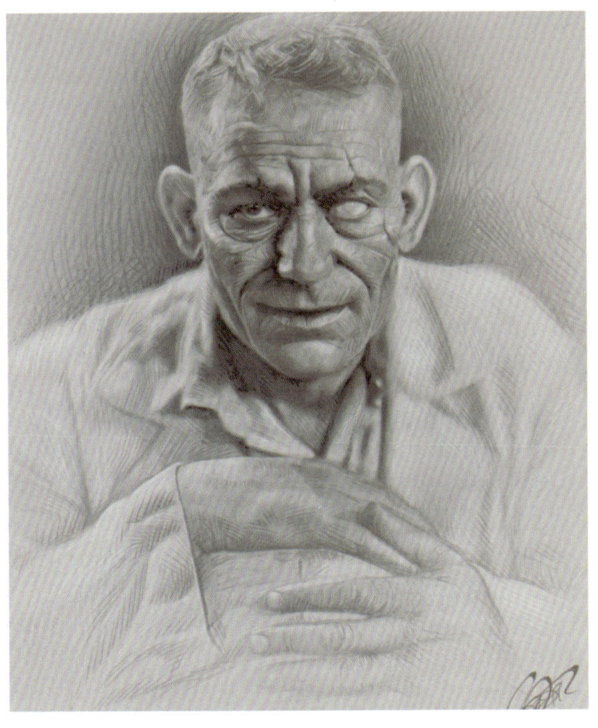

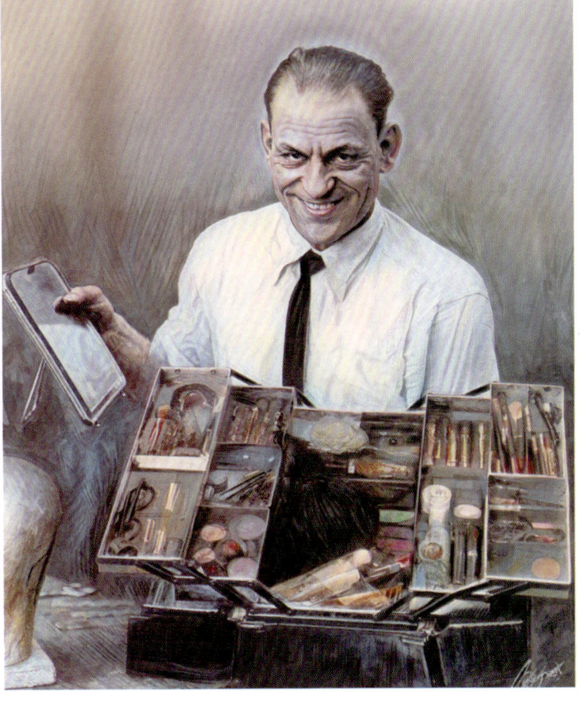

TOP *Man of a Thousand Faces* for James Cagney biopic of Lon Chaney Sr. by Graham Humphreys. Blu-ray cover art for Arrow Video. Mixed media, 2019.

FAR LEFT *Chaney in "The Road to Mandalay"* by Frederick Cooper. Pencil and marker on gray drawing board, 2019.

LEFT *Lon Chaney and Makeup Kit* by Frederick Cooper. Marker and pencil on Bristol board, 2024.

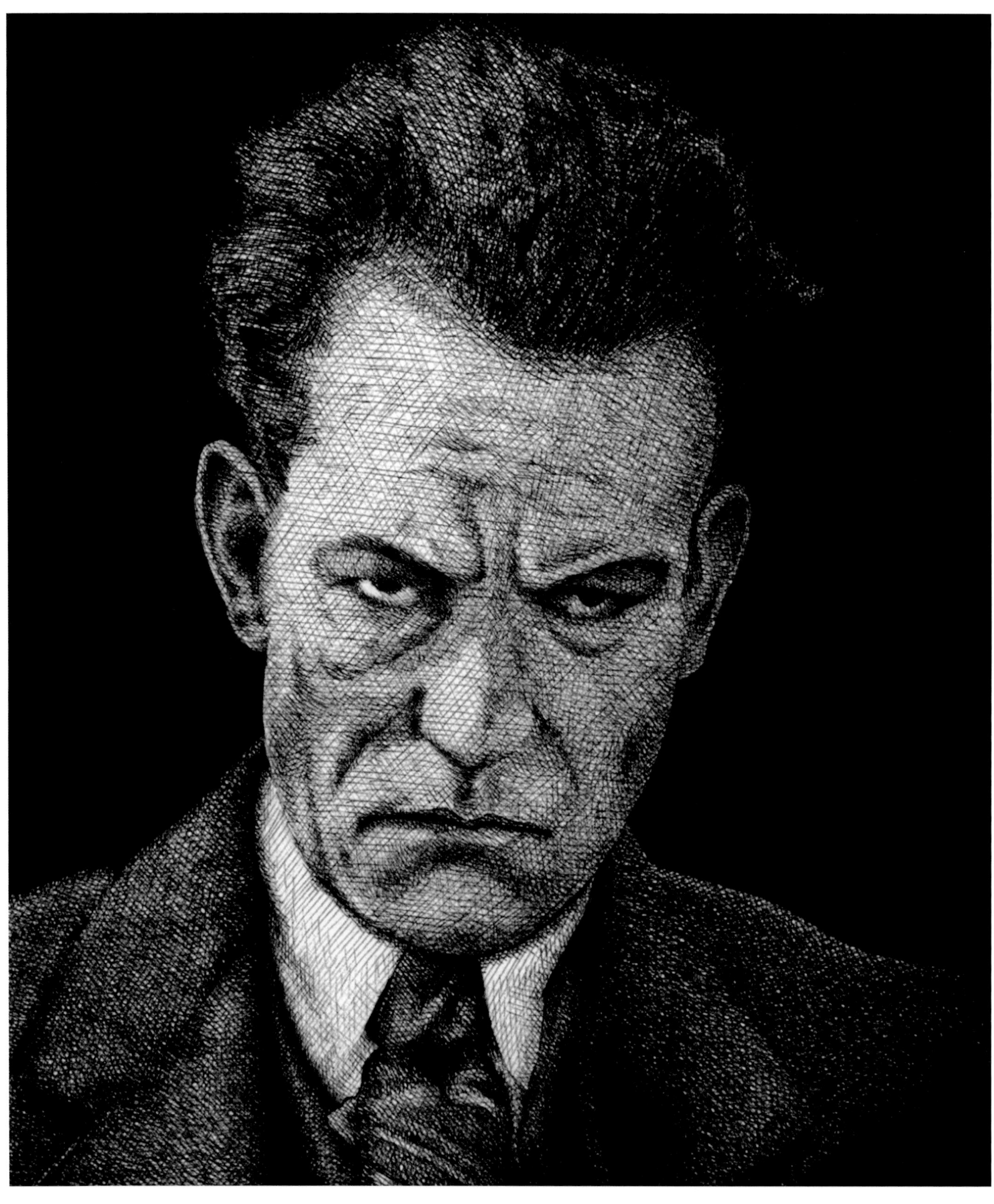

ABOVE *Lon Chaney* by Josh Ryals. Pen and ink on board, 2012.

OPPOSITE *Nosferatu* by Doug P'Gosh. Acrylic and pastel pencil on board, 2023.

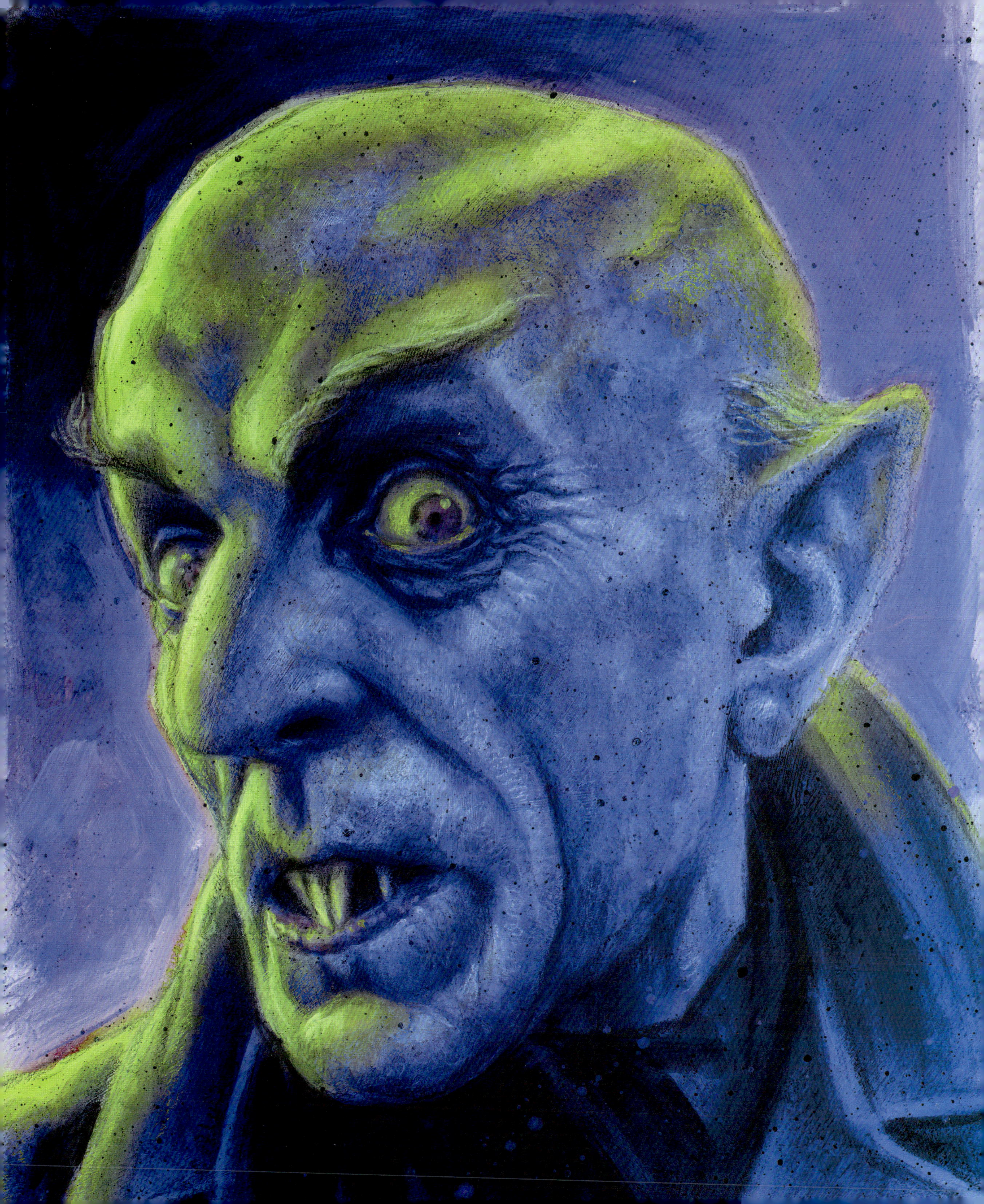

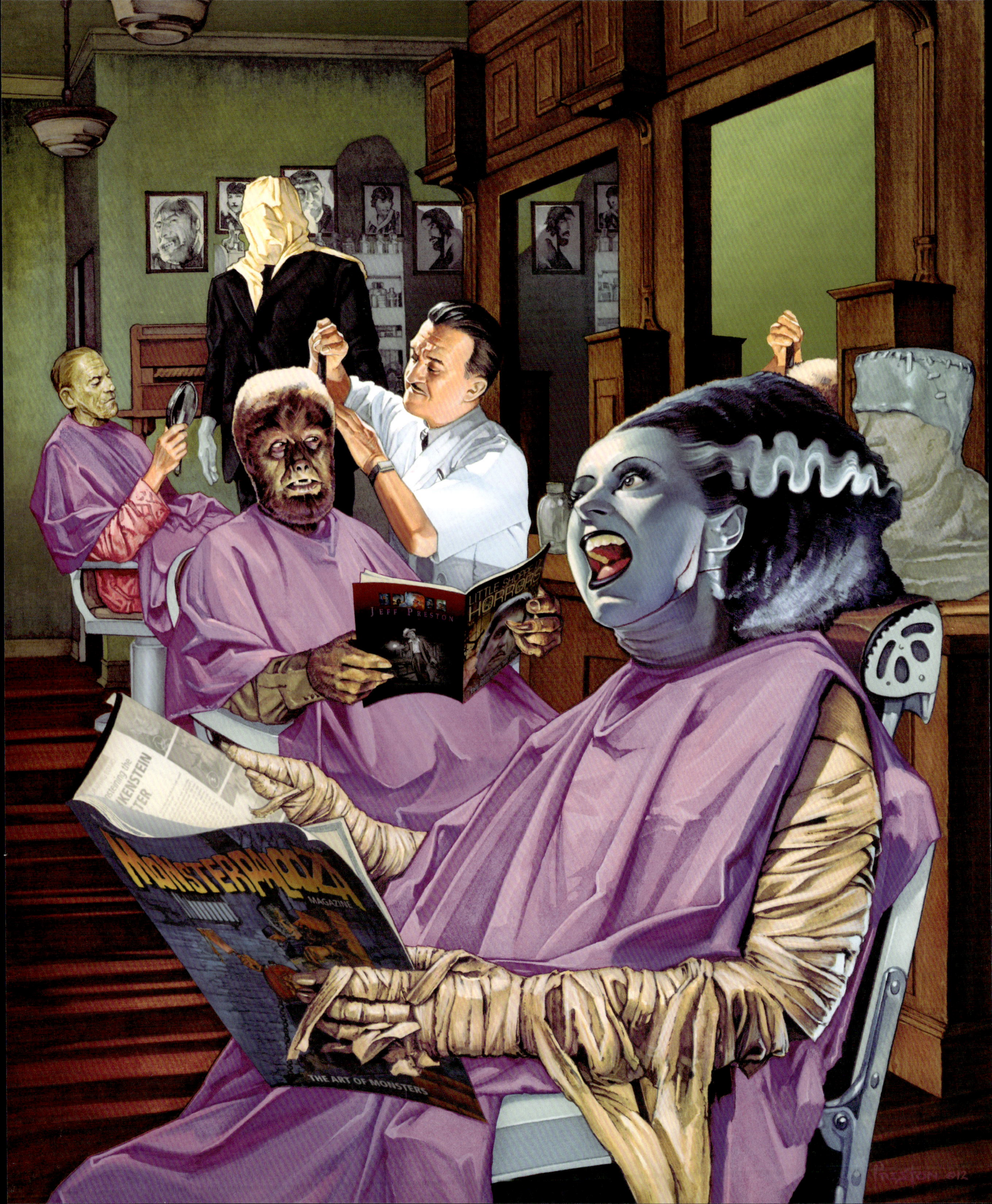
JEFF PRESTON
HORRORS
MONSTERPALOOZA
MAGAZINE
THE ART OF MONSTERS

CHAPTER 3

Universal Translation (1930–1939)

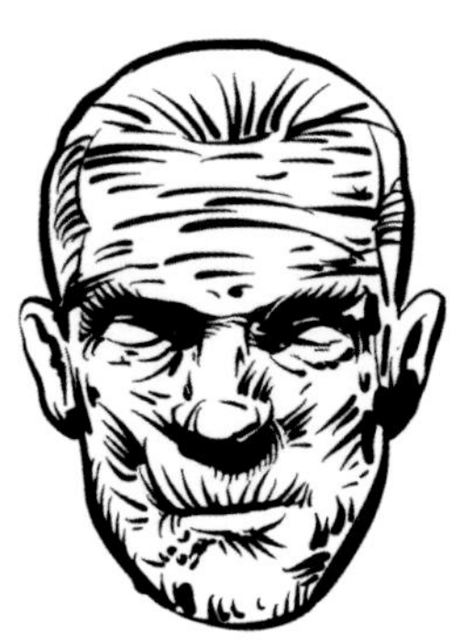
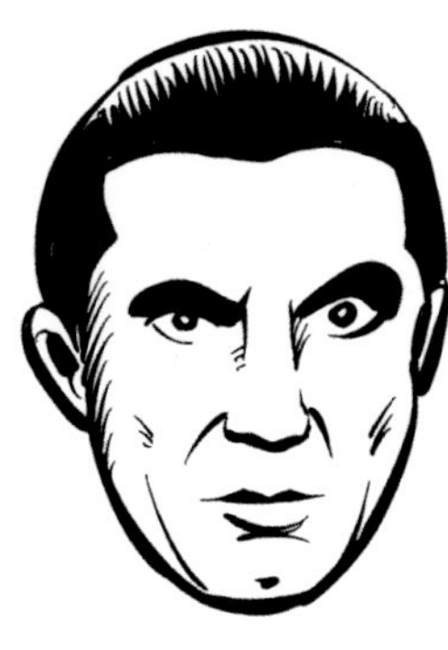
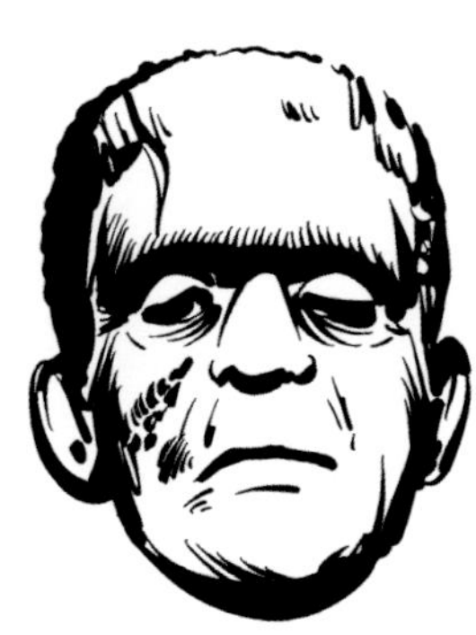

Like much of the folklore, myths, and fables that monster films are based upon, Bela Lugosi was forever inseparable from the old country in which he originated. Born in Lugos, the Kingdom of Hungary (now Lugoj, Romania), on October 20, 1882, Béla Ferenc Dezső Blaskó was picked by his own personal monster and became the face (and voice) of Dracula for time immemorial. To him, it was a blessing as well as a curse.

After the death of Chaney, director Tod Browning was left floundering to find a leading man for his film. Lugosi had appeared as the king of the vampires on Broadway and in national tours across the United States since 1927 to great success—but Universal Studios' Carl Laemmle Jr. was unimpressed and went through an army of possible Draculas (even Paul Muni, a big star at the time predominantly known for playing gangsters) before time grew short and a choice had to be made. In the most onerous, studio-friendly contract ever, Lugosi was signed for a mere $500 per week—a pittance in exchange for the profits reaped by the studio from his performance, even when adjusted for inflation—to make the movie that officially launched what would become one of the most popular film subgenres in history.

Author John Kenneth Muir reflects on why vampire films resonate with viewers: "Dracula and other vampires are reflections of our quest for immortality, and that quest remains as vital to humanity today as it was a century ago. The details of these monsters may change a little each time they are reimagined for modern audiences, but what they represent is something that all human beings intrinsically understand: belonging, loss, vengeance, and other familiar emotional states."

Although *Dracula* set the standard for vampire films, Lugosi never shows fangs—and he never has to. His peculiar speech pattern—attained when he had to learn his lines for the Broadway stage play phonetically because he barely spoke English—his intense facial expressions, and his unique gestures and body language spoke more loudly about the menace of the vampire than mere prosthetic teeth could have. His Dracula is unquestionably a creature of the night. The film was an unqualified success and propelled its leading man into stardom—of a sort. He would be forever associated with the role, and it with him, and found it difficult to break away from the stereotype of a supernatural villain and was relegated to playing similar parts for most of his life.

The success of *Dracula* begat *Frankenstein*. It also led to Lugosi turning up his nose at the role of the monster because he didn't want to cover his face for the

OPPOSITE *Universal Monster Barber Shop* by Jeff Preston. Unreleased magazine cover. Markers on paper, 2014.

ABOVE *The Mummy, Dracula, and Frankenstein* by Peter Bregman. Pen and ink, 2020.

movie (although a makeup test was done on him as a very different-looking creature than the one that made it to the screen). Instead, he chose roles in the 1932 features *Murders in the Rue Morgue* and *White Zombie*. *Frankenstein* director James Whale had only to look as far as a few tables over in the Universal Studios commissary, at lunch one day, to spot a hungry-looking William Henry Pratt, aka Boris Karloff, to find his monster.

James Whale, like Karloff, was British, and he was one of the directors who worked with Howard Hughes in 1929 to reshoot *Hell's Angels* as a talkie when synchronized sound burst onto the scene and made silent films passé. *Frankenstein* was his third Hollywood film. He was an openly gay man, something quite uncommon at the time. There were plenty of gay people in the film business, but few were able to admit it publicly for fear of forfeiting their careers to scandal.

"James Whale was the perfect director for *Frankenstein* and *Bride of Frankenstein* because, as a gay man, he could identify with Dr. Frankenstein's so-called Monster," says author and filmmaker Sam Irvin, a producer of *Gods and Monsters* (1998), the Academy Award–winning film starring Sir Ian McKellen as Whale. "This innocent creature was a freak of nature, misunderstood by society, judged, tried, and convicted by the court of public opinion and mob rule. In other words, just another day in the life of a member of the LGBTQ+ community. Whale made this outsider sympathetic. He may have looked scary, but he meant no harm and had a heart of gold. The true villain of the films was his creator, who abandoned him—and thus the confusion over the name Frankenstein. Was Frankenstein the Monster? Or the doctor who created the Monster? Or was the doctor really the creator *and* the Monster? These are the existential questions raised by the thinking man behind the first two classic Universal *Frankenstein* movies. Whale was not just making films for pure entertainment; he had a message that challenged us all. None of the sequels post-Whale had the depth nor pathos that this director infused. The first two movies are gut-wrenching and laden with real emotions that all of us 'Monster Kids' can identify with as outsiders. I certainly did. And still do." (Irvin's self-identification as a "Monster Kid" refers to the generation of youth raised during the 1960s monster craze.)

Whatever restrictions Whale may have been subjected to by the studio brass were off the table when *Frankenstein* proved to be an even bigger hit than *Dracula*

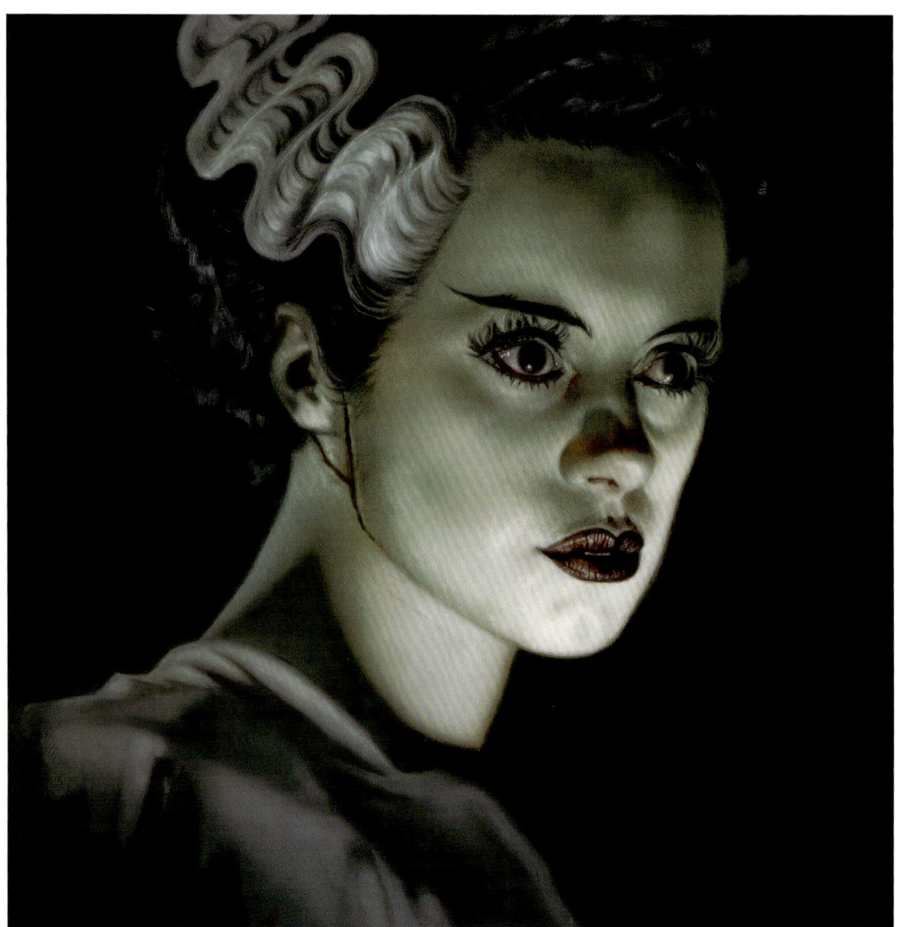

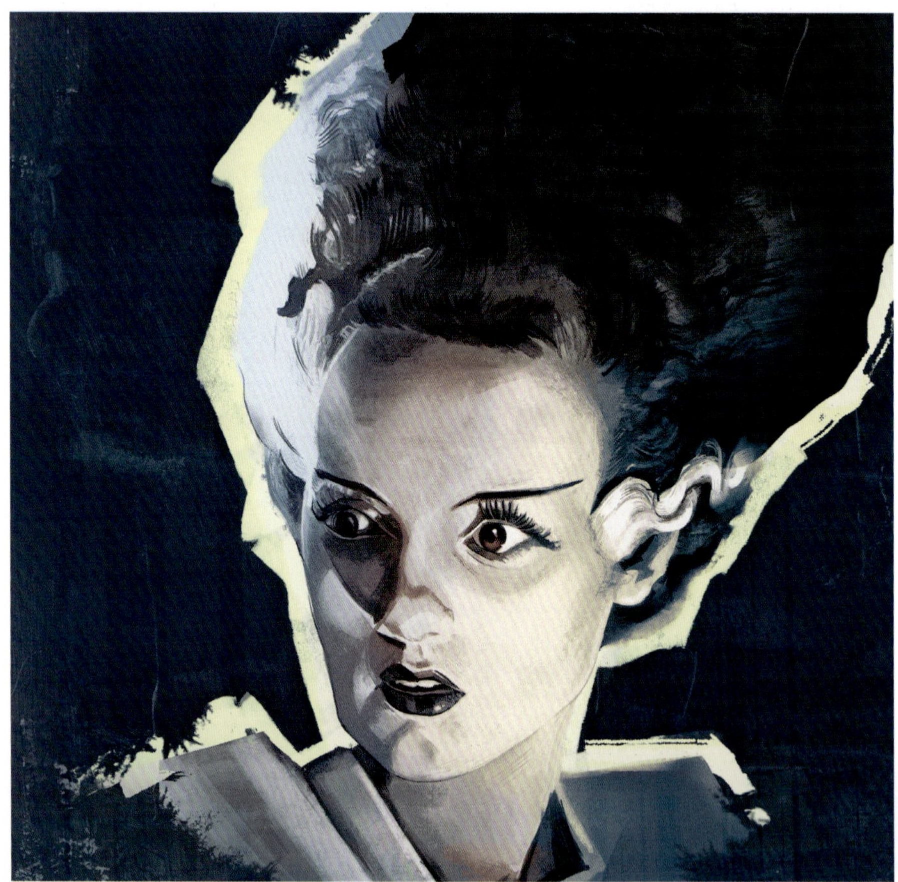

in 1931. By the time Universal talked him into directing a sequel in 1935, Whale had apparently decided that the subtext would be as flamboyant as he could make it. The result was the gloriously over-the-top *Bride of Frankenstein*, arguably one of the best monster movies ever made and a true fan favorite. *Frankenstein* would become Universal's first monster-film franchise. *Bride* was followed by *Son of Frankenstein* (1939), *The Ghost of Frankenstein* (1942), *Frankenstein Meets the Wolf Man* (1943), *House of Frankenstein* (1944), and *Abbott and Costello Meet Frankenstein* (1948). The monster also had a co-starring role in *House of Dracula* (1945).

"I remember seeing the monster's face in *Frankenstein* and literally gasping with complete adoration," recalls artist El Gato Gomez. "I had seen that face a million times, but the first time I watched the movie as an adult, it just took my breath away. Imagine going into that theater in 1931, having never seen that face—I think I would have peed my pants!"

Universal also made a series of *Dracula* sequels, including *Dracula's Daughter* (1936), *Son of Dracula* (1943), and the aforementioned *House of Dracula*, none of which starred Bela Lugosi. However, he did return as the Count in *Abbott and Costello Meet Frankenstein*. Lugosi would don the mantle of Transylvania's finest on-screen just once more, in a television appearance on *The Paul Winchell Show* in 1950.

The era of Universal's classic monsters began approximately two years after the Wall Street crash of October 1929. In the aftermath of that event, the country and, indeed, the world were plunged into an unprecedented financial depression. Unemployment was at an all-time high, with hundreds of thousands of people without jobs and suddenly unable to make mortgage payments, resulting in rising numbers of home foreclosures. The American Great Plains became a dust bowl where crops could not grow, further complicating an already untenable situation. Despair became the most frequent meal for a generation that was adrift in a sea of dread and confusion.

But movies survived. And they only cost a quarter.

In their darkest hour, many fled to theaters to help stave off the very real terror they felt about their own situation and the future. There, they could inhabit a world in which the troubles were someone else's, and the romance and reward came swiftly and brightened their hearts for a bit. Monster movies became the genre of choice for young and old alike because the horror on-screen was always vanquished by the end of the film. The personal anxiety of the viewer could be deferred while they experienced a fantasy version that could not harm them in any way. This fare became a salve for the culture, and it helped stop the metaphorical bleeding of deep psychological wounds. The images

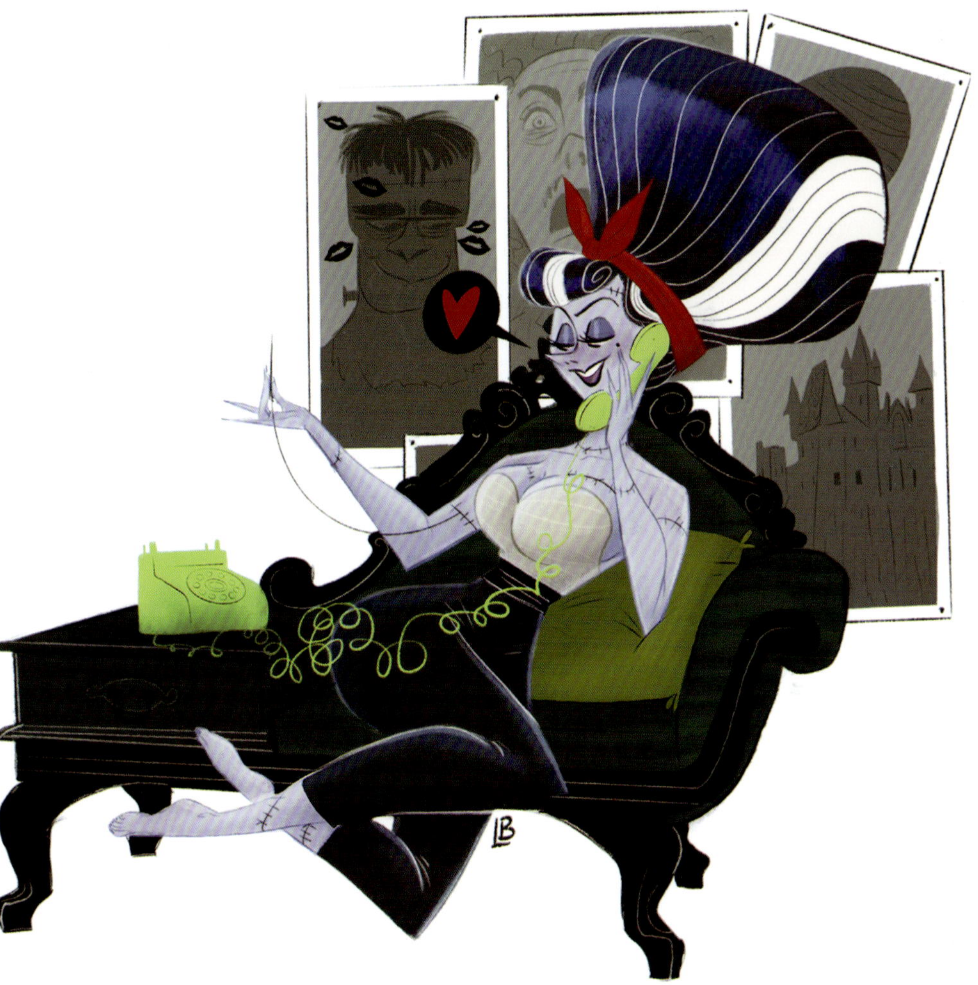

OPPOSITE TOP *The Bride* by Greg Staples. Poster design for Vice Press. Acrylic, 2022.

OPPOSITE BOTTOM *The Bride* by Adam Insam. Digital, 2022.

RIGHT *No, You Hang Up* by Lacie Barker. Digital, 2020.

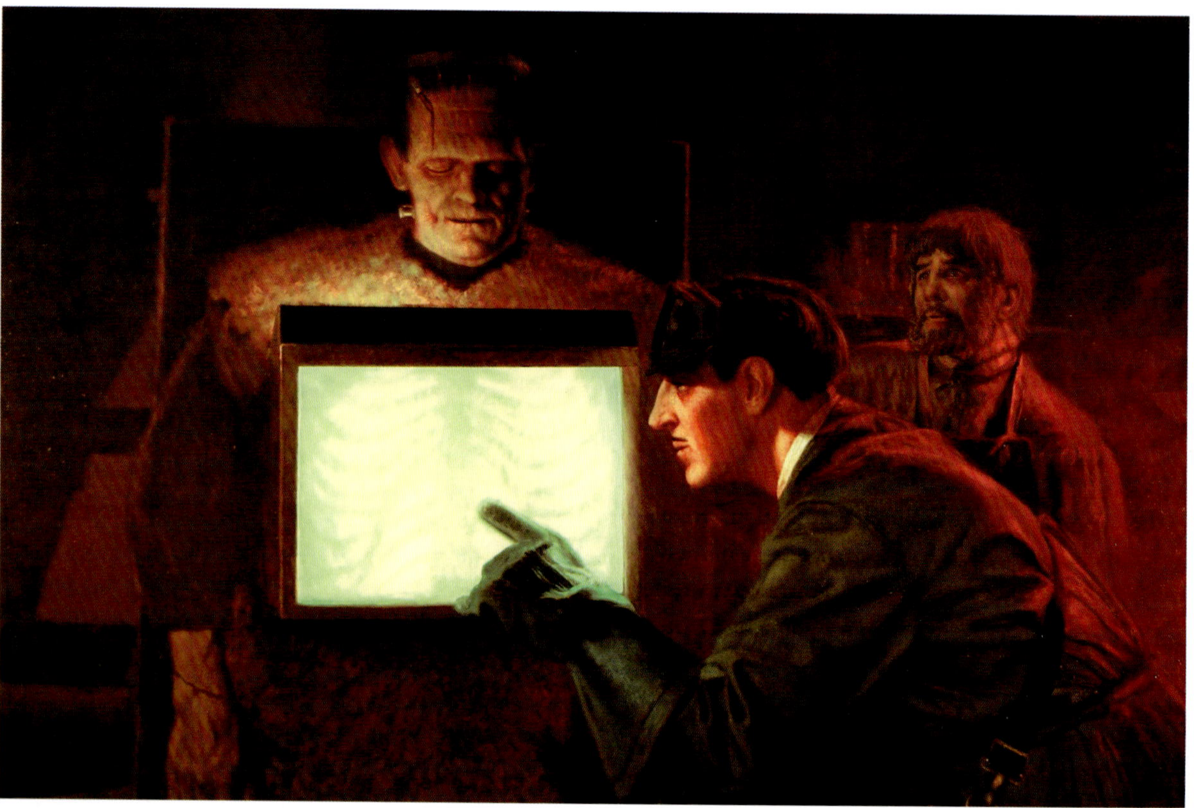

onscreen undoubtedly saved lives by offering hope to the hopeless.

Artist Erika Deoudes puts it succinctly: "Our fears speak in isolation, even as we engage with other people. When media reflects those fears, we realize we're not alone in them, even if we're watching alone. This effect amplifies exponentially with an audience: As fears mingle out in the open, we connect on deeper levels rarely accessed in social situations."

Film historian and author Mark Dawidziak agrees that there's a powerful connection between societal anxieties and screen horror:

"It's unsurprising that Barnabas Collins, the vampire on the *Dark Shadows* TV series, was the first to break the predator trap and reclaim his soul, and that happened in the 1960s—a decade of radical change and liberation movements. Similarly, two of the biggest vampire hits of the 1980s, *Fright Night* and *The Lost Boys*, dealt with the children of divorce in a decade when broken homes were increasingly common. Horror rarely doesn't reflect the cultural shifts of its time. You see this in the films produced during the 1950s' Red Scare, such as *The Thing*, *Invasion of the Body Snatchers*, and *The Return of Dracula*. You see this in every generation and decade."

As Universal's monster pictures took hold of the public's imagination, many of the so-called Poverty Row studios began to crank out low-budget B movie flicks to fill the gaps between releases. Monogram, PRC, Liberty, Mascot, and other studios threw what little money they had toward making films that promised a lot on their posters but in many cases delivered a less satisfying product. Movies like *The Devil Bat* (1940), *Invisible Ghost* (1941), and *Return of the Ape Man* (1944), all with Lugosi, as well as *Ghosts on the Loose* (1943) and *Strangler of the Swamp* (1945), are standouts in an otherwise mediocre crowd—which is nonetheless worth study and remembrance. These unassuming stories kept many kids up late on weekends in the 1960s when they were staples of the UHF television scene. Before the advent of cable TV, ultrahigh frequency channels—generally numbered 13 and up on the dial—were the refuge of retro and cult programming because these movies and shows were inexpensive time fillers for the generally independently owned and operated stations.

Apart from the Universal pantheon, several groundbreaking, classic films were born in the 1930s at other studios—chief among them *King Kong* from RKO. *Kong* was not the birthplace of the stop-motion animated monster, but it certainly heralded the forthcoming era of stop-motion beasts. The giant ape was the creation of sculptor and designer Marcel Delgado and animator Willis O'Brien, and wowed audiences when the movie was released in 1933. One audience member in particular was so inspired by the film that he eventually

ABOVE *The Son of Frankenstein* by Daniel Horne. Collection of Guillermo Del Toro. Oil on canvas, 2018.

OPPOSITE *The Monster* by Greg Staples. Print for Vice Press. Graphite and acrylic, 2022.

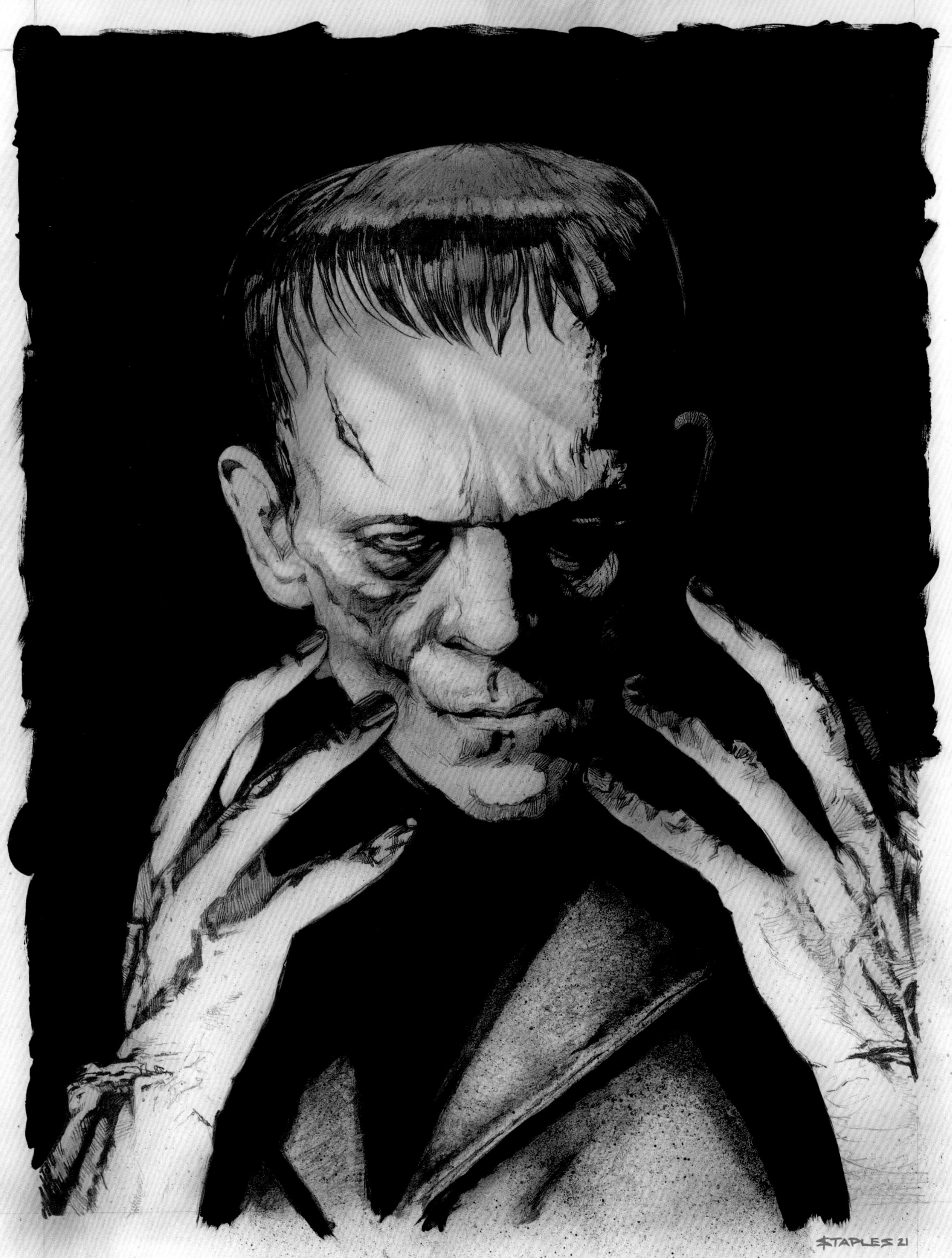
STAPLES 21

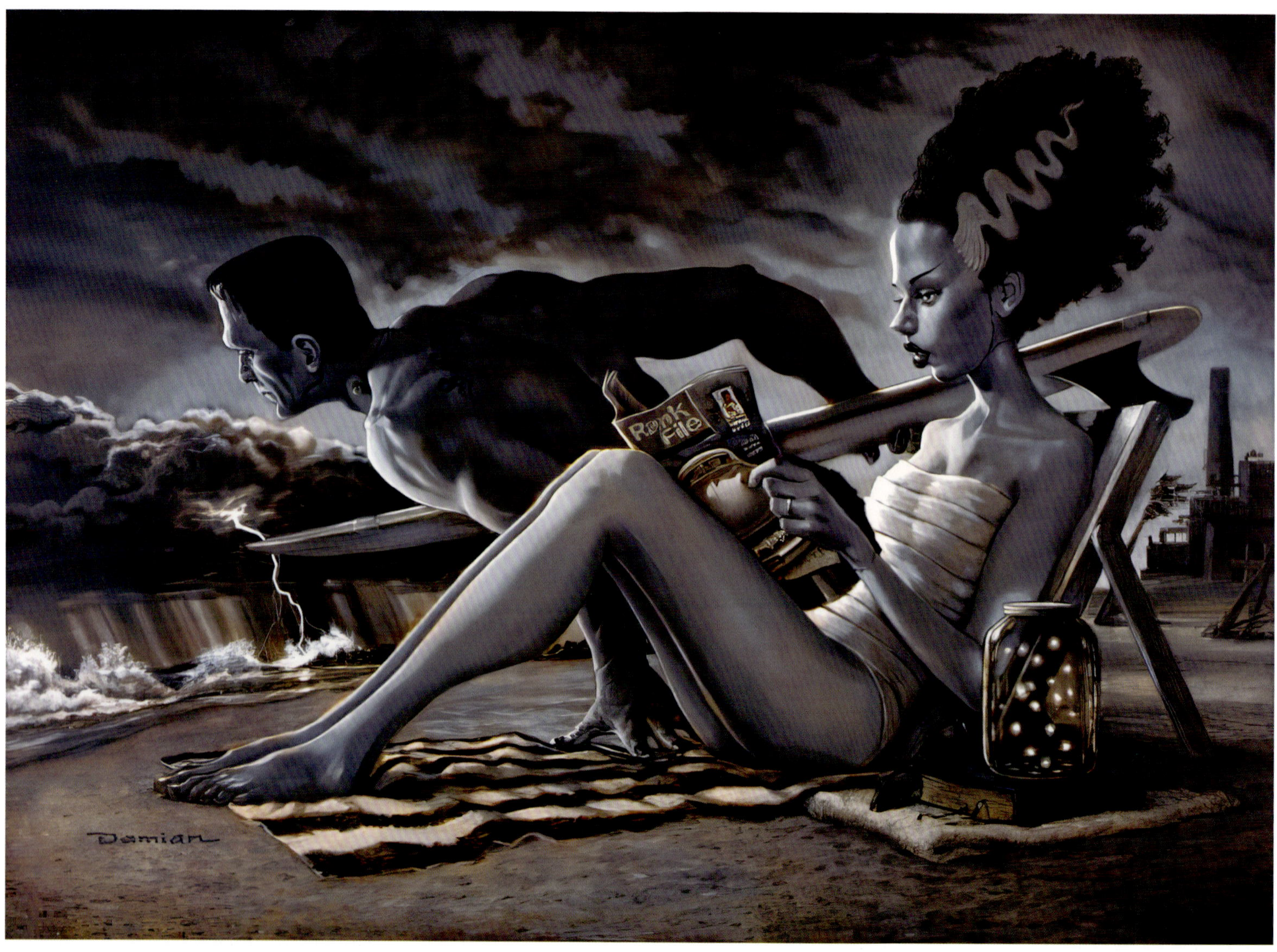

ABOVE *The Bathers* by Damian Fulton. Oil on canvas, 2013.

OPPOSITE *Hissing Bride* by Robert Laskey. Oil on board, 2021.

contacted O'Brien to show him his own efforts with a camera and articulated figures—Ray Harryhausen, who would become an assistant animator to O'Brien on *Mighty Joe Young* (1949) and move on to an impressive movie career of his own. *Kong* told a cautionary tale about messing with misunderstood natural forces and denying those forces their basic wants and needs in the name of commercialism.

Celebrated horror novelist Ramsey Campbell is a die-hard fan, declaring it his favorite monster movie. "*King Kong* now and forever," Campbell declares, "not just for its incomparably characterful creature and magical special effects but for its structure, which creates anticipation few films could satisfy. This one does, no matter how many times I revisit it. A masterpiece."

Among other movies with heads above the crowd was Paramount's *Dr. Jekyll and Mr. Hyde* (1931) with Fredric March, who won the Academy Award for Best Actor for his performance. Also of note were Lugosi as Murder Legendre, the scourge of Haiti, in United Artists' *White Zombie* (1932), Paramount's *Island of Lost Souls* (1932)—also with Lugosi, along with Charles Laughton—Tod Browning's *Freaks* (1932) from MGM, *Mystery of the Wax Museum* (1933) from Warner Bros., MGM's *Mad Love* (1935), and a gaggle of British and European releases including *The Ghoul* (1933), *Vampyr* (1932), and a second remake of *The Student of Prague* (1935). This small sampling of the first true decade of monster and horror film proliferation reveals there were many worthy films released during this period.

As the world began to right itself from the economic crisis, Europe became volatile again with the rise of the Nazi Party in Germany, and was, once again, plunged into war. The rise of fascism brought a new set of fears to be allayed in the dark but battled in earnest in the bright light of day.

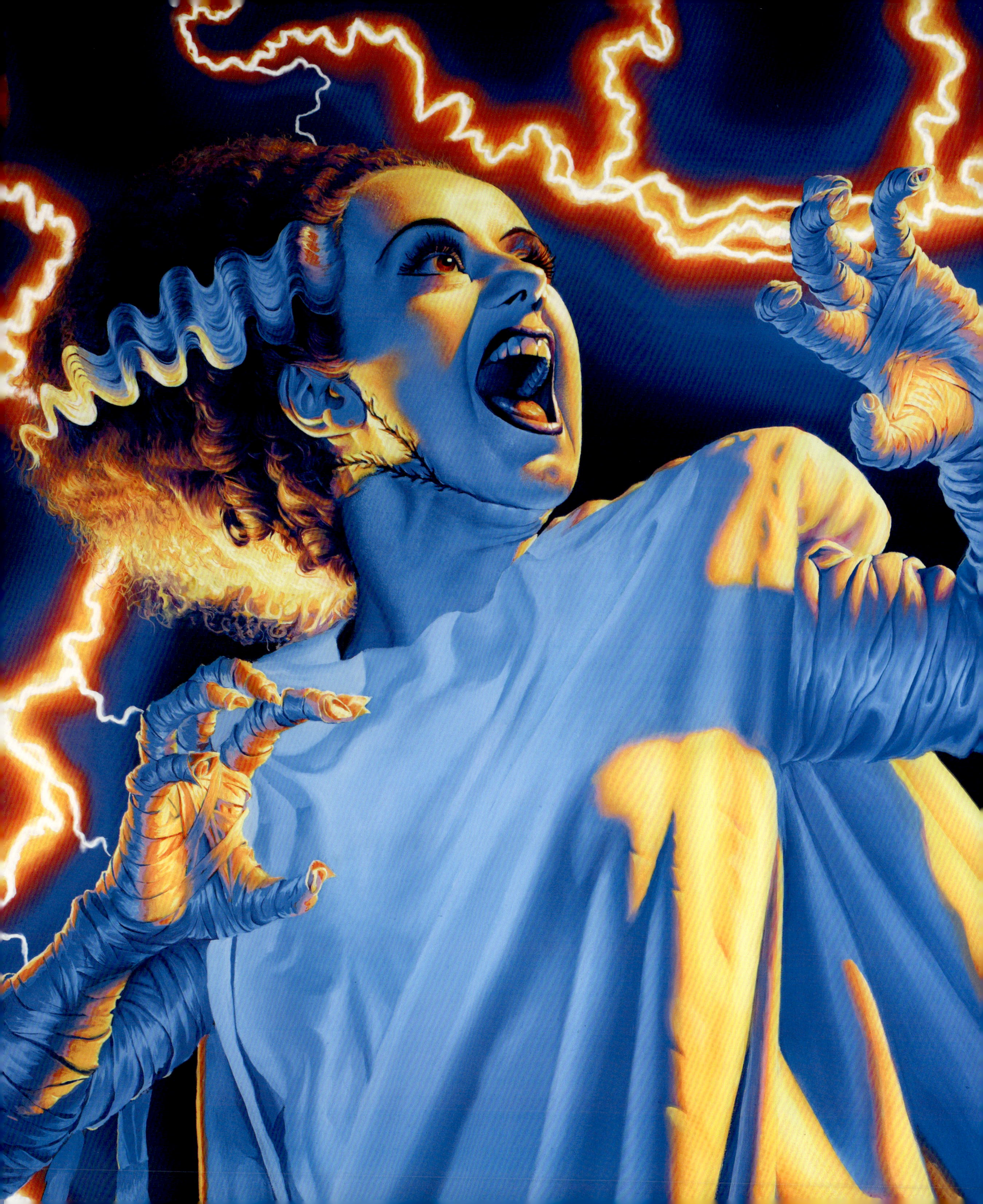

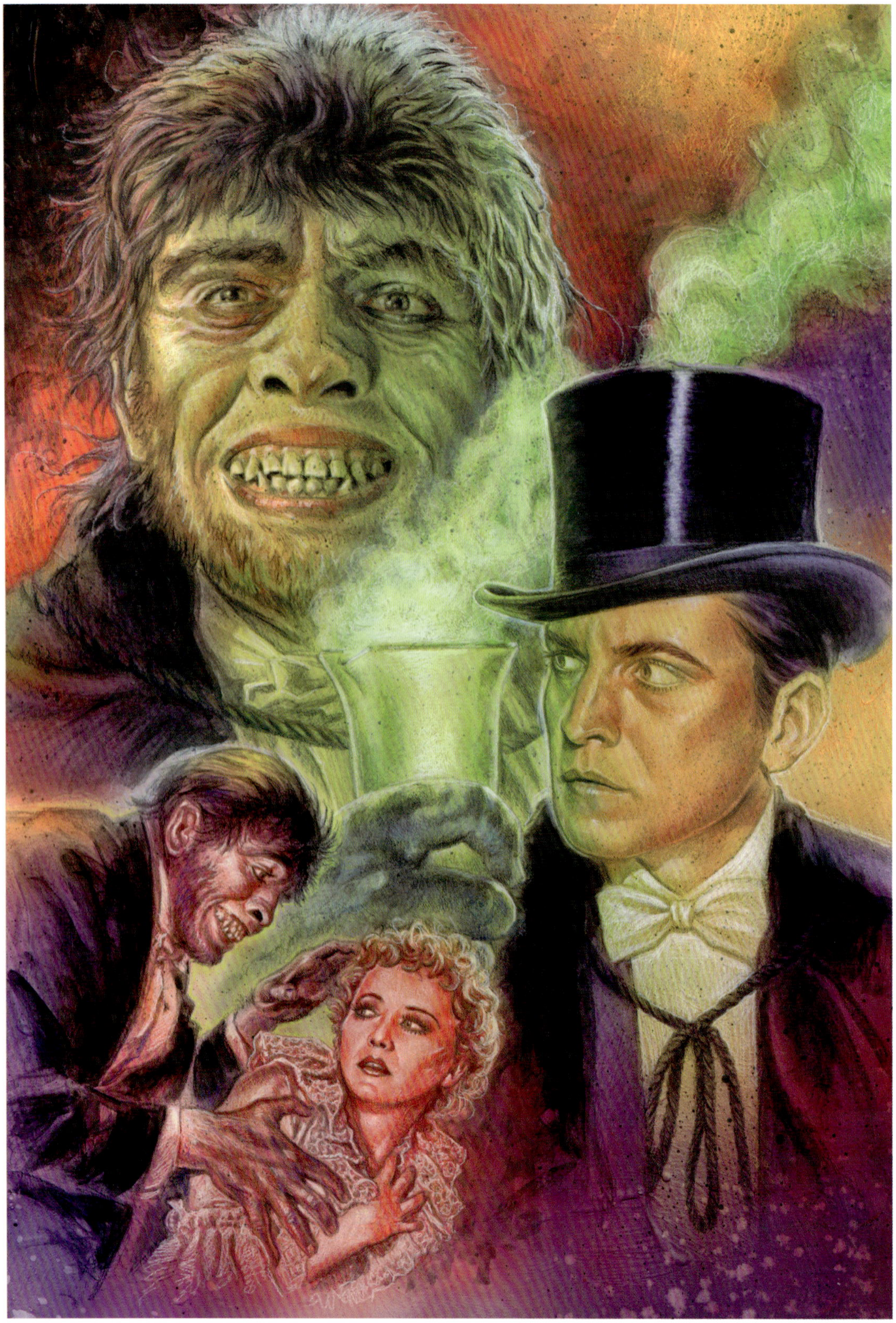

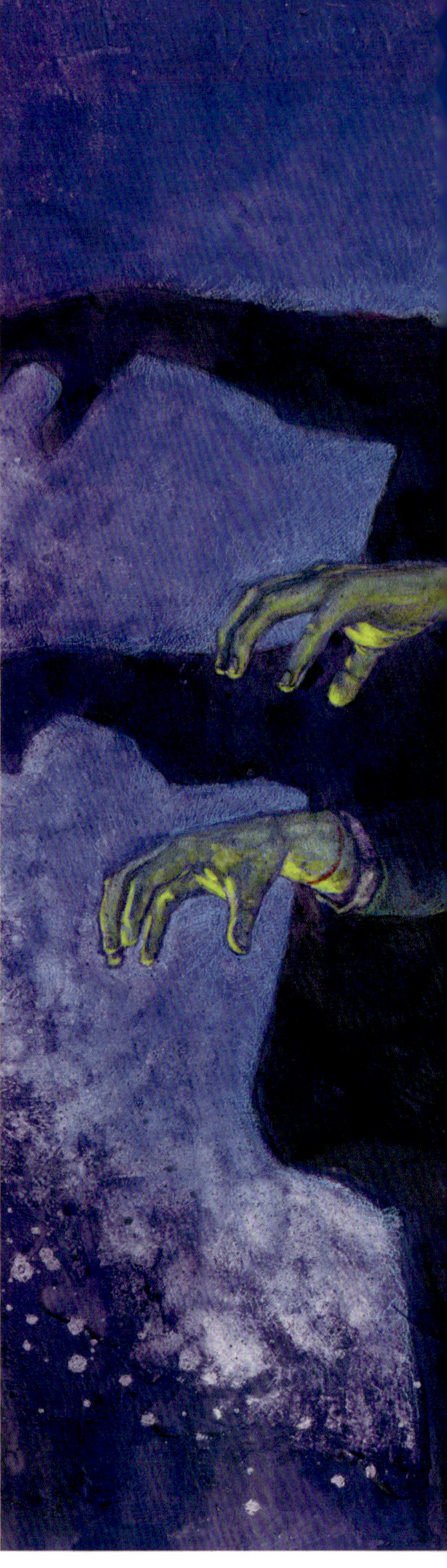

A trio of Doug P'Gosh works. **LEFT TO RIGHT** *"Dr. Jekyll & Mr. Hyde" Starring Frederic March*. Acrylic, airbrush, pastel pencil, 2021; *Glenn Strange Frankenstein Study*. Mixed media on illustration board, 2023; and *Dead Love: A Monstrous Love Affair*. Acrylic, airbrush, pastel pencil on illustration board, 2020.

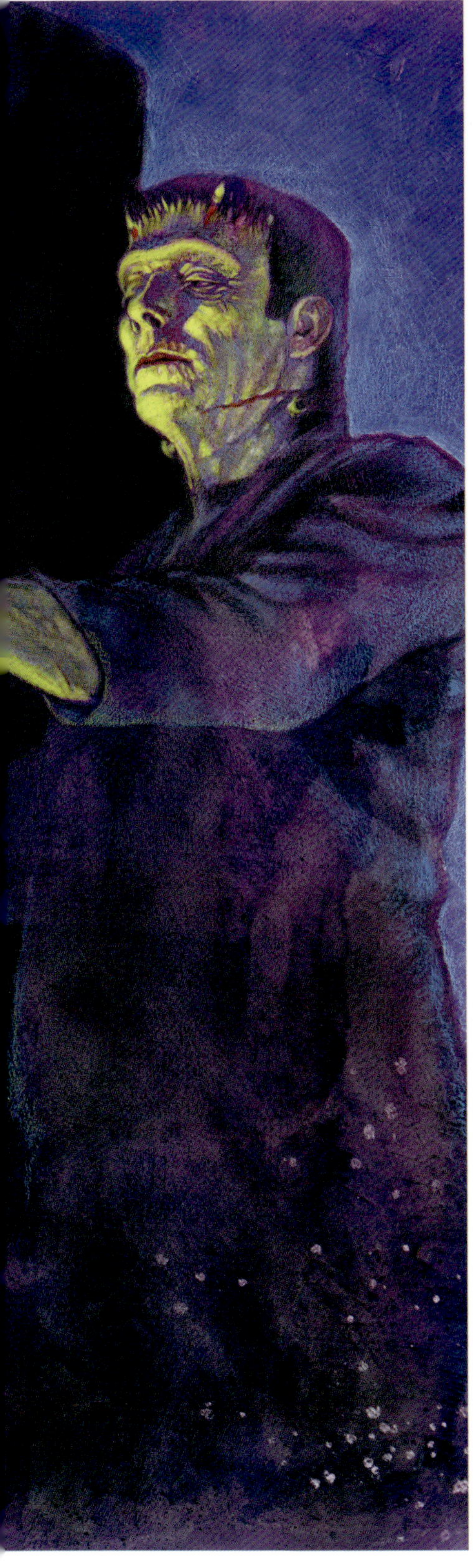

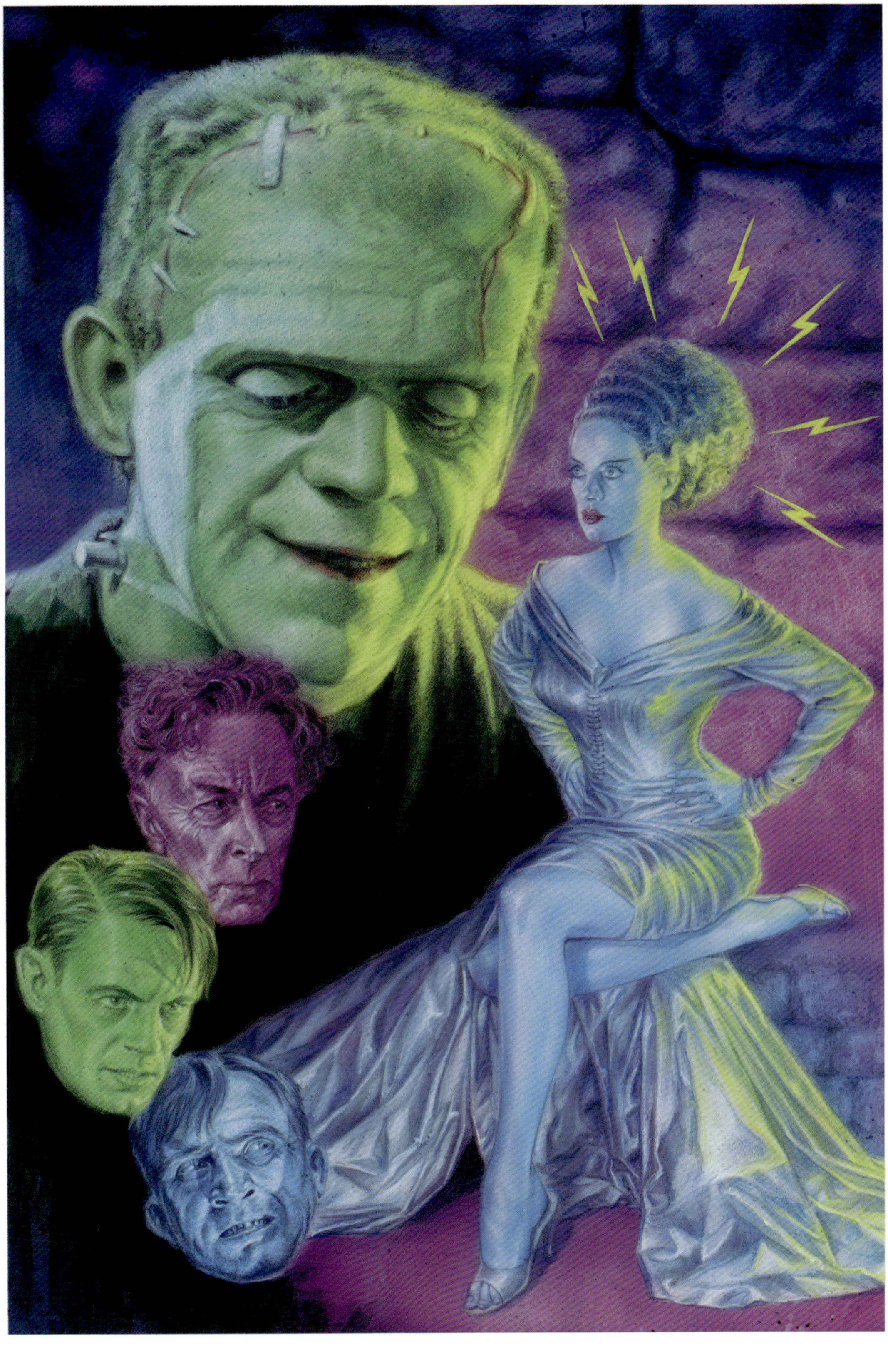

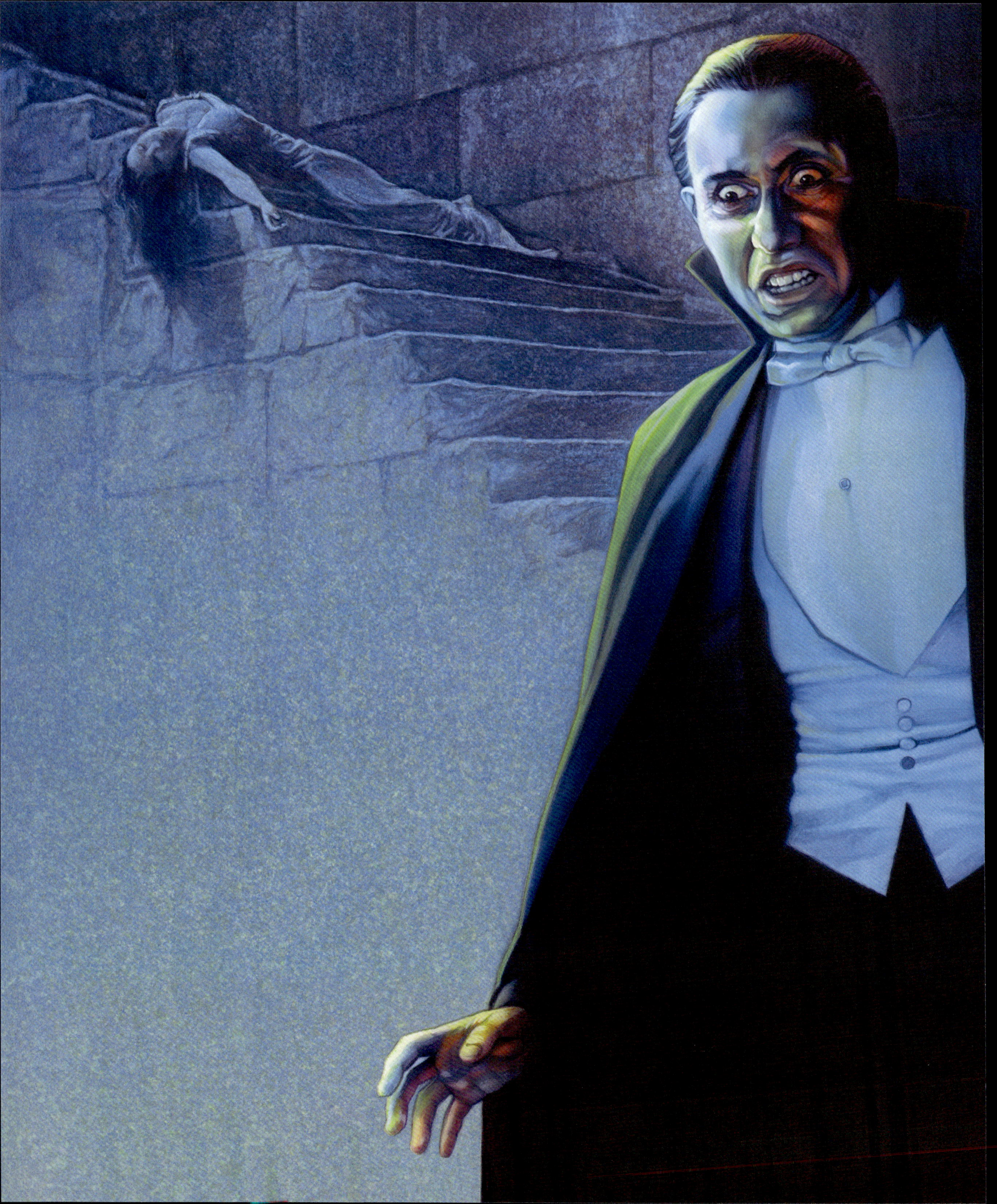

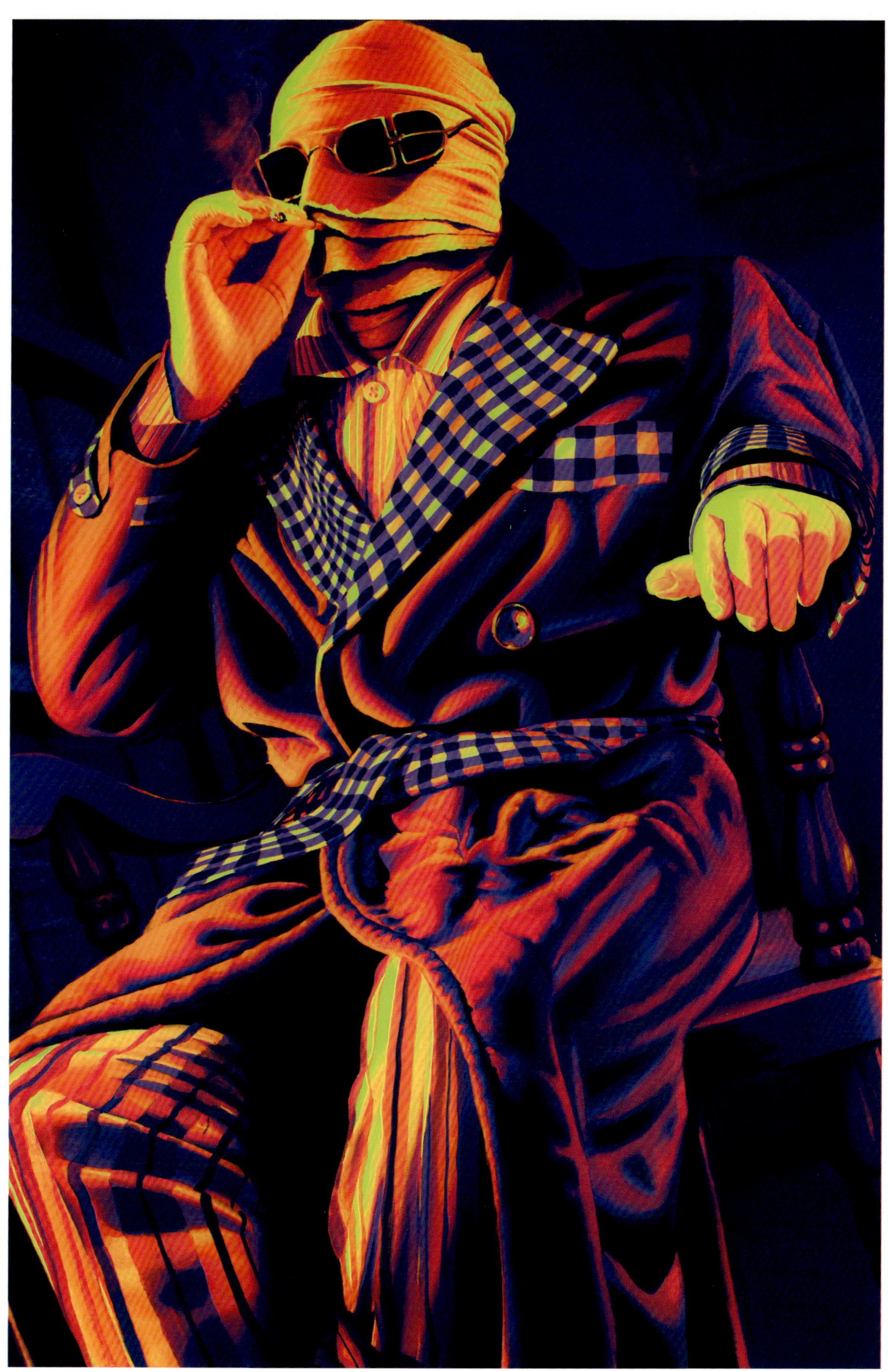

OPPOSITE *Spanish Dracula, Carlos Villarias* by Douglas Klauba. Poster art for the 1931 Spanish-language version of *Dracula* for the Northwest Chicago Film Society. Acrylic on board, 2019.

LEFT *The Invisible Man* by Robert Laskey. Oil on board, 2021.

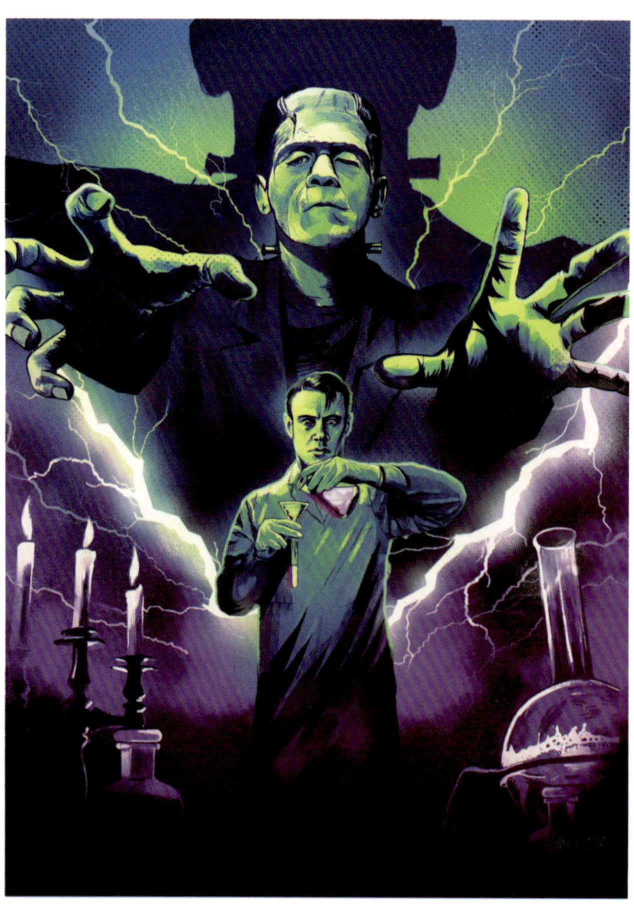

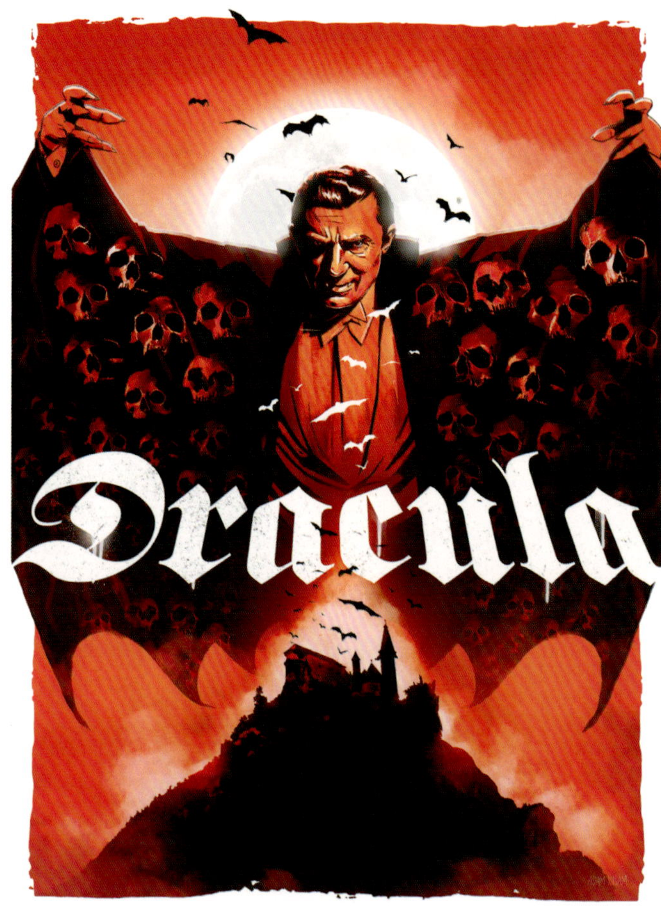

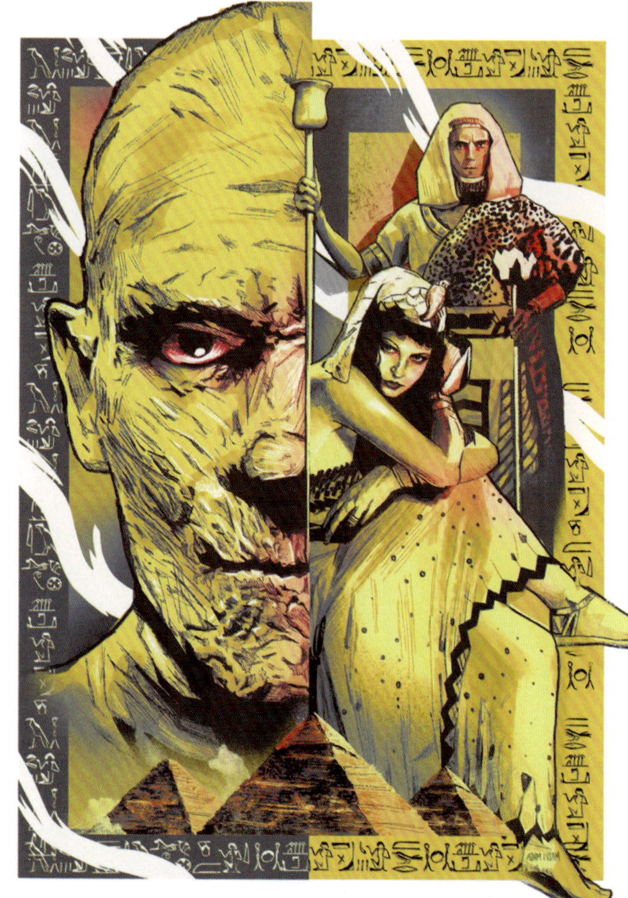

THIS PAGE A trio of reimagined Universal monsters poster designs (featuring Frankenstein's monster, Dracula, and the Mummy) by Adam Insam for his Spooky Season Series. Digital, 2021.

OPPOSITE *Boris Karloff as Imhotep, "The Mummy"* by Robert Laskey. Oil on board, 2020.

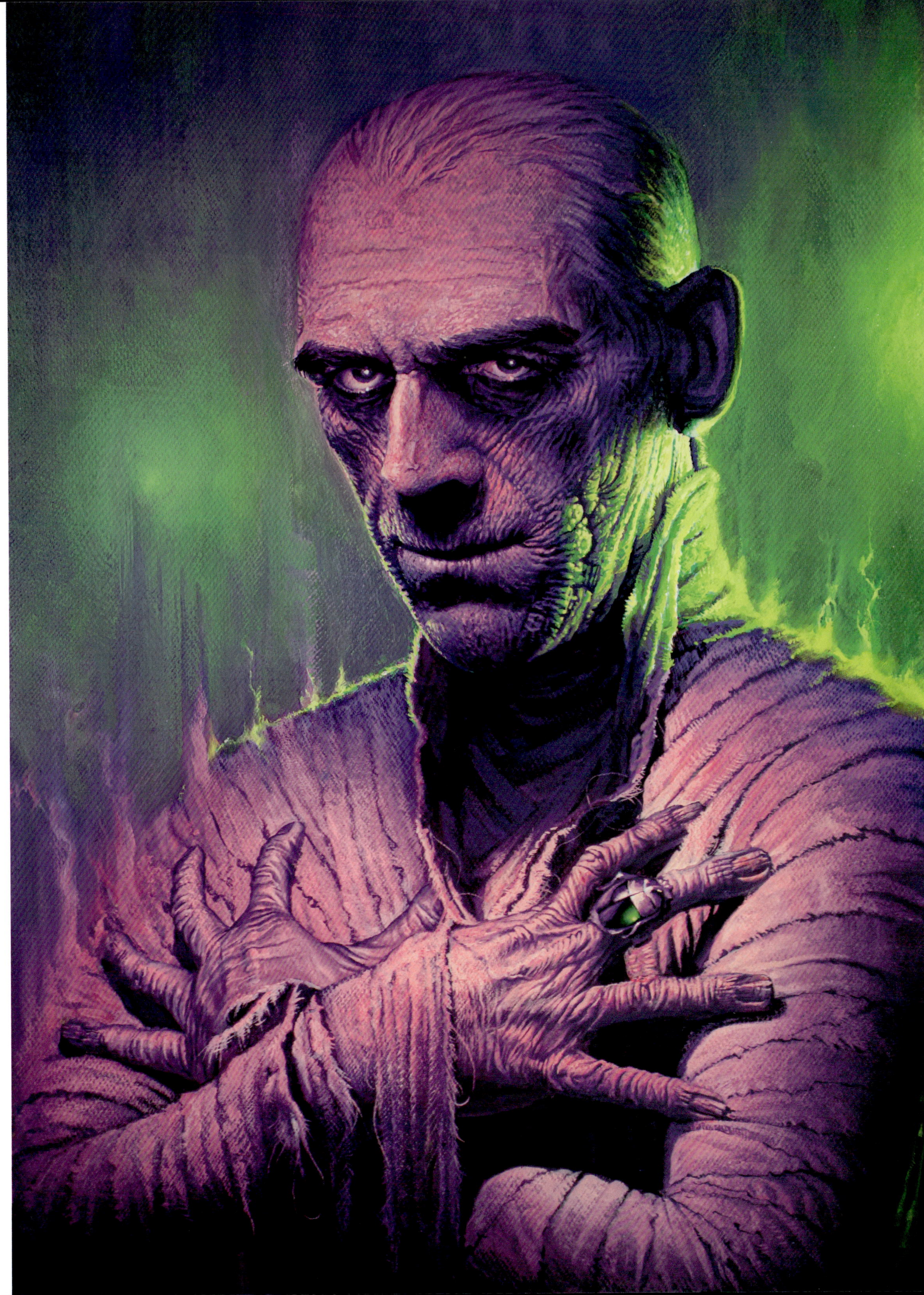

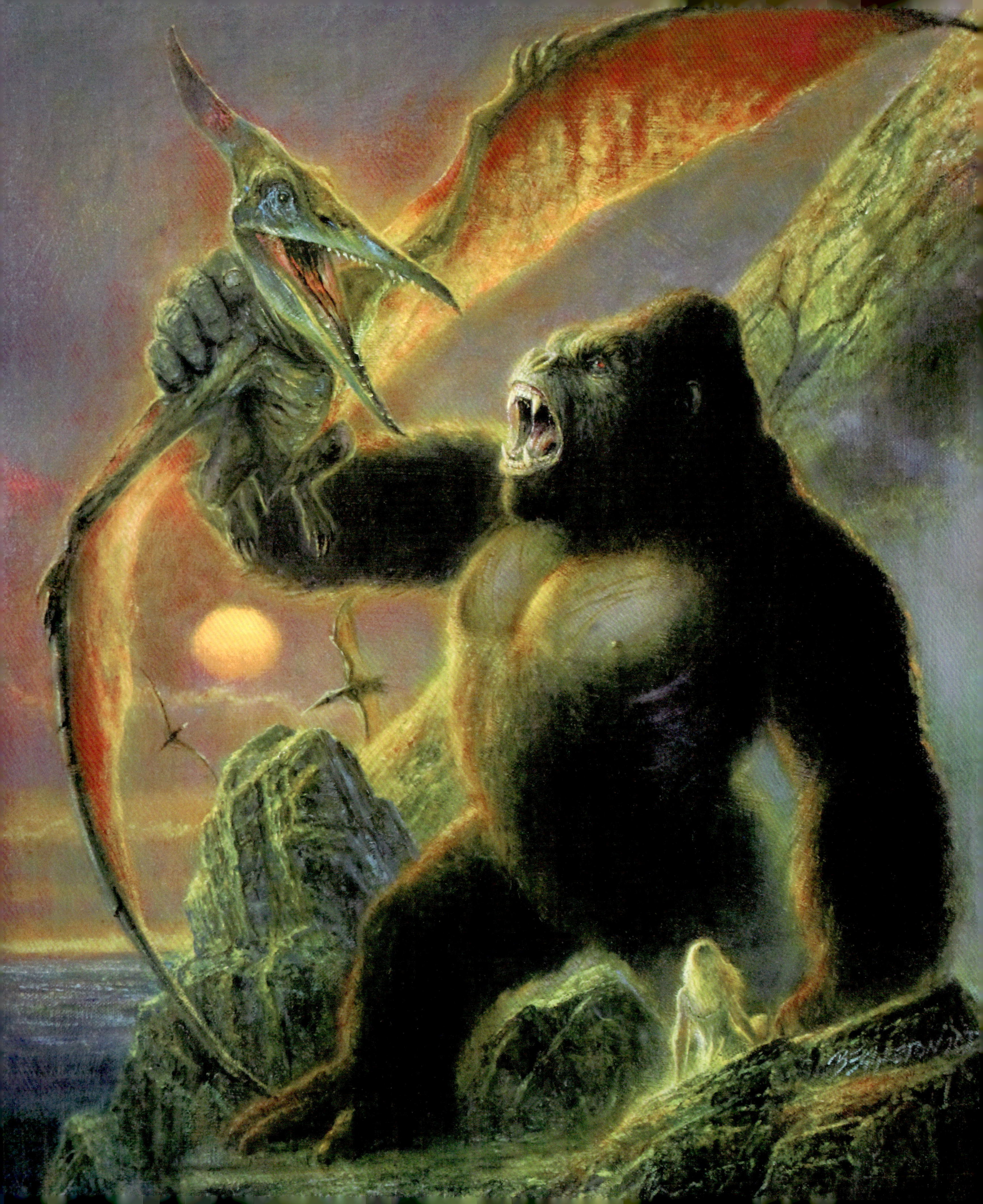

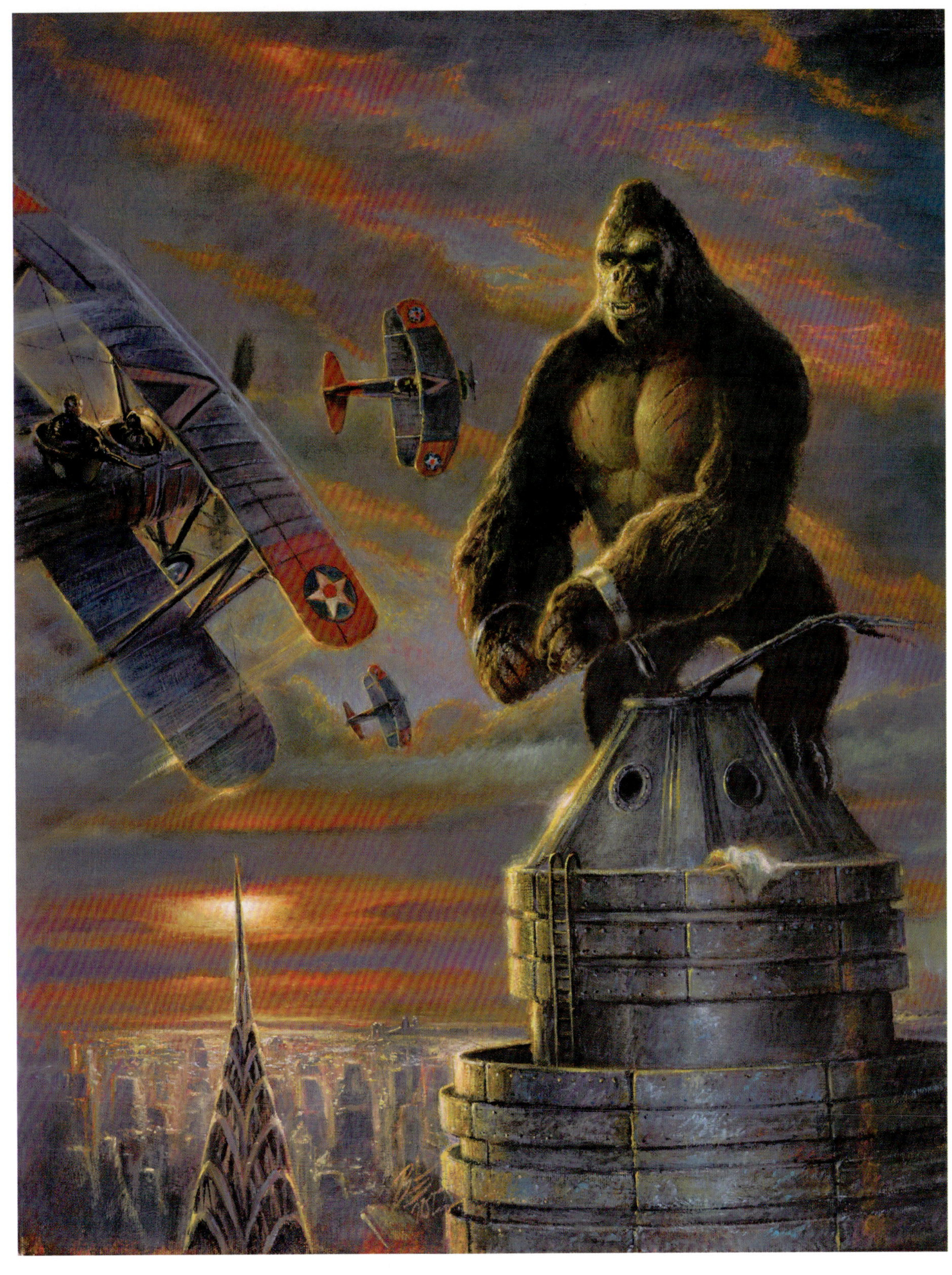

OPPOSITE *Skull Island Showdown* by Bob Eggleton. Oil on canvas, 2022.

ABOVE *The Last Stand* by Bob Eggleton. Oil on canvas, 2022.

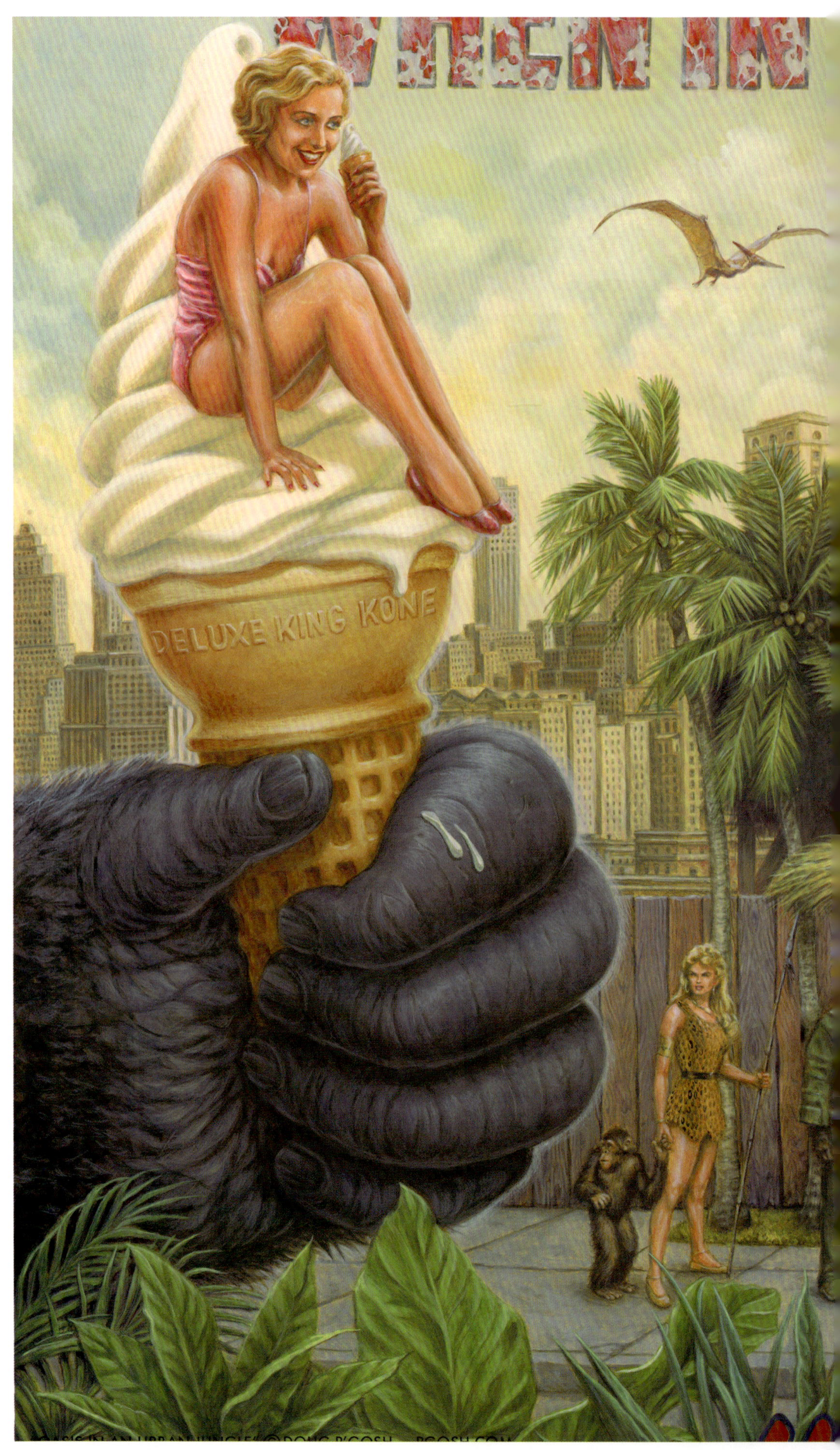

RIGHT *Oasis in an Urban Jungle* by Doug P'Gosh. Print for Retro-A-Go-Go. Acrylic on illustration board, 2021.

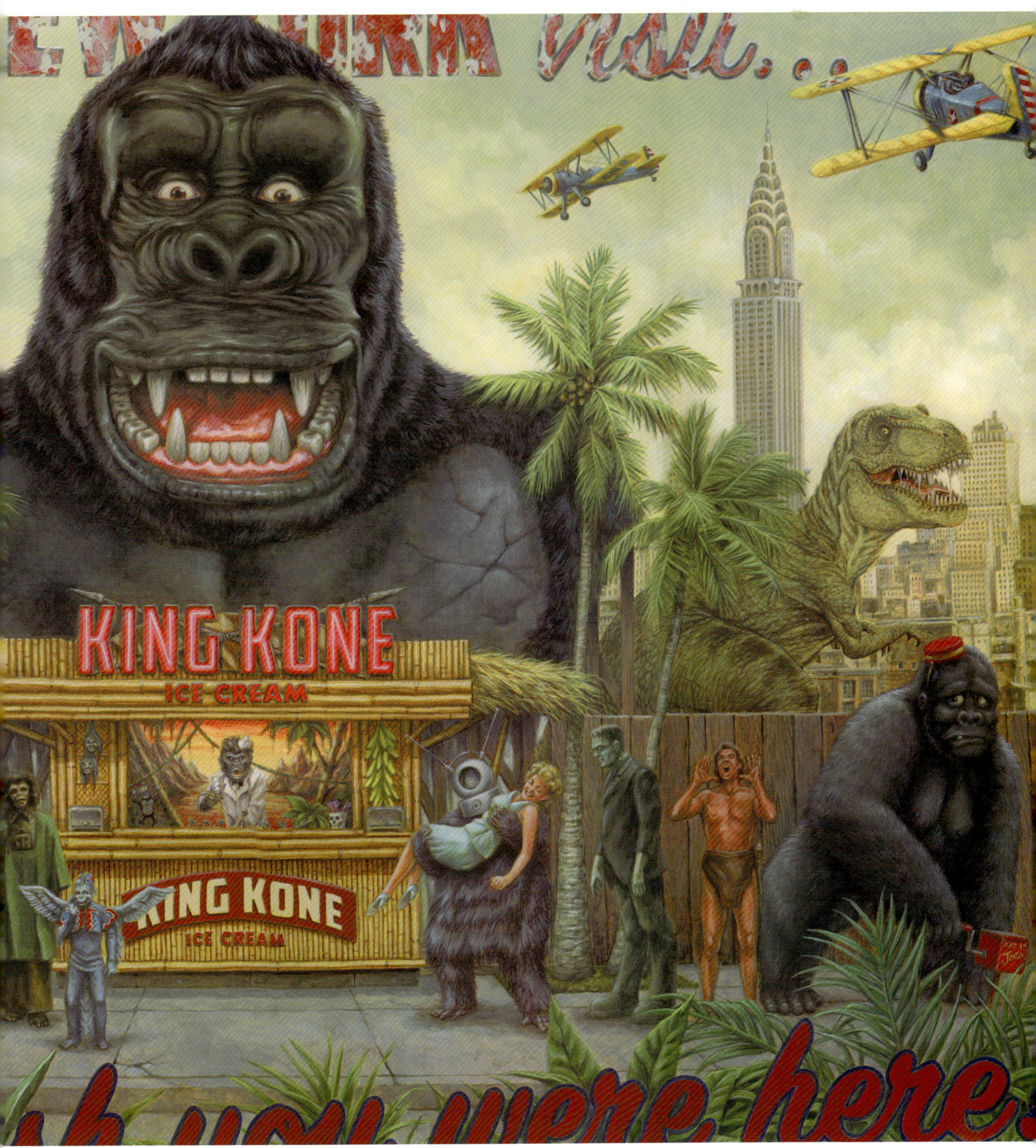
KING KONE
ICE CREAM
KING KONE
ICE CREAM

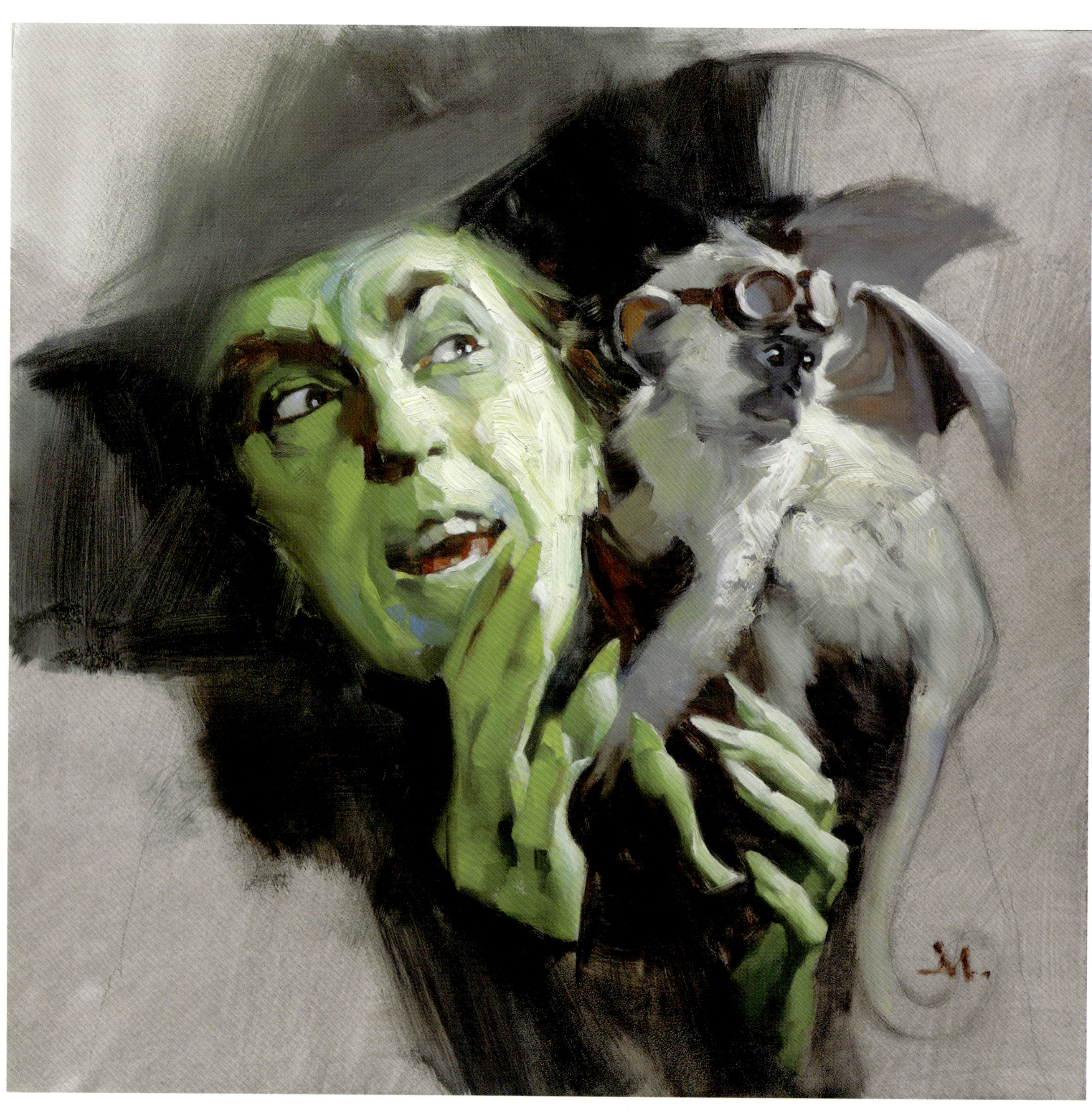

Two fast portraits by Gregory Manchess.

ABOVE *The Wicked Witch of the West*. Oil on canvas, 2022.

OPPOSITE *The Bride of Frankenstein*. Oil on canvas, 2022.

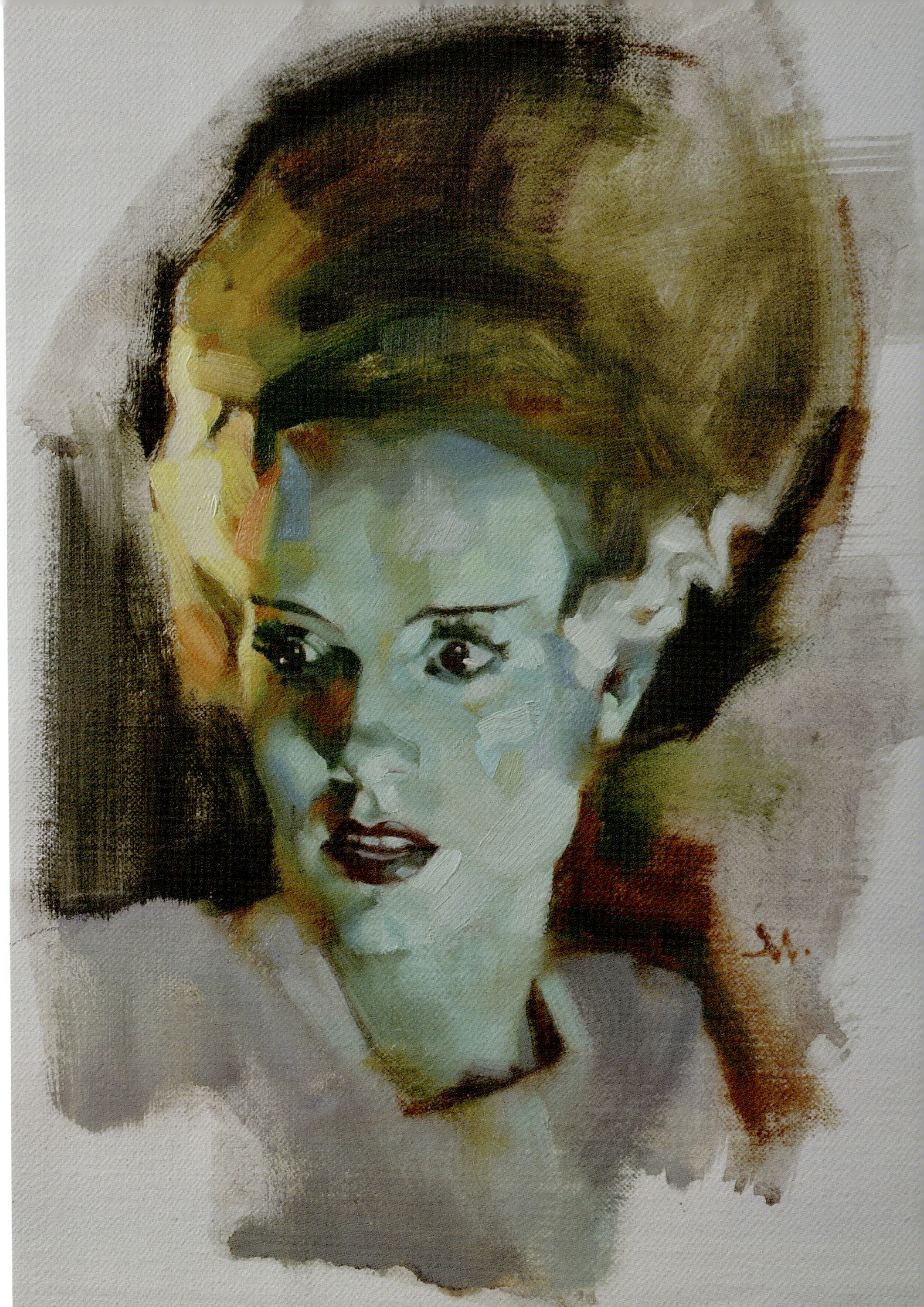

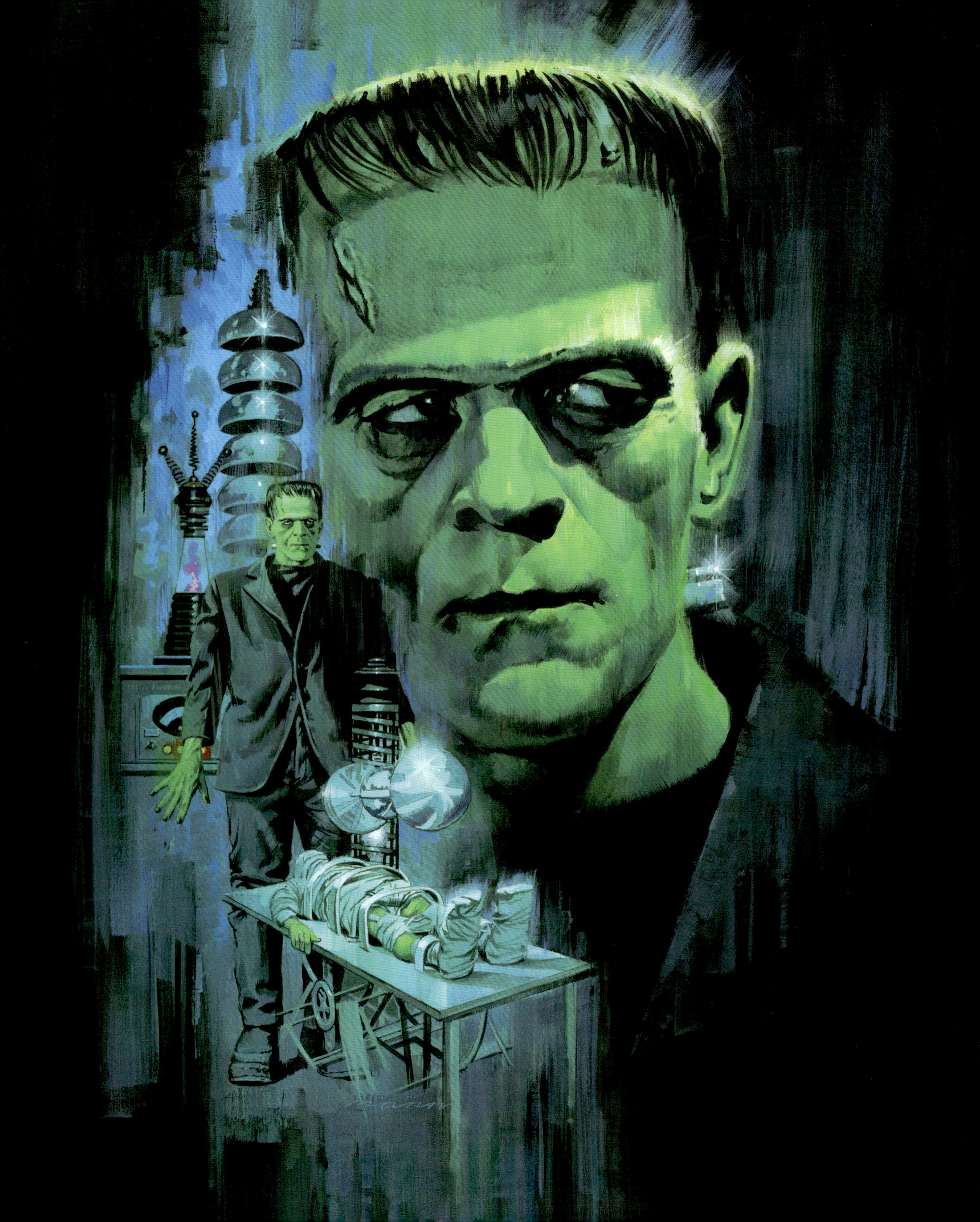

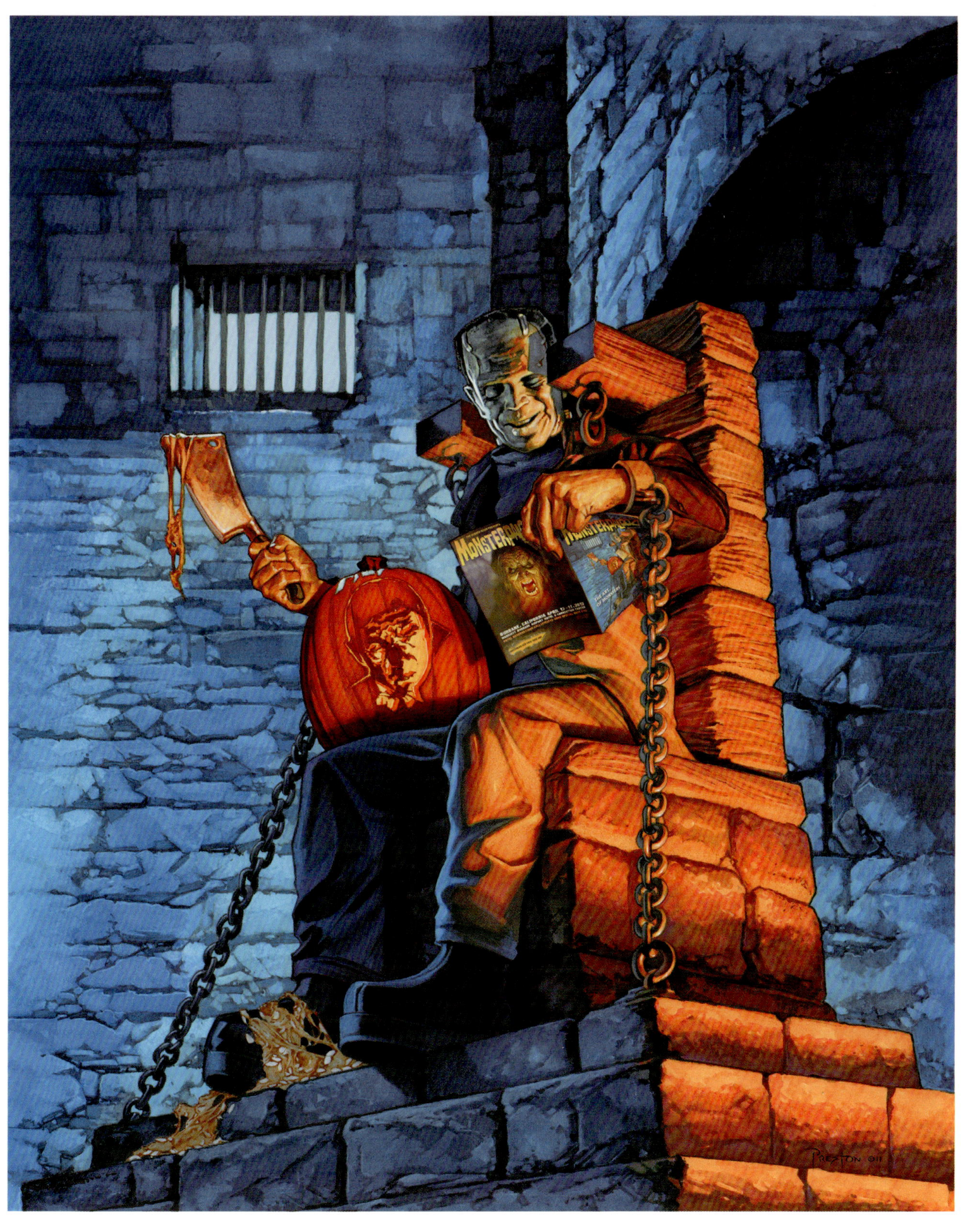

OPPOSITE *Frankenstein* by Paul Mann. Alternate movie poster for Vice Press. Acrylic on illustration board, 2020.

ABOVE *Monsterpalooza* magazine cover for issue #1 by Jeff Preston. Markers on paper, 2011.

Boris Karloff

Boris Karloff was a journeyman actor who became a star overnight when *Frankenstein* was released in 1931. The impact his performances have had on generations of horror and monster movie aficionados is immeasurable. Gordon B. Shriver, the author of *Boris Karloff: The Man Remembered,* has a unique insight on one of the true icons of horror and monster cinema:

"Born William Henry Pratt in a suburb of London on November 23, 1887, Karloff was the youngest of seven children, whose father was in the civil service. As a child, he became fascinated with acting and the theater after seeing *Peter Pan* on stage. As he matured, he had no interest in following in his father's footsteps and emigrated to Canada in 1909. There, he worked odd jobs and found his way into regional theater companies that toured the provinces. This despite having had no formal training as an actor at all. He took the stage name of Boris Karloff, figuring he couldn't be an actor with Pratt as a last name.

"He took the stage name of Boris Karloff, figuring he couldn't be an actor with Pratt as a last name."

"Karloff worked his way down to California and ended up in silent films, doing bit parts and extra work. In between pictures, he would drive a truck or haul bags of cement. During this struggling existence, he met Lon Chaney, the screen's 'Man of a Thousand Faces.' Chaney, famous for such works as *The Hunchback of Notre Dame* and *The Phantom of the Opera*, told Karloff to find something that no one can, or would, do, and pursue it.

"Fellow Brit James Whale, then Universal's hottest director, had seen Karloff in *Graft*, a minor gangster film, and was struck by the actor's looks and offered him the role of the Monster in his screen adaptation of Mary Shelley's *Frankenstein* (1931). Karloff at first was surprised, but accepted the role, which made him a household name. At forty-four, he became a star.

"Along with Bela Lugosi, who had earlier that year attained star status in Universal's *Dracula*, Karloff became synonymous with horror films. He was now the lead in such classics as *The Mummy* and *The Old Dark House* (both in 1932). Universal then put Lugosi and Karloff together, billed as the Titans of Terror. They would make eight films together, starting with *The Black Cat* (1934), followed by *The Raven* and *The Invisible Ray* (both in 1935), and *Black Friday* (1940). Karloff was able to freelance and work for other studios in mainstream films such as *The House of Rothschild* and *The Lost Patrol* (both in 1934). He was praised for the subtle underplaying and humanity he brought to all his characters, often with a quiet dignity to them, which was part of his own personality.

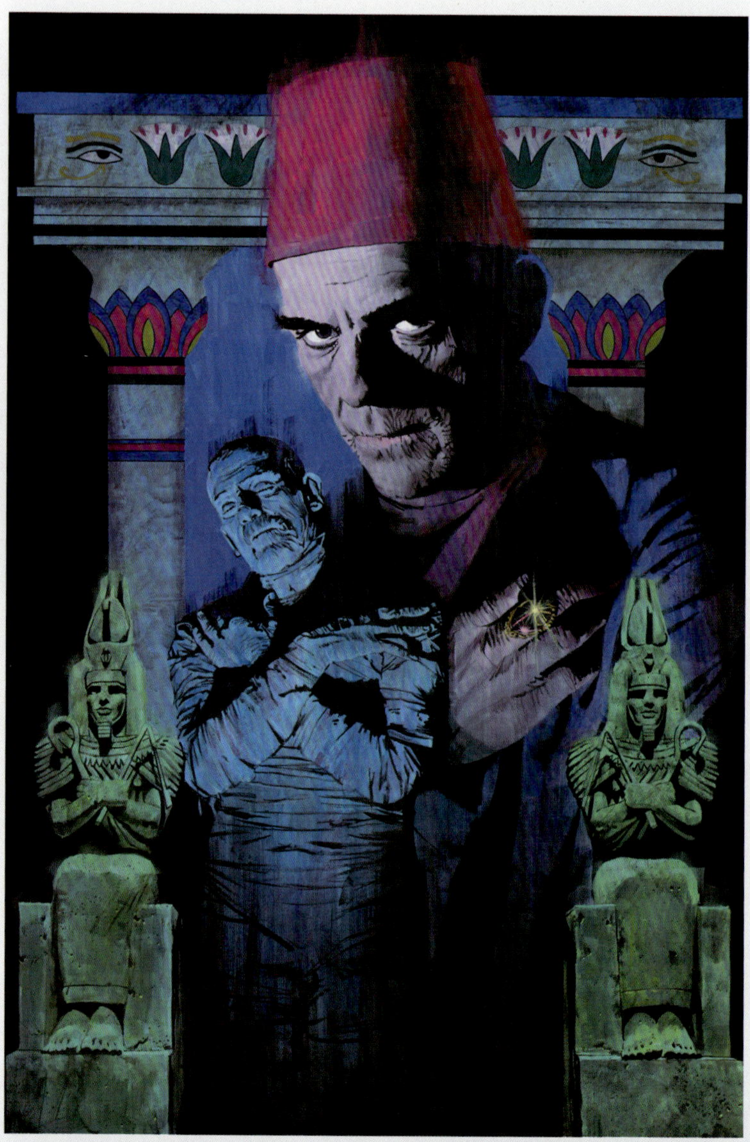

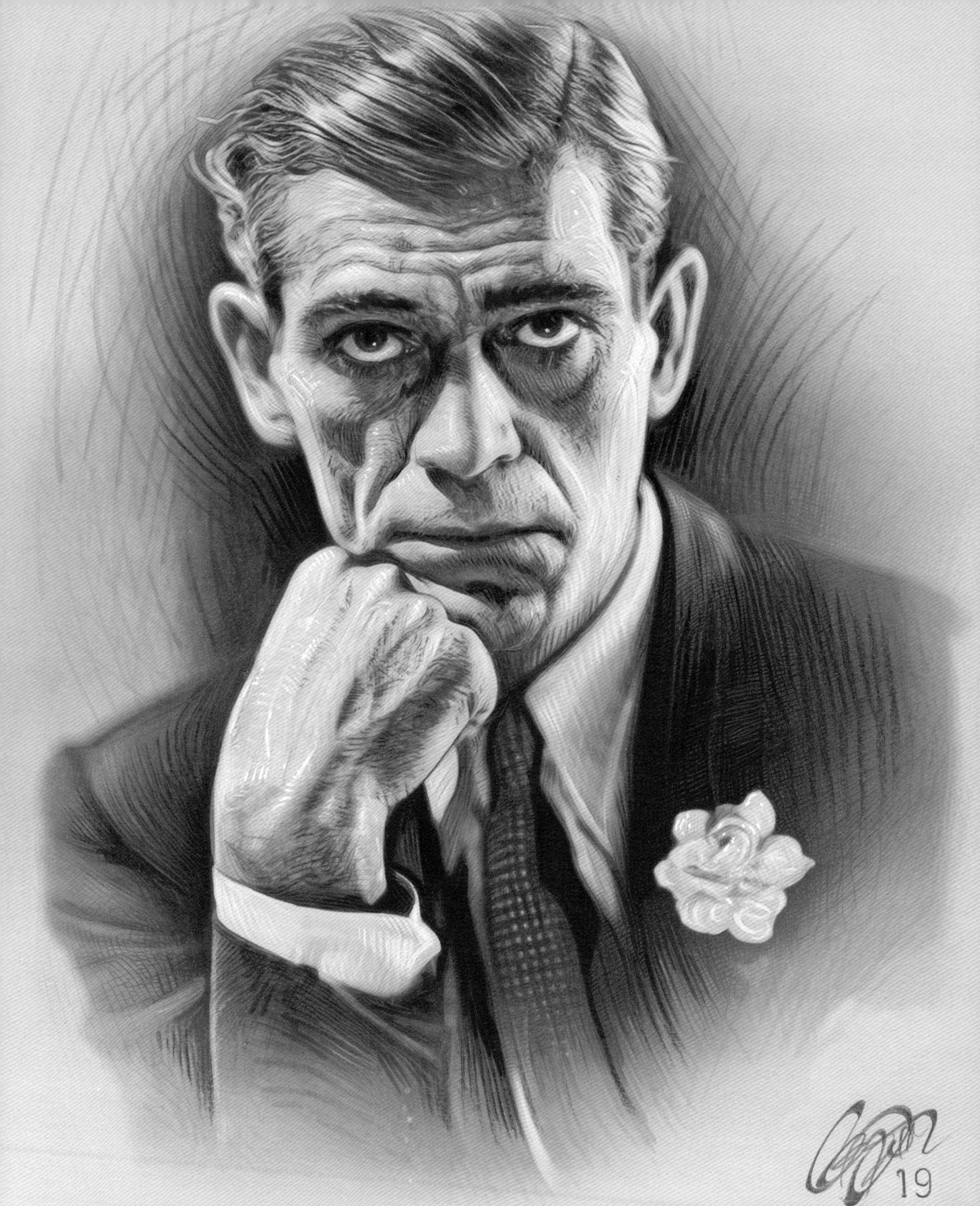

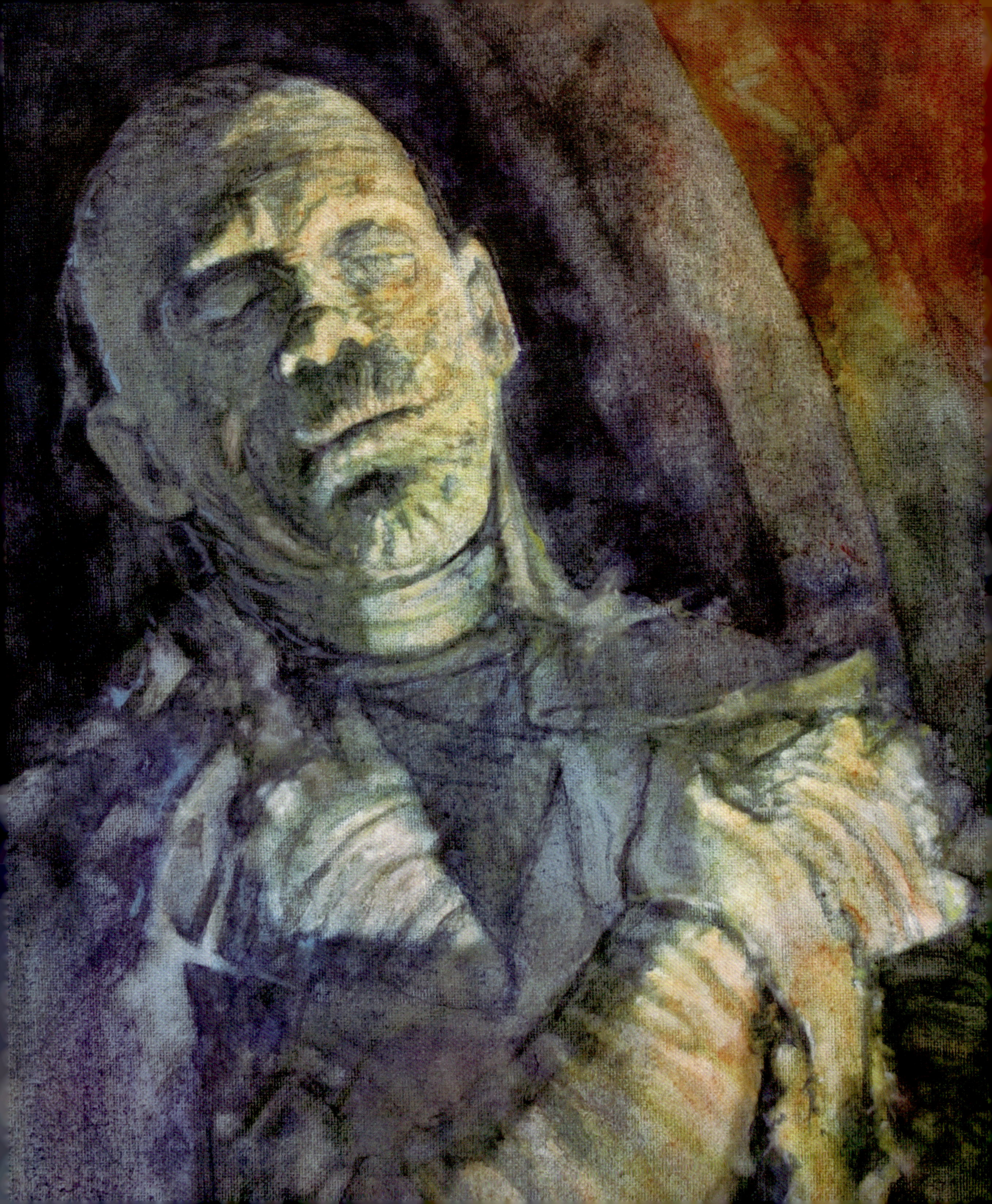

"He would reprise his role as the Monster in *The Bride of Frankenstein* (1935), James Whale's excellent follow-up to the original film, and for the last time in *Son of Frankenstein* (1939), also starring Basil Rathbone and Bela Lugosi.

"Always supportive of his fellow actors—particularly younger ones—Karloff was one of the original founders of the Screen Actors Guild. He served as a board officer on the Guild until the early '50s. Off-screen, he was a cultured British gentleman who enjoyed cricket, tennis, and gardening.

"In 1941, Karloff made his Broadway debut in Joseph Kesselring's horror comedy *Arsenic and Old Lace*. He felt Hollywood stars didn't belong on Broadway, but was talked into accepting the role of Jonathan Brewster (a homicidal maniac) when producers Howard Lindsay and Russel Crouse told him what one of his lines of dialogue would be; when asked why he killed someone, the character replies, 'He said I looked like Boris Karloff!' He took the part, which became one of his signature roles. Karloff went on to play Jonathan in over 1,400 performances, including on the radio, in US Army productions staged for the troops in the central Pacific, and later on television and in regional theaters.

"Radio was in its heyday, and with his wonderfully mellifluous voice, Karloff worked often and made many appearances on *Inner Sanctum* and *Lights Out*. He was not above poking fun at his own screen image and appeared on countless radio shows with comedians such as Fred Allen, Jack Benny, and Jimmy Durante. Later, he recorded many albums, often reading children's stories.

"Horror films began to decline in the '40s, and Karloff was seen to good effect in supporting roles in such films as *Lured* (1947), *The Secret Life of Walter Mitty* (1947), and *Tap Roots* (1948). For producer Val Lewton, he appeared in three of his career best, *The Body Snatcher* (1945), *Isle of the Dead* (1945), and *Bedlam* (1946).

"Now a great man of the theater, Karloff returned to the Broadway stage in two successful shows. In *Peter Pan* (1950), opposite Jean Arthur in the title role, he was both Captain Hook and Mr. Darling. Then, in 1955 (in what he thought was his best role), he played Bishop Cauchon in *The Lark*, opposite Julie Harris as Joan of Arc. Both Harris and Karloff were nominated for the Tony Award, as best actress and best actor. Harris won, but Karloff lost out to Paul Muni, who won for *Inherit the Wind*.

"Television was in full swing by then, and Karloff dove right into the new medium, which he found very exciting and felt like being on stage, with one chance to get it right, as much of it was broadcast live. Displaying his occasionally overlooked dramatic range, he often featured in non-horror roles for shows such as *Studio One*, *Climax!*, and *Playhouse 90*, working with a number of future film directors, including John Frankenheimer, Sidney Lumet, and Robert Mulligan.

"Horror in film and on TV had a resurgence in the '60s, so Karloff and his friends—such as Vincent Price and Peter Lorre—enjoyed a career boost and were much in demand. The three of them were in Roger Corman's *The Raven* (1963), and again—with the addition of Basil Rathbone—in Jacques Tourneur's *The Comedy of Terrors* (1964). A career highlight was his recording for television of Dr. Seuss's *How the Grinch Stole Christmas!* in 1966, which became an annual broadcast and won him a Grammy Award. In the twilight of his career, despite advancing age and declining health, Karloff never stopped working and capped it with a brilliant performance—as a character not unlike himself—in Peter Bogdanovich's debut film, *Targets* (1968). He died on February 2, 1969, from heart and lung disease, and is still revered for his talent, warmth, and wit."

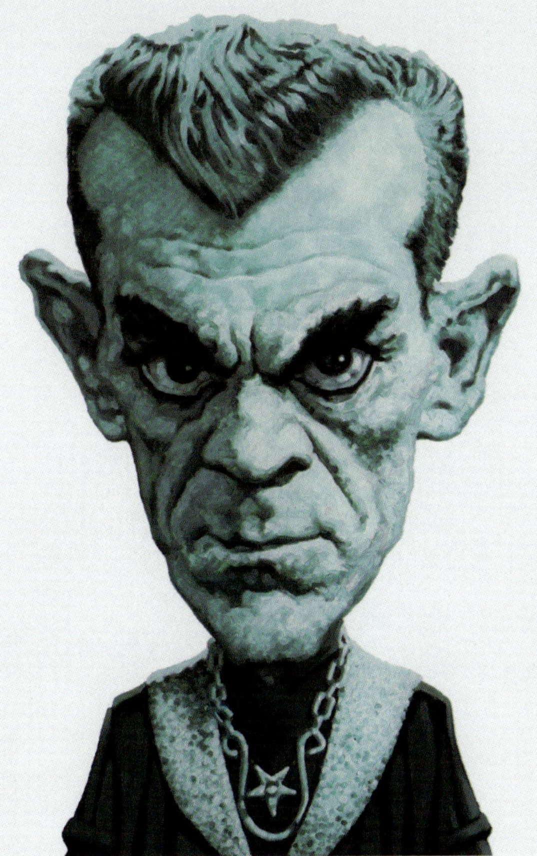

PREVIOUS PAGES *Boris Karloff as the Mummy* by Paul Mann. Alternative movie poster for Vice Press. Acrylic on illustration board, 2021; *William Henry Pratt AKA Boris Karloff* by Frederick Cooper. Mixed media, 2019.

OPPOSITE *The Mummy* by Jeff Busch. Oil on canvas, 2017.

LEFT *Karloff from "The Black Cat"* by Paul Garner. Detail from *Son of Unsung Horrors* cover illustration for We Belong Dead Publications. Mixed media, 2019.

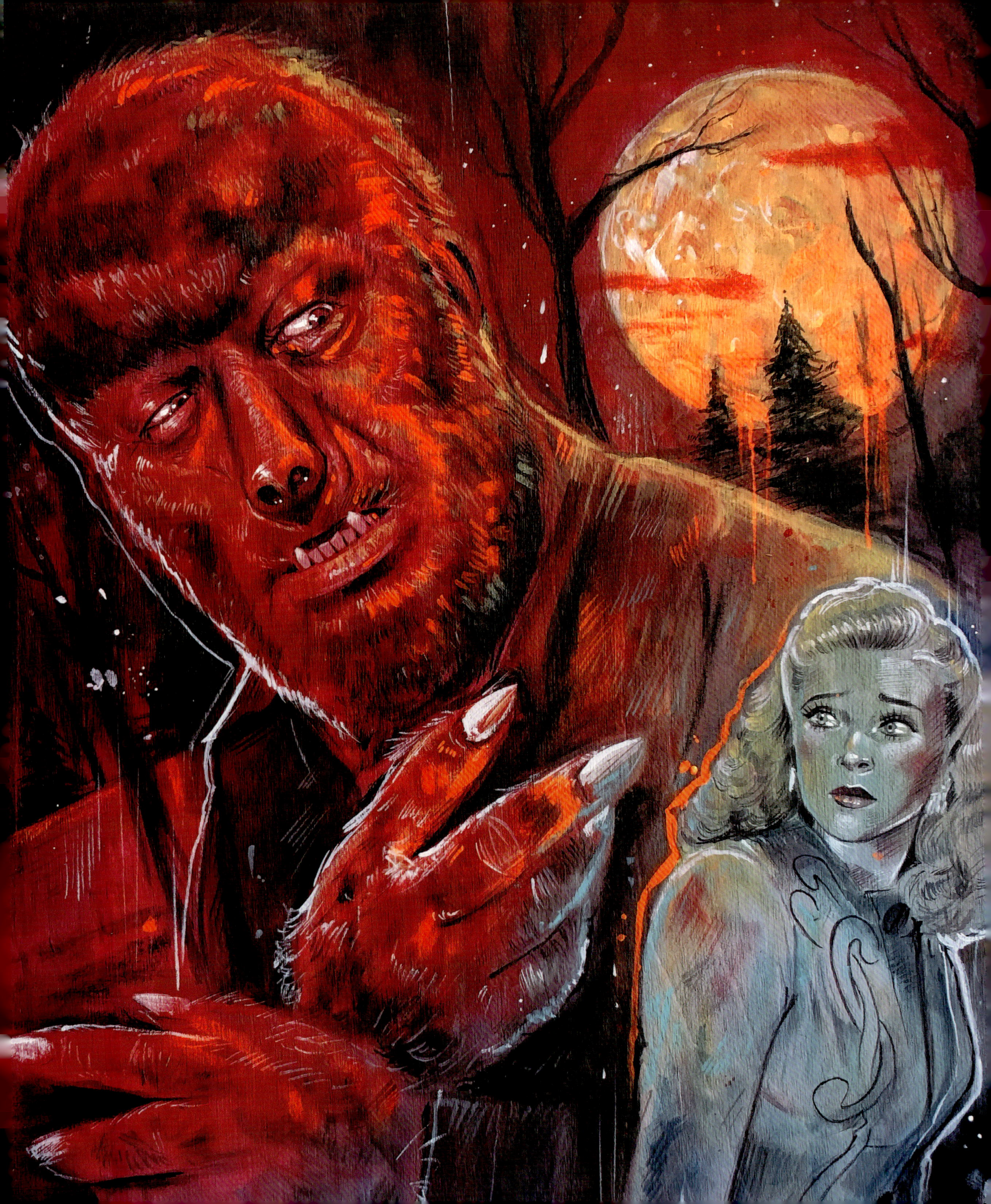

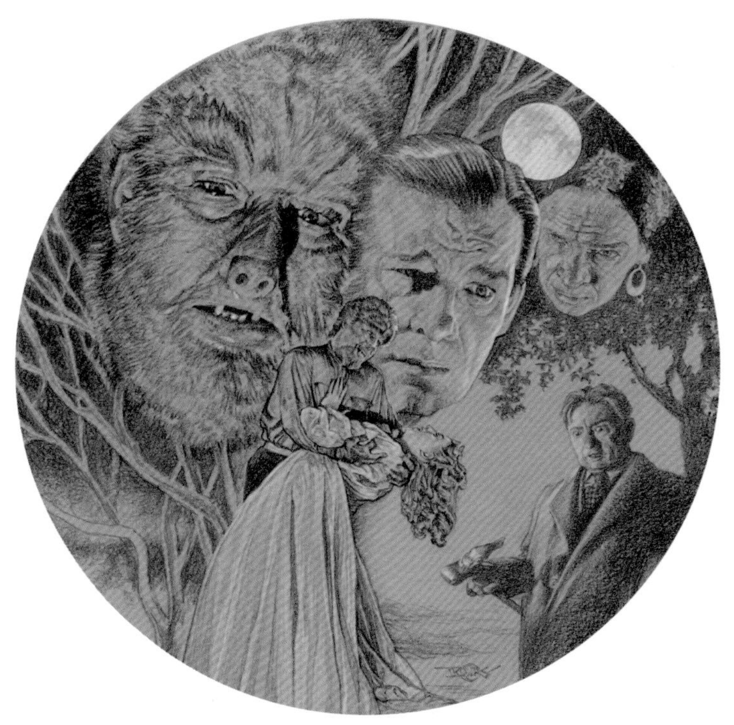

CHAPTER 4

Why We Fought (1940–1949)

Conflict breeds creativity. It's an accepted fact that when two opposing forces meet, energy is created, and in the early 1940s, opposing forces clashed in the most spectacular and devastating of ways—war. After what had erroneously been called "the war to end all wars," it seemed inconceivable that a mere twenty-one years later, the world was plunged once again into interminable combat when a joint attack on the Republic of Poland was mounted by Nazi Germany, the pro-Nazi Slovak Republic, and the Soviet Union on September 1, 1939.

Over the course of the war, many artists, writers, filmmakers, and musicians were drafted or joined the armed forces of their own volition to help in the battle against the Axis powers. Hollywood's top film directors, among them John Ford, John Huston, and William Wyler made documentary and training films for the US Army, and many actors went into active service—Brigadier General James Stewart, for instance, flew bombers in twenty combat missions over enemy territory. Future great names like Ted Geisel (Dr. Seuss), animator Ray Harryhausen, and composer Dimitri Tiomkin worked on films while enlisted in the Army's Special Services Division under Colonel Frank Capra.

In the days after the Allied forces' Normandy invasion on June 6, 1944, a US "Ghost Army" made up of the battalions under the 23rd Headquarters Special Troops entered France to follow the liberation forces through Europe and confuse and confound the Nazis by means of special tools and tactics. The 603rd Camouflage Engineers division was made up of artists and designers who had been recruited from New York's Pratt Institute and other schools and organizations. Their very cinematic mission: Utilize inflatable tanks, planes, trucks, and gun emplacements to convince the German army that troops and ordnance were in locations where they weren't.

These intrepid artists also painted jeeps and trucks with different unit markings to confuse collaborators left behind in towns that had already been liberated, and created fake patches to wear while impersonating officers and personnel in cafés throughout the region, leading to an enormous amount of misinformation being fed to the opposing forces. The Ghost Army was a classified secret until 1996, in case their special tactics might be needed again in later conflicts.

It's estimated that as many as thirty thousand allied troops' lives were saved by the creative work of the personnel of the 23rd Headquarters Special Troops. In

OPPOSITE *Wolfman* by Susana "Suspiria" Vilchez. Acrylic on canvas, 2020.

ABOVE *Wolfman* by Douglas Klauba. Mixed media on toned paper, 2000.

2024, all members were awarded the Congressional Gold Medal for their service. Many went on to careers of note in the arts, such as trend-setting mid-century menswear designer Bill Blass, renowned music and fashion photographer Art Kane, famed abstract painter Ellsworth Kelly, and illustrators Vic Prezio and George Wilson, both of whom would contribute to the pantheon of monster art in the 1960s and '70s as comic book and paperback cover artists. These men wielded brushes and pens as swords and saw firsthand the power that art has when used as a force for good.

And although the world was focused on war, movie production continued regardless.

In Hollywood, Universal's monster franchises moved forward and added a newcomer to their list of stars—Lon Chaney Jr. Creighton Tull Chaney was not terribly fond of taking his father's first name at the behest of studio brass in 1935, but certainly understood the marketing power behind the move. He had appeared in several of his father's films as a child but was discouraged from pursuing a career in show business by his dad. After Chaney Sr. died, Creighton went into the film business and worked steadily in Westerns, melodramas, and other films produced solely to fit a theater programming bill before breaking through with his unforgettable performance as Lennie in *Of Mice and Men* (1939).

Universal gave him a tryout for one picture, *Man Made Monster* (1941), and based on its box office success, signed him to a regular contract. Later that year, his portrayal of Larry Talbot—the accursed fellow who, though he is "pure in heart and says his prayers by night," becomes a wolf "when the wolfbane blooms and the autumn moon is bright"—cemented his place in the monster film hall of fame and took him out of the shadow of his father. *The Wolf Man* (1941) became an instant classic, reflecting the tensions people felt worldwide upon entering the war. In that conflict, sides were drawn into areas of nearly black-and-white resolution, but Talbot's conflict was with grayer forces that could not be reckoned with or vanquished by a show of might. Nature itself (and, metaphorically speaking, the duality of man) was his tormentor. As Stephen King opined in his book *Danse Macabre*, "Some werewolves are hairy on the inside."

In reality, the Allied powers fought to defend freedom and vanquish fascism, while the Axis powers unapologetically attacked with an iron glove to subjugate the entire world. It was easy enough to choose a side, but the growing anxiety, unrelieved until the D-Day invasion and subsequent liberation of Europe, was enormous and ever-present.

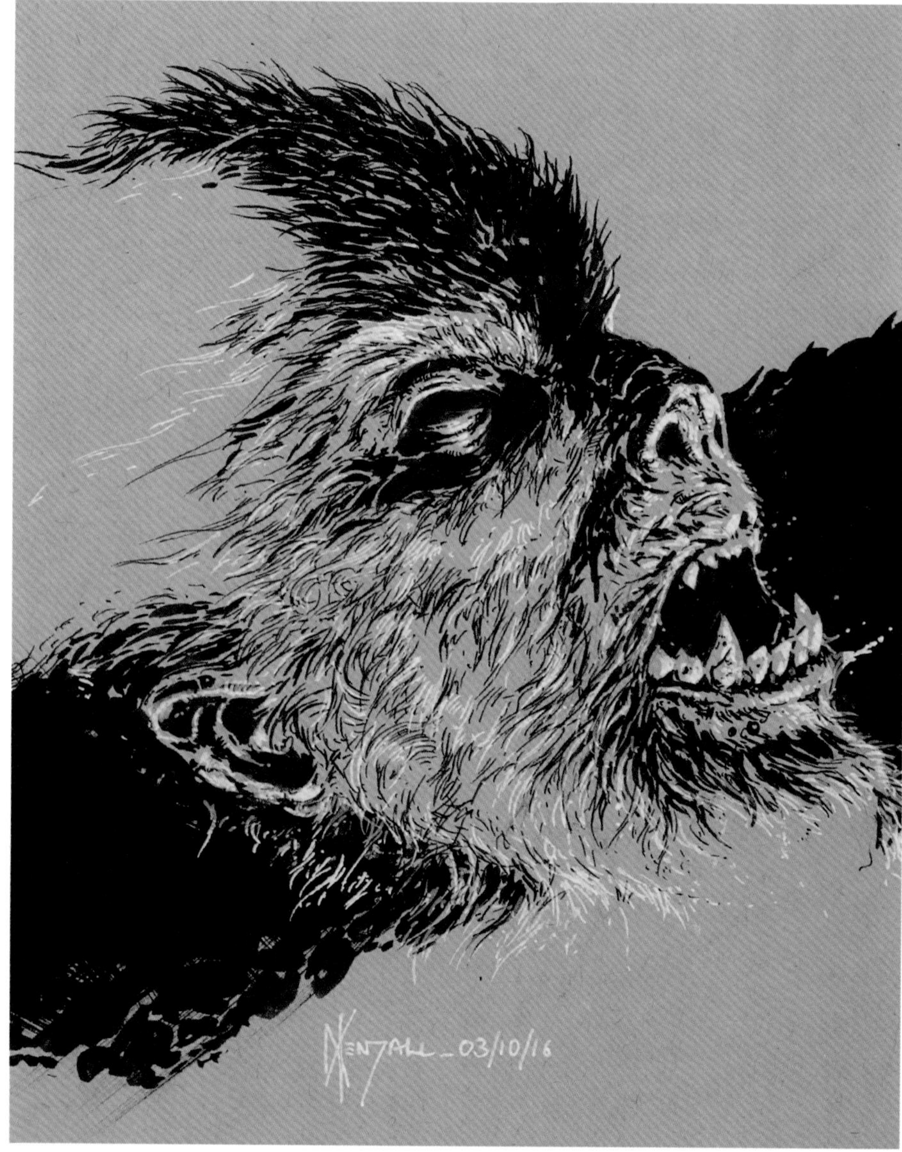

Artist Erika Deoudes connects the nature of horror-fiction beasts with the apprehension they instill regarding our humanity; how we relate to monsters is how we relate to ourselves. "We've overcome many fears as a species: We've conquered the dark, contained a lot of disease, controlled pests, domesticated beasts, neutralized threats, solved mysteries, grasped natural phenomena, colonized the whole planet and parts of the universe, and dethroned gods, but we haven't gotten control of ourselves. We haven't conquered human nature, painful emotions, unreasonable desire, mental 'illness,' our internal conflicts. So, we outsource those to monsters in an attempt to contain and subdue them. But we also fear that conquest, because if we defeat our minds and hearts, we're no longer human; we're

ABOVE *The Wolfman* by Dave Kendall. Colored pencil on gray Crescent board, 2016.

OPPOSITE *Full Moon* by Doug P'Gosh. Gouache and acrylic paint on illustration board, 2019.

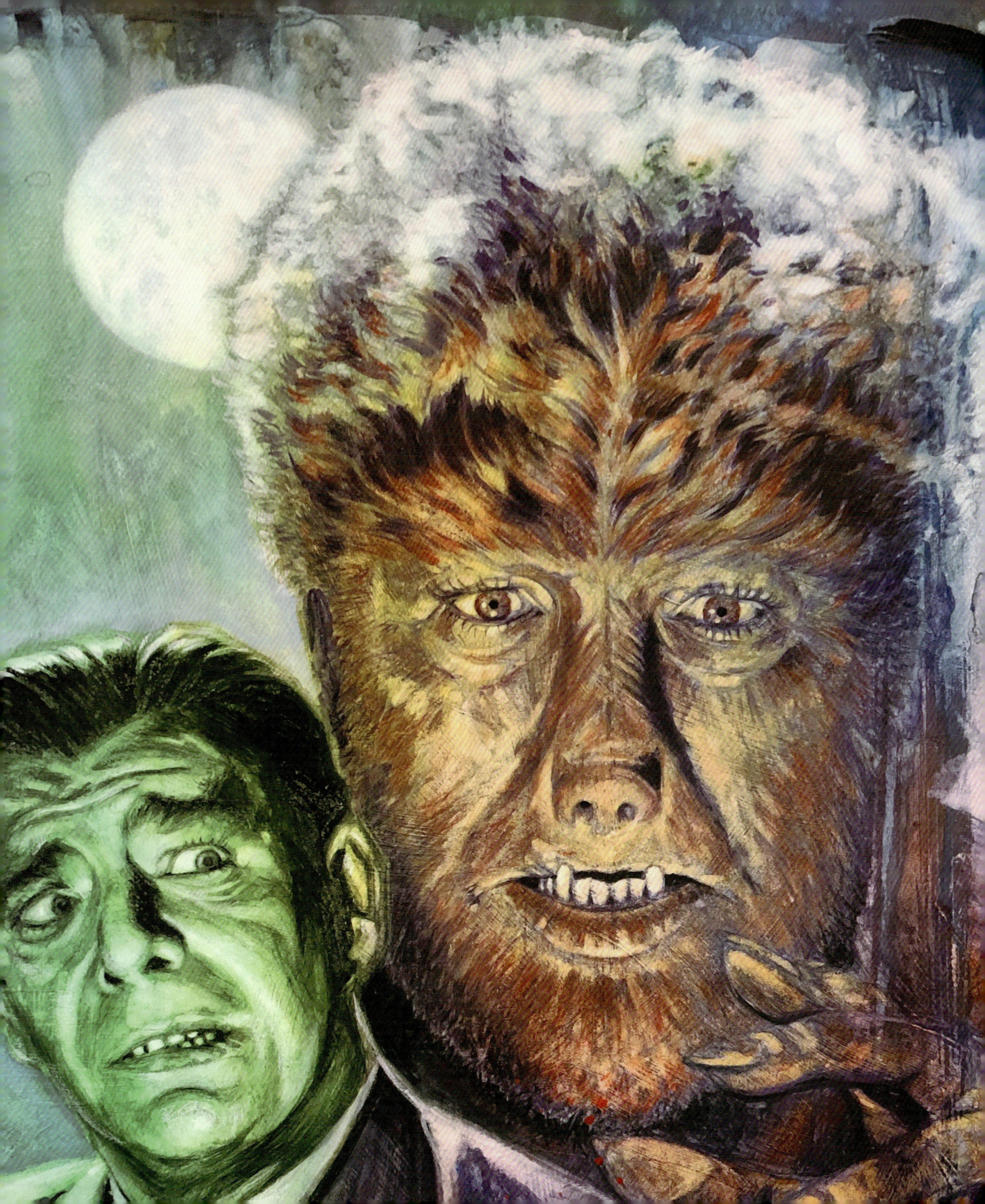

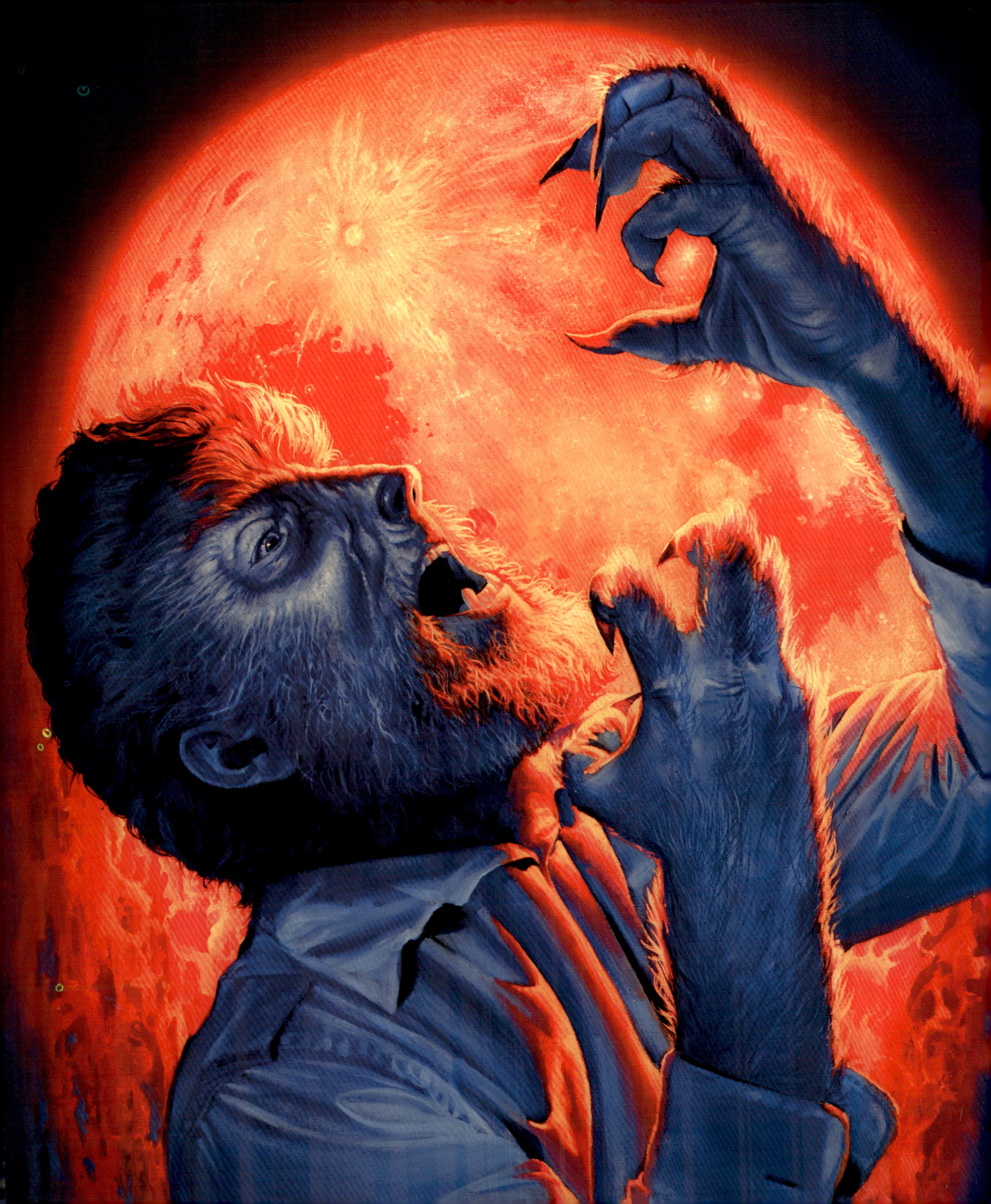

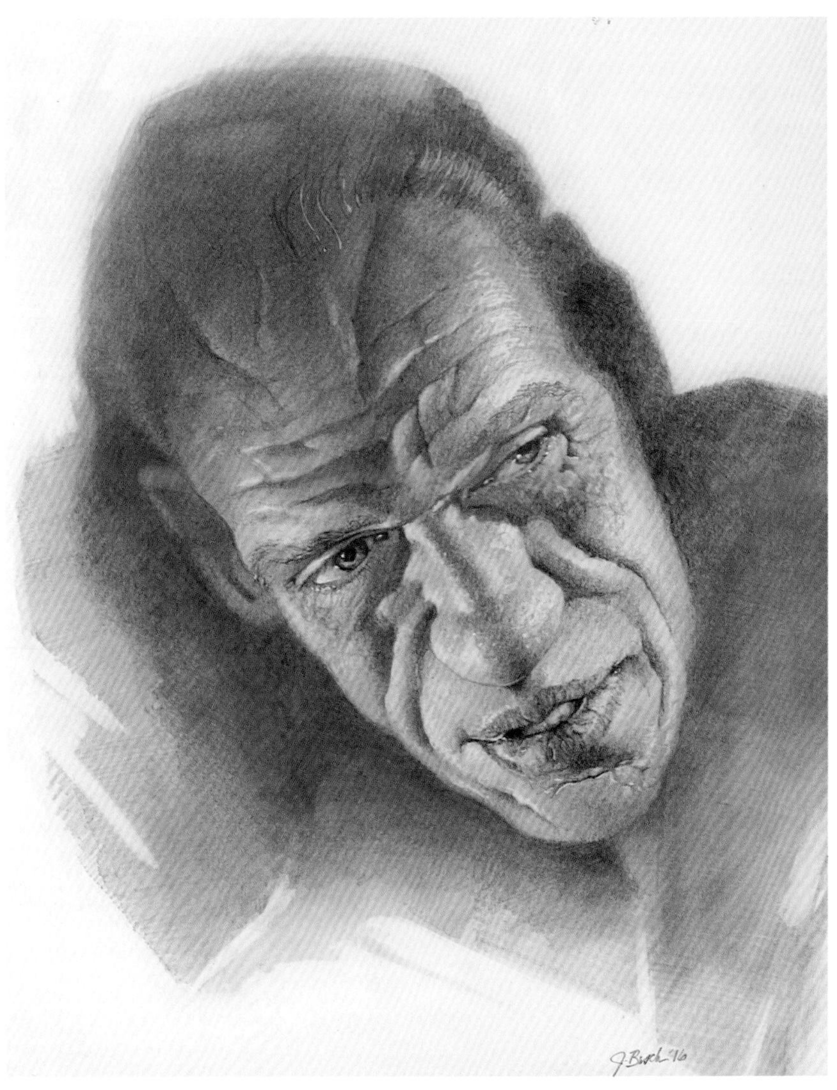

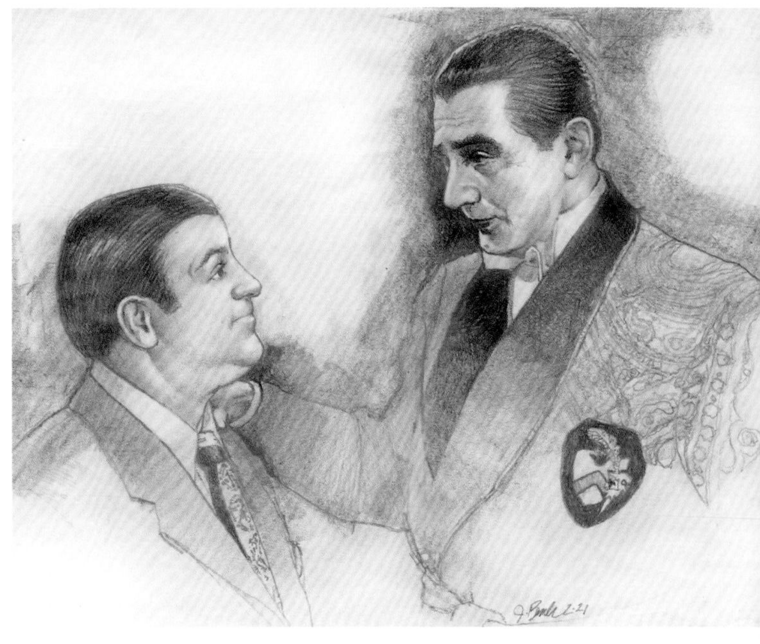

cyborgs, insects, body snatchers. The thing that makes us better than beasts is also our bane."

It's interesting to note that during the Second World War, readers all over the globe, including troops on active duty, embraced the exploits of superheroes in comic books with great enthusiasm. These depicted such iconic images as Hitler being punched in the face by Captain America and gave comfort to the masses that good people would win over the monsters that were hell-bent on forming a new world order in which they ruled unchallenged.

But another real-life monster loomed on the horizon: the atom bomb. The bomb changed everything quickly and efficiently when it was dropped on Japan—Emperor Hirohito surrendered unconditionally in the face of the horror wrought in Nagasaki and Hiroshima. Germany had surrendered three months earlier, when Berlin had been taken by the Allies and Hitler found his own personal final solution.

The war was over, and the world faced new prosperity and potential peace. The monster and horror movies that had sustained fans for the decade had begun to fade at the box office and entered their final stage of relevance—self-parody. *Abbott and Costello Meet Frankenstein* (1948) ushered in a new era of humorous disdain for monsters founded in folklore and superstition. In the bright light of a new world of atomic destruction, they no longer seemed quite so frightening or unvanquishable. Science had usurped superstition, and now fears and nightmares revolved around what dangers lay in the universe as we unlocked its secrets in laboratories, classrooms, and test facilities. In creating the ultimate weapon, scientists had provided a cure that was almost certainly worse than the disease. And what of the strange sightings of so-called flying saucers spotted in the sky after the war? Were they related to this fearsome new atomic power somehow?

What would be the unavoidable consequences of splitting the atom?

OPPOSITE *Wolfman* by Robert Laskey. Oil on canvas board, 2023.

ABOVE LEFT *Rondo Hatton, the Creeper* by Jeff Busch. Pencil, 2016.

ABOVE RIGHT *Costello Meets Dracula* by Jeff Busch. Pencil, 2021.

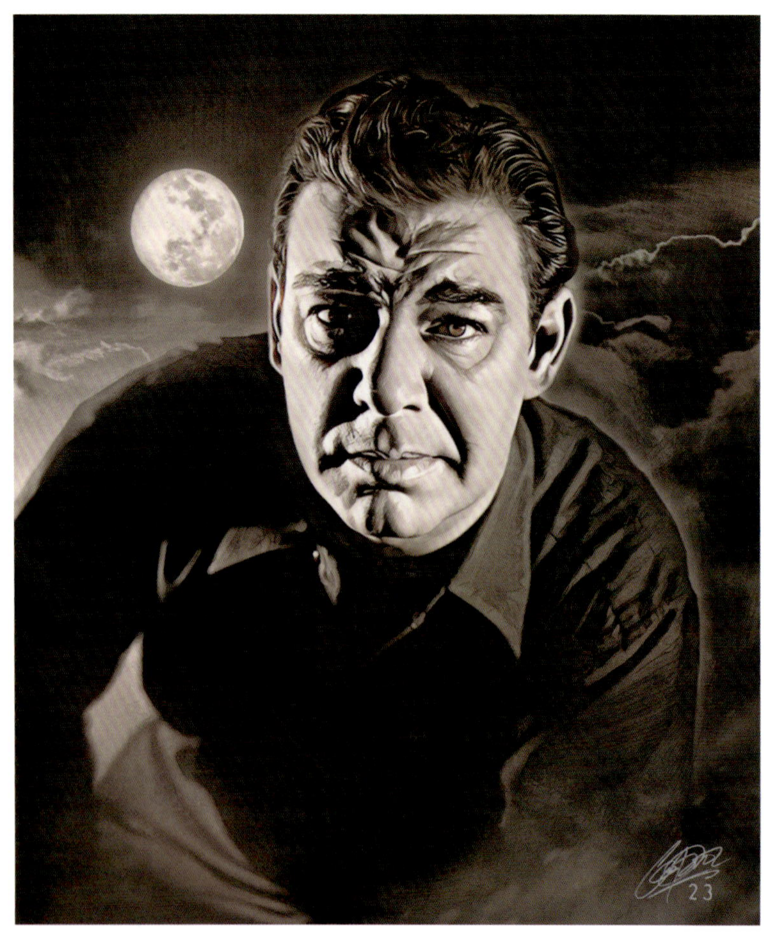

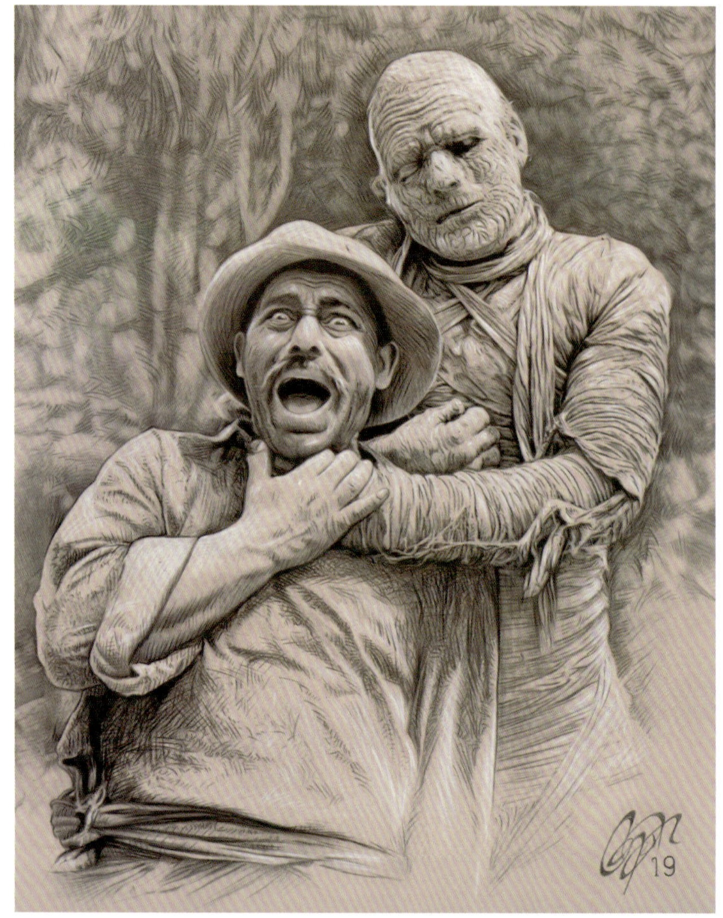

A spread of Frederick Cooper portraits.

TOP *Lon Chaney Jr. as Larry Talbot, aka the Wolfman*. Acrylic, 2023.

TOP RIGHT *The Mummy's Curse*. Colored pencil on toned paper, 2019.

RIGHT *Son of Frankenstein*. Mixed media, 2019.

OPPOSITE *Glenn Strange as the Monster*. Marker, pencil, and paint on sepia drawing board, 2019.

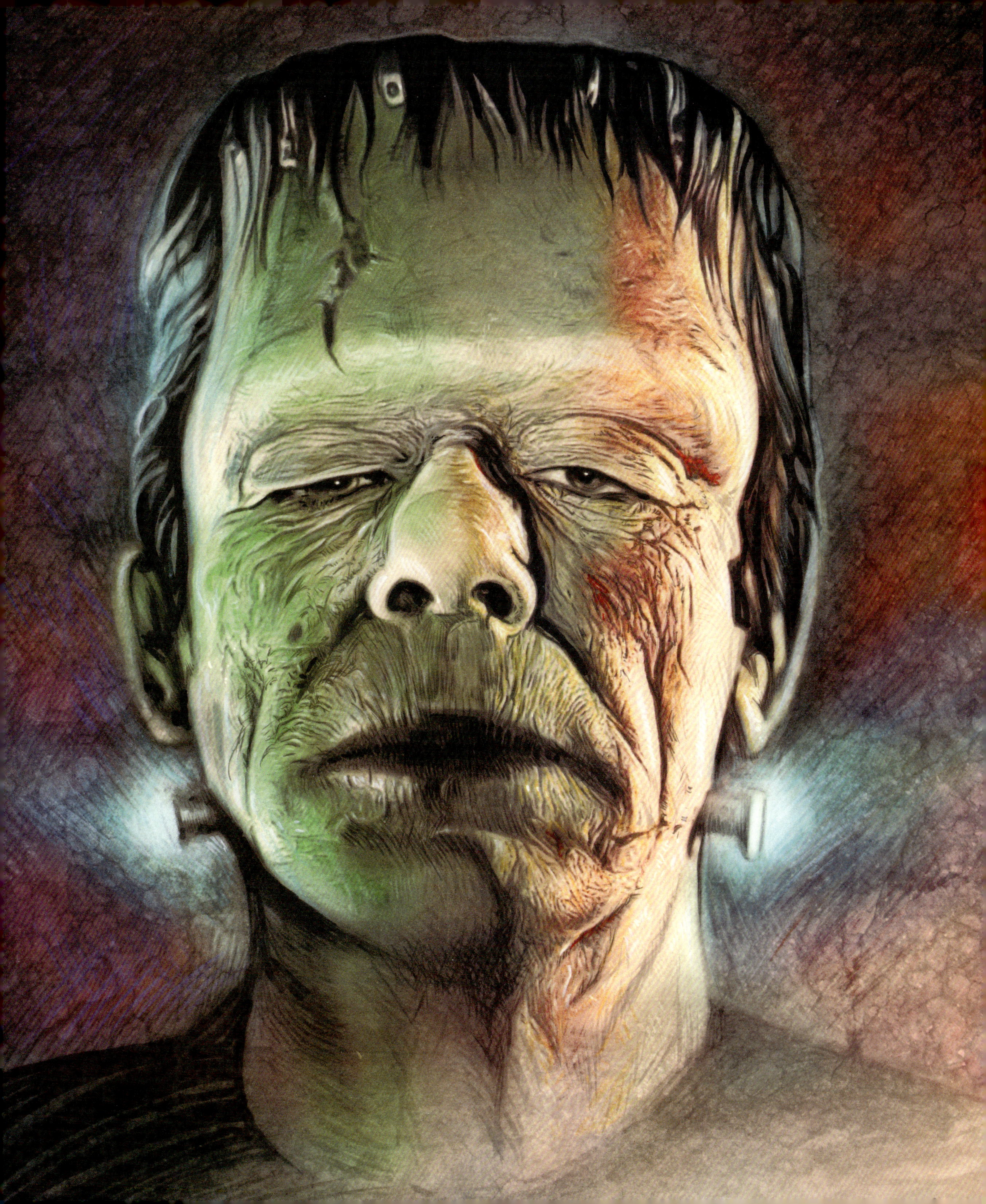

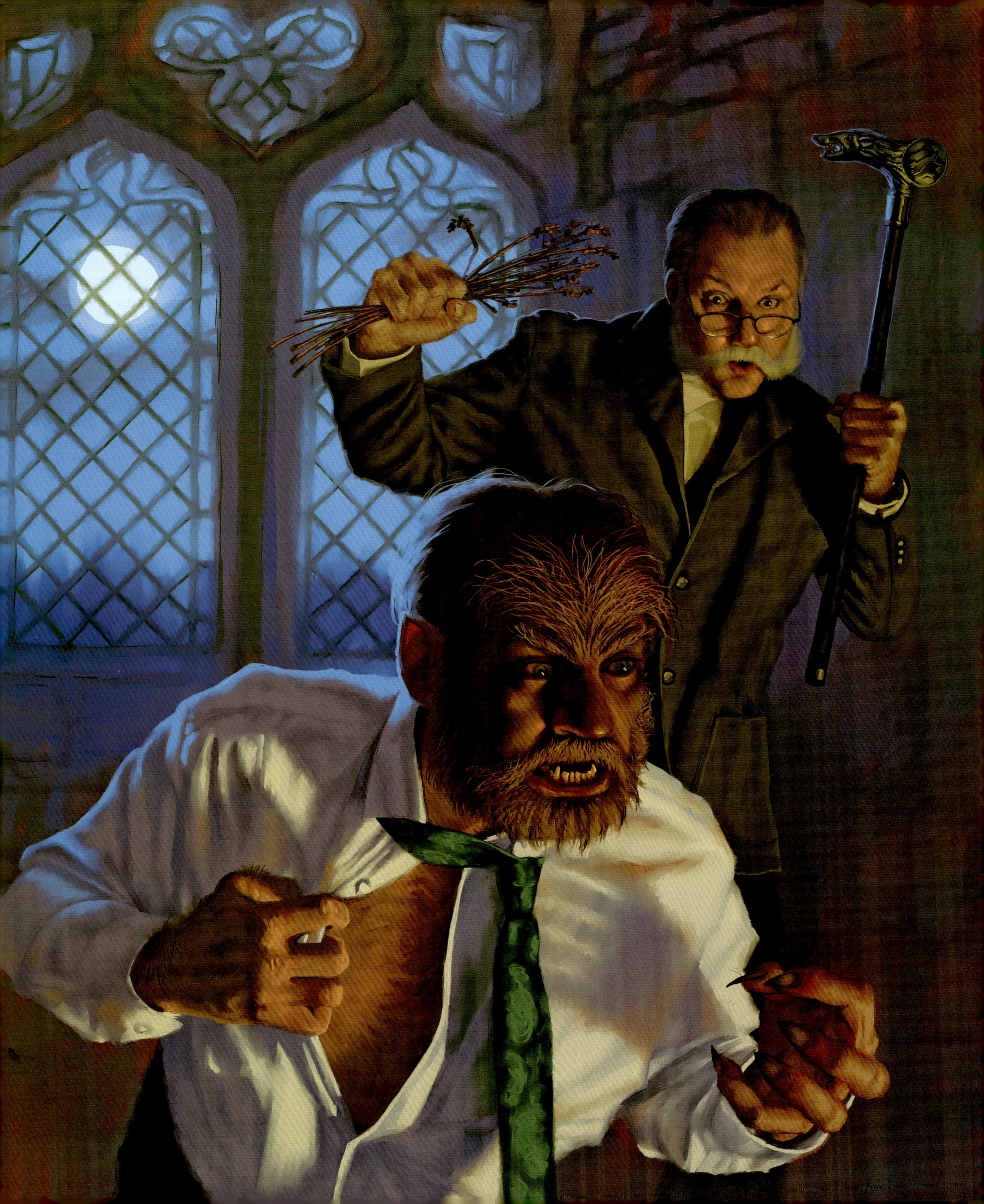

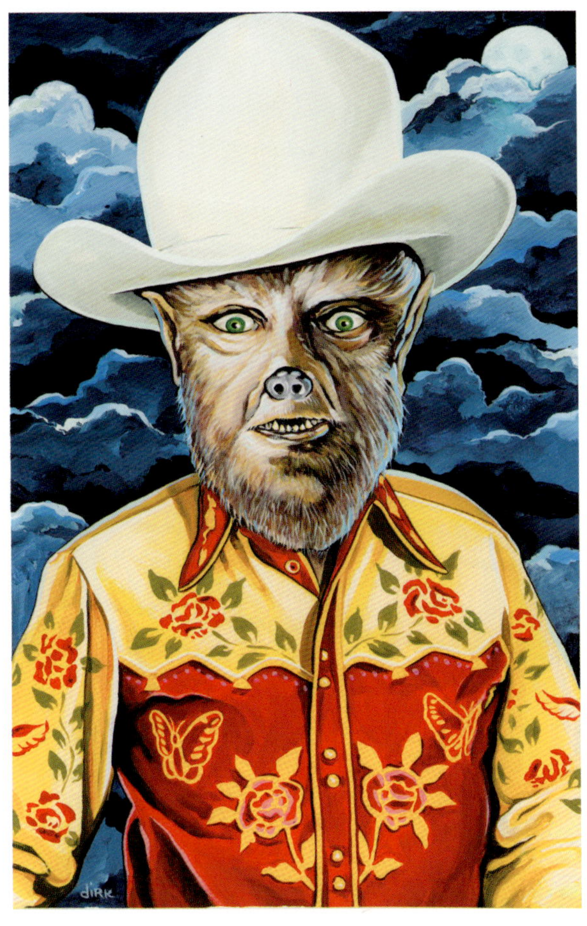

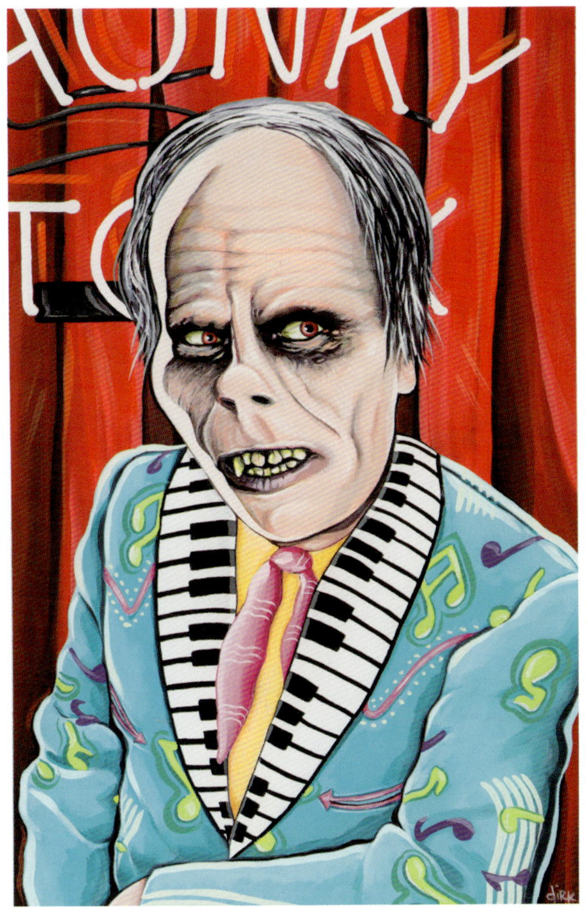

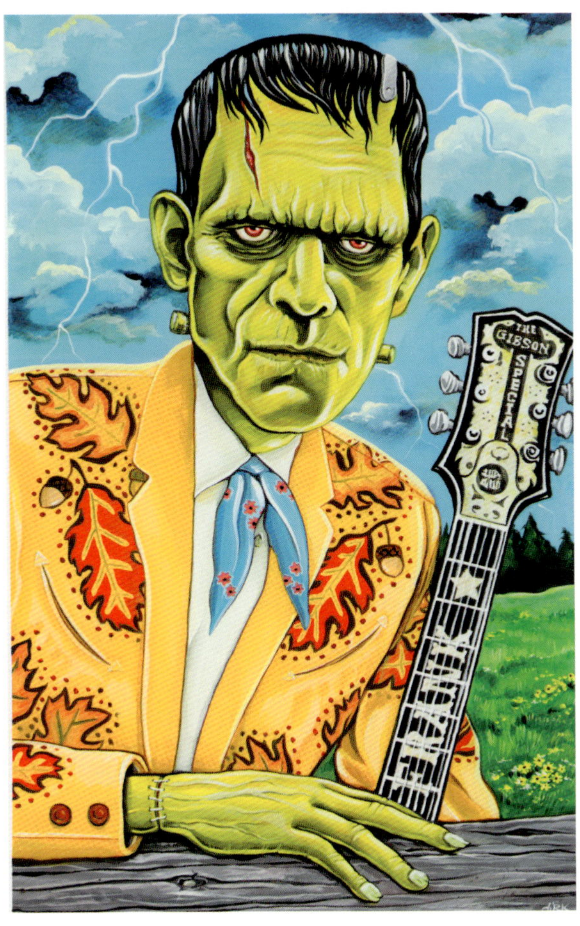

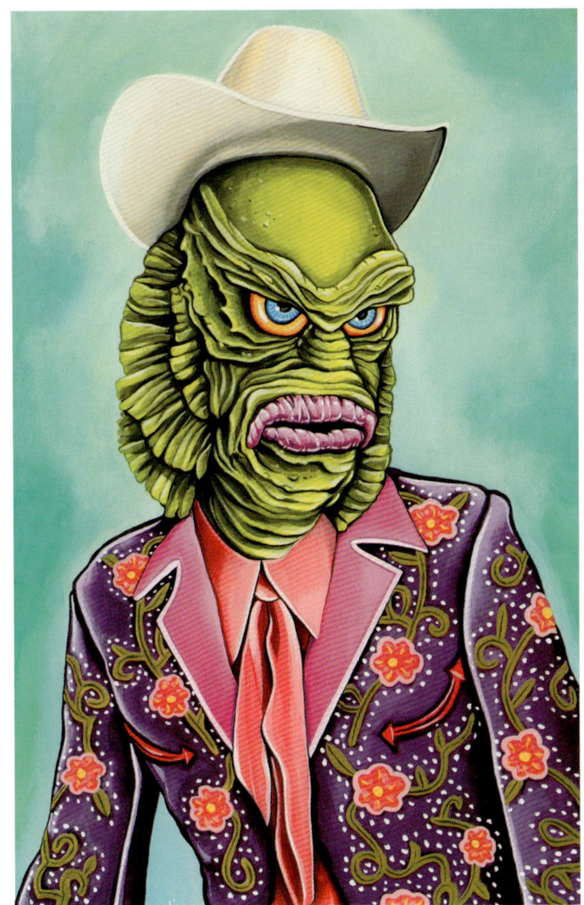

OPPOSITE *Wolfmen* by Daniel Horne. Card game art for Trick or Treat Studios. Oil on board, 2024.

LEFT *A Quartet of Nudie-Suited Famous Monsters of Country Music* by Dirk Hays: the Wolfman, the Phantom, the Monster, and the Gillman. Acrylic on board, 2017.

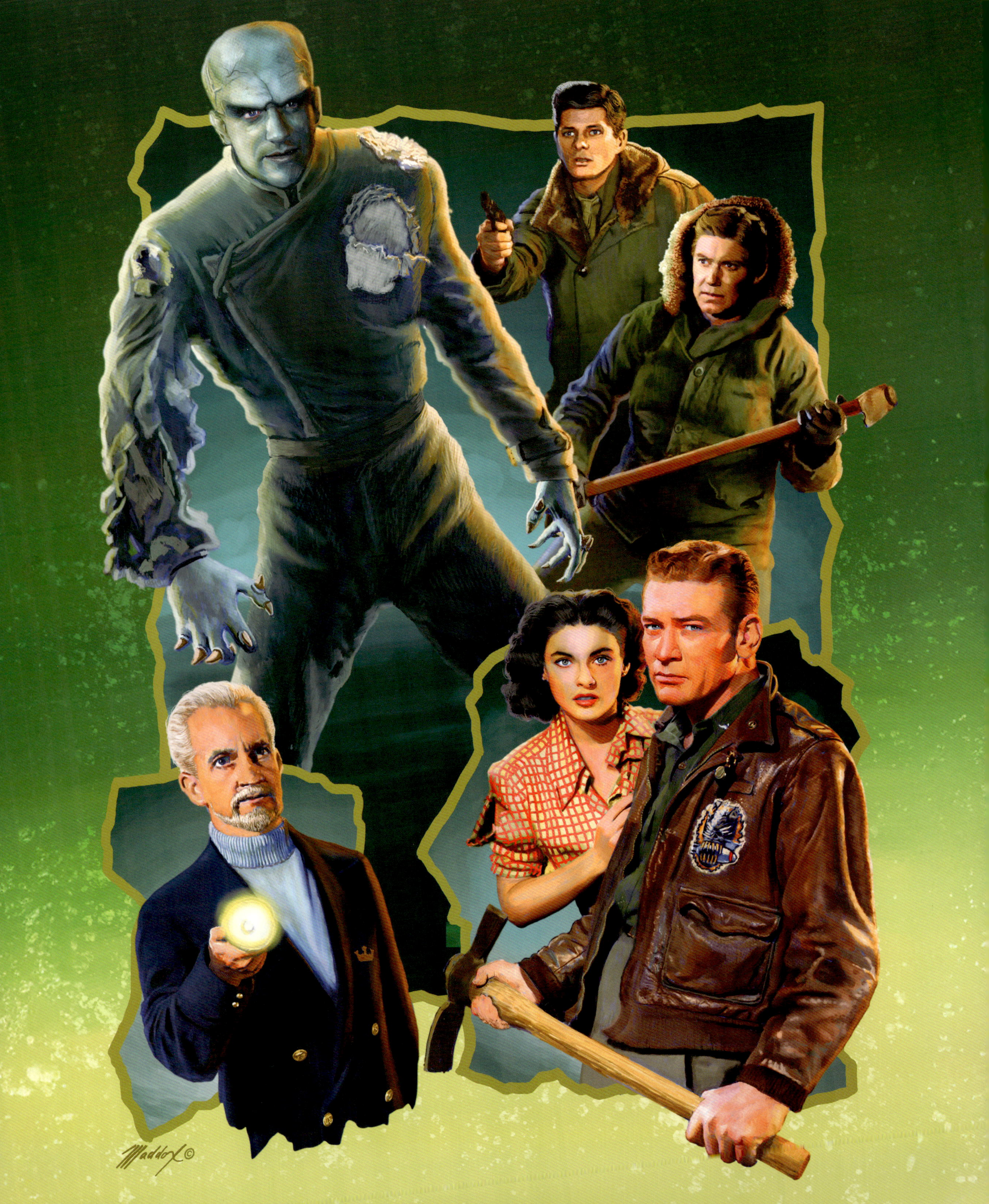
Maddox©

CHAPTER 5

Science Goes Too Far! (1950–1959)

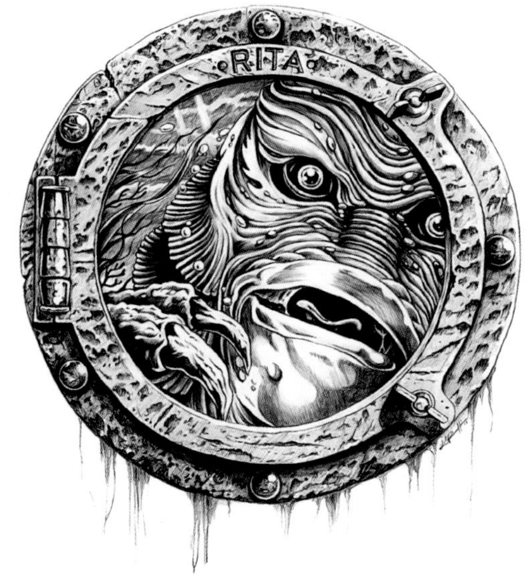

People often visualize fictional monsters as villains. This is not generally the case—a villain may be monstrous, but in twentieth-century mass media representation, monsters are rarely villainous. Indeed, they are often portrayed as sympathetic characters unable to fit into polite society because of physical, emotional, or cognitive disabilities—they are outsiders, shunned by the "normal" characters surrounding them because they are different.

"King Kong and the Creature from the Black Lagoon are destructive," says author John Kenneth Muir (*Horror Films FAQ*), "but we register them as tragic, lonely outsiders, and we've all felt lonely, or like outsiders in our lives, at one point or another."

This experience is a universal formative process for all humans, and means that we are all capable of feeling kinship with this type of monster. Not everyone identifies as an outsider throughout their lives, but all of us go through a period—normally surrounding puberty and into early adulthood—in which we feel ostracized by parents, family, or peers. These ordeals form the foundations of artistic and creative interaction, with metaphor and allegory creating empathy for others in similar situations—the basis of humanity at its most basic level. Catharsis comes with understanding the self and purging the unrealistic expectation of rescue from without. Monsters, as proxies for the viewer, provide an external vessel in which to pour frustration, anger, longing, loneliness, and other cumbersome emotional baggage. It's a rite of passage.

Muir continues, "Monsters feel pain, loss, and sadness, just like we do. For kids, that's a very powerful model. And the monsters lash out when hurt, which I think is also human instinct, and one which children recognize (and have a hard time controlling). Children relate to monsters because monsters can be awkward, angry, confused, etc. Those are emotions we all feel and have trouble controlling, even in adulthood. Accordingly, I think children often feel real empathy for the silver screen monsters."

As an award-winning writer and one of the world's most prominent creators of horror fiction, Ramsey Campbell is perched with a keen eye on its effects on readers. He offers a different perspective: "I've never viewed it that way. I think [monster/horror fiction] engages the imagination, and that's justification enough. At its best, like all good art, it can make us look again at things we've taken for granted, not least notions of the monstrous and of supposed normality. I'm reminded of film critic Robin Wood's (*On the*

OPPOSITE *The Thing from Another World* by Mark Maddox. Cover for *We Belong Dead* magazine #20. Digital, 2023.

ABOVE *The Creature Invades the Rita* by "Ghoulish" Gary Pullin. Alternate art for Mondo poster. Pencil, 2018.

Horror Film) formulation: 'Normality is threatened by the monster,' the purpose of which is to encourage us to interrogate both concepts."

The comic book superheroes, so popular in the 1940s, found themselves fighting a different kind of battle in the 1950s—the battle for newsstand space, which was being eaten up by the increasingly popular horror and true crime comics. Publisher William Gaines's EC Comics published a full slate of grisly fright titles like *Tales from the Crypt*, *The Vault of Horror*, and *The Haunt of Fear*, filled with provocative and explicit art from exceptionally talented artists like Joe Orlando, Wally Wood, Reed Crandall, Jack Davis, Graham Ingels, Johnny Craig, and John Severin.

Inspired by Dr. Fredric Wertham's book *Seduction of the Innocent*, which inaccurately blamed the rise in juvenile delinquency on this type of comic book imagery, Senator Estes Kefauver, a Democrat from Tennessee, opened an investigation in 1954 into the comic book industry. This, in turn, led to the formation of the Comics Code Authority, a board appointed by the publishing companies to police themselves and clean up the gruesome content of companies like EC and other independents. Needless to say, the "offensive" horror and true crime comics soon disappeared from stores and newsstands.

As science began to supplant superstition in the representation of monstrous characters in the late 1940s thanks to the new frontier of atomic weapons, science fiction began to dominate the concepts presented in media as a vessel for these characters. Films like *The Day the Earth Stood Still* and *The Thing from Another World* (both in 1951) brought invaders from outer space into local theaters to sensational effect and respectable box office receipts.

Perhaps the most terrifying and subversive story of this genre was 1953's *Invaders from Mars,* resplendent in glowing Technicolor. Young David MacLean spots a flying saucer landing in a field behind his house one night and, within a day, his parents, neighbors, and all other authority figures have been turned into thralls of a malevolent power from beyond Earth. The film, and others that followed, is a thinly veiled allegory for the

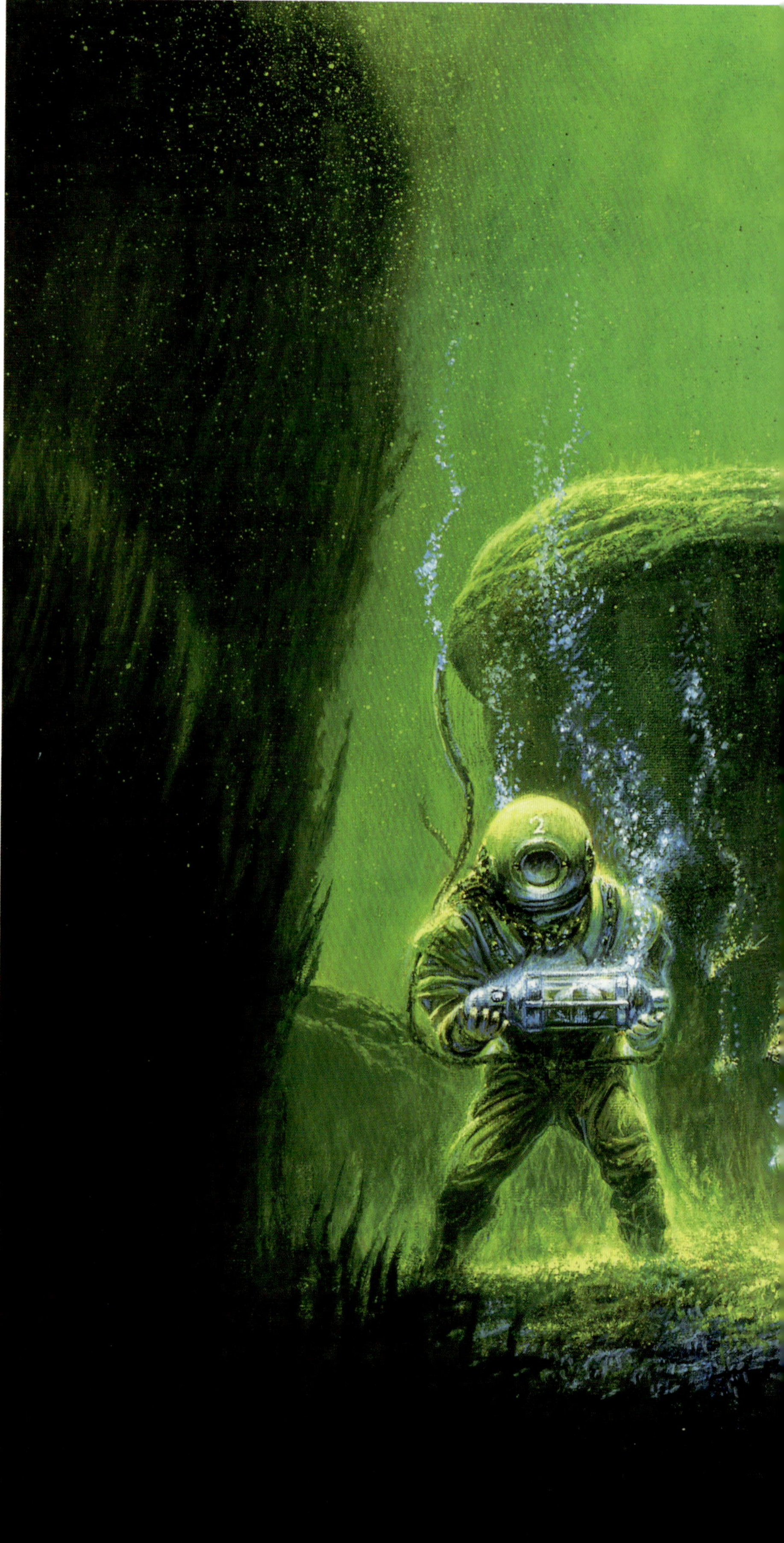

RIGHT *Serizawa's Last Stand* by Bob Eggleton. Oil on canvas, 2004.

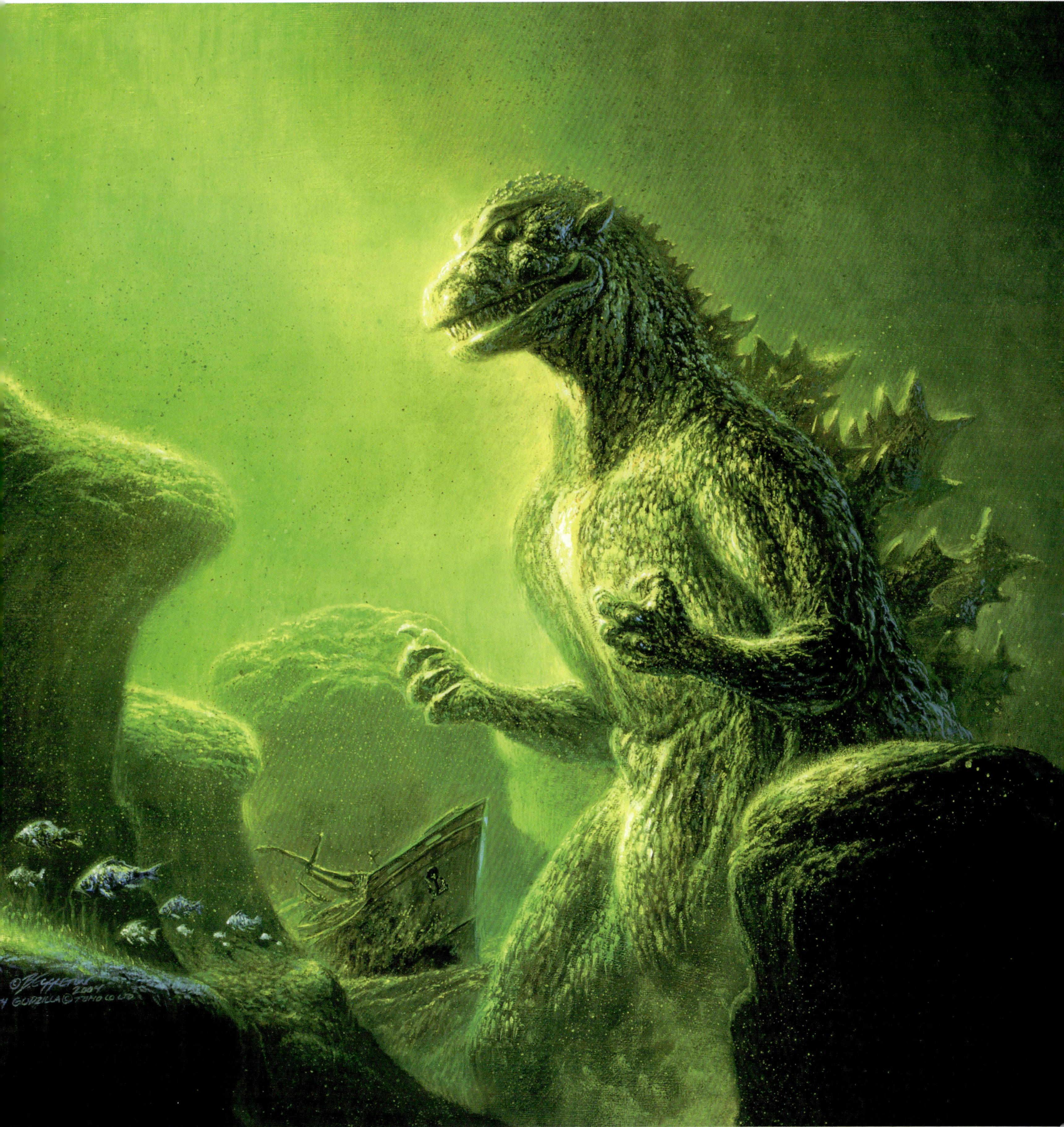
2004
GODZILLA © TOHO CO LTD

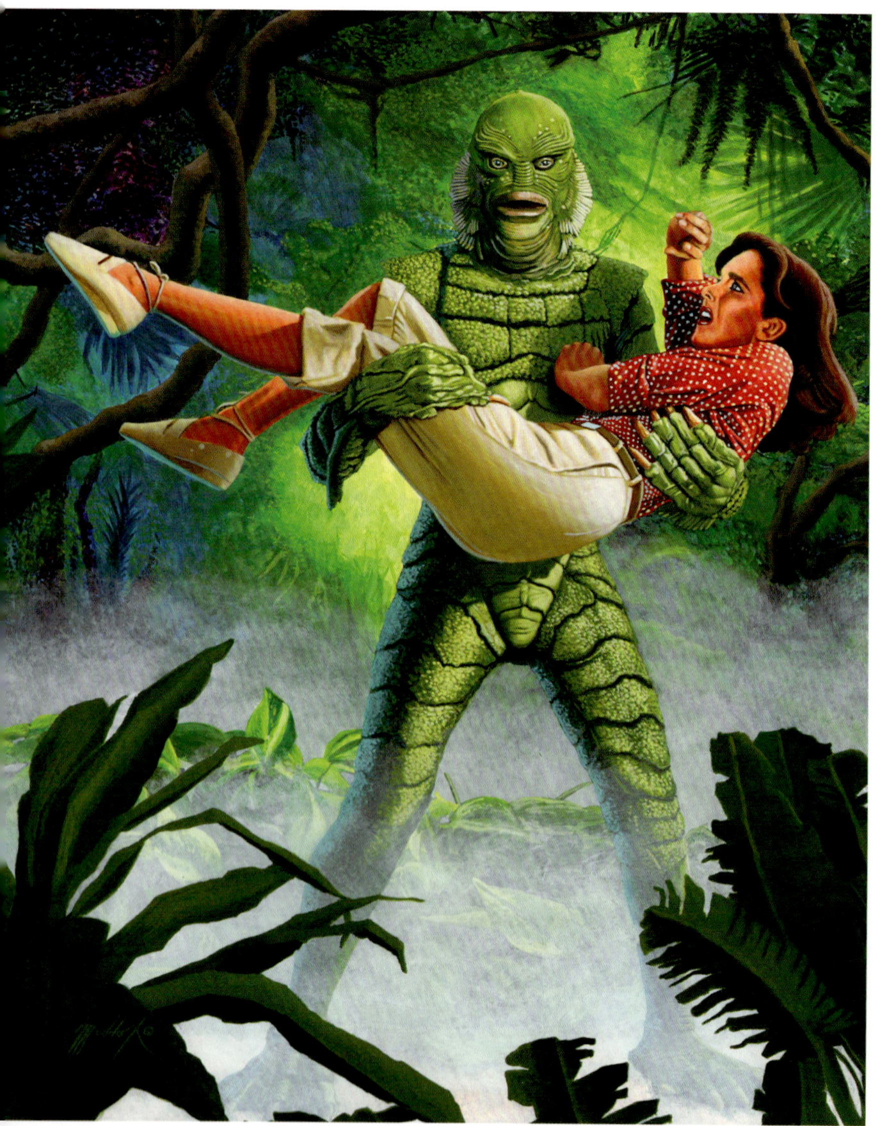

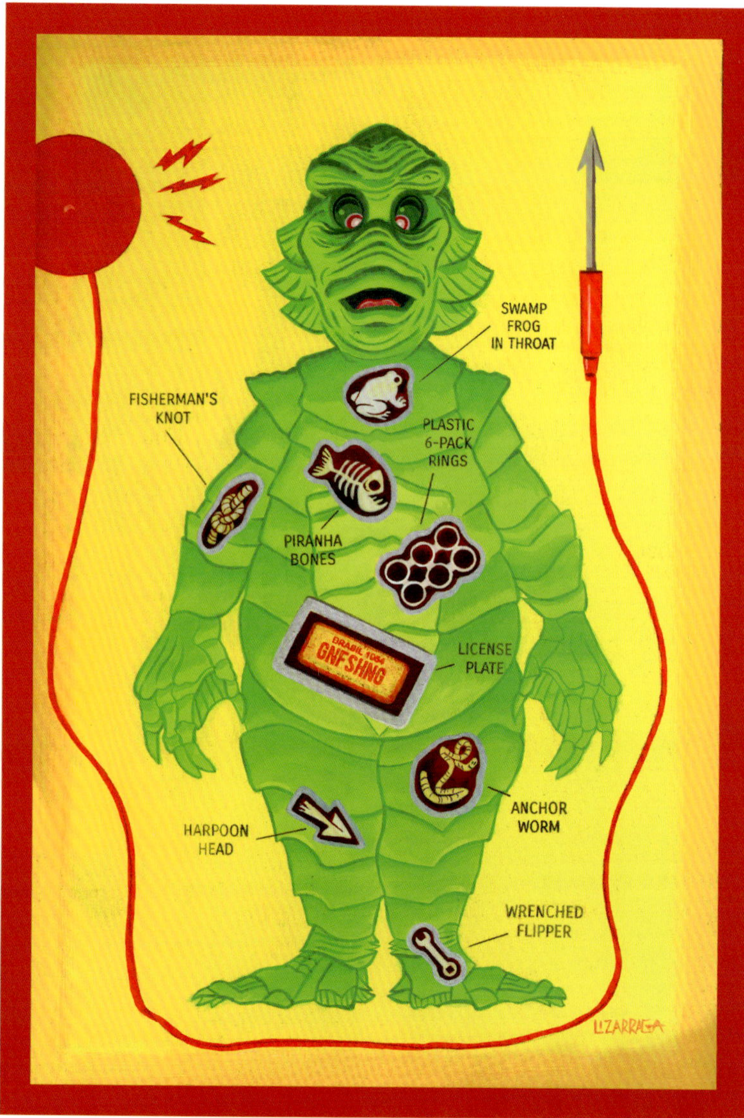

ABOVE LEFT *Creature and Kay* by Mark Maddox. Cover for *Screem* magazine. Mixed media, 2023.

ABOVE RIGHT *Creature Operation Game* by Bob Lizarraga. Acrylic, 2022.

OPPOSITE *Creature from the Black Lagoon* by Bob Eggleton. Oil on canvas, 2005.

Cold War that was taking place between the Soviets and the Americans, and a warning of the dangers of communist infiltration. Oh sure, they *look* like us, but do they *think* like us? The ideological split the world was experiencing was beginning to turn even the most idyllic settings and relationships asunder, and filmmakers wanted to make sure we understood the underlying mechanisms of propaganda.

Slightly less sinister, the aliens in *It Came from Outer Space* (1953) crash-land on Earth accidentally, but still traipse about impersonating humans and wreaking havoc with the locals. The granddaddy of all alien invasions takes place in producer George Pal's film of H. G. Wells's *The War of the Worlds*, released that same year. Using state-of-the-art photographic effects, Pal and director Byron Haskin depict the end of the world as we know it—almost. When all seems lost, nature steps in to save what's left of humankind and a brighter day dawns.

Invasion of the Body Snatchers (1956) takes the fear of invasion and loss of identity to new heights as Kevin McCarthy and company find themselves being replaced by emotionless clones born of alien plant pods from outer space—while they slept! Fear of the dark is a common phobia, and we are always most helpless and vulnerable while we sleep. Jack Finney's source novel amps the stakes, and director Don Siegel's film delivers some seriously knuckle-biting moments.

These four films took advantage of the Red Scare happening across America, and to some extent around the world, to sell tickets to a public who were finally living free of the economic hardships of the 1930s and the war of the 1940s. Yes, there were still homeless people and "police actions" taking place around the planet,

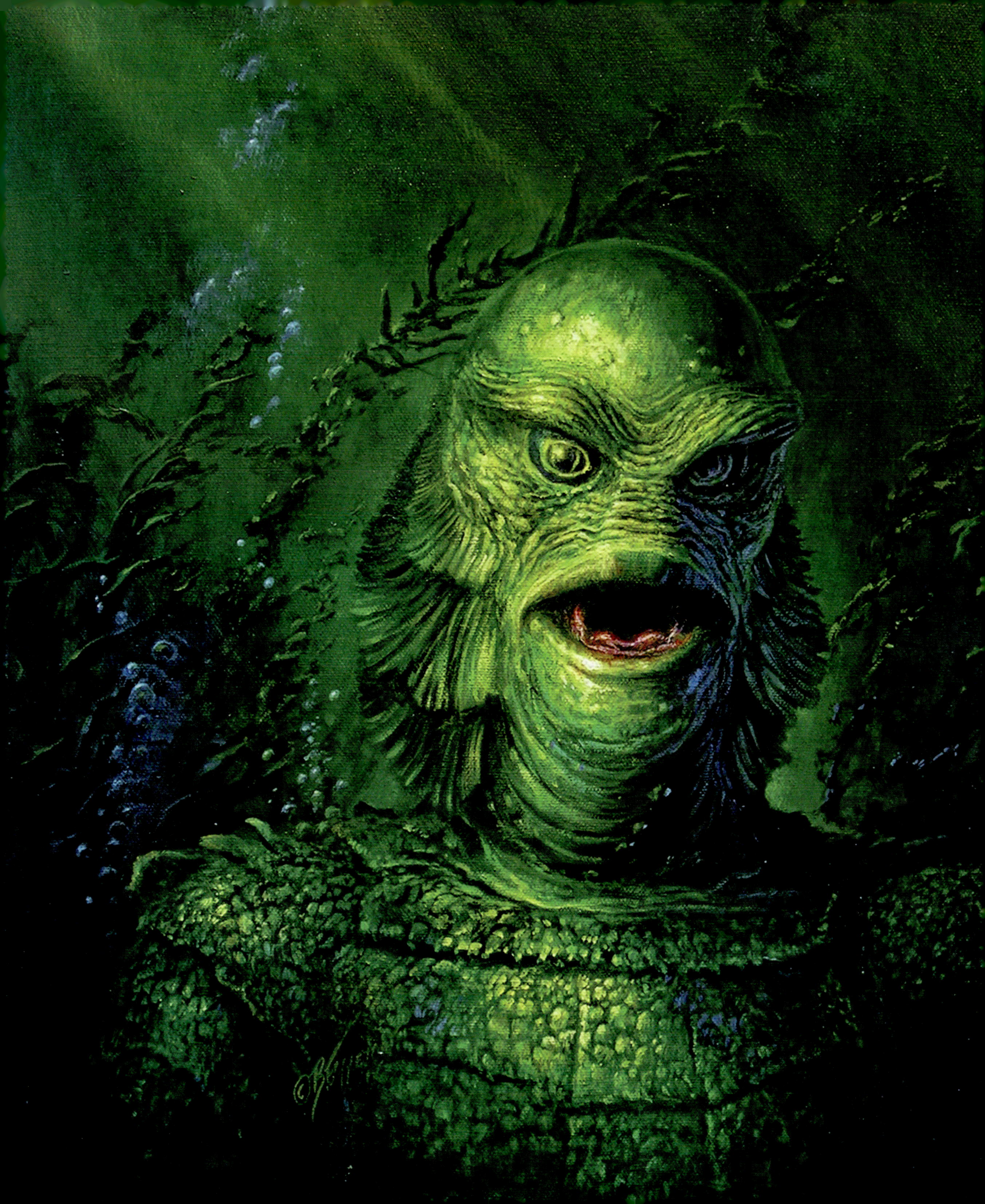

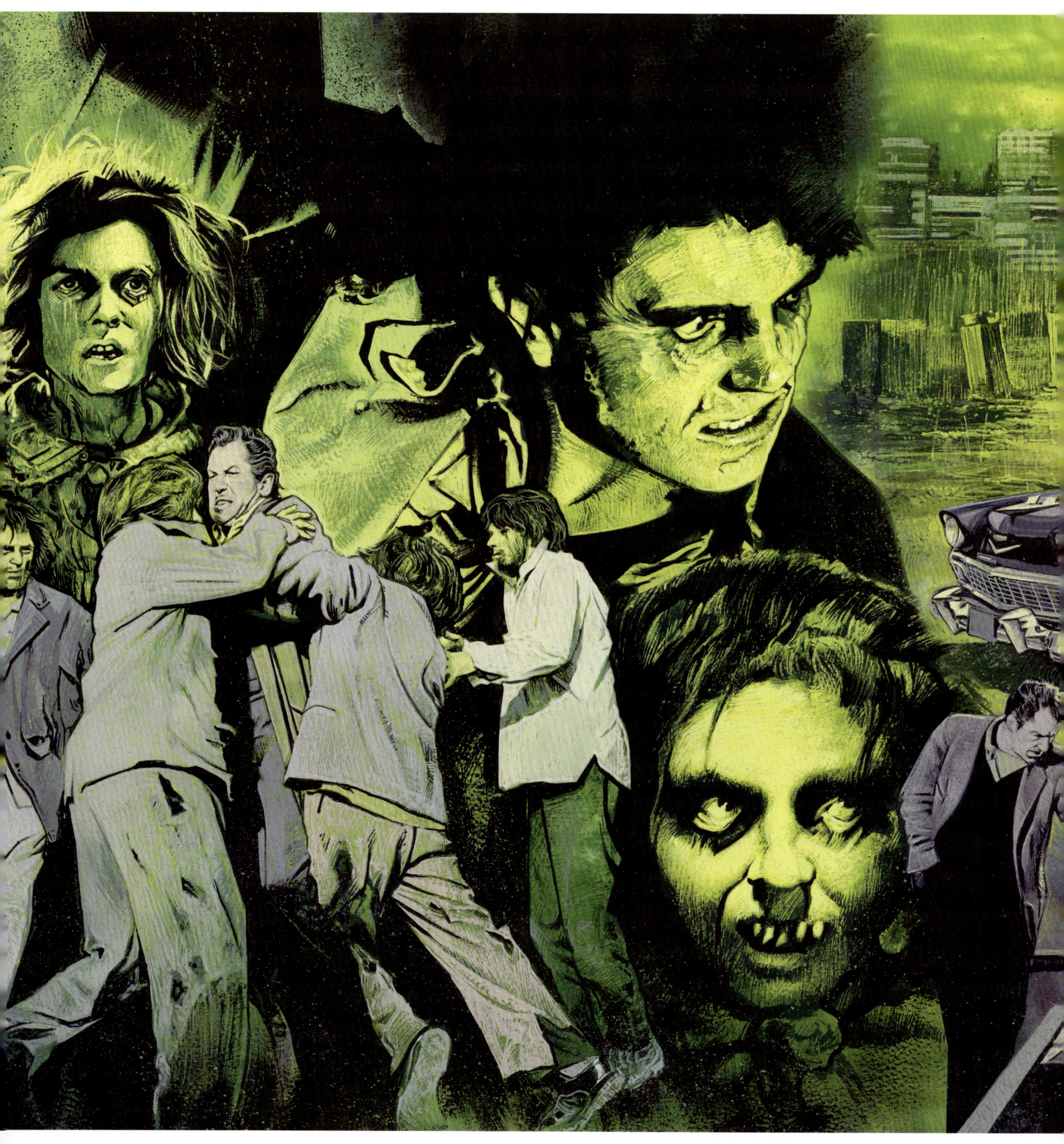

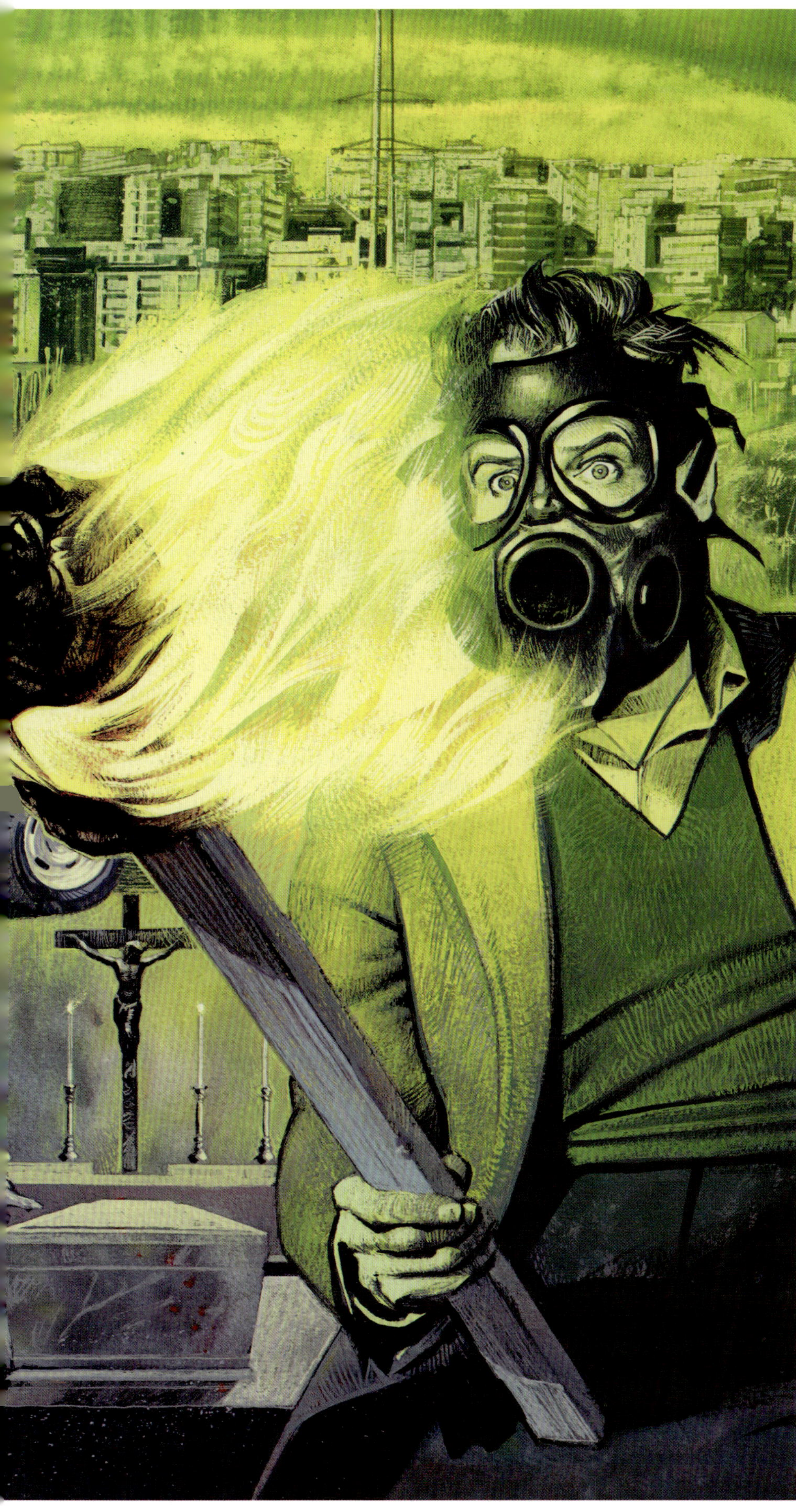

but the general nostalgia for this period is that it was a time of plenty. What self-respecting alien from a dying world wouldn't want to take advantage of that scenario and seize it for themselves? By the end of the decade, many more films—a myriad of them low-budget B movies by independent filmmaking greats such as Roger Corman—dotted this landscape, including classics like *This Island Earth* (1955) and *The Quatermass Xperiment* (1955), along with *Earth vs. the Flying Saucers* (1956) and *20 Million Miles to Earth* (1957), which both featured stop-motion special effects by the incomparable Ray Harryhausen.

So, we kept watching the skies. But what about the seas?

Harryhausen had been busy there as well, generating a lonely dinosaur and a giant octopus that ran amok in cities in, respectively, *The Beast from 20,000 Fathoms* (1953) and *It Came from Beneath the Sea* (1955). Also enraged, and thoroughly mutated by nuclear radiation from the Hiroshima and Nagasaki atomic bombs, the title creature in *Gojira* (1954) burst from the Sea of Japan and tore through Tokyo like a living explosion, creating an entirely new genre of monster films in the process (although he was in fact inspired by *The Beast from 20,000 Fathoms).* Godzilla, as he is known in English-speaking countries, is literally the physical embodiment of the nuclear fears and loathing the Japanese people were left to process after the war, a giant creature that breathes fire and is uncontrollable—at least in his first appearance. The movie was edited and amended to add Raymond Burr as American journalist Steve Martin and released in America a year and a half later as *Godzilla, King of the Monsters!* (1956). And Godzilla truly became the king, going on to spin off dozens of sequels and characters in what the Japanese termed *daikaiju*, or "giant strange creature" films. Before the decade was out, more giant creatures saw the light of day in Japanese films like *Godzilla Raids Again* (1955), *Half Human (Jû jin yuki otoko)* (1955), *Rodan* (1956), *Warning from Space* (1956), *The Mysterians* (1957), and *Varan* (1958), while American and British productions, including *The Deadly Mantis* (1957), *The Giant Claw* (1957), *The Spider* (1958), and *The Giant*

LEFT *The Last Man on Earth* by Graham Humphreys. Album gatefold for Waxwork Records. Mixed media, 2024.

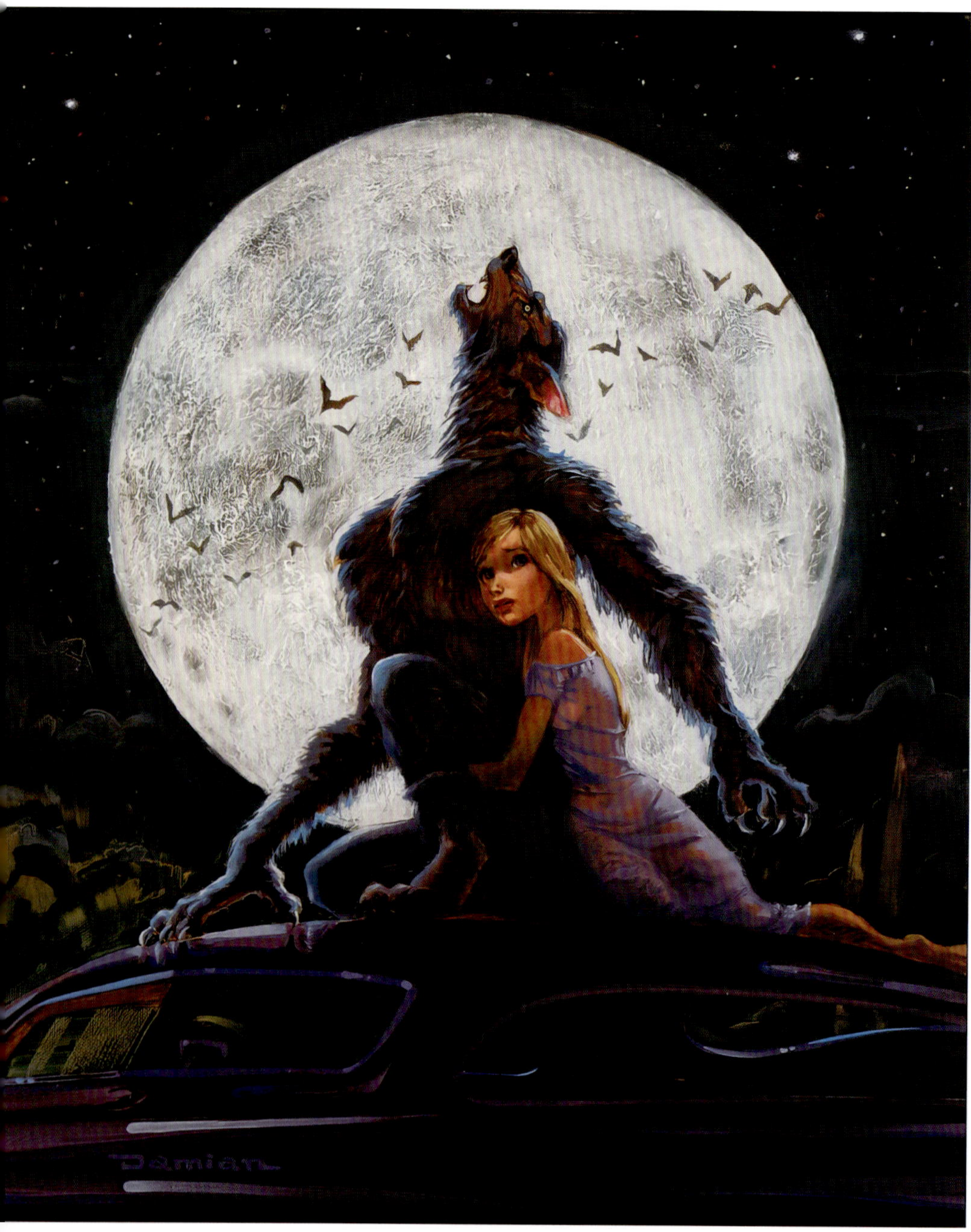

ABOVE *I Was a Teenaged Werewolf* by Damian Fulton. Oil on canvas, 2010.

OPPOSITE *An Eye for an Eye* by Damian Fulton. Oil on canvas, 2010.

Behemoth (1959), brought their own monstrous creatures to international audiences.

1954's *Creature from the Black Lagoon* is one of the most beloved monster movies of all time. A newcomer to the Universal Studios monster crowd, the Gill-man, as he's known, is a throwback to the prehistoric Devonian period, a walking fish-man with an eye for the ladies. Sporting possibly the greatest movie monster suit an actor ever wore, the film offers similar themes as *King Kong* and has an unforgettable—if very repetitive—musical score. The Creature was so popular, he returned for two sequels and spawned a handful of imitators such as *The Monster of Piedras Blancas* (1959).

What about other environments—the deserts, the mountains, the plains, the cities? No place was immune to mutated monsters on the loose.

In the American desert, giant irradiated ants by the thousands attacked in *Them!* (1954), in what could also be considered a US *daikaiju* movie. *Them!* is a perennial favorite of genre aficionados for its deadly serious attitude and excellent performances. The eerie sounds the ants make before they attack are unforgettable. The following year, *Tarantula* (1955) pulled a similar stunt with a giant—wait for it—tarantula in the Arizona desert. In Mexico City, *The Black Scorpion* (1957) terrorized the barrio after a volcanic disturbance, and back in Texas, *The Giant Gila Monster* (1959) couldn't resist hanging out in the hot rod street-racing scene.

In the realm of mad scientists, *The Fly* (1958) starred Al (later David) Hedison as Andre Delambre, an egghead dead set on cracking the formula for station-to-station teleportation who gets mixed up when a house fly enters the chamber in which he's using himself as a guinea pig. An unforgettable denouement with co-star Vincent Price makes the film a classic. 1957's *I Was a Teenage Werewolf* substitutes science with the bite of the man-wolf, and *Fiend Without a Face* (1958) is a semi-psychedelic trip through an attack of flying brains, complete with spinal cords, thanks to an errant scientist.

A side benefit of the rise of science fiction and horror movies in the '50s was an influx of truly wonderful poster art for the films. American illustrators like Reynold Brown, Albert Kallis, and Mort Künstler—and, in the UK and Europe, Tom Chantrell, Enrico De Seta, Boris Grimsson, and Guy-Gérard Noël—created unforgettable art that elevated even the lowest-budget B movie to great heights, establishing a foundation and raising the bar for the generation of poster artists to come.

As these modern marvels menaced kids and adults, to their delight, in theaters, a couple of interesting developments occurred that brought the older-style monsters back to the public eye.

First, Hammer Films in the UK had the bright idea to take two public domain characters, Dracula and Frankenstein's monster, out of mothballs and release new color films complete with blood, heaving bosoms, and semi-tame violence—all to great success. *The Curse of Frankenstein* (1957) and 1958's *Dracula* (*Horror of Dracula* in the US) made stars of actors Peter Cushing and Christopher Lee and led to multiple sequels as well as a cadre of other, similar gothic horror films that stretched into the 1970s.

Second, a new syndicated package of monster movies from Universal—which included their classic films from the 1930s and '40s—called *Shock Theater* was released to television stations across America in October 1957. Adopting the show as late-night weekend programming, many stations created a host character for these films, which fueled a culture of viewing that became almost irresistible to youngsters. Preschoolers may have had *Captain Kangaroo*, *Romper Room*, or *Bozo the Clown* catering to their television whims, but now middle schoolers and high schoolers had Ghoulardi, Vampira, Zacherley, and others to latch onto. *Shock Theater* (and the similarly named shows that broadcast the films from the syndication package) became essential viewing for the nine- to seventeen-year-old crowd and the equivalent of what was called "watercooler TV" in the 1990s.

One more element was needed to turn the tide from still waters into a tsunami—a nexus for the nascent crowds of fans to form around. It came in the form of a magazine called *Famous Monsters of Filmland*, which burst onto the scene in 1958. Published by James Warren and edited by sci-fi (he created the term!) superfan Forrest J Ackerman, *Famous Monsters* was like an atomic bomb aimed directly at the *Shock Theater* crowd, and when it exploded, the metaphorical shrapnel blanketed the world.

The Monster Kid movement was born.

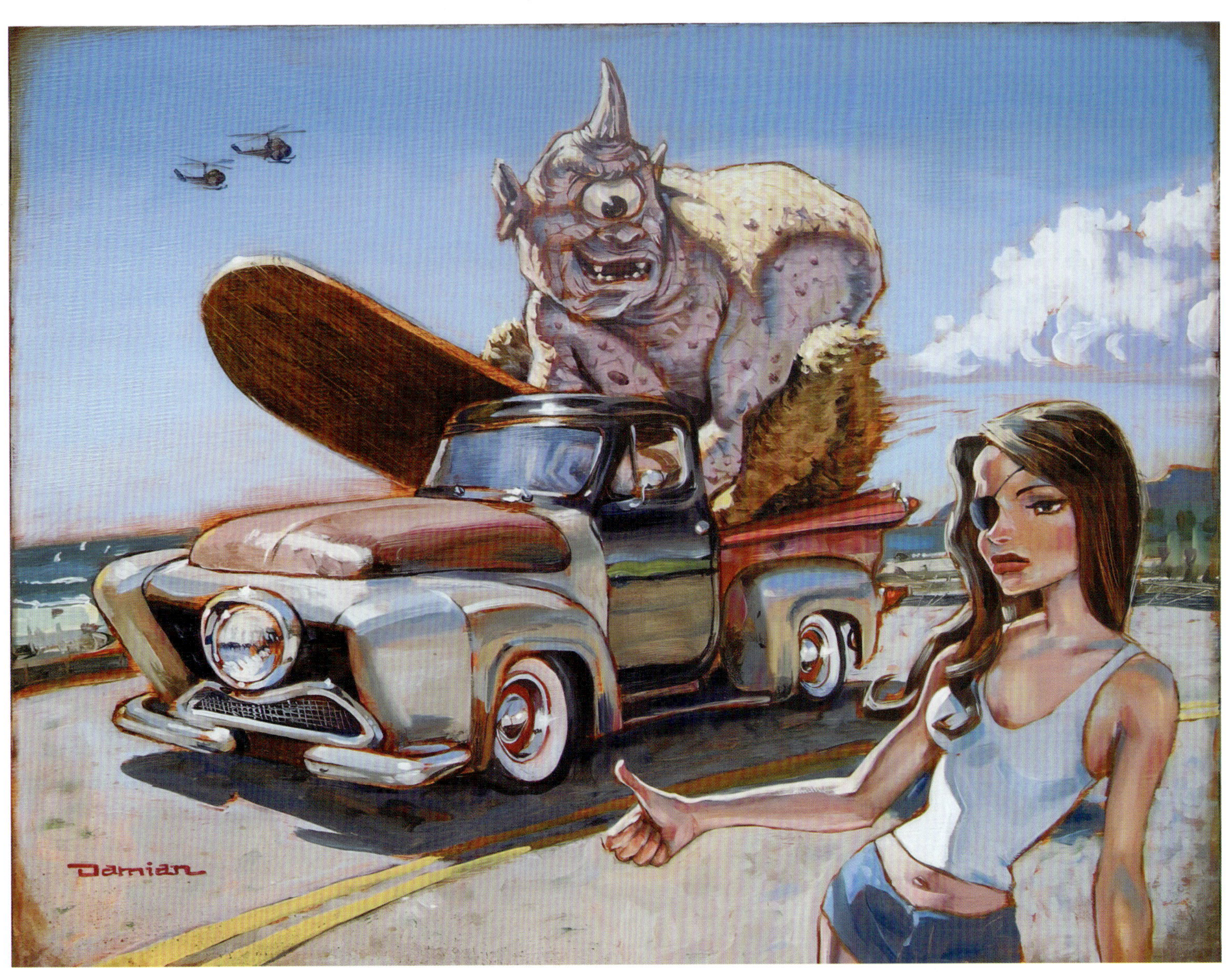

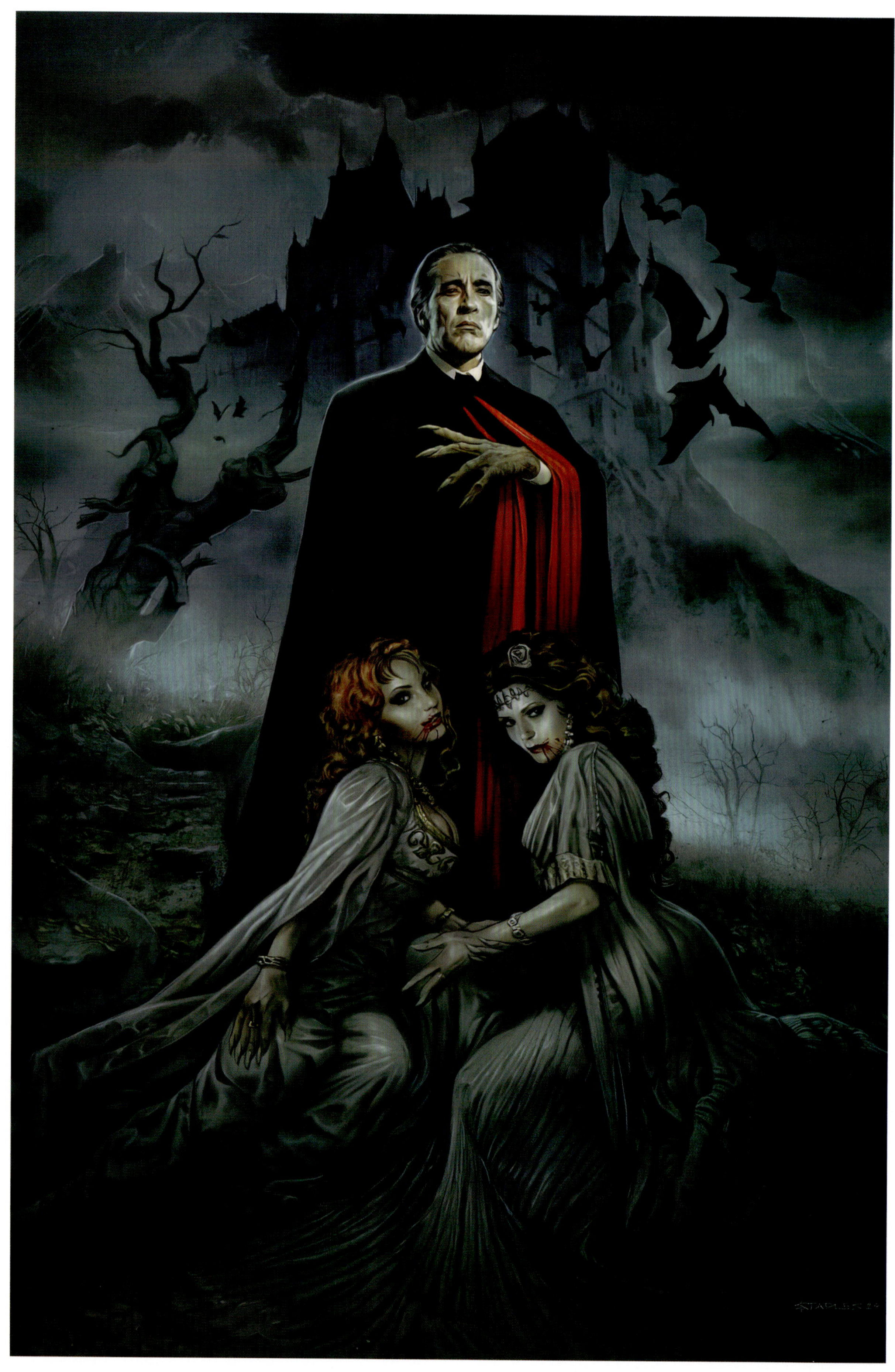

RIGHT *Hammer Dracula* by Greg Staples. Acrylic on art board, 2024.

OPPOSITE *The Horror of Dracula* by Bob Lizarraga. Illustration for *Little Shoppe of Horrors* magazine #46. Acrylic, 2021.

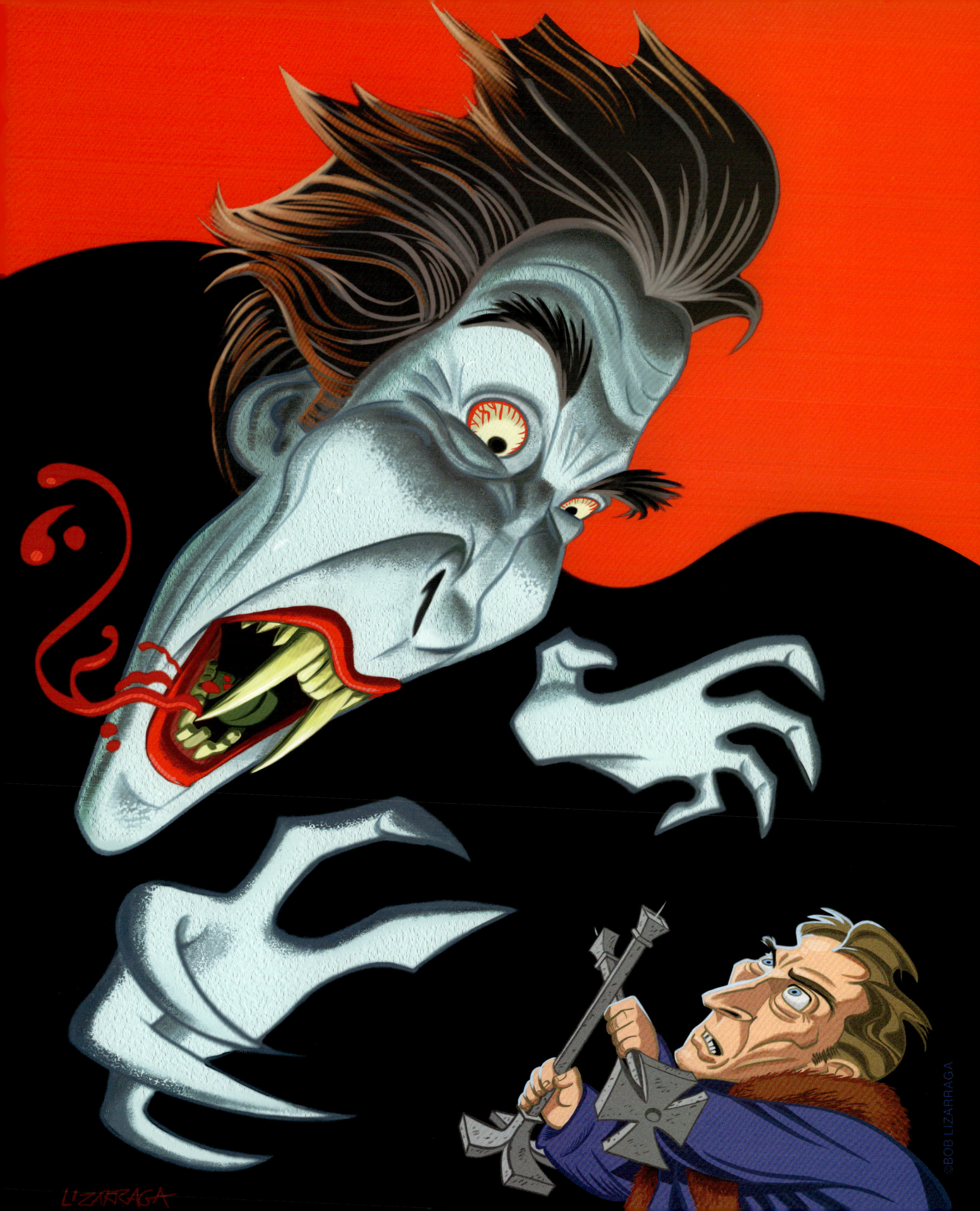
LIZARRAGA
©BOB LIZARRAGA

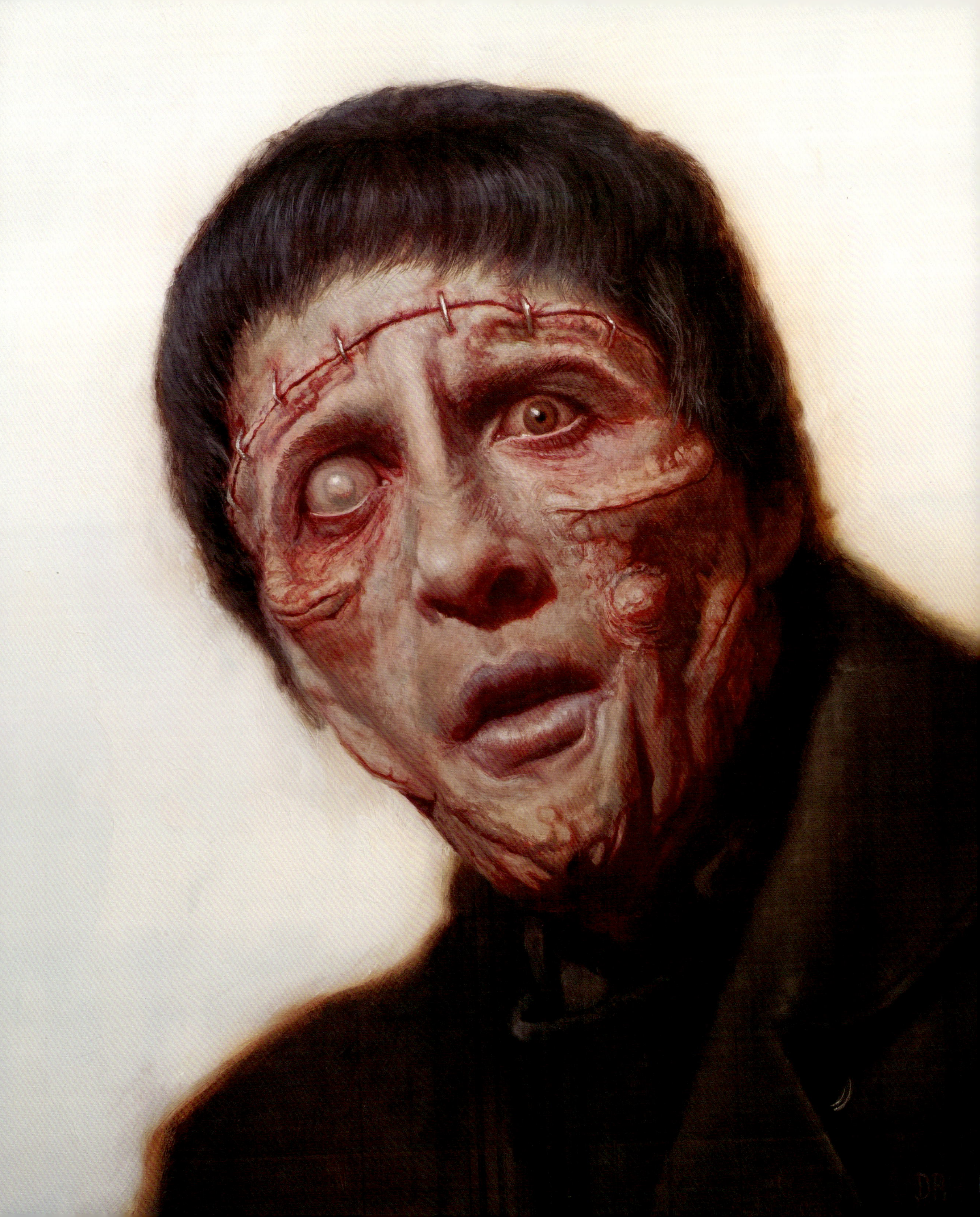

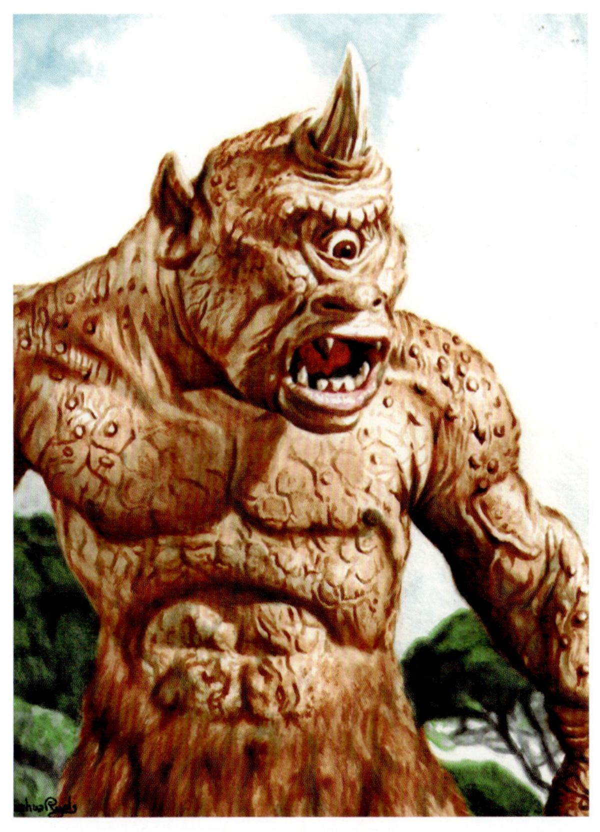

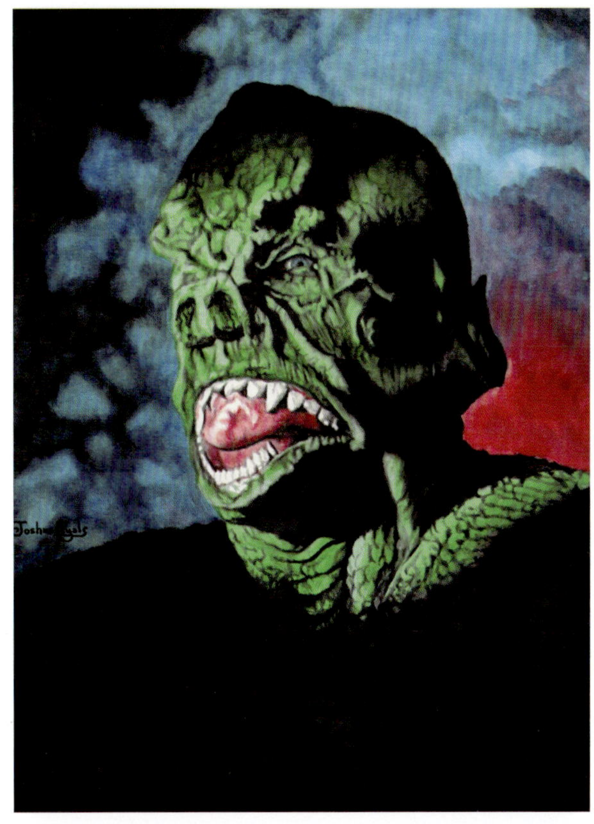

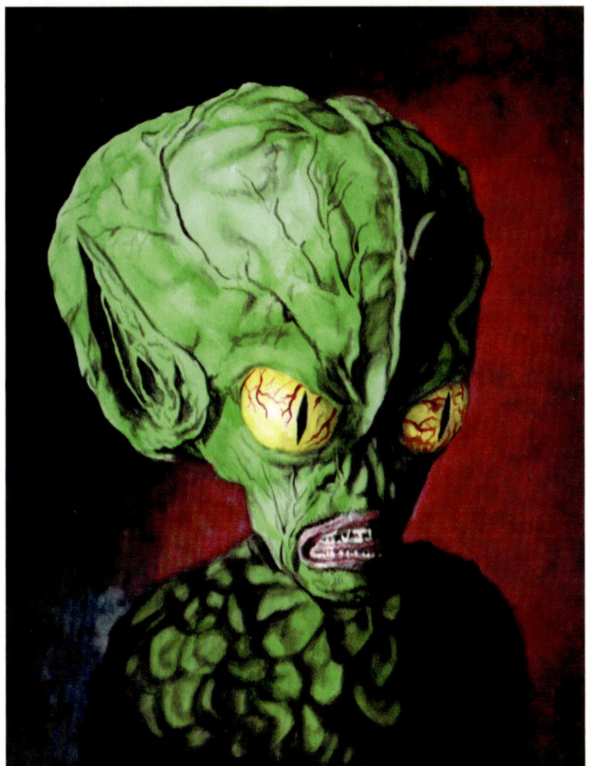

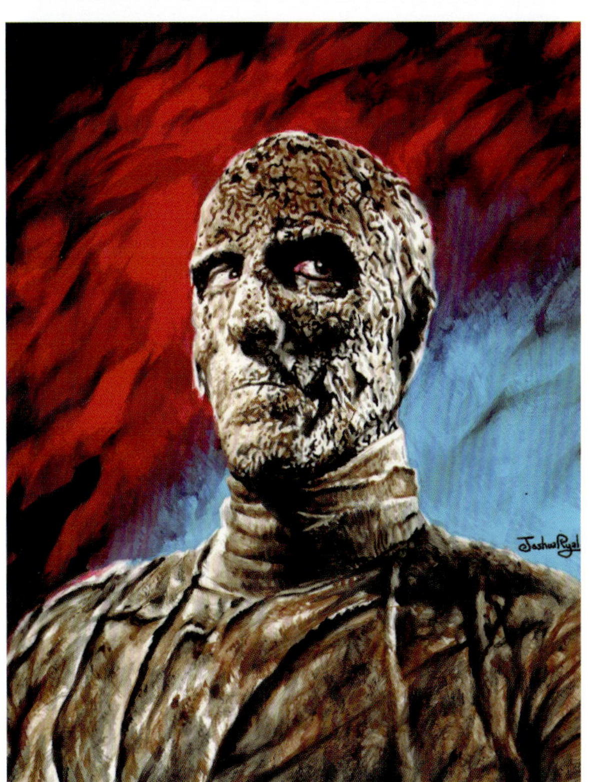

OPPOSITE *Christopher Lee in Curse of Frankenstein* by Daniel Horne. Oil on board, 2016.

THIS PAGE A quartet of monster portraits by Josh Ryals. Clockwise: *Cyclops from "The 7th Voyage of Sinbad"; "It! The Terror from Beyond Space"; Hammer's "The Mummy"; "Invasion of the Saucer Men."* Watercolors on watercolor paper, 2020–2024.

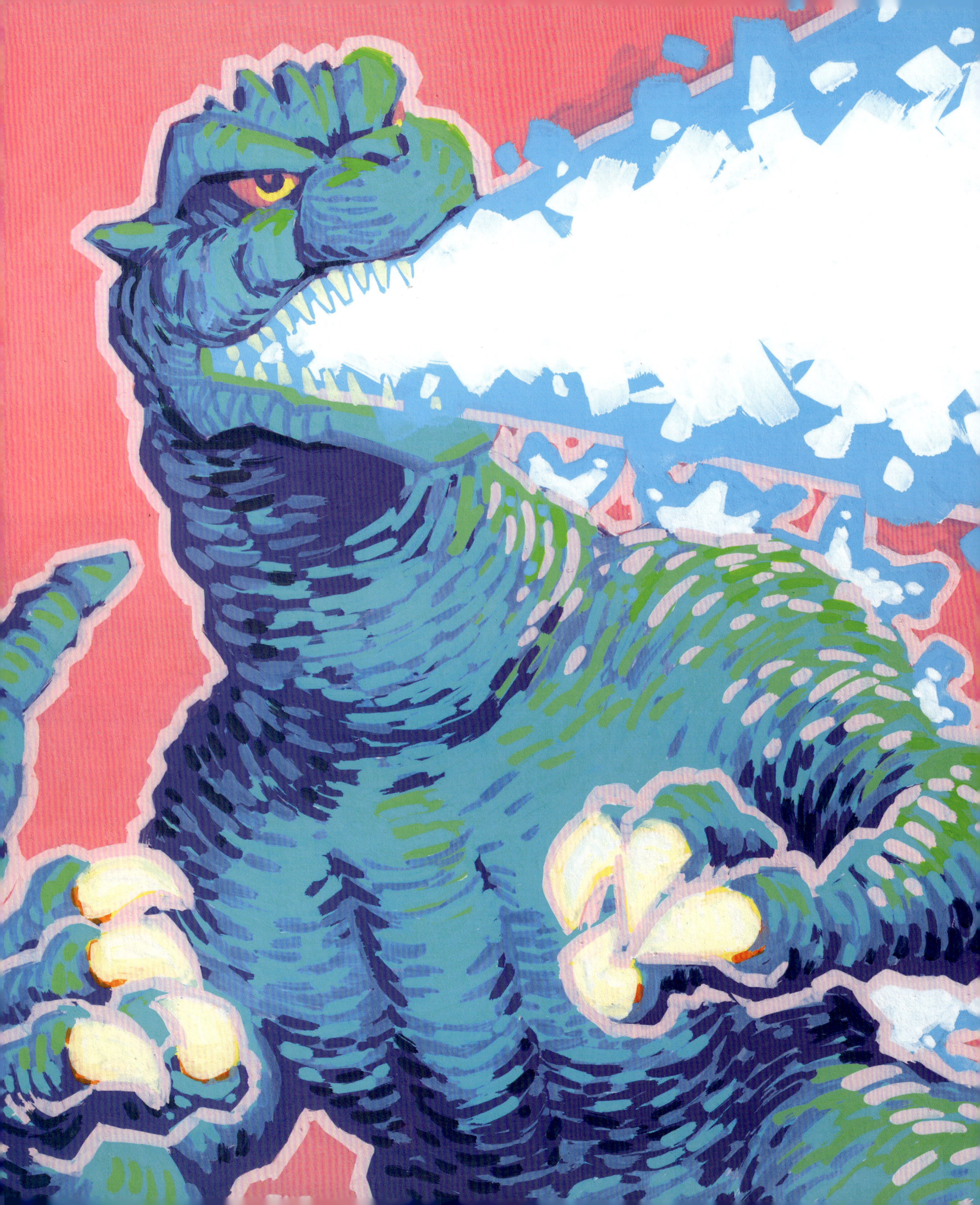

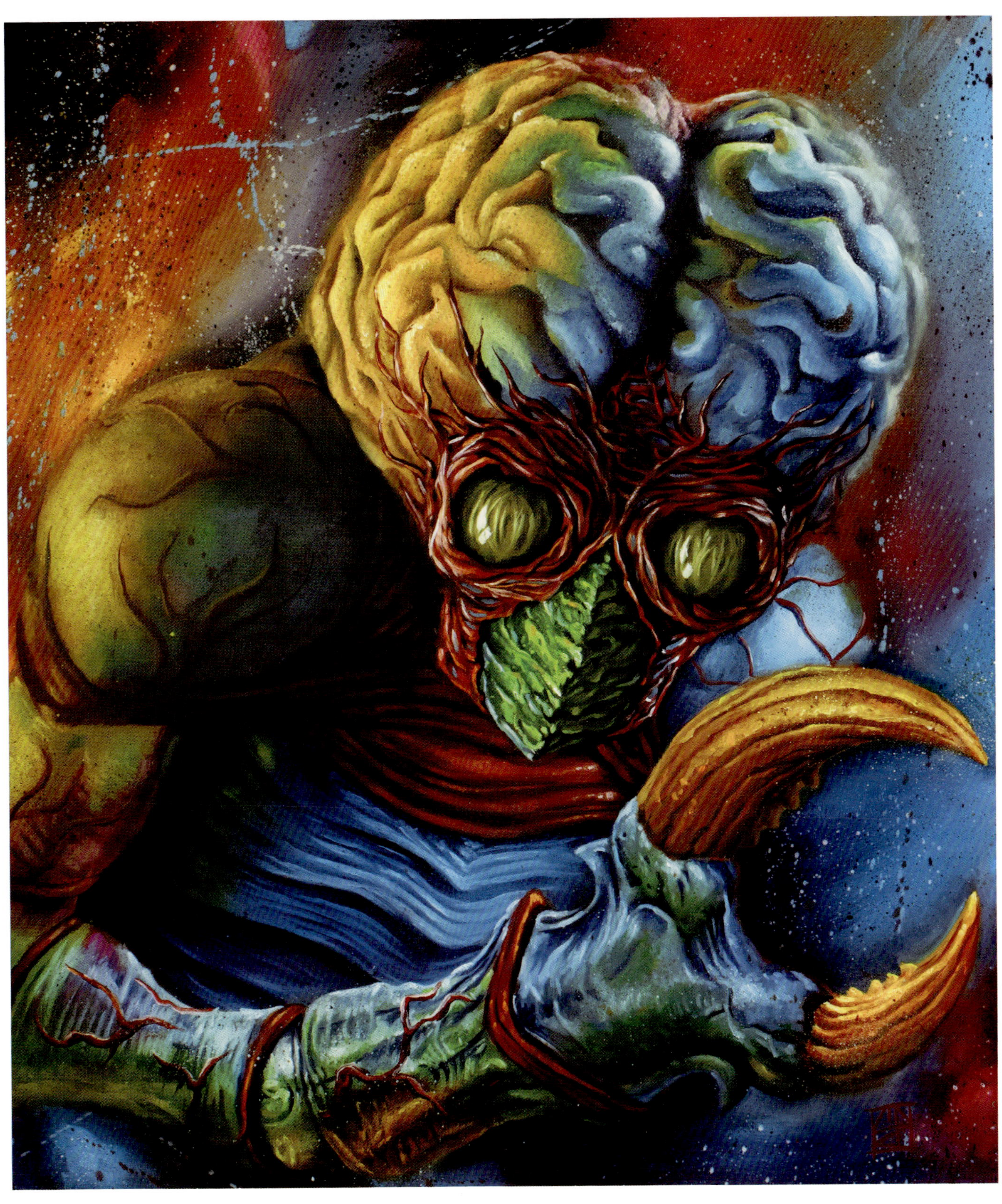

OPPOSITE *Toho Mojo* by Jared P. Foust. Acrylic on board, 2024.

ABOVE *The Metaluna Mutant* by Cecil Porter. Oil on board, 2020.

Horror Hosts

ABOVE *Svengoolie 45th Anniversary Print* (detail) by Mitch O'Connell. Pen and ink, digital color, 2024.

OPPOSITE *Mystery Date* by Mitch O'Connell. Pen and ink, digital color, 2019.

Having played Dr. Gangrene on Nashville, Tennessee's television screens on and off since 1999, Larry Underwood is not only a horror host but also a fan of the hosts who came before him. His knowledge of these television presenters runs deep.

"The television horror movie host is a uniquely American tradition that began in the 1950s and was directly influenced by the horror comic books of the day," Underwood explains. "Chief among those was EC Comics, which featured the wisecracking characters the Crypt-Keeper, the Vault-Keeper, and the Old Witch hosting tales of terror and the supernatural in *Tales from the Crypt*, *Vault of Horror*, and *The Haunt of Fear*. The first of these comics hit the newsstands in 1950, and the books were tremendously popular at the time. Their influence is directly felt in the pun-filled intros and macabre humor of the television hosts.

"EC and its fellow horror comics of the early '50s were in turn influenced by old-time radio horror and mystery programs such as *Lights Out*, *Suspense*, and *Inner Sanctum Mysteries* (with host Raymond Edward Johnson). The very first horror radio program was *The Witch's Tale*, which premiered in May 1931 and featured a cackling witch named Old Nancy and her cat, Satan, introducing each evening's eerie offering from her bubbling cauldron.

"Interestingly, the first recorded television horror movie host was also a woman."

"Interestingly, the first recorded television horror movie host was also a woman. On April 30, 1954, viewers in the Los Angeles area were treated to a blood-curdling surprise when a black dress–garbed graveyard ghoul named Vampira appeared on their screens, dripping with sarcasm and sex appeal to introduce the evening's horror movie on *The Vampira Show*. Vampira was played by Maila Nurmi, a model and aspiring actress. She drew inspiration for the part from the Charles Addams character Morticia in the *Addams Family* cartoon, which ran in *The New Yorker* magazine. The show became a hit in the Hollywood viewing area but was canceled after just one year over rights issues. Nurmi revived the show on a rival station in 1956, but again, it was short-lived, lasting less than a year.

"Nineteen fifty-seven was the year horror programming exploded across America with the release of the *Shock!* movie package. This was a collection of fifty-two films from Universal Studios that were packaged together and released through Screen Gems, a television subsidiary of Columbia Pictures. The films were syndicated across the country and stations were encouraged to have a costumed host on the program to increase interest. The concept caught on, and suddenly there were vampires, mad scientists, and spooky ghouls on the airwaves across the nation. The host was often an employee of the station, a weatherman or sports announcer coerced to dress in a silly costume and introduce the evening's offerings, returning during the breaks to keep audiences entertained. The shows became wildly popular in their markets and the hosts became local celebrities.

"Perhaps the most popular of the early hosts was a character played by John Zacherle, who began his career as Roland in Philadelphia, on October 7, 1957, hosting

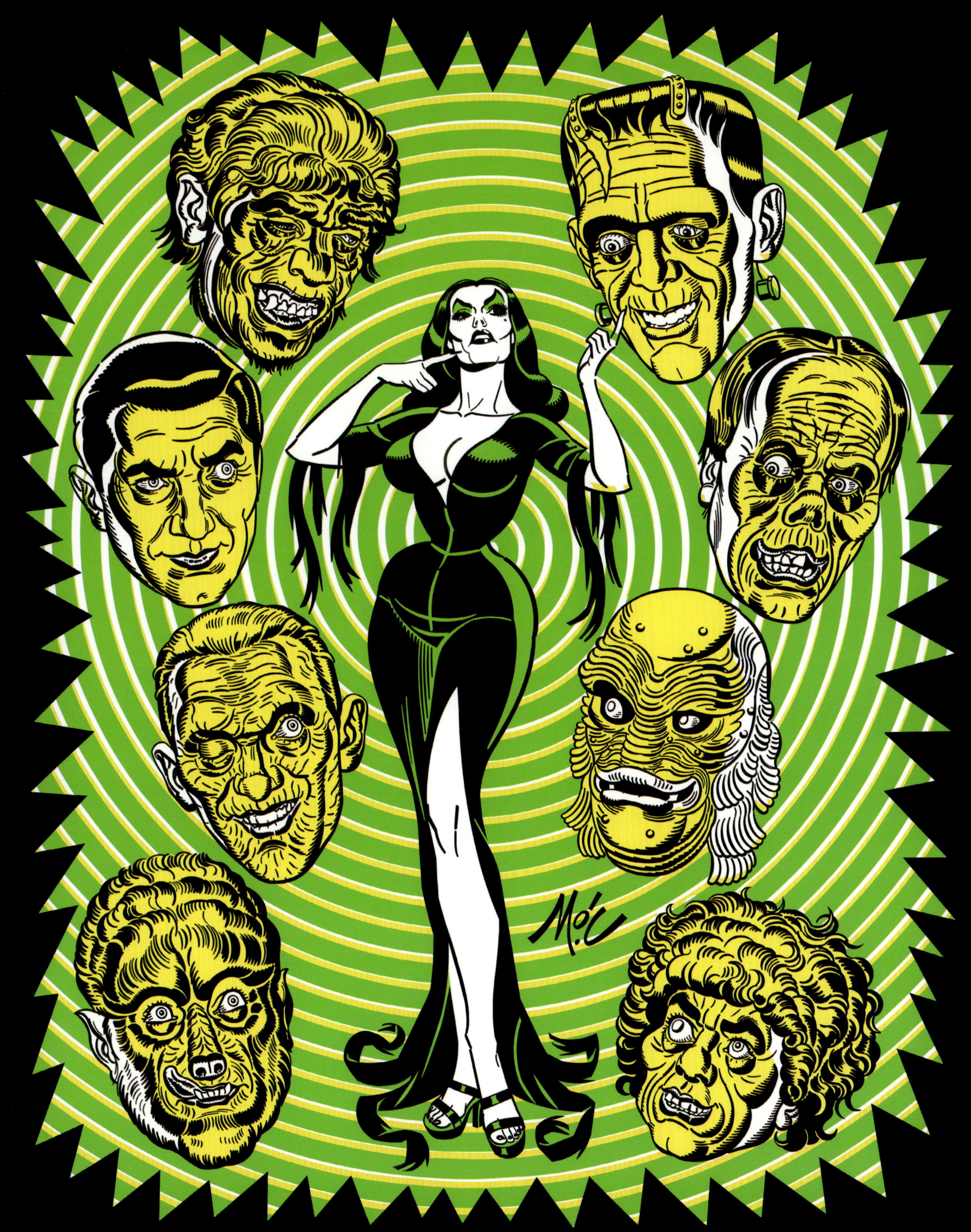

Shock Theater. While in Philadelphia he also recorded a novelty song called 'Dinner with Drac,' which made it to number six on the Billboard charts. He hosted *Shock Theater* in Philadelphia for a year before leaving for New York in 1958, where he changed the name of his character to Zacherley. His show was broadcast by the ABC affiliate out of New York City and brought him national fame, along with appearances in magazines and a legion of fans who referred to him affectionately as the Cool Ghoul. He was the first host to cut himself into the films, playfully interacting with the movies, a technique carried on by hosts ever since.

"It would be impossible to mention all the hosts through the years, but some of the most influential ones were Ghoulardi in Cleveland (played by Ernie Anderson), a madcap beatnik in a lab coat and Vandyke beard who openly mocked the films and blew up items with firecrackers on the air; Morgus the Magnificent in New Orleans (played by Sid Noel), a wacky mad scientist broadcasting from his secret laboratory and performing zany 'experiments' throughout the broadcast; Sammy Terry from Indianapolis (played by Bob Carter), a green-faced ghoul in hood and cape with a talking spider sidekick named George; and Sir Graves Ghastly in Detroit (played by Lawson J. Deming), the Motor City vampire with the cackling laugh.

"However, not all hosts wore costumes. Most famous among these was Bob Wilkins in Sacramento, California, who began his hosting career in 1964. The cigar-chomping host became famous for appearing as himself, doling out facts about the films with a soft-spoken voice and a dry sense of humor. When he retired, he turned the reins over to John Stanley, a *San Francisco Chronicle* film critic, who ramped up the tradition of talking about the films by delivering copious amounts of behind-the-scenes information, an unusual approach given that many of the earlier hosts seldom referred to the films at all, relying instead on skits that would run in the segments around commercial breaks. Stanley and Wilkins, by contrast, relied entirely on facts and interviews with people in the industry.

"In Pittsburgh, another non-costumed host began his career in 1964. Bill Cardille hosted *Chiller Theater,* where he became known as Chilly Billy Cardille. He also appeared in a small part in George Romero's *Night of the Living Dead*, which would later fall into the public domain because of a copyright error and become a staple of programming for later horror hosts.

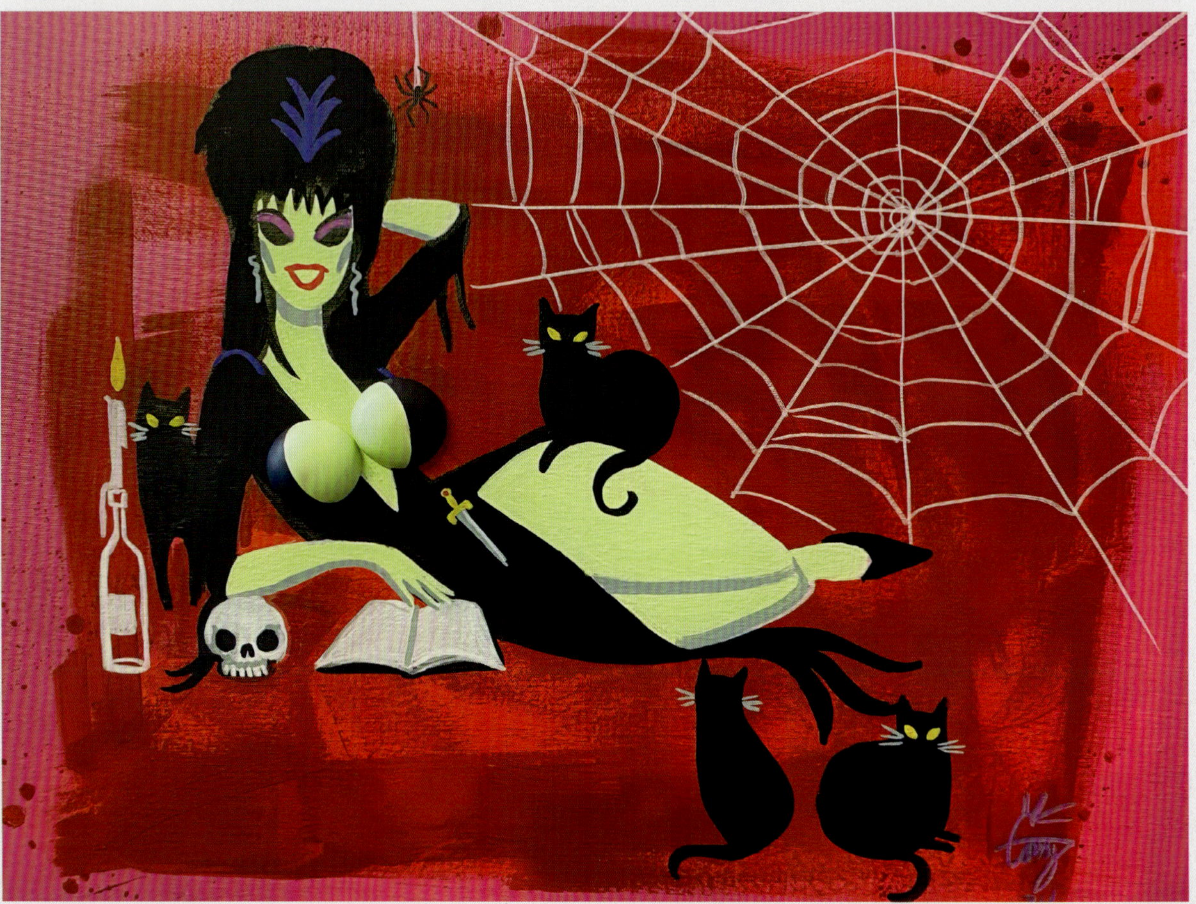

RIGHT *Elvira 3DD* by El Gato Gomez. Acrylic on canvas with "highlights," 2023.

OPPOSITE *Elvira—High Priestess of Horror* by Doug P'Gosh. Acrylic on board, 2022.

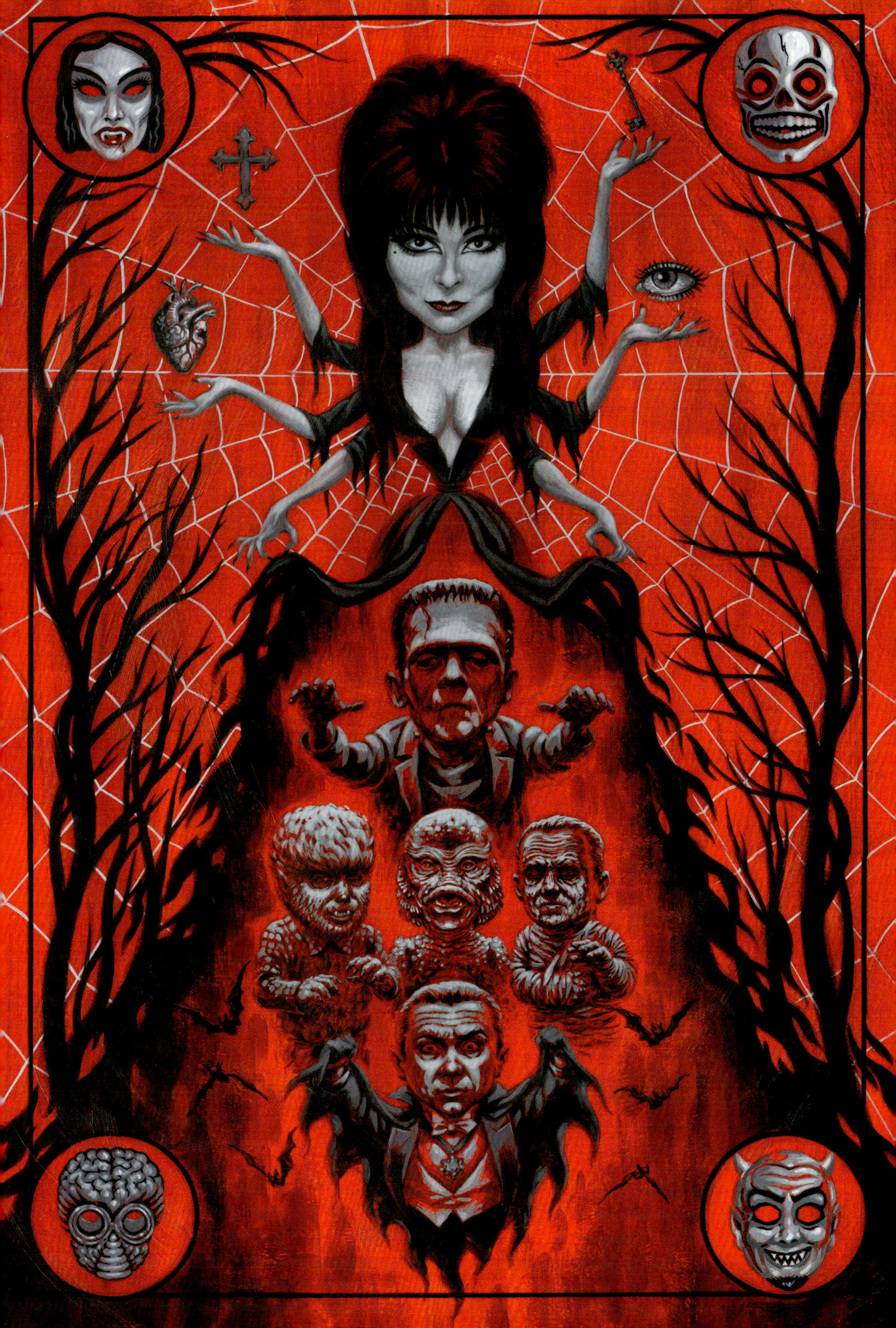

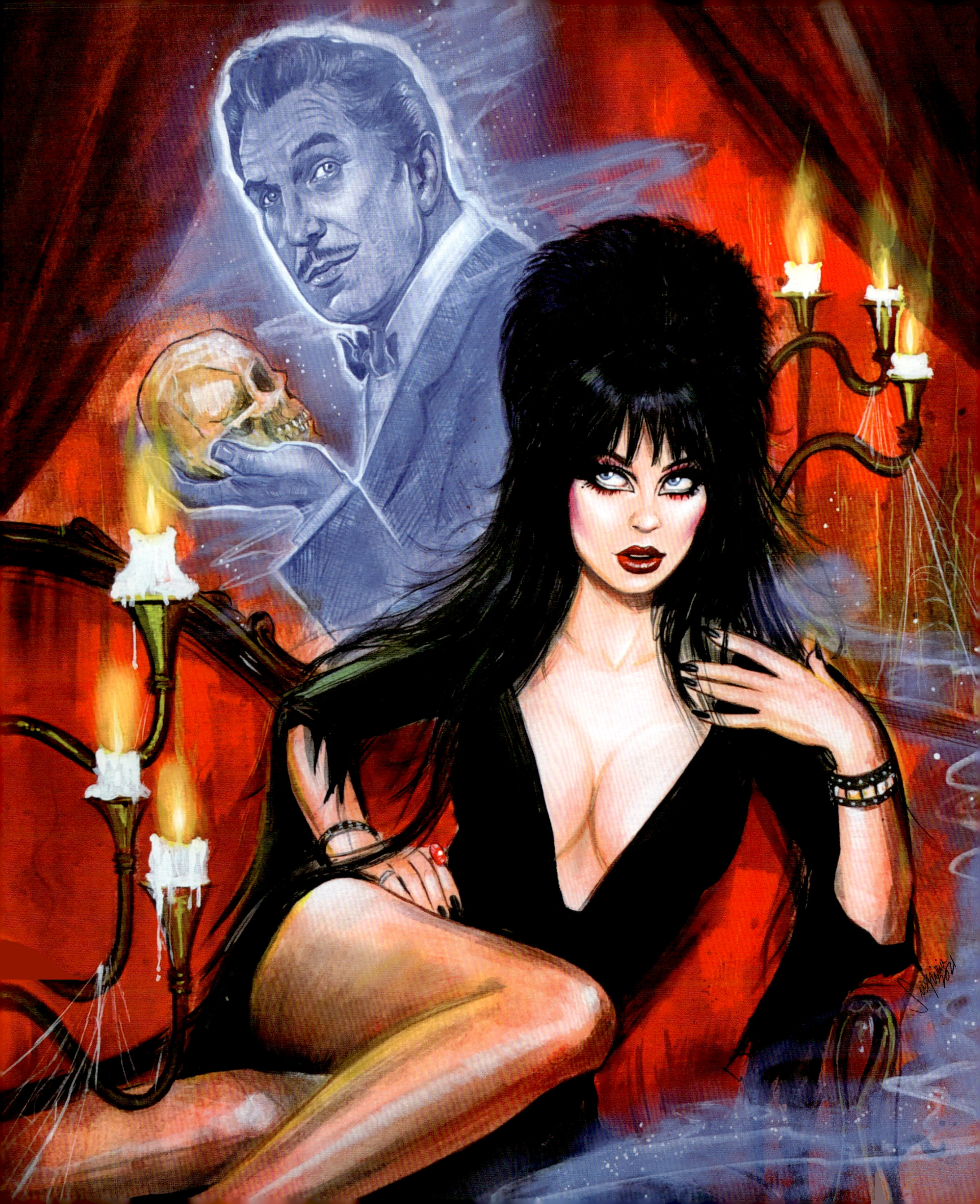

"After Ghoulardi left Cleveland, the show was taken over by Charles M. 'Big Chuck' Schodowski and Bob 'Hoolihan' Wells. The pair appeared as themselves, hosting *The Hoolihan and Big Chuck Show* in 1966. Hoolihan left the show in 1979 and was replaced by John Rinaldi, and the show was retitled *The Big Chuck and Lil' John Show*, as Chuck stands over six feet tall and John is four foot three. Both shows consisted of host segments, live audience interactions, and heavy use of prerecorded skits, making the show as much a comedy sketch show as a movie program. Chuck would work on the air for an impressive (and uninterrupted) forty-one years.

"A second wave of hosts surfaced throughout the '70s, including such notable names as Dr. Paul Bearer (Dick Bennick) in St. Petersburg, Florida; Sir Cecil Creape (Russ McCown) in Nashville, Tennessee; Count Gore De Vol (Dick Dyszel) in Washington, DC; the Bowman Body (Bill Bowman) in Richmond, Virginia; Seymour (Larry Vincent) in Los Angeles; and Svengoolie in Chicago, played by Jerry G. Bishop.

"The first host with a nationally syndicated show was Elvira, Mistress of the Dark, played by Cassandra Peterson. She hosted *Movie Macabre* in 1981 and the show became a national sensation, running till 1986, and was revived between 2010 and 2011. Elvira became so popular that she became practically synonymous with Halloween, with heavy marketing and commercial appearances around the holiday. Over the years, with the advent of cable television, many other hosts would appear in syndicated programming. Notable among these is Joe Bob Briggs, played by film critic John Bloom; Rhonda Shear and Gilbert Gottfried, hosts of *Up All Night*; Commander USA, played by Jim Hendricks; and the latter-day Svengoolie, played by Rich Koz, the most well-known horror host currently working.

"The popularity of television horror movie hosts has waned since the heyday of the 1960s through the 1980s. The internet brought a nearly endless variety of entertainment options that, in combination with the natural sophistication of modern audiences, made the quaint tradition of horror hosting seem a bit old-fashioned. The number of hosts dropped dramatically over the years—but they never completely vanished and continue to haunt our screens to this day. There are a handful of hosts still on traditional broadcast television in their local markets, a few have syndicated shows, and many deliver entertainment through the internet. With cheaper, better equipment and nearly instantaneous internet delivery, producing a show has never been easier. But it's also a double-edged sword, as it's harder to get the viewer's attention. However, these hosts are a resilient bunch and continue to adapt to the constantly changing technological and entertainment landscapes, and their shows offer lighthearted entertainment, something that is much needed today, so don't expect them to vanish anytime soon. As the Bob Wilkins slogan read, 'Watch horror films, keep America strong.' These quirky entertainers are certainly doing their part to keep this eerie tradition alive!"

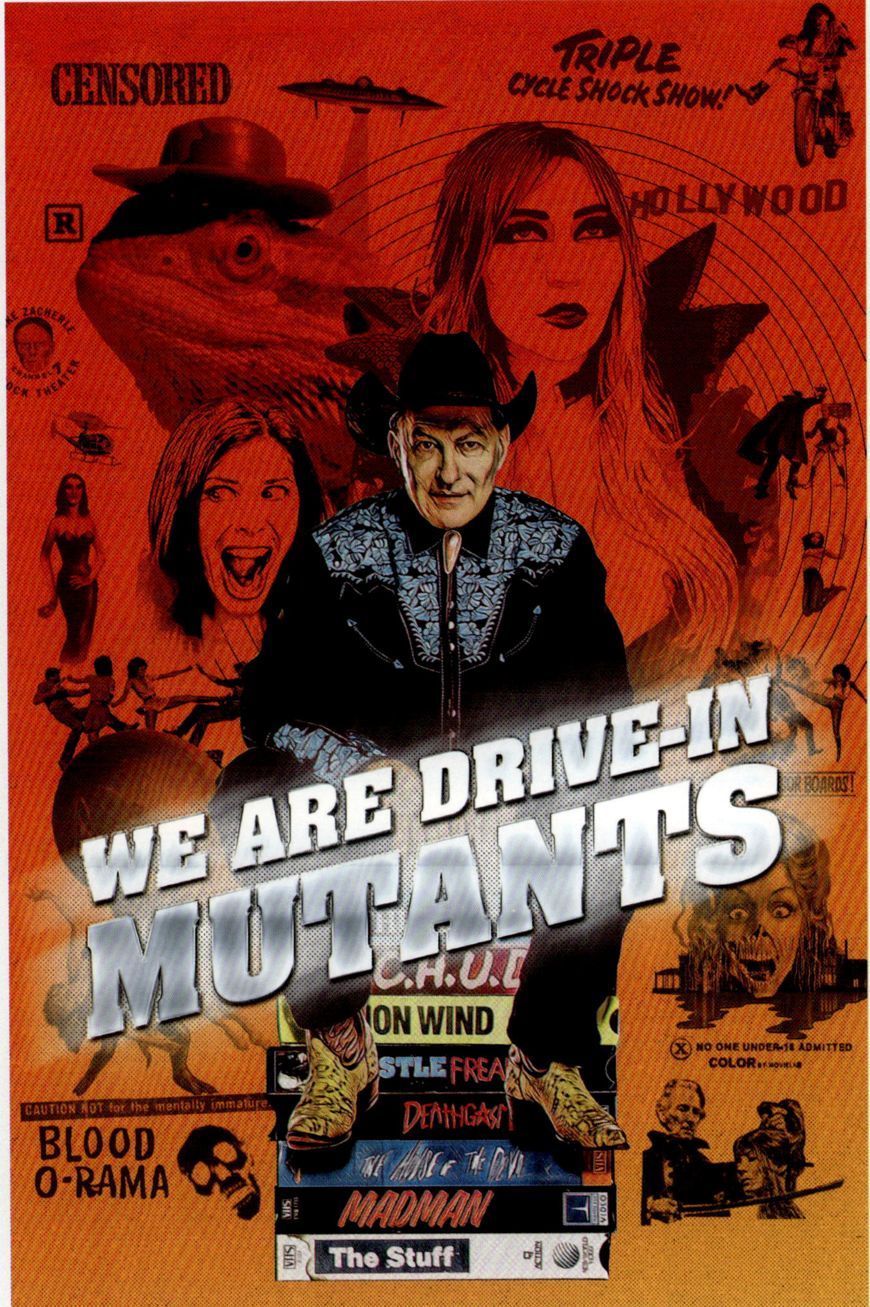

OPPOSITE *The Price of the Dark* by Susana "Suspiria" Vilchez. Acrylic on canvas, 2021.

ABOVE *We Are Drive-In Mutants* by Unlovely Frankenstein. Poster to celebrate season 1 of *The Last Drive-In with Joe Bob Briggs*. Digital, 2018.

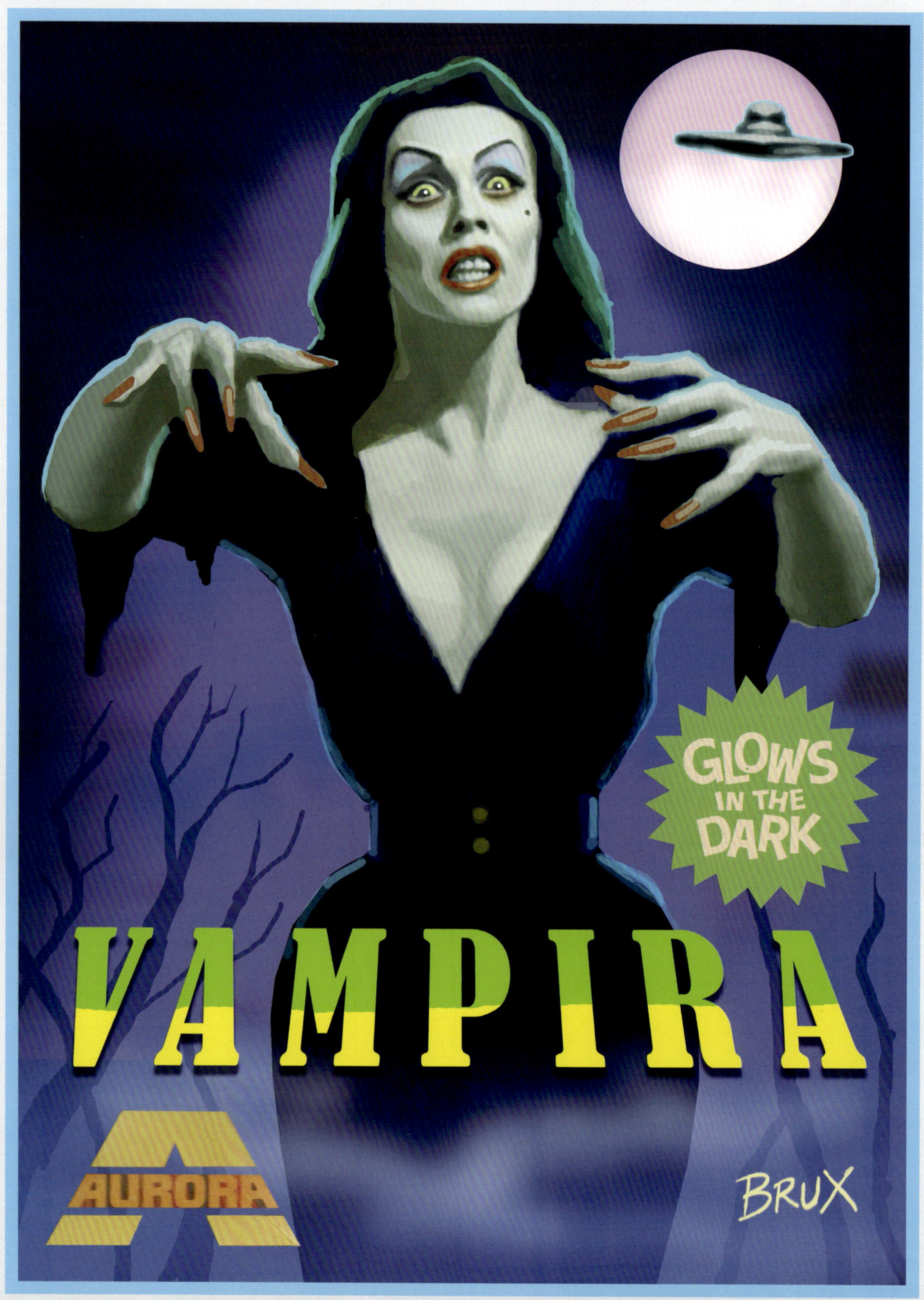

RIGHT *Aurora Glow in the Dark Vampira* by David Brooks (Brux). Digital, 2021.

OPPOSITE *Vampira Takes a Walk Among the Tombstones* by Unlovely Frankenstein. Digital, 2023.

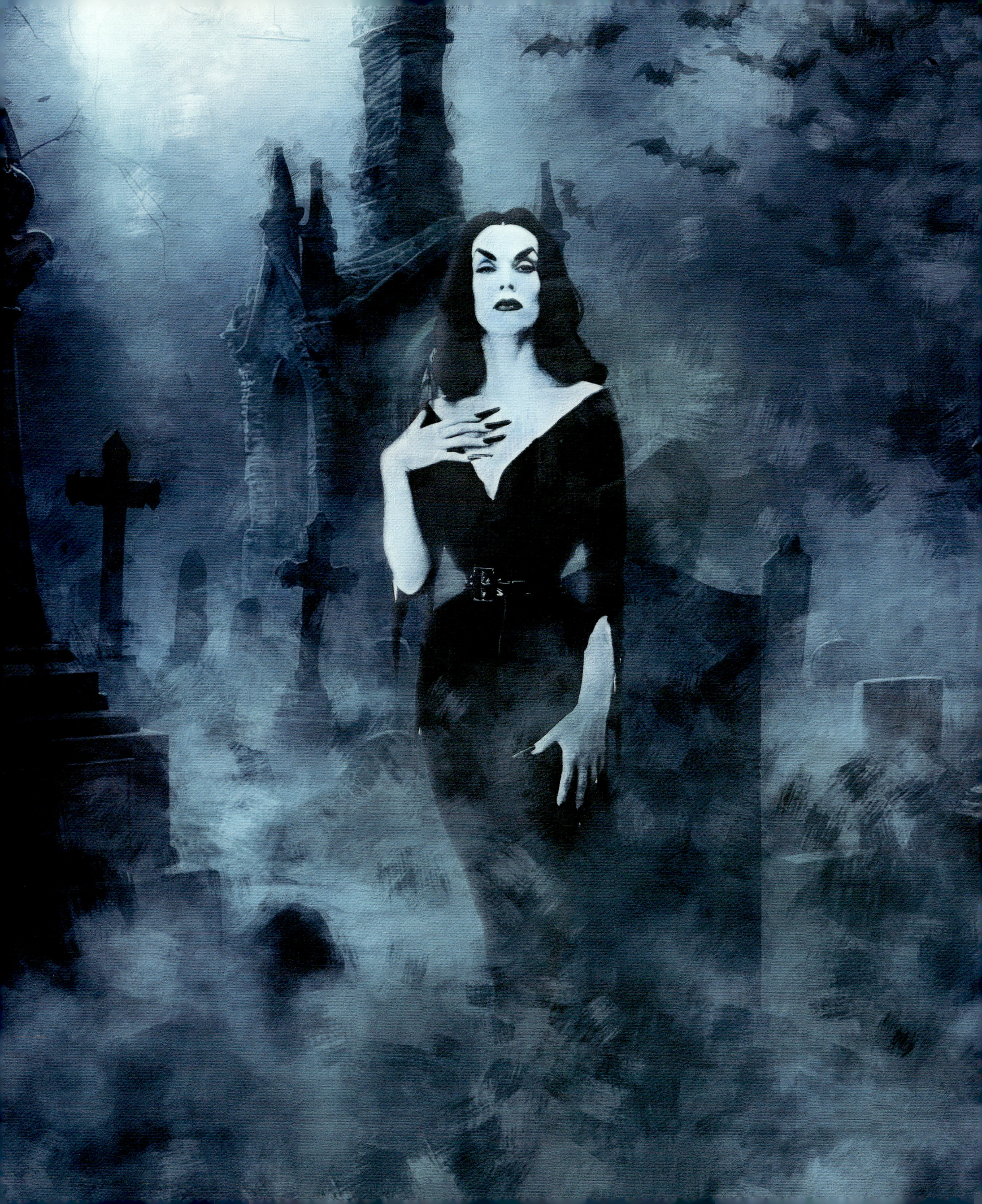

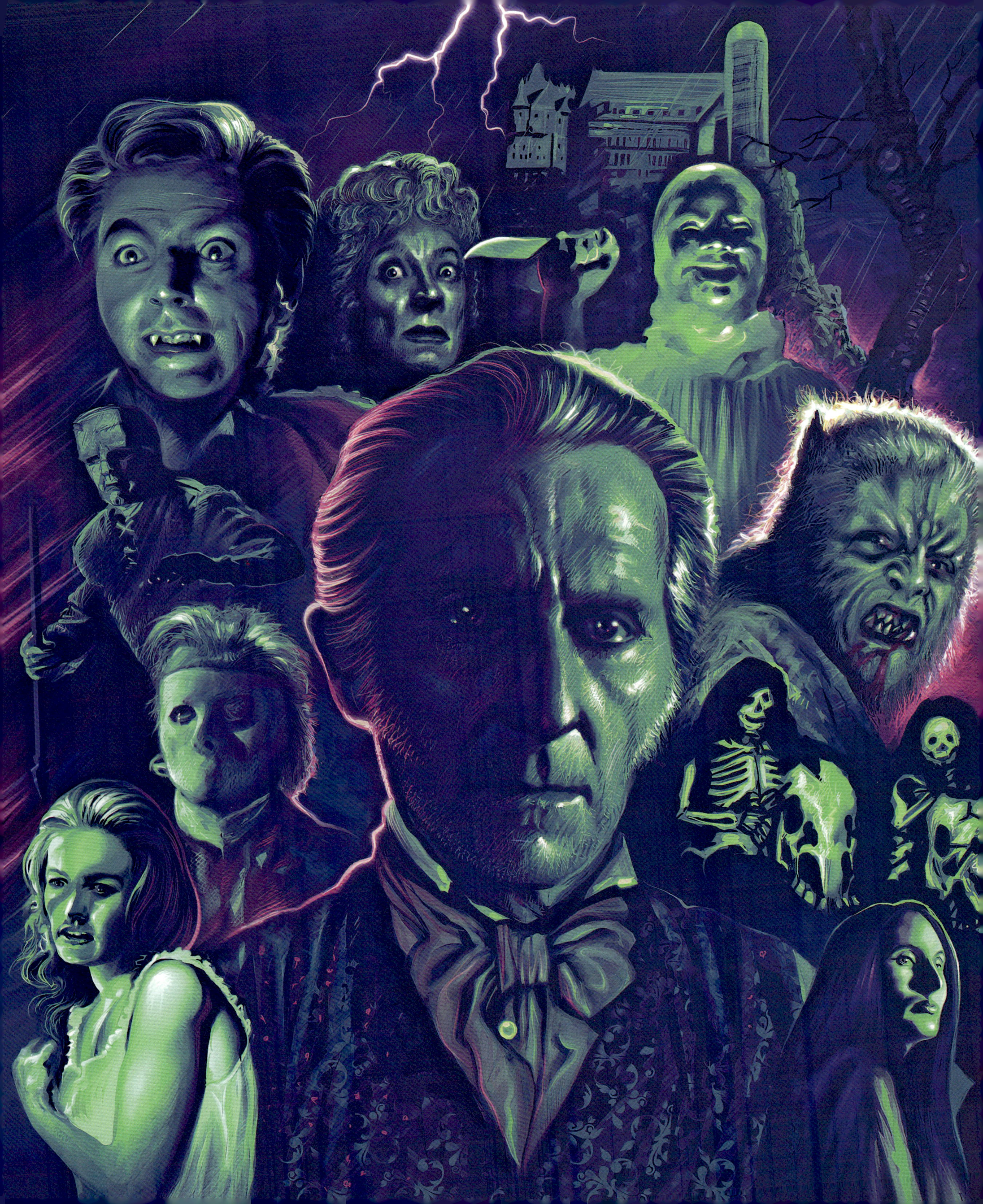

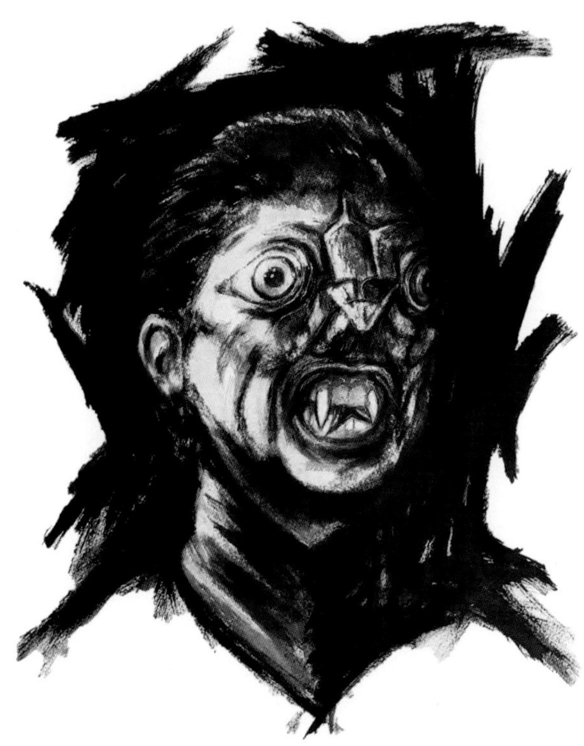

CHAPTER 6

A Dark Shadow at the Door (1960–1969)

Why are monster and horror films so popular, especially with young adults? Monsters like King Kong or Godzilla appeal to the young because they represent a growth phase we all experience, defined by frustration and rage at our inability to express deeper feelings or accomplish tasks to completion. But what about horror films of a darker slant?

Artist Robert Laskey has some experience with this question at an academic level. "My college thesis was on the psychology of horror in art and entertainment," he recalls. "I believe the human mind comes into this world with the ability to absorb and process all manner of natural horrors, and we experience this process as fear. Those horrors were once commonplace, but now, as a society, we have almost completely insulated ourselves from them. As a result, there is a part of our brain that isn't being utilized, [so] it seeks out fear so that it can be made useful again. Horror media provides this outlet as a safe place to experience the fear this part of our brains crave."

The Monster Show: A Cultural History of Horror author David J. Skal mused that "invariably, when I'm introduced to people as an expert on Dracula and other monsters, they will just light up and relate some anecdotes about their first discovery of horror movies. Even if it scared the crap out of them at the time, they're smiling nostalgically about it now. Frightening masks have always played a part in initiation rituals, and I've come to think people often experience horror as having a coming-of-age significance.

"As we mature, we search for, and ingest, more mature subject matter as entertainment. As children, we may find the delight of watching giant monsters stomping cities is the highest form of gratification from film viewing, but by the time we're adults, we appreciate the nuance and storytelling of a movie like *Godzilla Minus One* (2023), which tells a very human story of loss and acceptance. Both are entertaining, both give comfort, and both use fantastic elements to tell their stories. When it comes down to it, the reason we watch films, read books, play video games, listen to music, or create art is less to alleviate boredom and more to catch a glimpse of ourselves in what we take in from these sources. We search for the pieces of ourselves that aren't readily visible in a mirror, and when we find them, we embrace and integrate them."

Author Mark Dawidziak believes horror and monster media can influence cultural shifts beyond the singular personal experience. "They certainly can give shape, sympathy, understanding, and empowerment of those shifts," he says. "I believe the one time where there was a profound influence was when the first generation of what we now call Monster Kids identified themselves as horror fans—a baby boom generation from the early '50s and *Tales from the Crypt* comics to the mid-'70s. That generation, and its embrace of horror, went on to

OPPOSITE *Hammer Horror Montage* by Daryl Joyce. Digital, 2019.

ABOVE *Hammer Films' "The Reptile"* by Gustavo Rapela. Gouache, 2020.

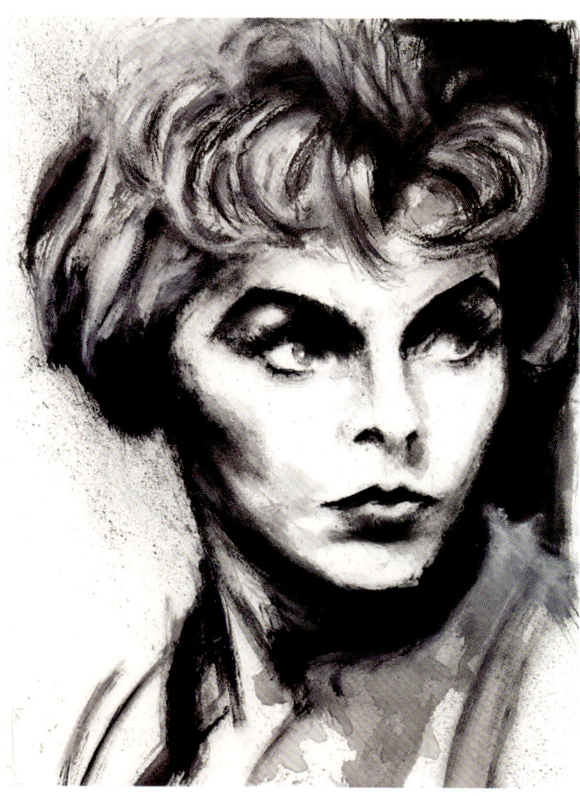

have an immense influence on entertainment and culture from the late '70s to today. There's little they don't influence." Many of these young fans were led into their adult careers and cultural pursuits by the films, comics, and art they experienced as children.

Danielle Gelehrter, better known as horror host Penny Dreadful, notes that this happens even more so as marginalized groups assert their identities. "An interesting and unexpected [case] is how *The Babadook* (2014) inadvertently became an LGBTQI icon, via some initially jokey memes. I guess [another] big one would be clown-themed horror and how that has sort of seeped into the pop cultural consciousness. It's kind of strange, because I almost feel that these days clowns are less associated with fun, friendly, circus characters and more with unhinged, and disturbing agents of evil. That makes me a little sad in a way. I remember talking to a professional clown one time. He was out of makeup and character, and I mentioned 'evil clowns.' He turned to me with a serious expression, almost of hurt, and said: 'There's no such thing as an evil clown.' That genuine reaction never left me, but there's no denying that

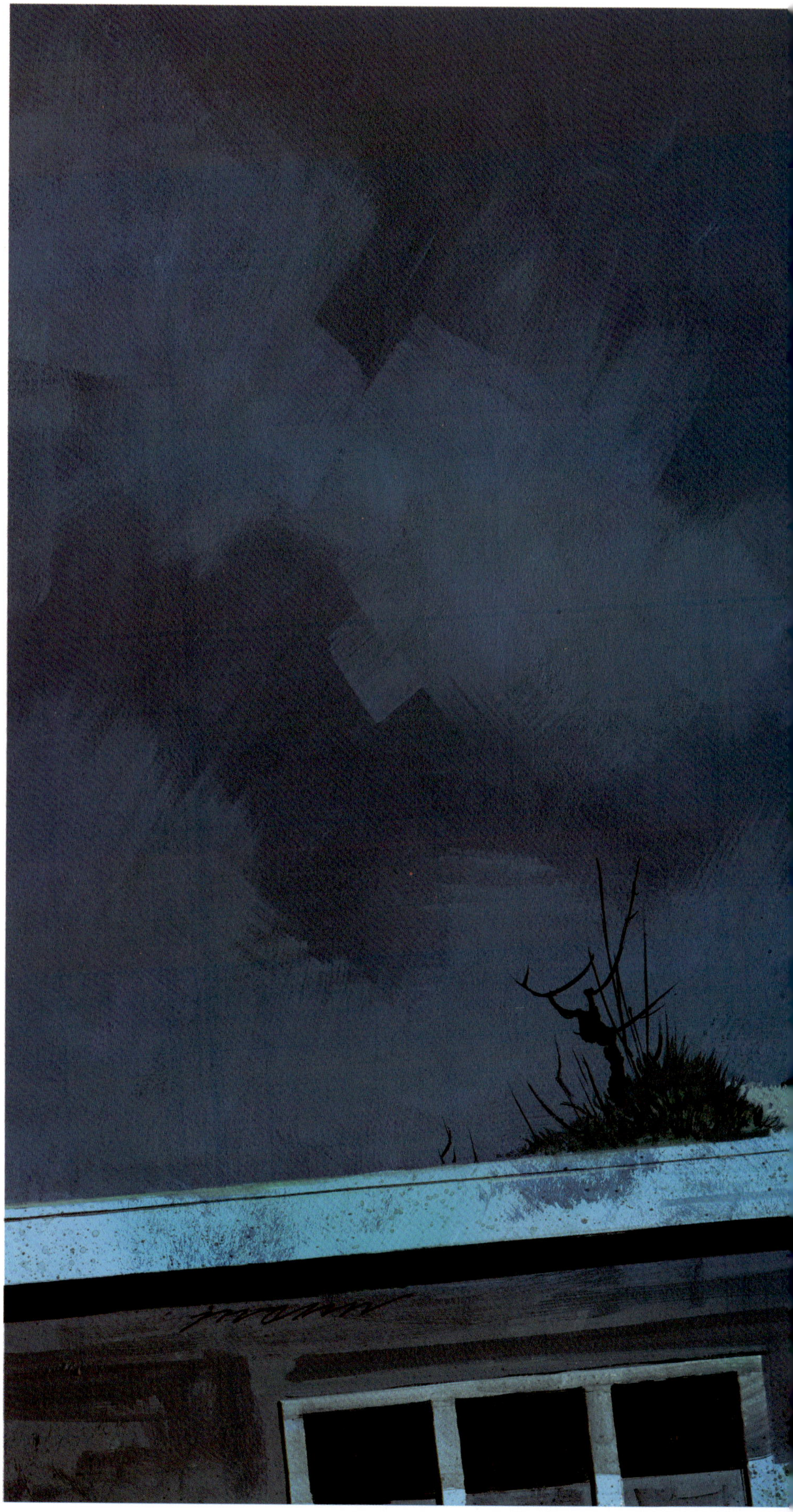

ABOVE *Janet Leigh from "Psycho"* by Gustavo Rapela. Gouache, 2021.

RIGHT *Bates Motel* by Paul Mann. Dust jacket for Suntup Editions' *Psycho* by Robert Bloch, artist edition. Acrylic on illustration board, 2023.

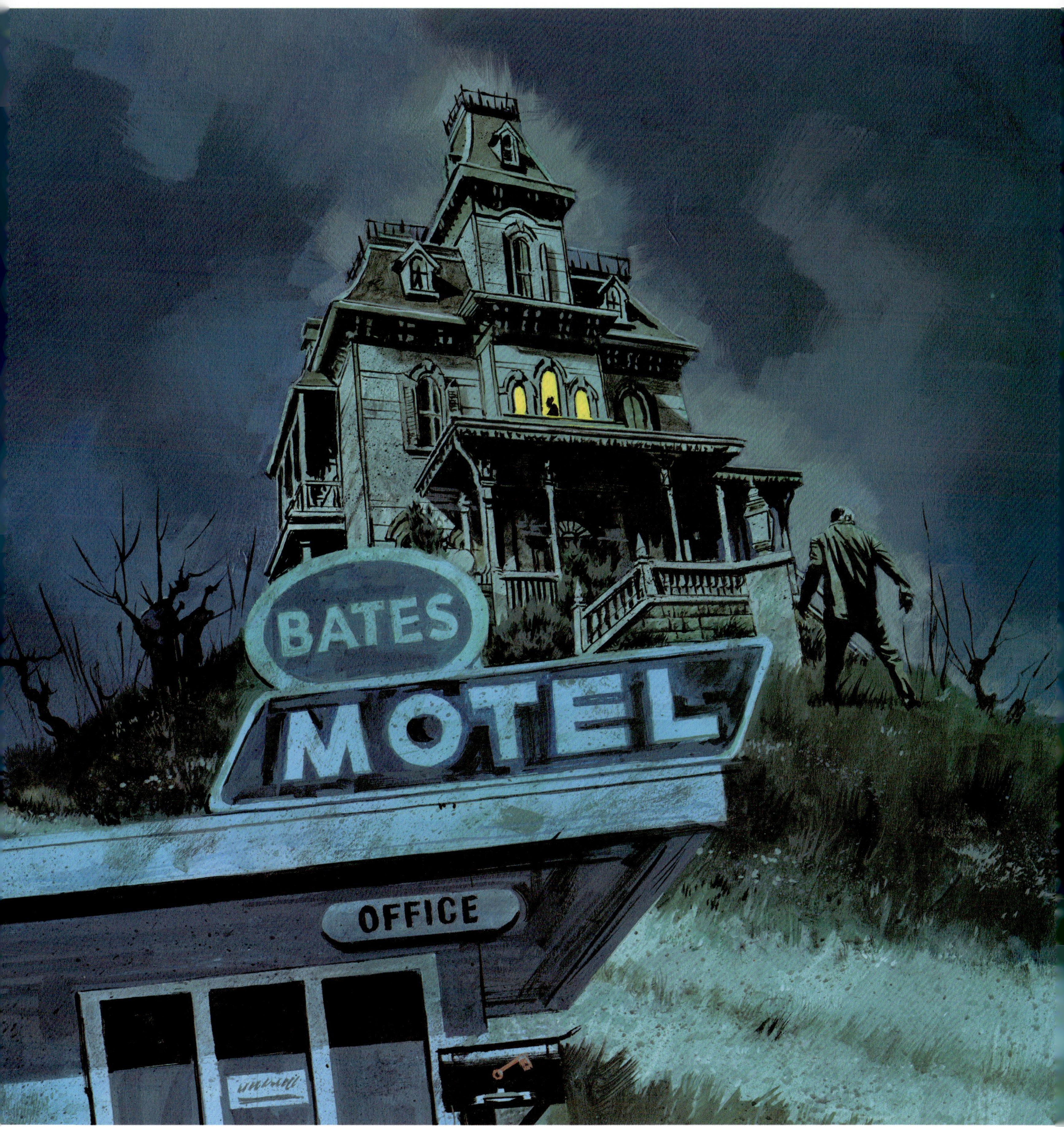
BATES
MOTEL
OFFICE

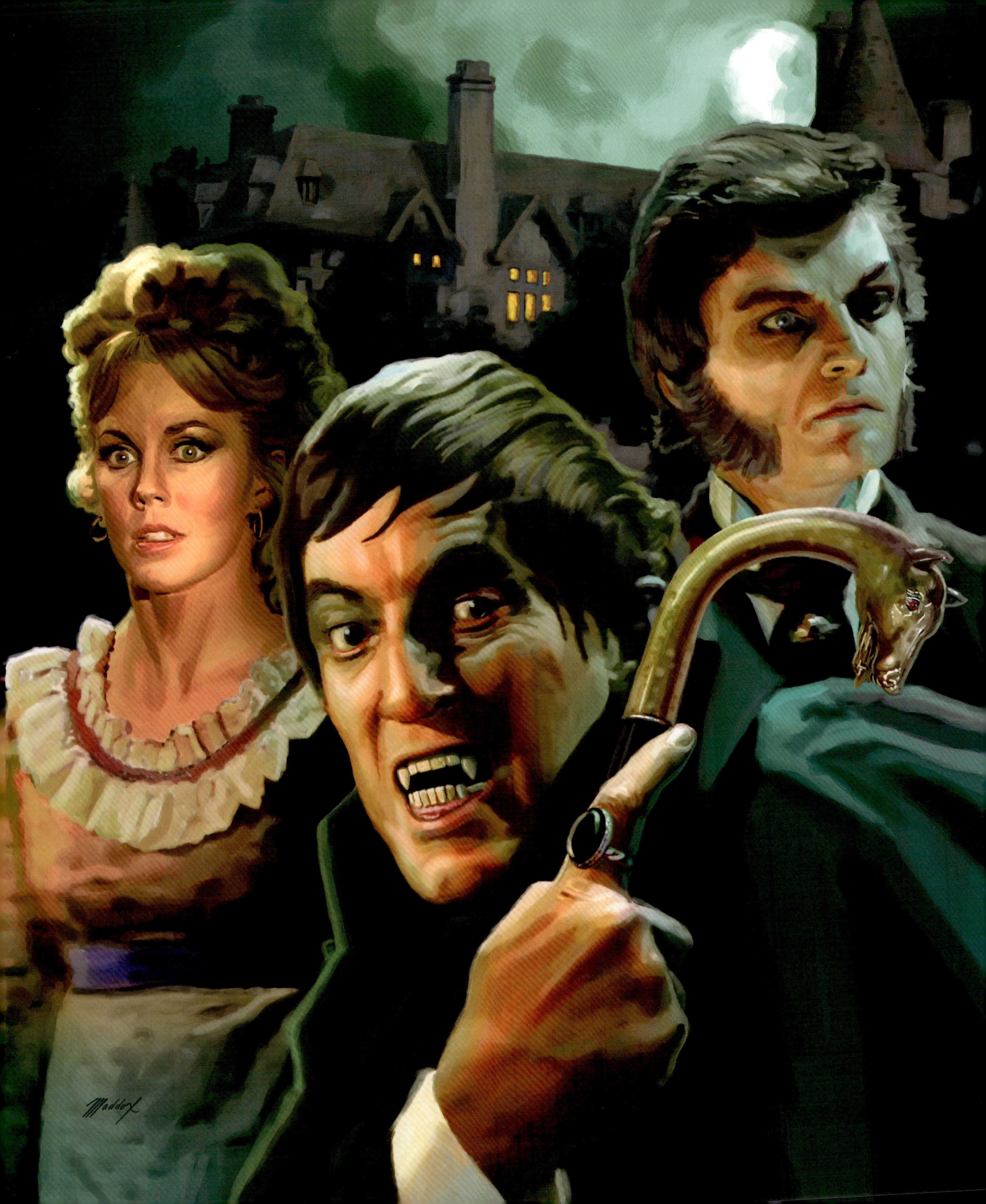
Maddox

'evil clown' is an image that one sees constantly at horror conventions these days."

The 1960s saw the proliferation of the Monster Kid generation all over the world, the civil rights movement in the United States, hippies and antiwar protesters, and countercultures of all stripes. Black Power, passive protest, drug culture, and lowbrow art all propelled these years into a swirling fusion that challenged and changed traditional thinking on a fundamental level. For the first time, youth had many voices in how things ran, and once the establishment started listening, they realized they had a lot to say. This decade was an island upon which many waves overlapped.

As the *Famous Monsters of Filmland* magazine juggernaut continued to attract young readers, it eventually attracted aficionados of adjacent fandoms. Hot rod and car culture adopted monster mascots, with Ed "Big Daddy" Roth's Rat Fink by far the most recognizable and durable.

"I enjoyed the character so much that it actually made me look up Ed Roth and read up on him," recalls television and Topps trading card writer Richard J. Schellbach (*ALF, Are You Afraid of the Dark?*). "It was pretty much the first time I realized that there was a cartoonist behind the cartoons, as silly as that sounds." Rat Fink's popularity created a wave of merchandise including T-shirt transfers, model kits, and toys, and it spawned similar lines such as Weird-Ohs by Bill Campbell and the Louis Marx toy company's plastic Nutty Mads figure series.

Monsterscene magazine publisher Steve Smith also had an early affectation for the Fink. "I had a Rat Fink T-shirt in second grade as well as some stickers. I started buying Silly Surfers and Weird-Ohs model kits by age nine. Then I found the original Rat Fink model kit. I had no interest in hot rod or custom cars, but I knew Ed 'Big Daddy' Roth's name at a young age. I sent away for stickers from an ad in some magazine at age ten and received a handwritten letter from Big Daddy that said, 'Thanks for the root beer money' along with my Rat Fink stickers," Smith recalls. "I would say Rat Fink opened the door for me liking Basil Wolverton's art, and Bill Campbell's art for Weird-Ohs and Silly Surfers, and may even have opened the door for my very early love of surf culture."

Surfing and tiki imagery and totems crossed over in a big way, creating a scintillating blend of *moai*, batik, Polynesian, and monster cocktail culture. This magnetically linked foursome formed the basis of what would become the "lowbrow" art movement—which remains even more prevalent today than in the '60s, though not as widely embraced as it was then.

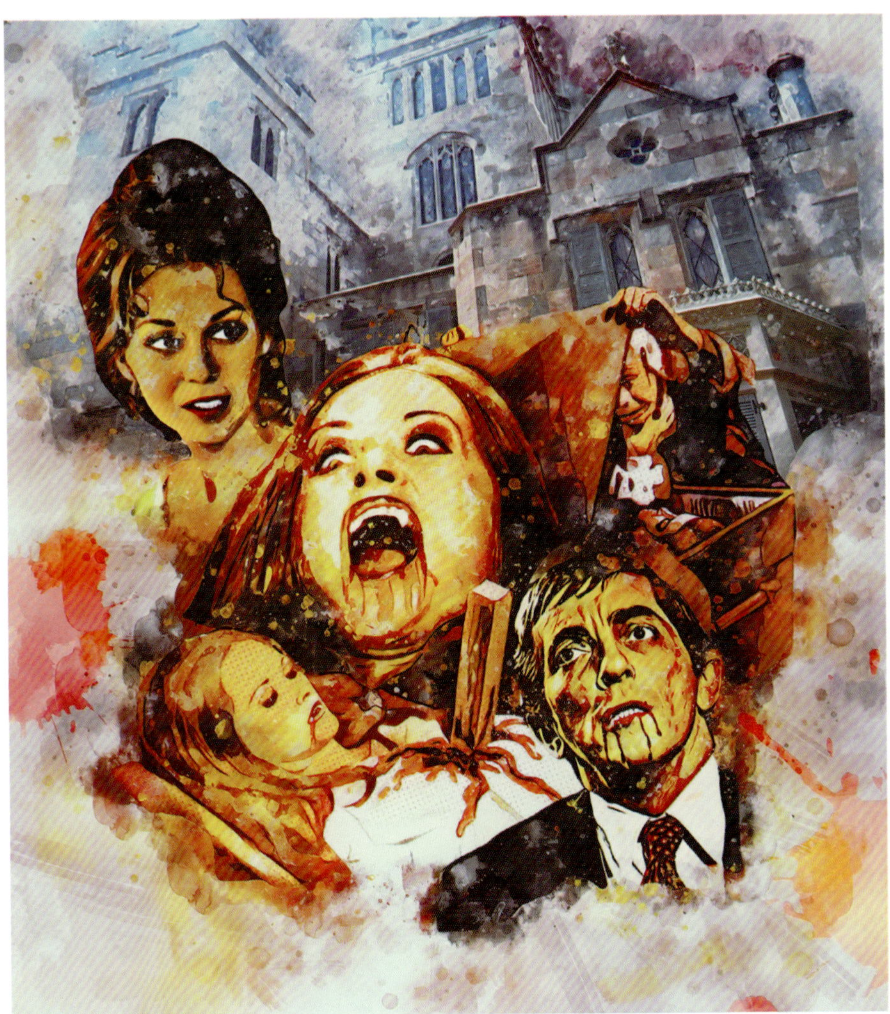

As Madison Avenue began to grasp the width and breadth of the monster craze, more and more products aimed at Monster Kids appeared.

Aurora Plastics Corporation's advertising and promotional manager, Bill Silverstein, witnessed a line of teenagers and kids wrapped around a city block in New York waiting to see a double feature of Universal's original *Dracula* and *Frankenstein* films in 1961 and an idea occurred to him: Why not make model kits of the monsters? Silverstein tried to convince the company's product managers for months before they gave in, licensed the monsters, and created tooling for Frankenstein's creation as a figure kit to show at the next Hobby Industry Association marketplace in Chicago, where retailers ordered products for the upcoming season.

For four days, no one looked twice at the prototype on display. Finally, on the last day, a retailer brought his sons to the Aurora booth and they became very excited

OPPOSITE *Collinwood Trio* by Mark Maddox. Diamond Distributors variant cover for *SCREEM* magazine #24. Digital, 2012.

ABOVE *Dark Shadows Behind the Screams/House of Dark Shadows* by Unlovely Frankenstein. Poster art for Sleepy Hollow Film Festival screening. Mixed media, 2019.

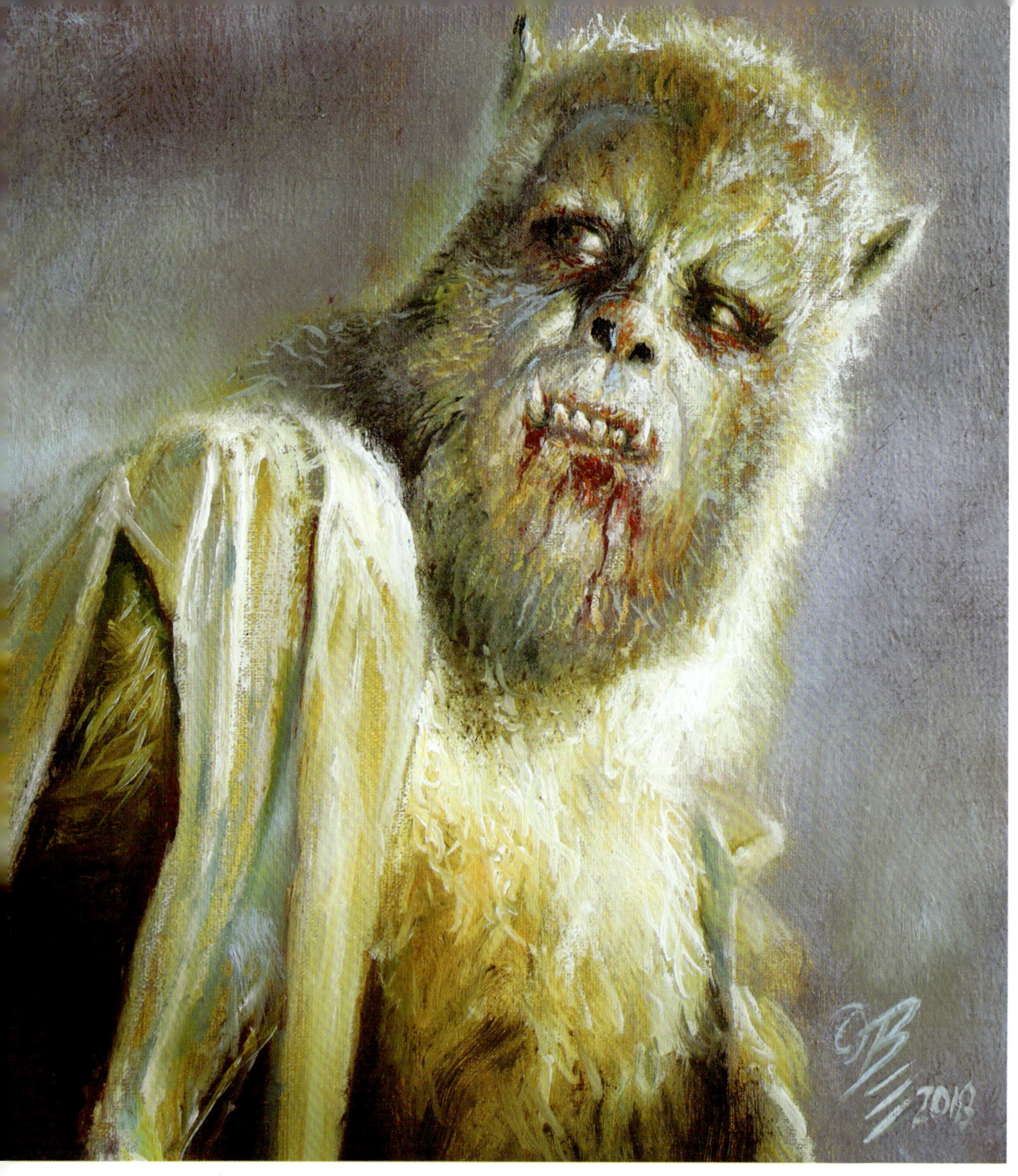

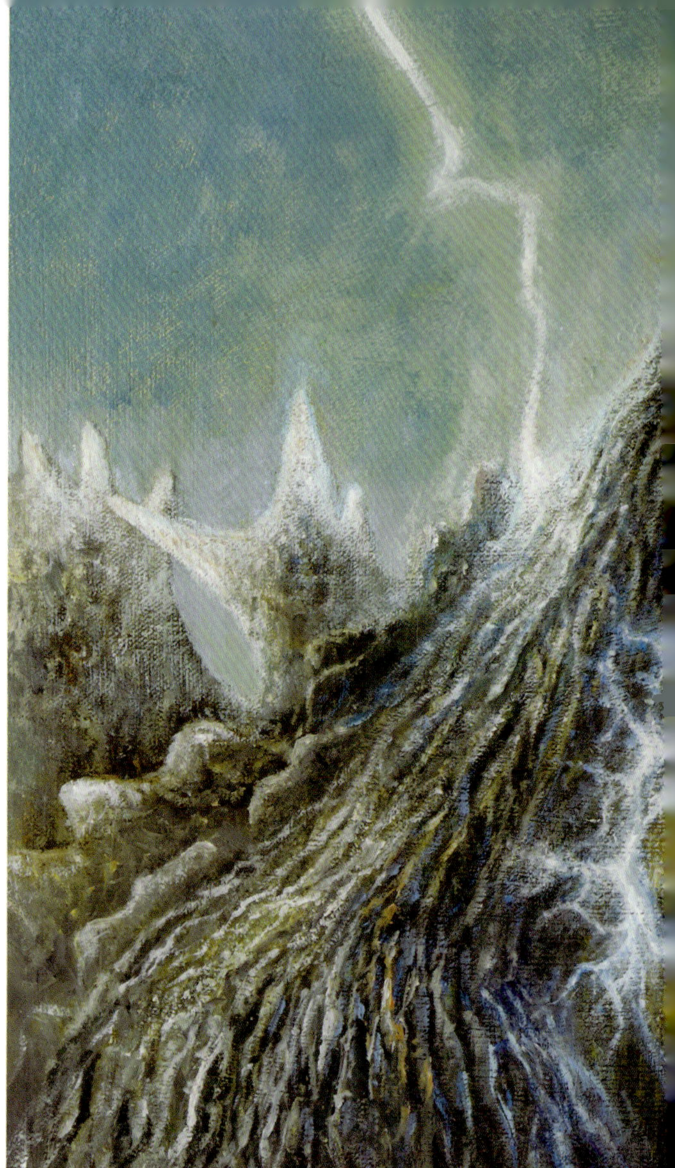

TOP LEFT *The Curse of the Werewolf* by Bob Eggleton. Oil on canvas, 2018.

TOP RIGHT *King Kong vs. Godzilla* by Bob Eggleton. Oil on canvas, 2023.

about the model; this was witnessed by a California distributor who also placed orders, and Aurora entered into the most profitable period of the company's life. By August 1964, they had sold almost eight million monster model kits, and demand was still strong.

"During the high point of the monster reissue renaissance of the '60s, I was a voracious monster model builder," says artist Damian Fulton. "Every time my mom took me shopping with her, I scoured the isles of our local department store for the latest Aurora plastic model kit. They cost about a buck back then, exactly my weekly allowance. I built them all—except 'Big Frankie,' the grandest of them all, and at $5.00, out of my price range. When I finally had enough saved to pull the trigger on Big Frankie—his big, colorful box featuring a close-up painting of the monster by Basil Gogos—it was no longer available. Sigh. Fast forward to the twenty-first century. Big Frankie was reissued by Moebius Models, and he now sits among my other classic monster model kits."

A major attraction of Aurora's kits—which grew to include Dracula, the Wolf Man, the Mummy, the Creature from the Black Lagoon, and many more—was the box art. Painted in rich secondary and tertiary colors, the art depicted the kits in their best light possible, sometimes less than accurate to the finished products themselves. Two of the men responsible for these paintings were James Bama and Mort Künstler, New York commercial illustrators who had both been providing art for paperback book covers, magazines, product advertisements, and promotional materials for years. Both artists became well-known for their book covers and promotional art for genre subjects, and interestingly, both later retired and took up painting nineteenth-century Americana; Bama became one of the most popular cowboy and Western artists, while Künstler was a renowned Civil War painter.

Another artist doing a lot of monster-related heavy lifting at the time was Basil Gogos, the house cover artist at *Famous Monsters of Filmland*. Gogos applied a vivid

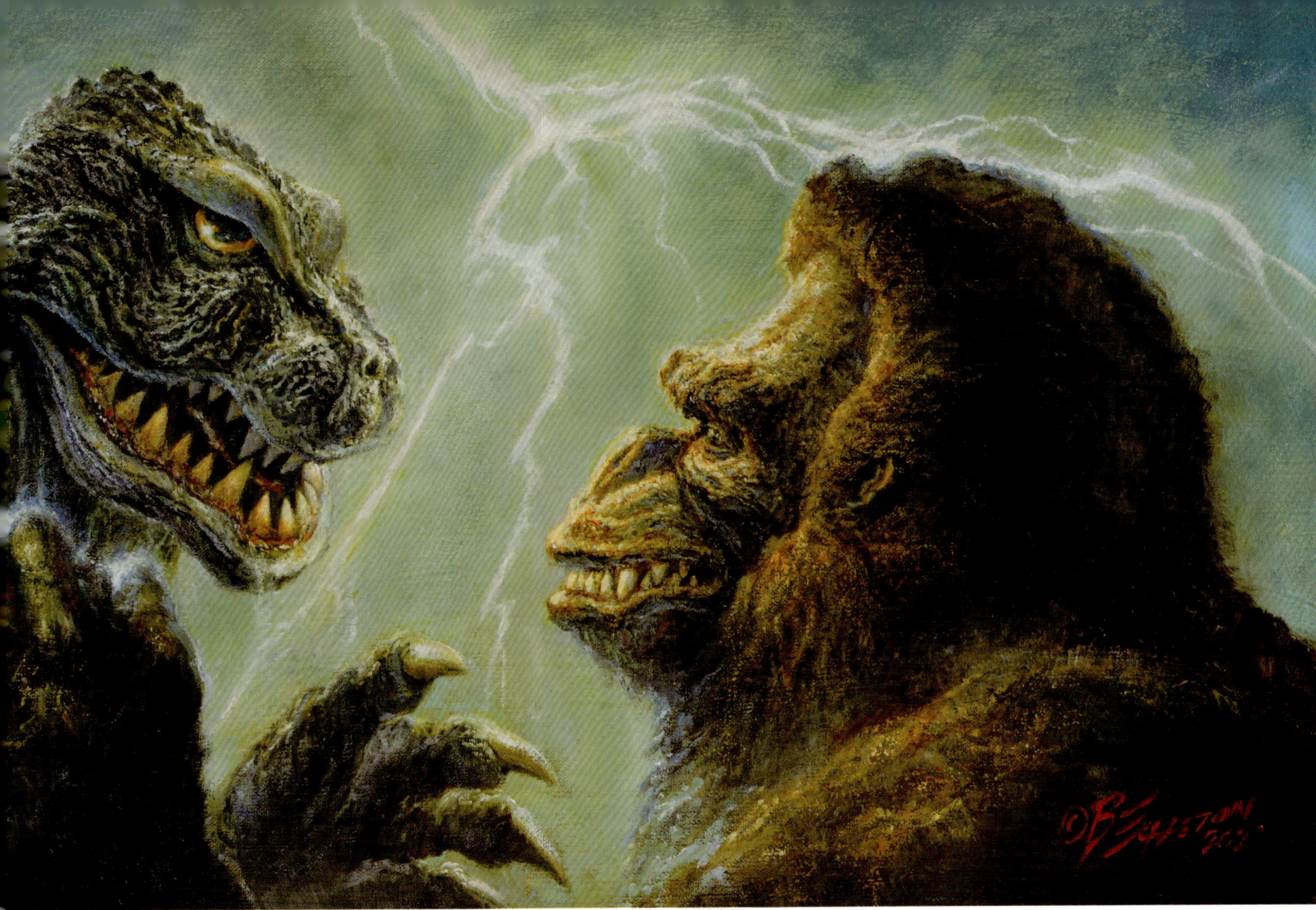

palette to characters who had mostly been seen only in black and white, creating striking color images that fired the imaginations of the magazine's young readers. Like Bama and Künstler, Gogos had been a constant provider of illustrations to publishers, ad agencies, and magazines in New York for years before the monster craze made him an icon for a generation of fans.

In theaters, Hammer Films continued to provide gothic horrors such as *Brides of Dracula* (1960), *The Curse of the Werewolf* (1961), *The Evil of Frankenstein* (1964), and *Dracula: Prince of Darkness* (1966), while MGM scared the pants off filmgoers with films like *Village of the Damned* (1960), *The Haunting* (1963), and *Children of the Damned* (1964), as well as showcasing memorable monsters in features such as *The Time Machine* (1960), *7 Faces of Dr. Lao* (1964), and *The Green Slime* (1968), in association with Toho of Japan, Godzilla's home studio. More monsters from the nimble hands of animator Ray Harryhausen followed in the wake of his first color film—*The 7th Voyage of Sinbad* (1958)—in such releases as *Mysterious Island* (1961), *Jason and the Argonauts* (1963), *First Men in the Moon* (1964), and *The Valley of Gwangi* (1969). There was a proliferation of amazing films from Europe by directors like Mario Bava and Roger Vadim, and so many memorable movies directed and produced by Roger Corman.

In 1968, Pittsburgh filmmaker George A. Romero's *Night of the Living Dead* set a benchmark for a nascent genre that would become very popular over the next few decades: the zombie film. Romero's talent for masking political and societal commentary within the trappings of a horror film would influence upcoming genre directors and set the stage for sequels of his own.

Meanwhile, monsters made their way to television in a big way in the form of *The Munsters* (1964–66) and *The Addams Family* (1964–66) competing for the loyalty of young viewers on different networks. Rod Serling's award-winning series *The Twilight Zone* (1959–64) had its fair share of creatures, but for maximum monster coverage, nothing beat the similar and sublime anthology series *The Outer Limits* (1963–65). Additionally, creatures of the night (including Karloff, Lugosi, and other genre stars) stepped outside their usual niche to make appearances on *Route 66*, *The Red Skelton Show*, and many other programs in the first half of the decade.

By the mid-'60s, the monster craze began to fade as James Bond and his spy friends came along, but the real blow was *Batman* (1966–68). The Caped Crusader and Robin, the Boy Wonder, fundamentally changed the game, prompting other popular shows to mimic their campy delivery and oversaturated color. Though they burned in the television airwaves for only three years, they burned very brightly, eclipsing the mania of the monsters.

But as we all know, monsters never die.

In 1966, producer-director Dan Curtis unleashed *Dark Shadows* (1966–71) upon the world, and a new resurgence of monster mania occurred—specifically, Barnabas Collins mania. The series was the first soap opera to feature the kind of gothic, supernatural characters that appeared so prominently in the movies released by Hammer Films. Every day, housewives and swift-footed schoolchildren sat rapt before their TV sets to see the latest happenings in Collinsport, Maine, home to vampires, ghosts, werewolves, and the like. Star Jonathan Frid (who played Barnabas) and sidekick David Selby became heartthrobs overnight.

Famous Monsters of Filmland magazine catered to a very specific crowd, and the fans were creative and industrious. They made monster models, wrote stories, and created their own Super 8 films featuring creatures of all stripes. Many of them never turned away from that early obsession with films about monsters, and became professionals in the movie industry. Academy Award–winning makeup artist Rick Baker was a faithful reader of the magazine, as was film director and fellow Academy Award winner Peter Jackson. Stephen King—arguably the most popular writer in the world, and certainly the most popular writer of horror fiction—had his first published work, a letter to editor Forrest J Ackerman, printed in *Famous Monsters*.

Literally hundreds of men and women who create films, make special effects, write books, produce visual art, and write and perform music so beloved by huge fandoms started their journey to a creative career because they saw others doing it in the pages of *Famous Monsters*. The effect of this—and the influence of those who loved comic books and other fantastic media in their formative years—is that popular culture is now nerd culture. The things kids were laughed at or scolded for liking in the 1960s now generate billions of dollars in theaters, on television, and in bookstores, as well as merchandise sales.

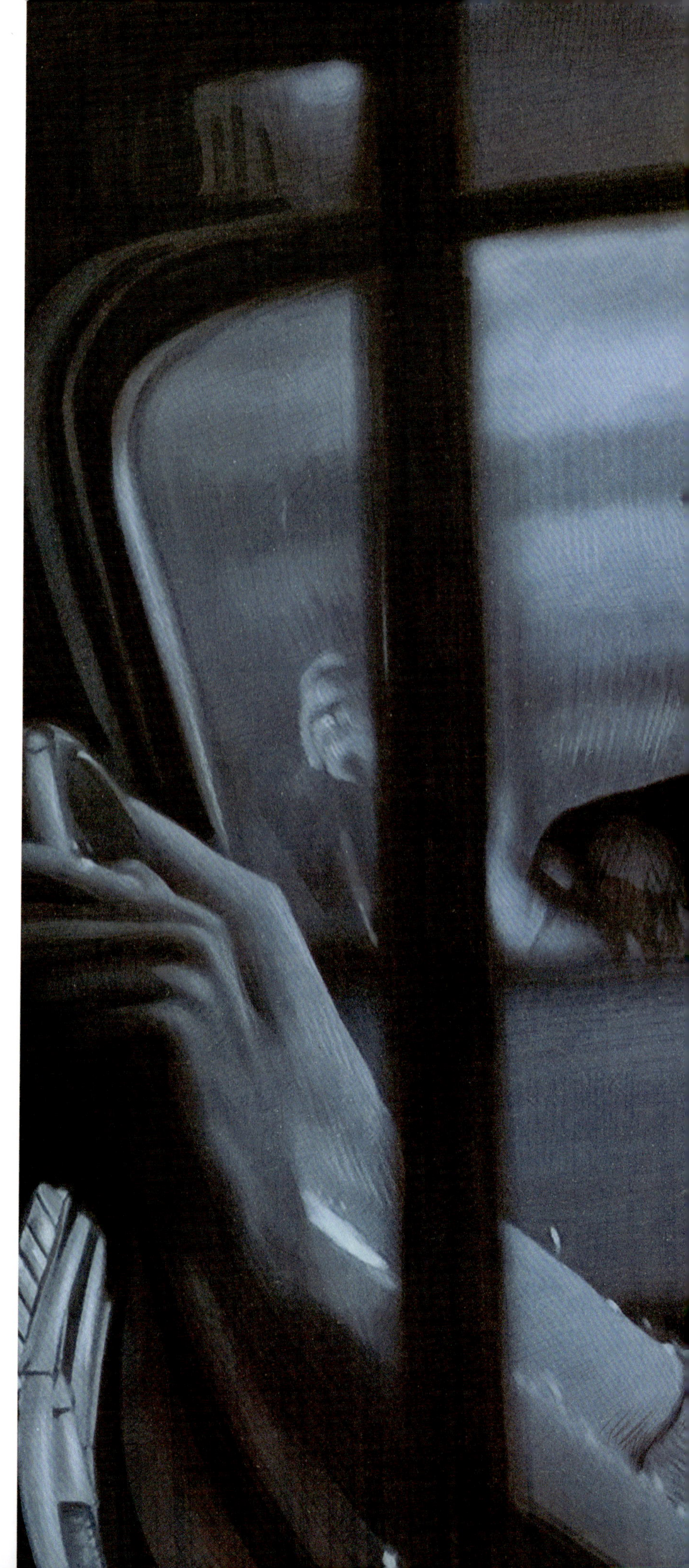

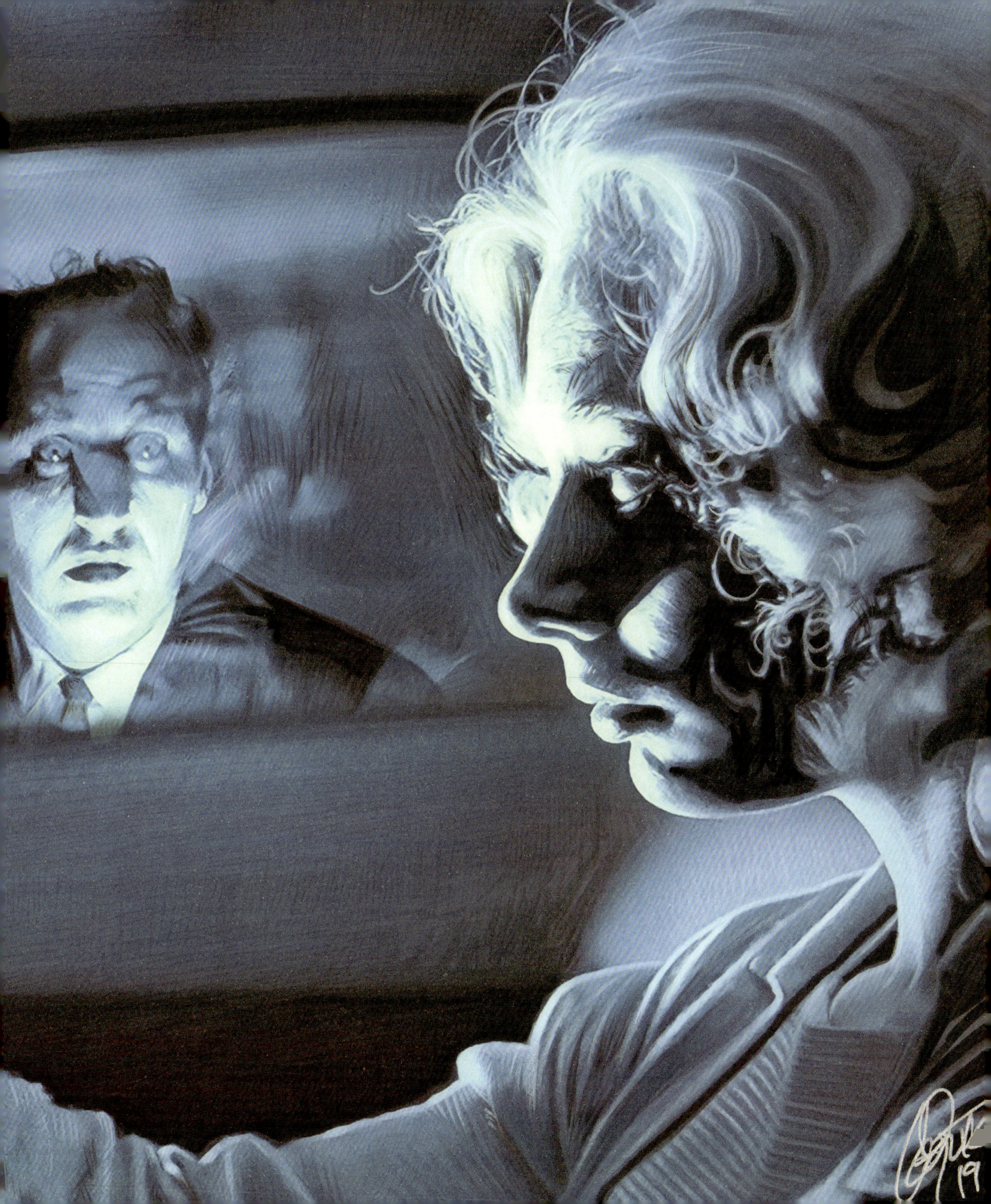

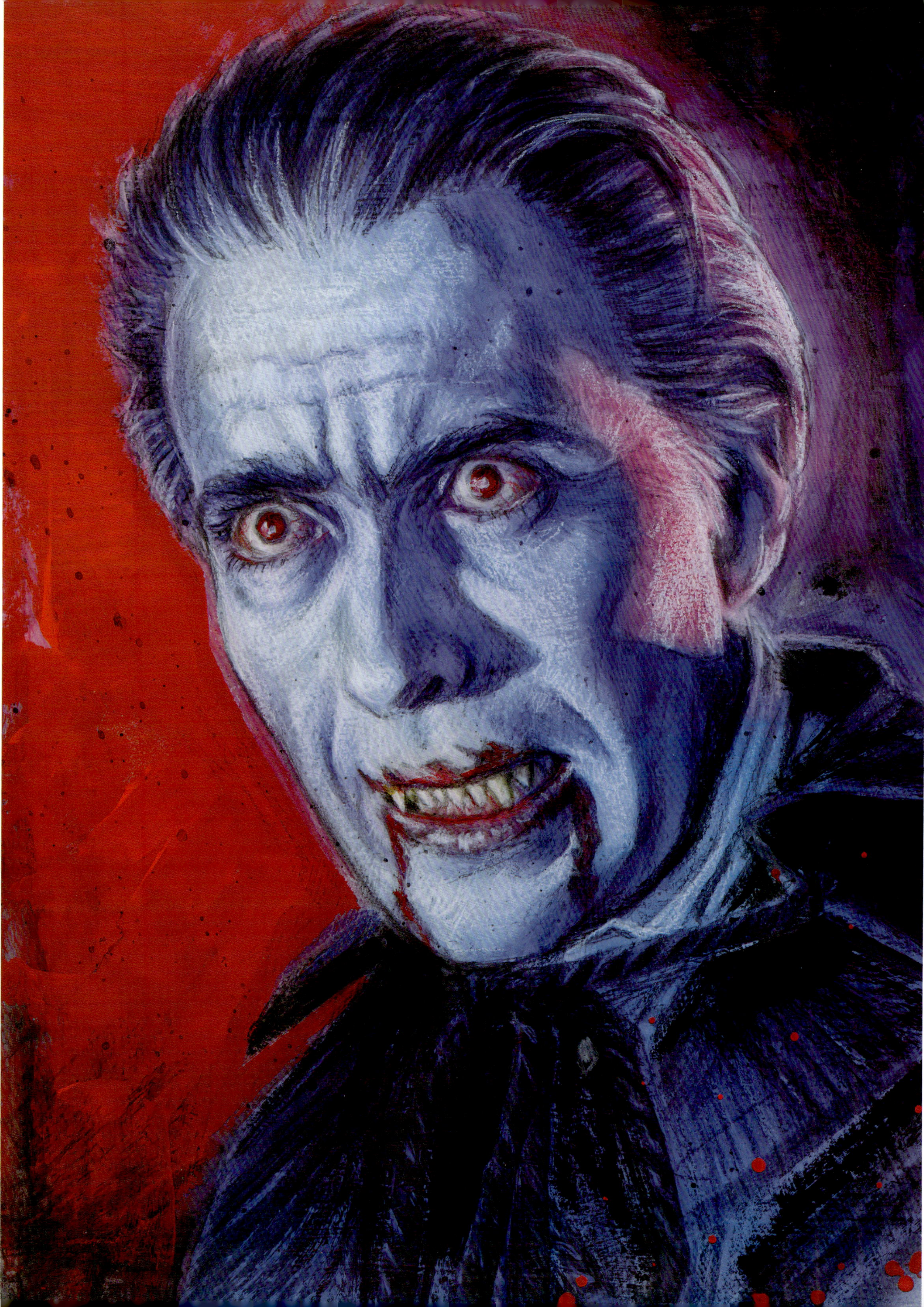

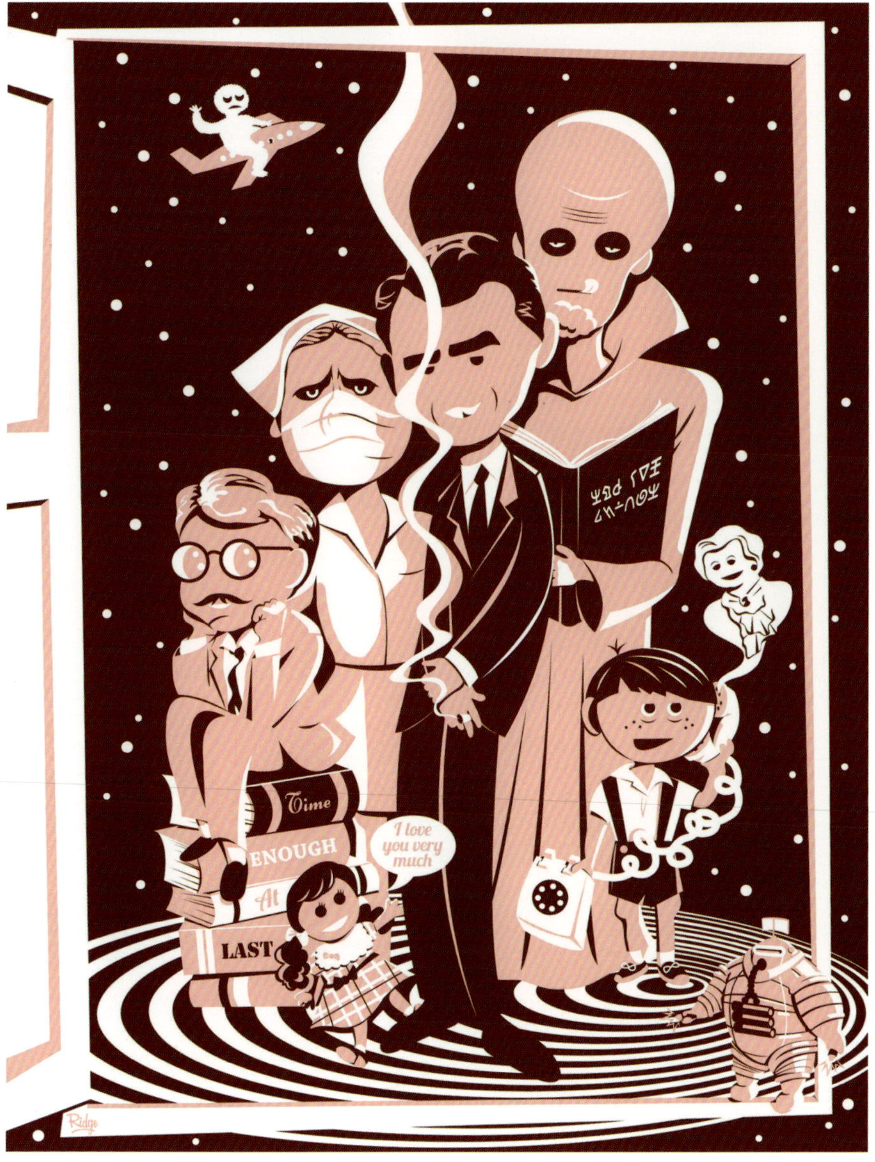

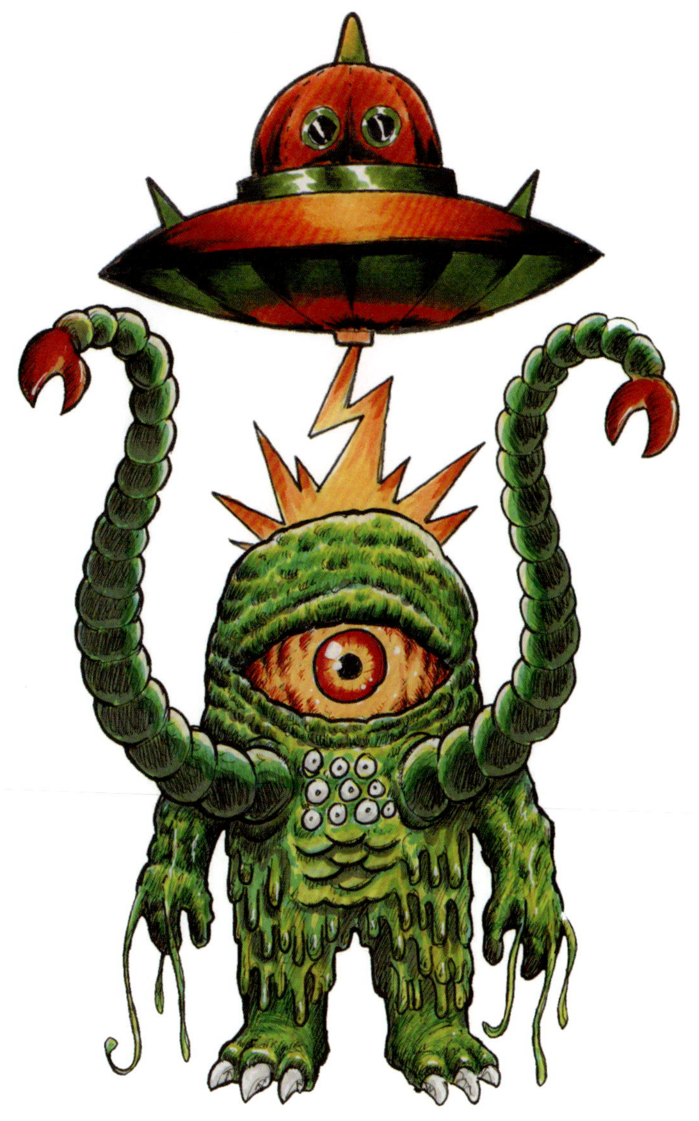

PREVIOUS PAGES *Carnival of Souls* by Frederick Cooper. Marker and pencil on cyan drawing board, 2019.

OPPOSITE *Christopher Lee as Dracula* by Doug P'Gosh. Acrylic and pastel pencil on illustration board, 2023.

ABOVE, LEFT *Spoiled for Your Approval* by Ridge Rooms. Digital, 2015.

ABOVE, RIGHT *The Green Slime* by Stephane Willemy. Markers, 2019.

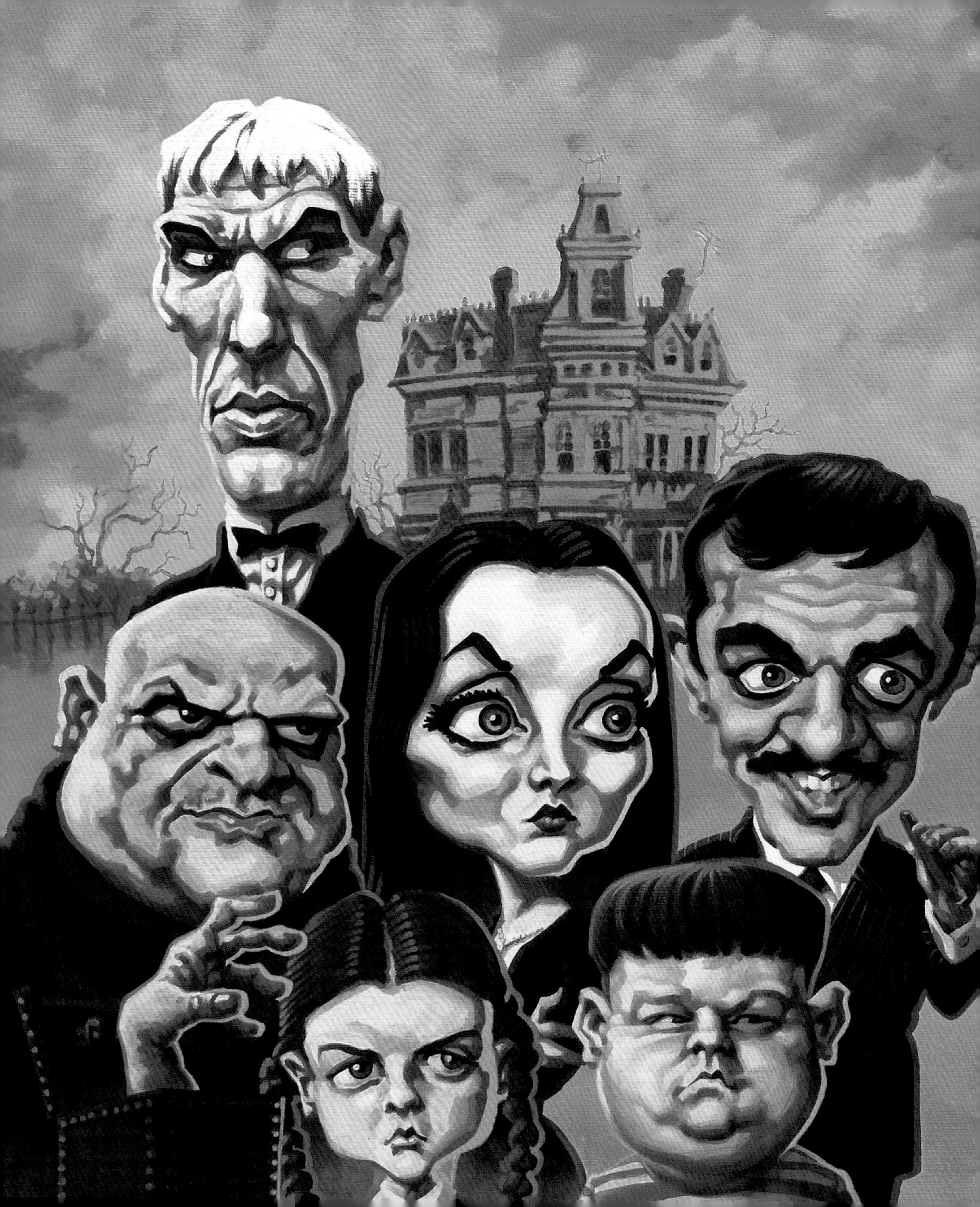

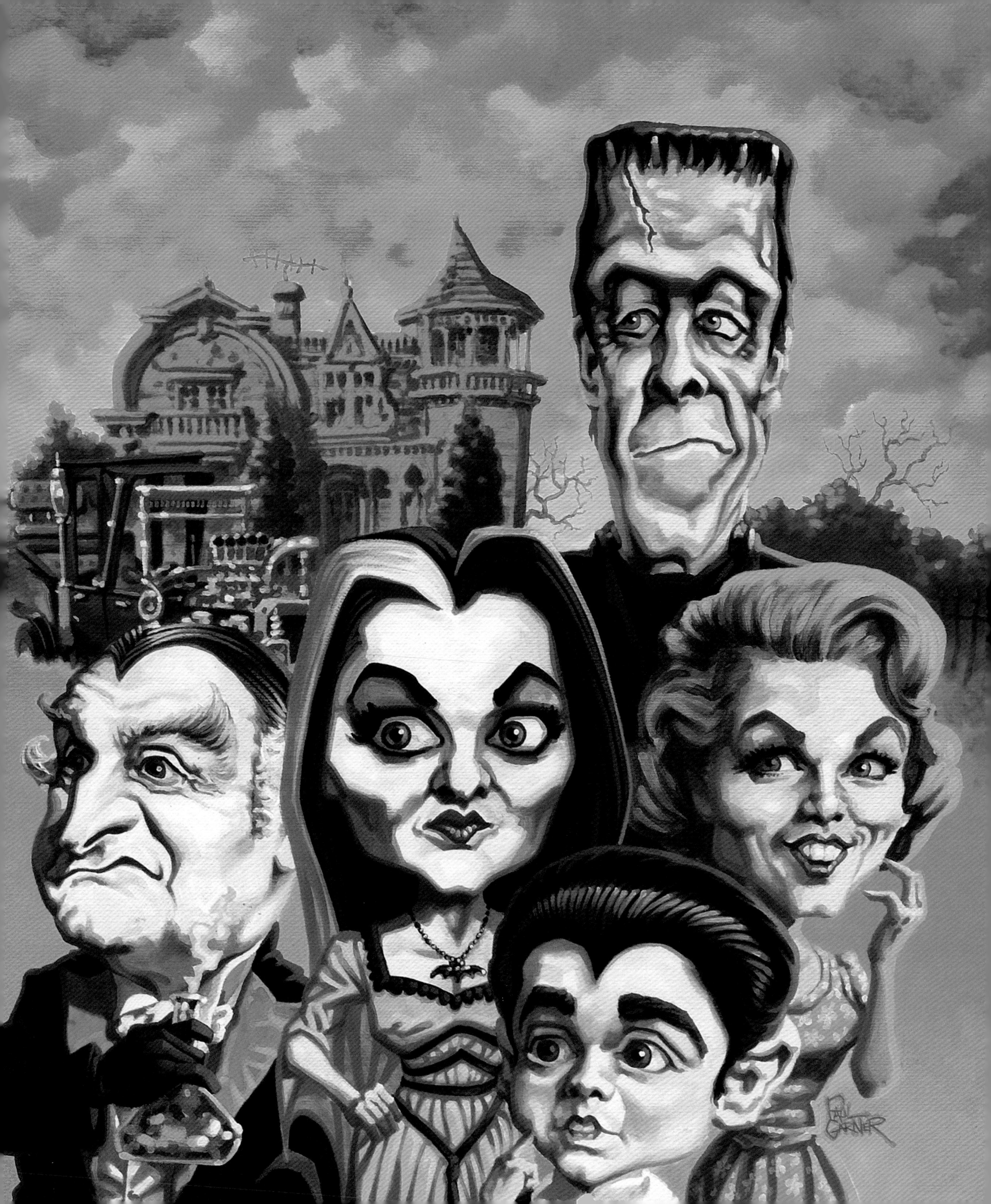
PAUL GARNER

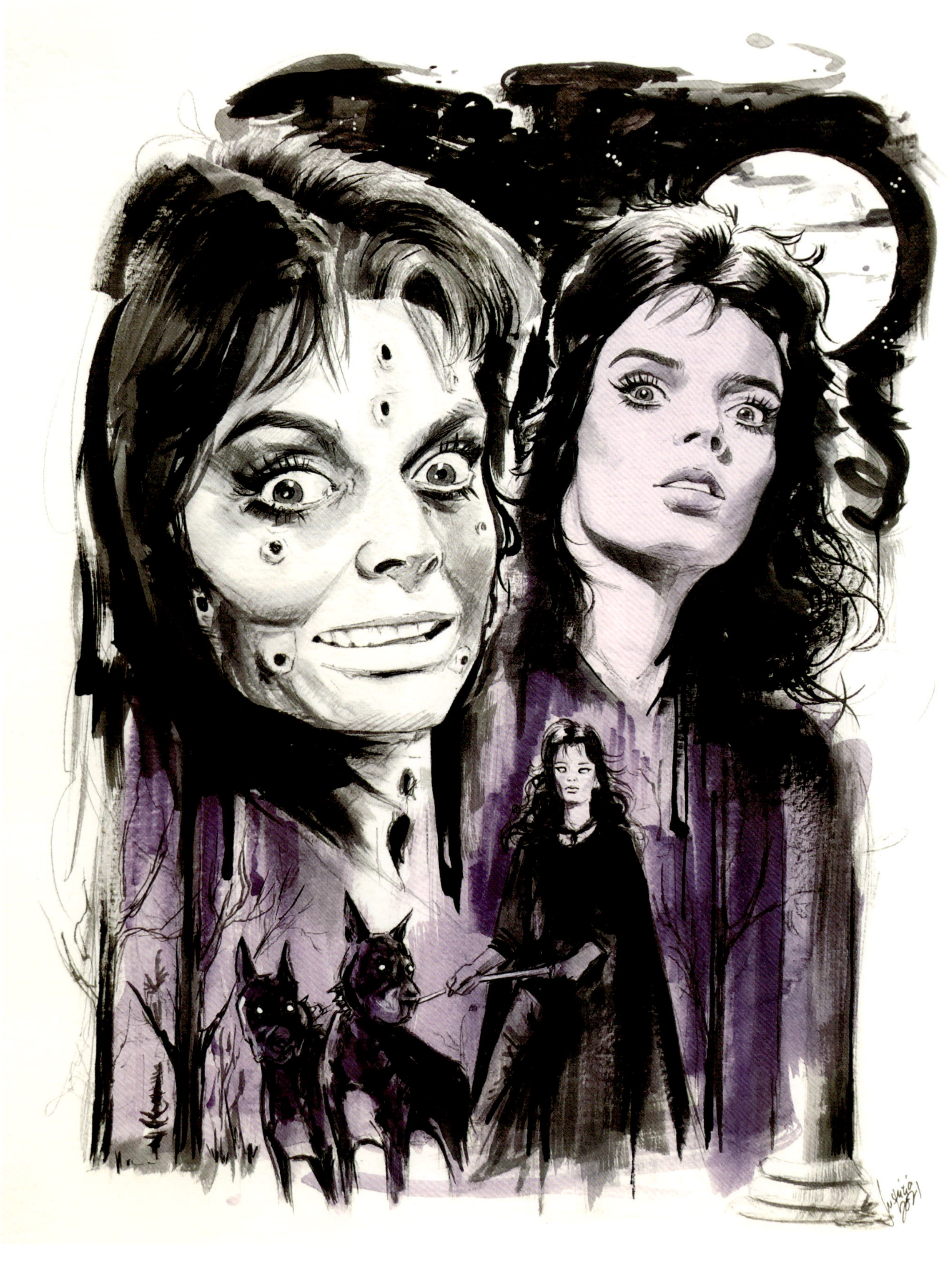

ABOVE *Black Sunday* by Susana "Suspiria" Vilchez. Acrylic on board, 2021.

PREVIOUS SPREAD *Monster Television Showdown* by Paul Garner. Cover art for *Famous Monsters of Filmland* magazine #268. Acrylic on board, 2013.

OPPOSITE *Psycho Montage* by Paul Mann. Alternative screen-printed poster for Spoke Art Galleries. Acrylic on illustration board, 2024.

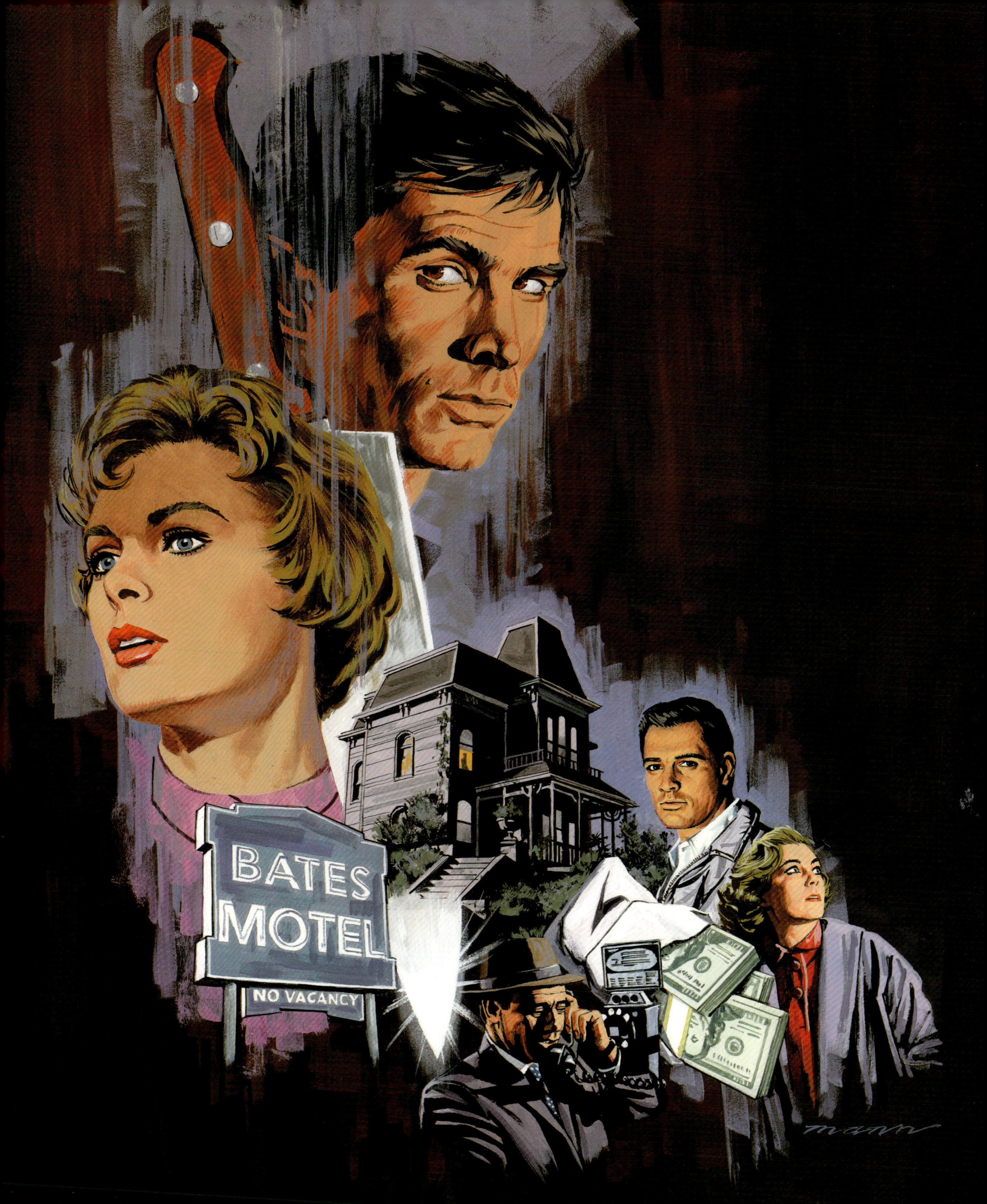
BATES
MOTEL
NO VACANCY
mann

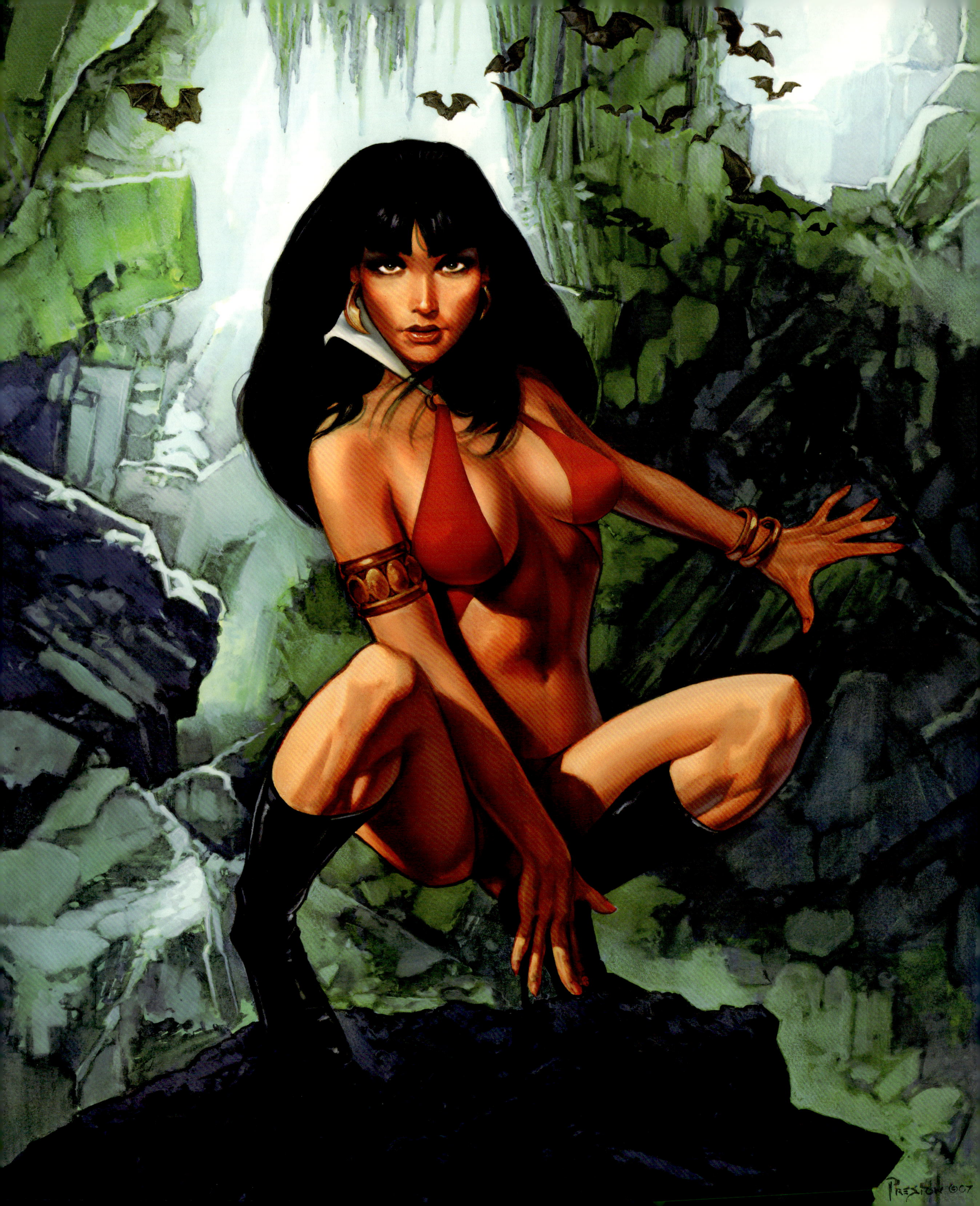
PRESTON ©07

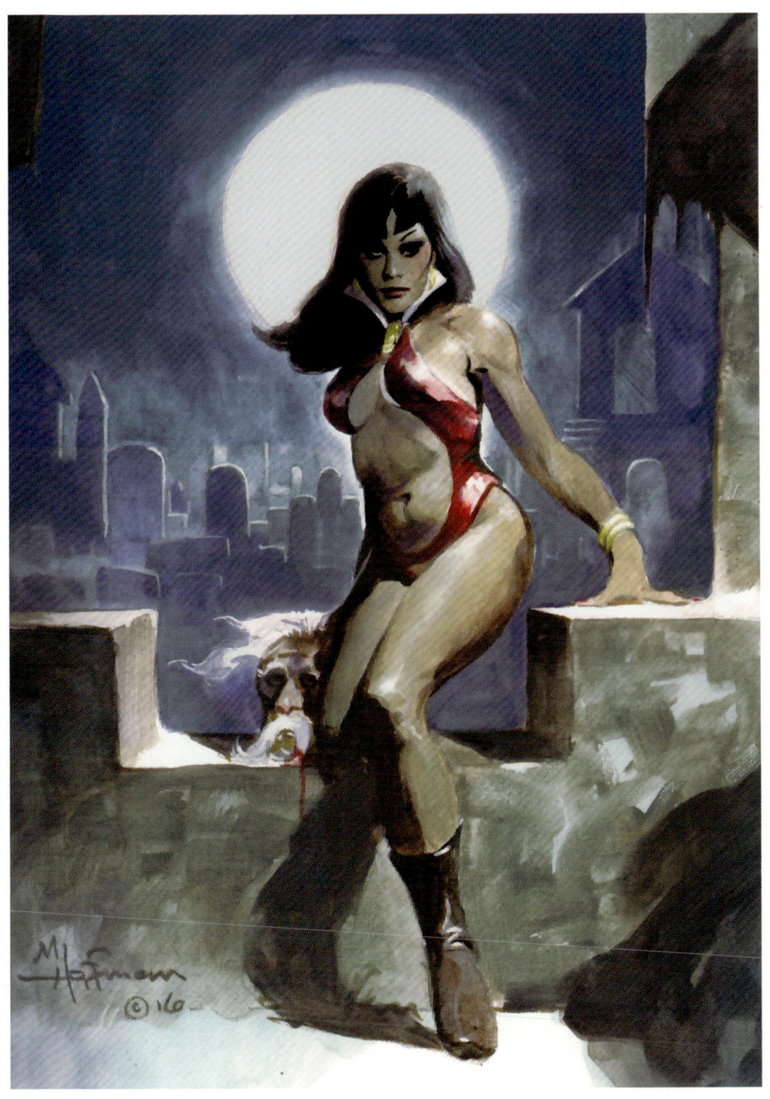

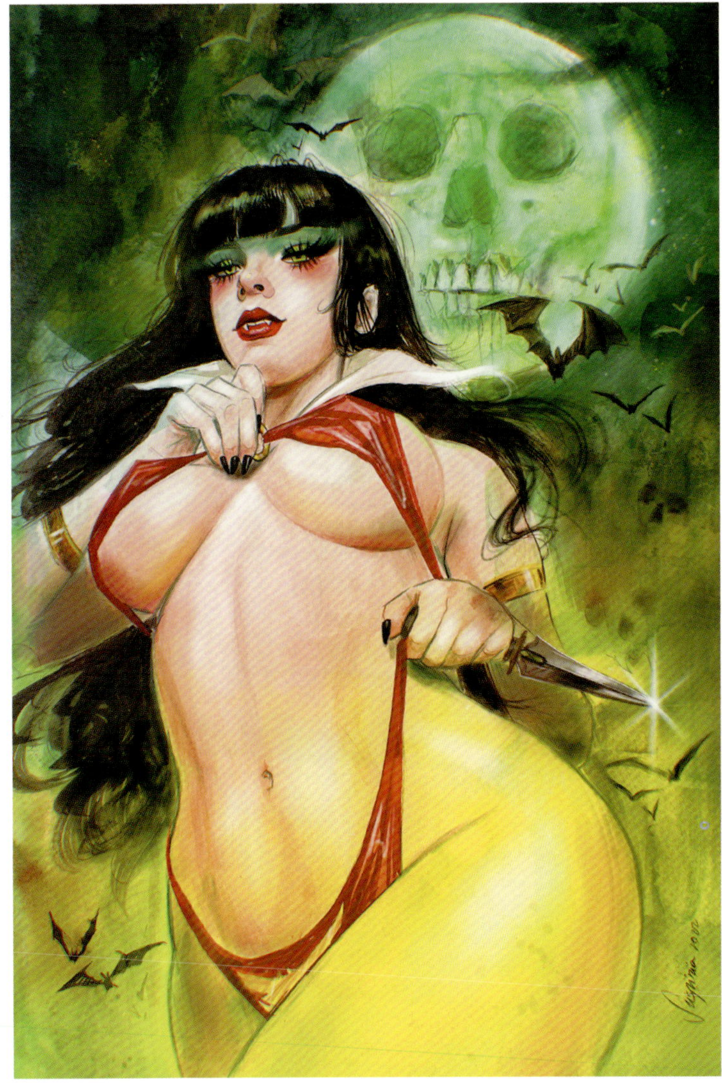

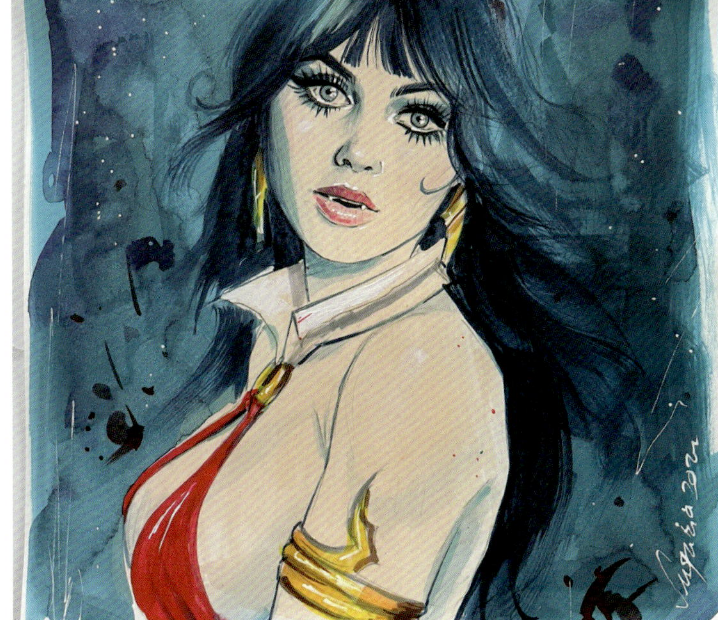

OPPOSITE *Vampirella* by Jeff Preston. Markers on paper, 2007.

TOP LEFT *Draculonian* by Mike Hoffman. Oil on board, 2016.

TOP RIGHT *Vampi* by Susana "Suspiria" Vilchez. Acrylic on board, 2002.

RIGHT *Vampirella* by Susana "Suspiria" Vilchez. Mixed media, 2022.

Dino De Laurentiis's *King Kong*

Though youth monster culture peaked in the 1960s, the following decade had unmistakable event-viewing moments for young creature film lovers. Writer John Michlig (*Kong: King of Skull Island*) once again shows his colors as a monster expert—specifically a giant-monkey movie enthusiast—with his remembrance of De Laurentiis's remake of *King Kong*:

"Modern genre enthusiasts below a certain vintage are not going to grasp this, but there was a time when the appearance of a mid- to high-budget movie about an oversized-to-giant beast of any kind was very, very rare. Sure, we had periodic late-night TV revisitations with the likes of *Godzilla* and *Mothra*—and, don't get me wrong, they were lots of fun—but a straightforward, mid-'70s modern portrayal of a colossal beast was just not happening.

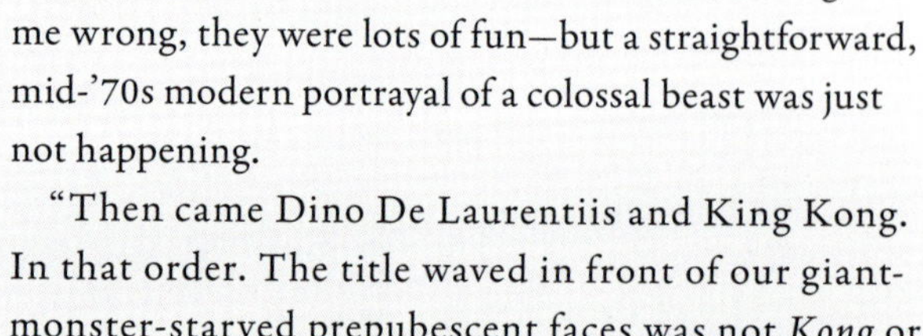

BELOW *'76 King Kong Montage* by Daryl Joyce. Digital, 2024.

OPPOSITE *Kong and Dwan* by Adam Insam. Digital, 2021.

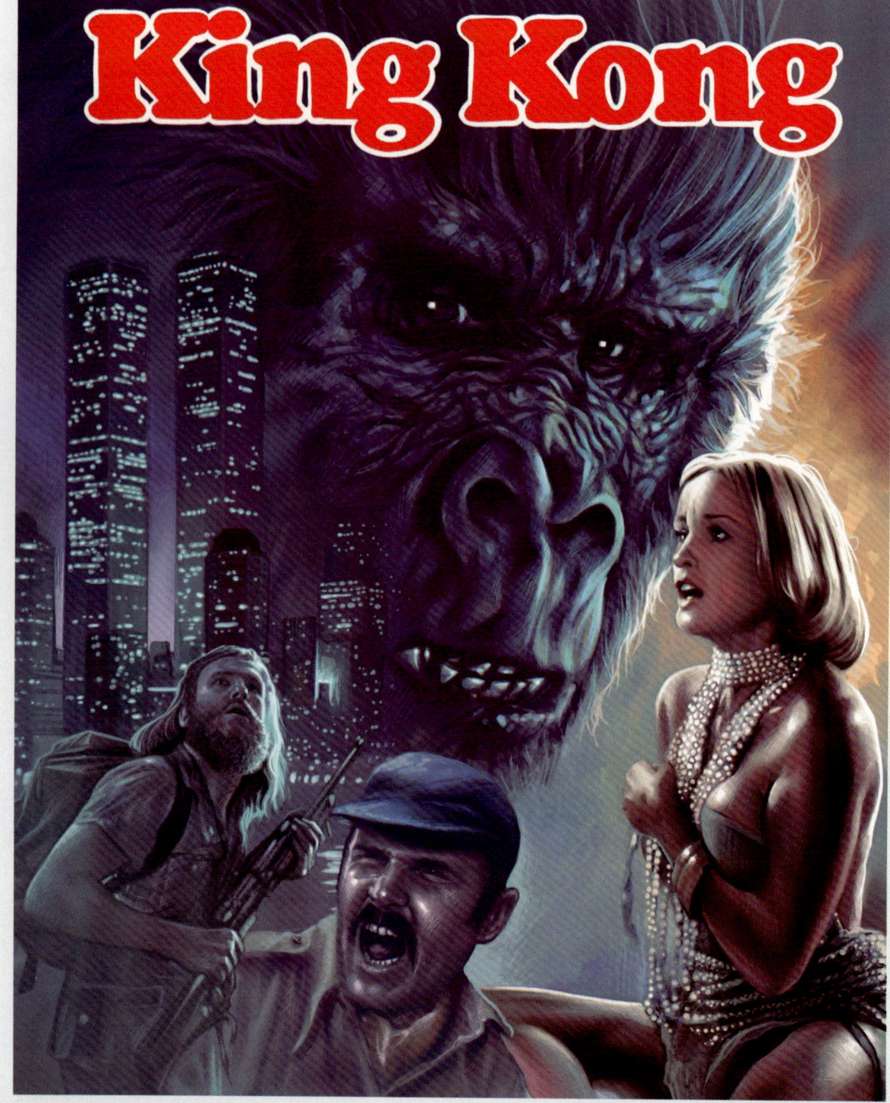

"Then came Dino De Laurentiis and King Kong. In that order. The title waved in front of our giant-monster-starved prepubescent faces was not *Kong* or *King Kong*; it was *Dino De Laurentiis's King Kong*.

"On November 30, 1975, *The New York Times* printed an ad for a film that wouldn't be released for over a year. Across the top of the image were the words 'There still is only one King Kong'—a calculated stab in the eye aimed at Universal, which had run their own Kong ad weeks before in their quest to produce a remake—and at the bottom was a coupon offering a free copy of the poster. Paramount assigned a single person, Christabel Winerman, to deal with the anticipated requests. The day after the ad ran, Winerman was presented with a box containing 219 letters. The next day, four thousand appeared. On the third day, eight thousand letters showed up. Winerman was given some help; eventually, sixty thousand requests for the poster came in!

"Still, none of this filtered down to flyover country. With no internet in 1975, information and images did not disseminate at today's lightning speed. My first glimpse of the promo occurred in my sixth-grade classroom as I unfolded the poster from the back of a brand-new *Dynamite* magazine, the Scholastic School Book Club's 'hip' periodical. Our teacher had just handed out the new book orders, and I couldn't wait to see the giant gorilla.

"The poster, by artist John Berkey, was in the back of the magazine, folded twice. By happy accident, when you flipped it open you saw the upper half of the poster: Kong revealed from the waist up, blonde captive in one hand and crushed fighter jet in the other. The face jumped right out, and it was one of those moments where guys simultaneously emit a drawn-out 'Whoooaa!' We were taken aback; it was a quite surprising and quite frightening image. Not really a gorilla, but sort of Yeti-like creature with a *Phantom of the Opera* skull-like nose. Glorious. Unambiguously awesome. It hung on my bedroom

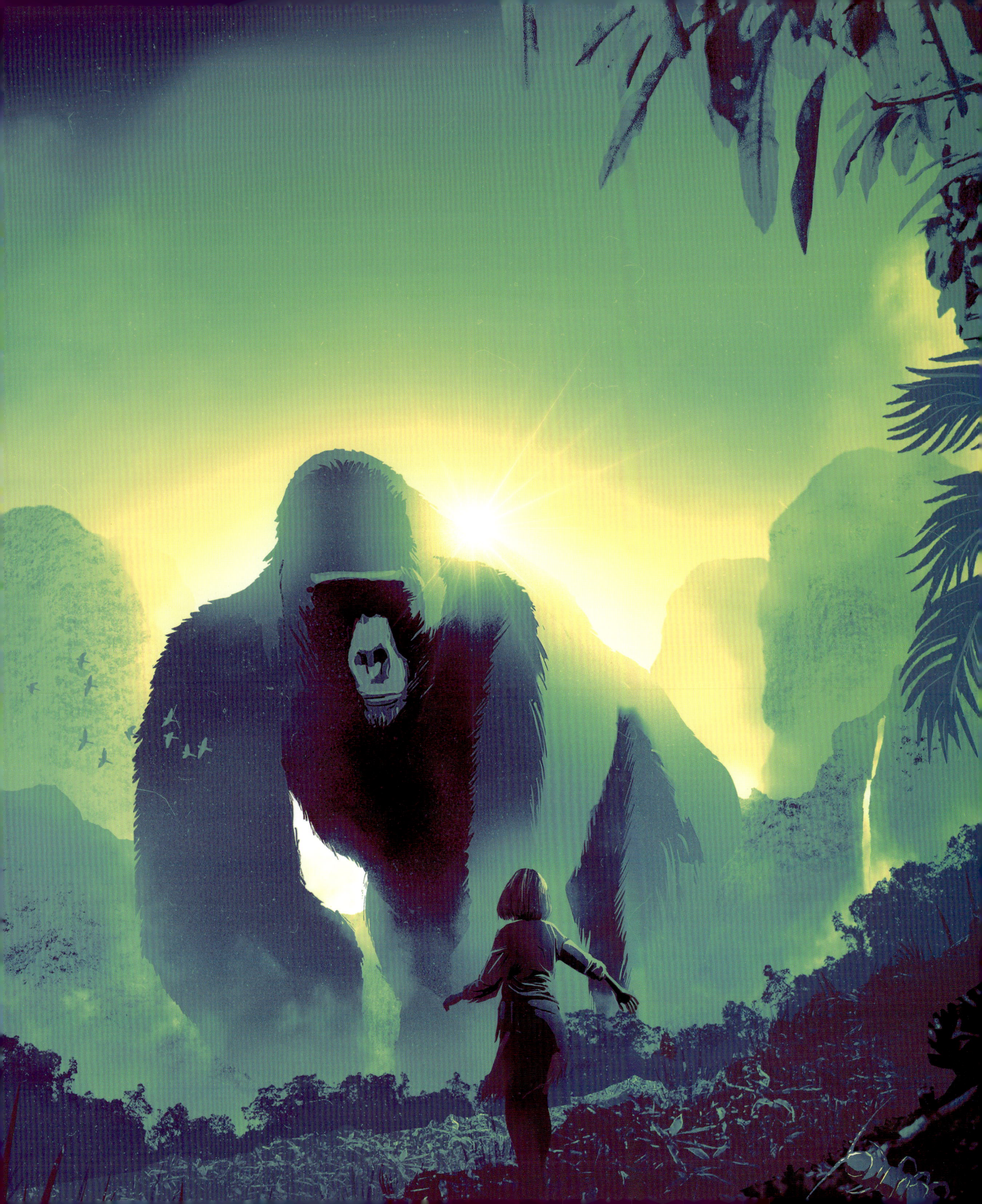

wall for the rest of the decade, and I still own that very poster. But the stirring image was not the only audacious aspect of what became the visual center point of a brilliant campaign.

"'We—Steve Rose and Jeffrey Katzenberg, who was my assistant—were about to make the presentation to Barry Diller and Charles Bluhdorn [head of Paramount

"There is still only one king Kong. The most exciting motion picture . . ."

and CEO of Gulf and Western, Paramount's parent company] when we realized that there wasn't any text,' remembers the vice president of Paramount's worldwide marketing, Gordon Weaver. 'The three of us huddled and came up with the copy: "There is still only one King Kong. The most exciting original motion picture event of all time."'

"That hubris and hyperbole ultimately doomed the film, but at this stage of the game it utterly buried Universal's hopes to produce their own remake. The ad hit like a ton of bricks, and nothing could stop the Paramount promotional juggernaut.

"Of course, the attention drawn to the remake also spotlighted the original—and, to my preteen sensibilities, ancient—1933 RKO classic. I was able to secure a copy of Ballantine's newly republished *The Making of King Kong* by George E. Turner and Orville Goldner, a book I read cover-to-cover at least three times before I was able to actually see the 1933 film."

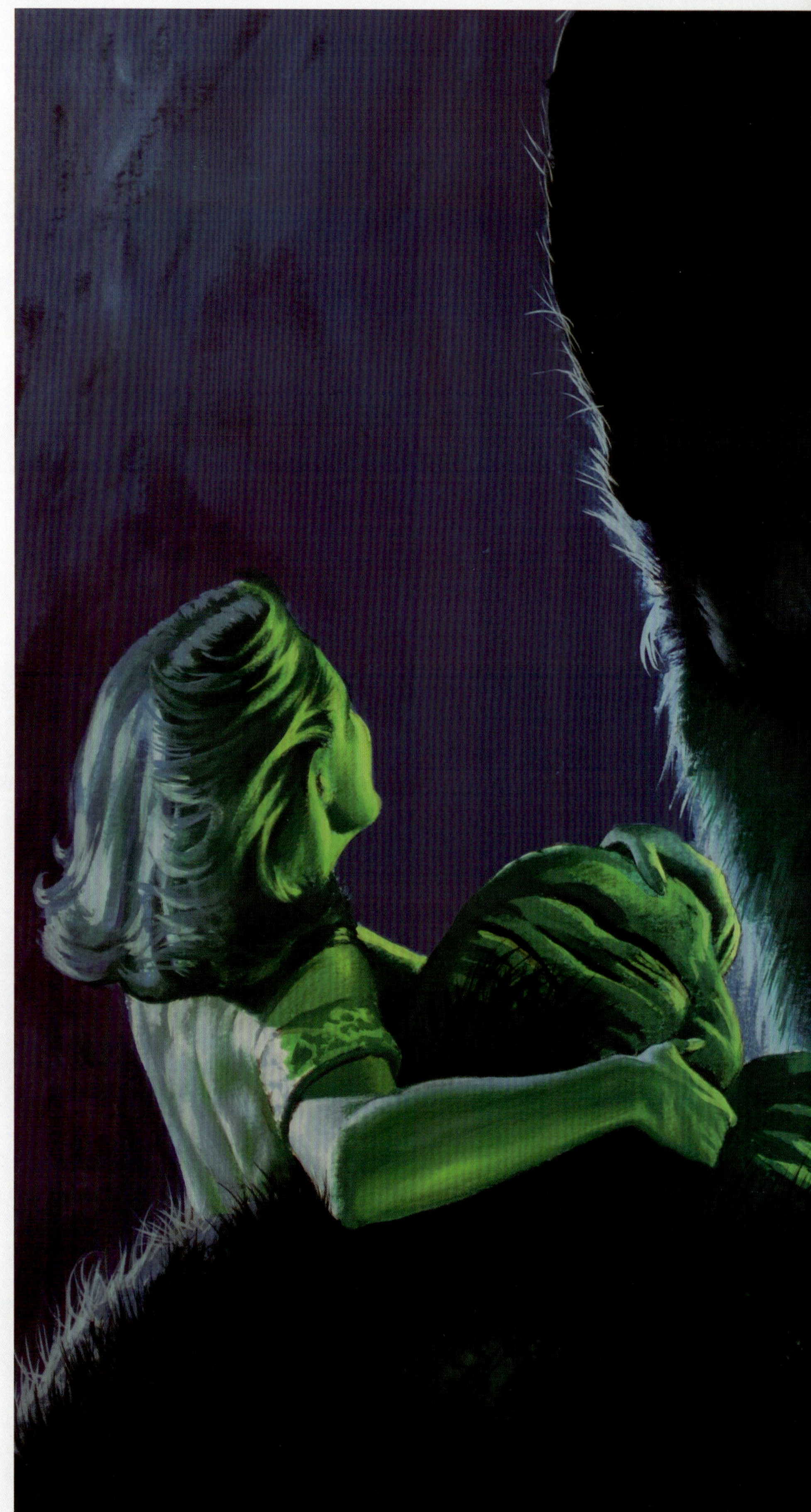

RIGHT *The Dwan of Kong* by Robert Laskey. Exclusive to this book. Acrylic, 2025.

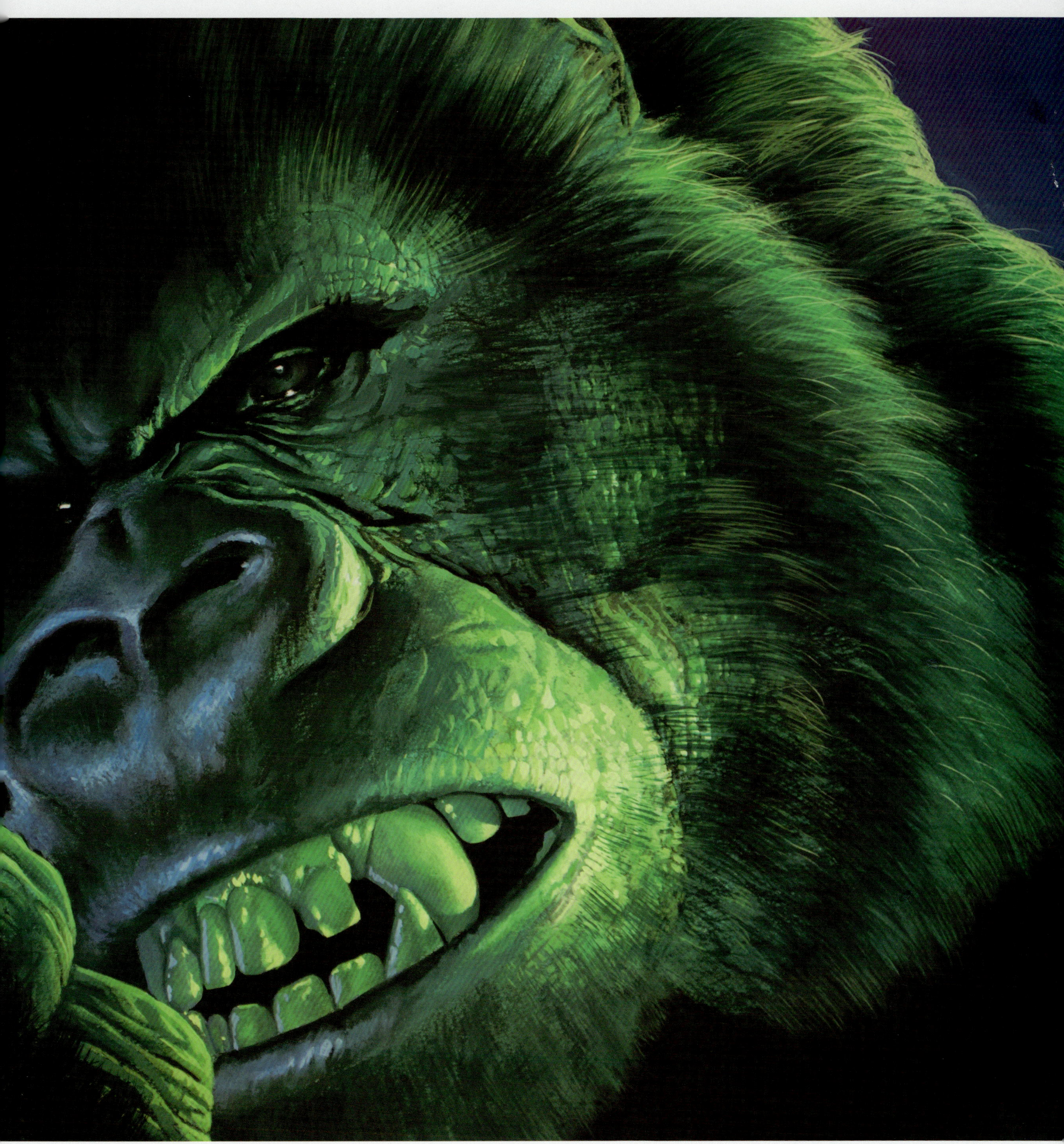

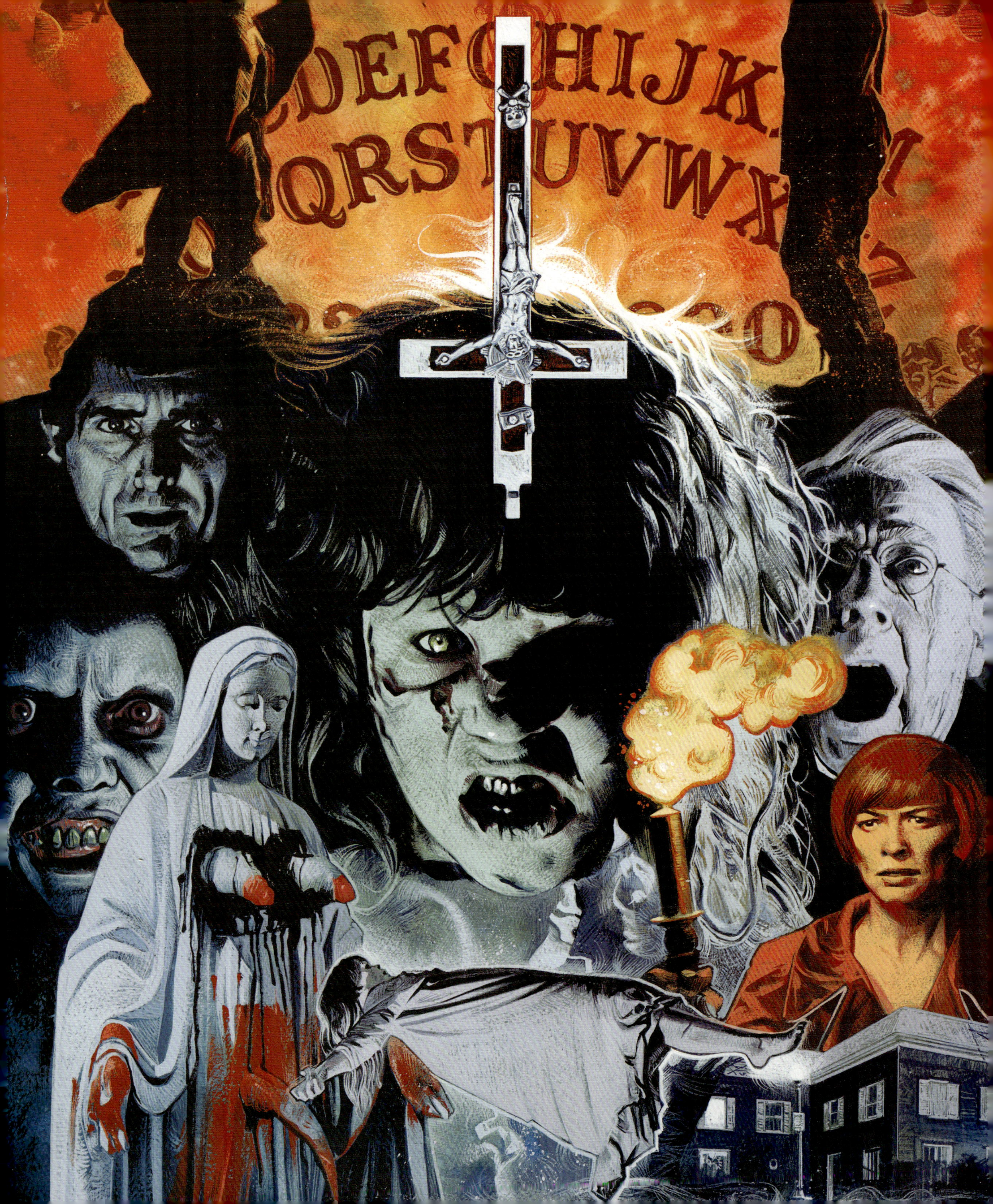

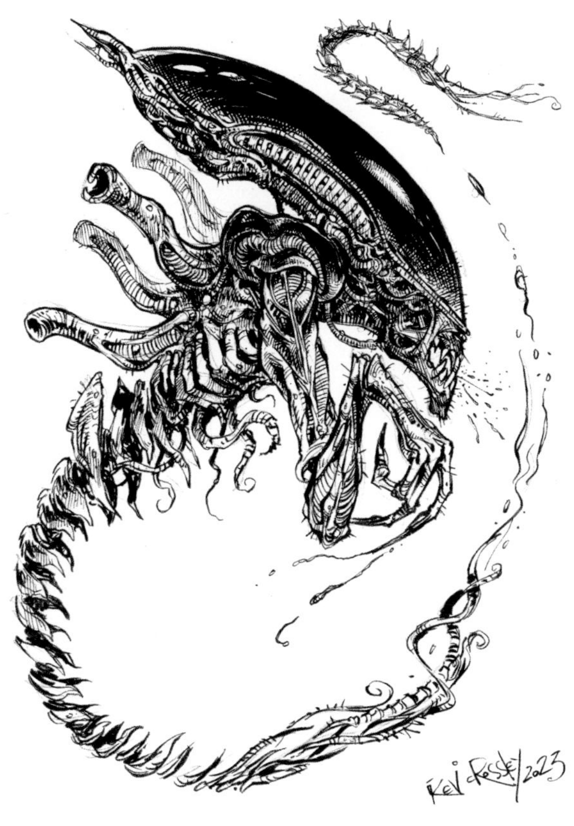

CHAPTER 7

It's All Happening (1970–1979)

Though it's a popular aphorism that the 1960s didn't end until 1973, nothing could be farther from the truth. While the epitome of '60s pop culture, the Beatles, held on until April 1970, they were finished a year earlier, when they walked off that rooftop after the third performance of "Get Back" was interrupted by the police. Though they recorded the album *Abbey Road* after that, they were no longer a band but, rather, a group of people in a room trying to ignore each other and finish a job they were contractually bound to complete.

Though the entity that created so many amazing songs and recordings ended, the creativity went on, with individual members continuing to record and perform, and the original works were preserved for future generations to enjoy.

But what about works that are created but do not survive, either through neglect or the willful destruction of their creator? Do they matter? Do they have an impact?

Absolutely.

In the Hindu religion, Creation and Dissolution are both acts of the Lord, along with Maintenance, Concealment, and Bestowal of Grace. For our purposes, let's just consider the first two.

For thousands of years, Buddhist monks have lovingly created large mandalas from colored sand—great works of art that take days to painstakingly make—and then swept them away and enjoyed a feast afterward.

Arguably the greatest fantasy writer of all time, Ray Bradbury wrote a short story almost every day of his adult life. His story "In a Season of Calm Weather" (*Playboy*, 1956) tells the tale of George Smith, a Picasso fan on vacation in the South of France, where Picasso has been recently seen. After searching the town high and low for the artist, he finally gives up and takes a walk on the beach, where he unexpectedly encounters the man himself.

As Picasso begins to draw in the sand with a long stick, George is enthralled to witness the act of creation by his idol, but as the tide comes in and washes away the imagery, he becomes despondent. Later, when his wife asks if anything interesting happened while he was out, a listless George responds, "No."

The point that George—and so many—misses is that the act of creation is art unto itself. Art need not be permanent to engage the mind of those who view it, even if only for a moment. Art is active in this equation, as are those who experience it. Art is not necessarily an object, an image, or a melody. Art may in fact be the

OPPOSITE *The Exorcist* by Graham Humphreys. Movie poster art for AMP Posters. Mixed media, 2025.

ABOVE *Alien* by Kev Crossley. Pen and ink, 2023.

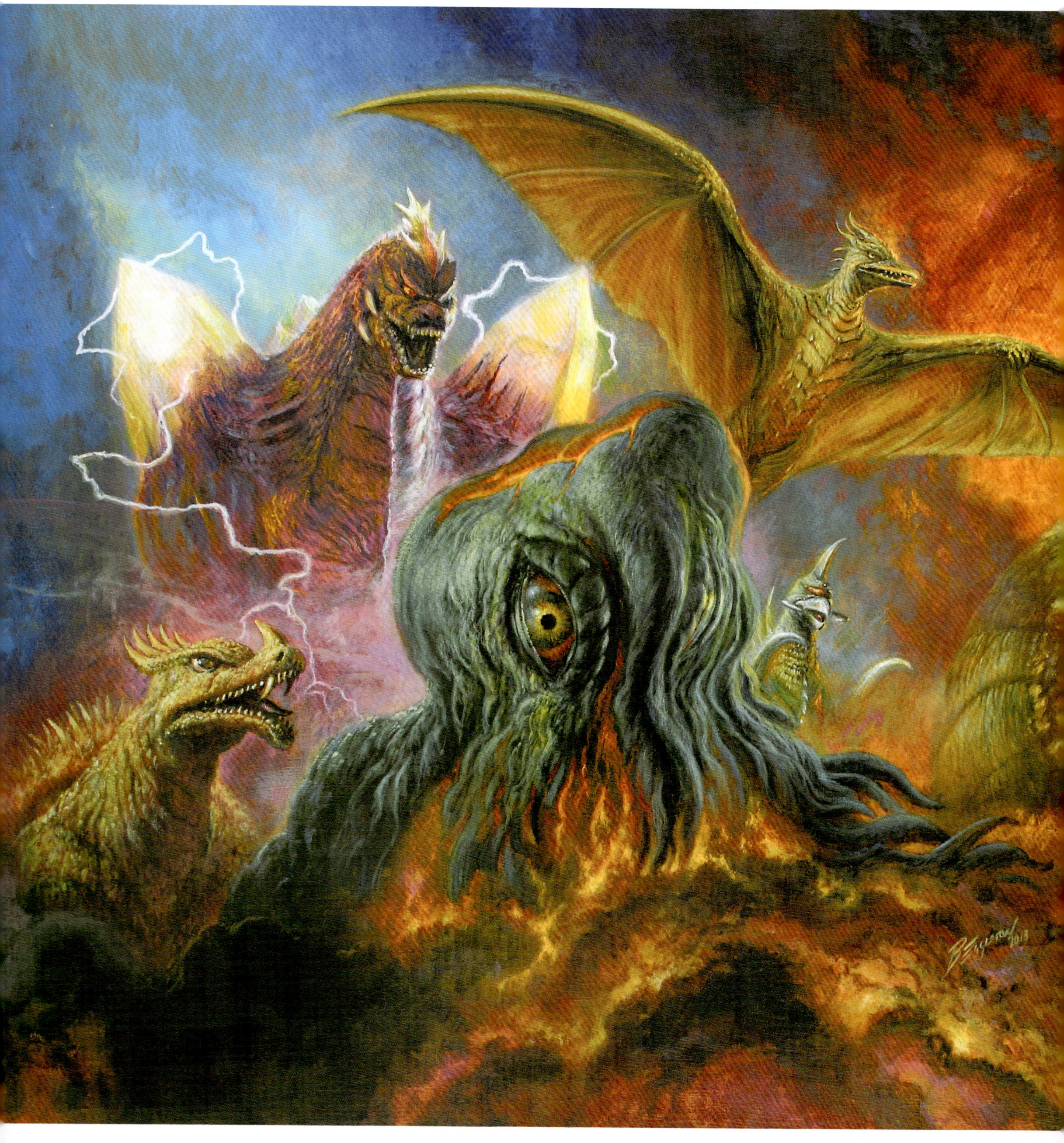

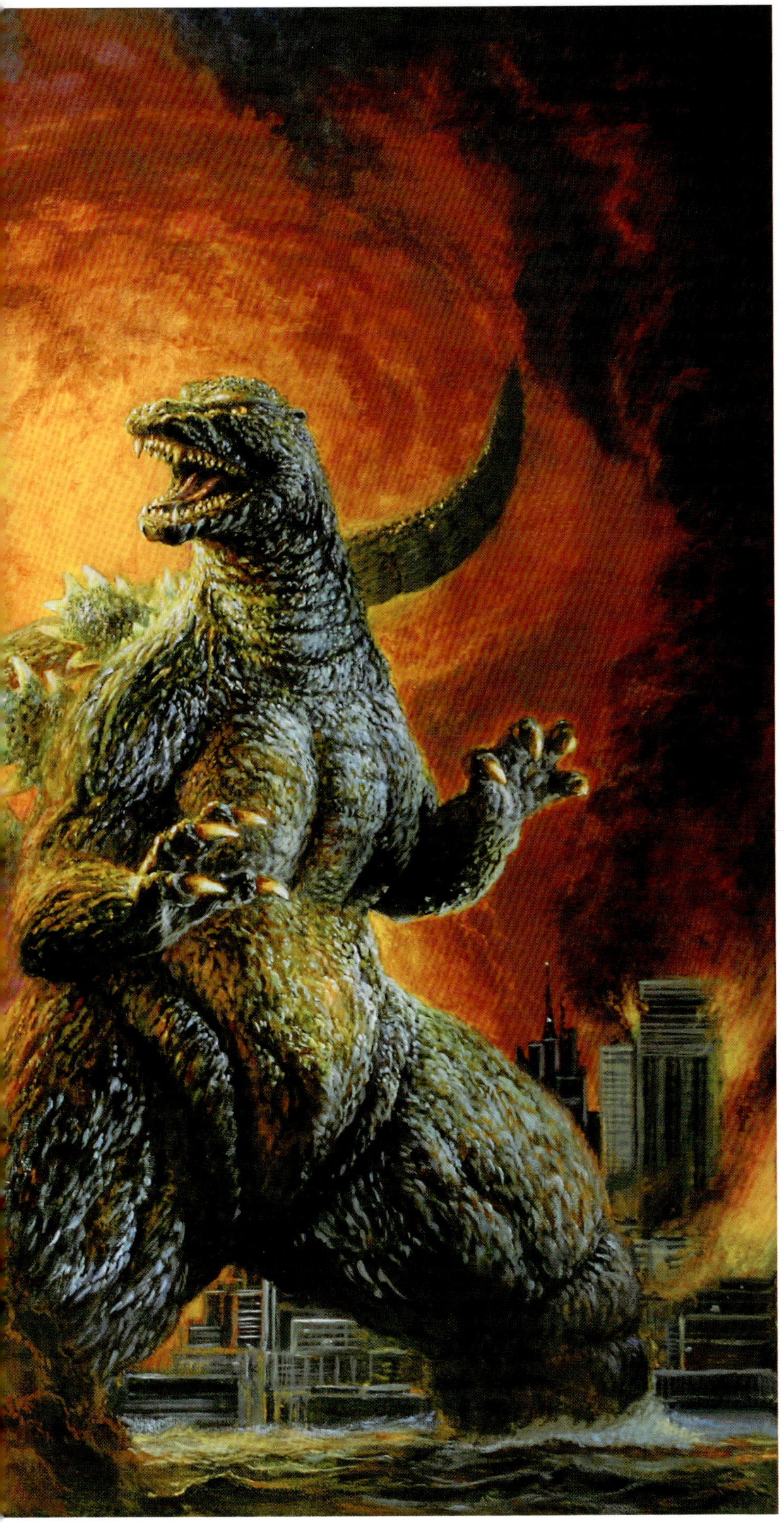

thoughts, emotions, or actions inspired by those things, and in the end, art must inspire to be relevant on any level. There are lost horror films that still influence us, such as Tod Browning's *London After Midnight*, starring Lon Chaney Sr.

This is a book about monster art, but it's also a book about how art that depicts characters we feel affinity toward affects us on multiple levels. The more we understand about the experience, the deeper the experience embeds itself within us and shapes our opinions and outlook on other subjects. The chosen media in this case is visual art.

Having ruled the monster craze with his magazine *Famous Monsters of Filmland*, James Warren doubled down on horror and monsters in the mid- to late '60s by resurrecting the classic EC-style comics with his *Creepy*, *Eerie*, and *Vampirella* titles. In a canny move to subvert the machinations of the Comics Code Authority, Warren made his titles magazine size so they wouldn't fit on comic book spinner racks and retailers would have to place them on the magazine shelves. Warren also printed the comics with black-and-white interiors and full-color cover art by artists like Frank Frazetta, Ken Kelly, and, later, Bernie Wrightson and Richard Corben.

In the early 1970s, Warren stumbled onto a studio of Spanish artists that began doing much of the art for his comics line. These artists included José González, Esteban Maroto, Manuel Sanjulián, Enric Torres-Prat, and others, and their distinctive work made the magazines favorites with readers.

"In terms of horror art, my earliest influences were Basil Gogos's covers for *Famous Monsters of Filmland* and the artists who drew for *Creepy* and *Eerie*, especially Bernie Wrightson, Reed Crandall, and Frank Frazetta," relates screenwriter and producer Mark Protosevich (*The Cell*, *I Am Legend*). "I pored over every frame on the pages of those Warren publications. The impact of those graphic works during my formative years cannot be underestimated—and that impact reverberates to this day."

Other comics publishers entered the horror comics fray but adhered to CCA rules for titles such as DC Comics' *The House of Mystery*, *The Witching Hour*,

LEFT *Seventies' Toho Kaiju Parade* by Bob Eggleton. Cover of *Godzilla, History's Greatest Monster* comic book trade paperback for IDW. Oil on canvas, 2013.

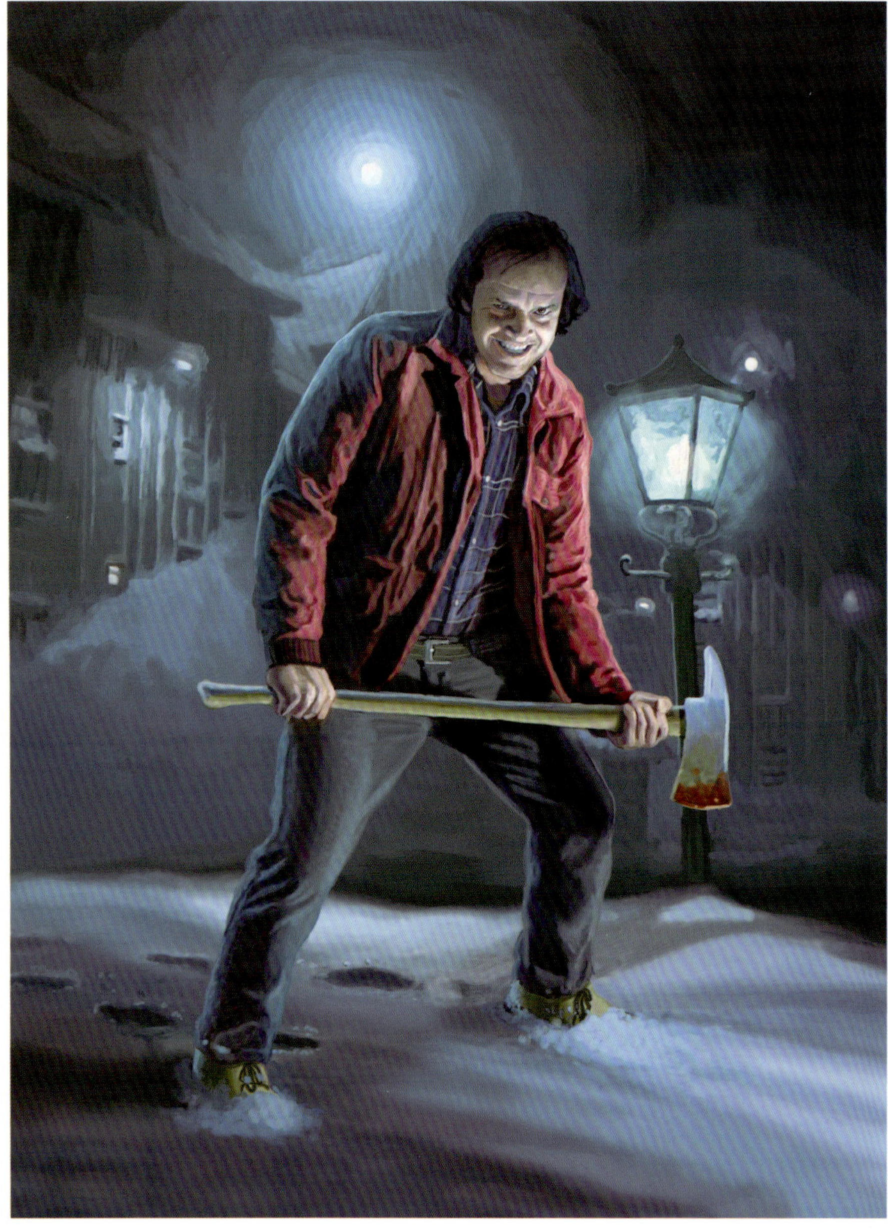

ABOVE *All Work and No Play* by Mark Maddox. Cover for *SCREEM* magazine #23. Digital, 2011.

OPPOSITE Parody posters by Paul Garner for *Jaws*, 2021, and *The Shining*, 2022. Mixed media.

and *House of Secrets* and Marvel Comics' *Monsters Unleashed*, *Chamber of Chills*, *Where Monsters Dwell*, *The Tomb of Dracula*, and others. Artists like Bob Larkin and Earl Norem similarly provided wonderful cover art for Marvel's off-the-comics-rack black-and-white horror and science fiction magazines.

"As a kid, finding back issues of the amazing Marvel comic series *Tomb of Dracula* changed my attraction to the entire horror genre," says author and podcaster Rod Barnett. "Having a serialized comic tale about the villain was mind-bending, and seeing the dreamy, smoky artwork of Gene Colan left a permanent impression about how horror stories can excite and chill. To this day, when I see Colan's work on anything I get an anticipatory thrill related to his work on *Tomb of Dracula*."

The monster craze had seen better days, but *Famous Monsters of Filmland* continued until 1983, although its focus shifted toward *Star Wars* and other popular science fiction and space opera films and television in the last few years before it shut down. It would be subject to several revivals in more recent years, but it never again got the kind of traction among fans that it had in the 1960s.

Monsters on television in the 1970s fared well, however: films like *The Night Stalker* (1972), *The Night Strangler* (1973), and *Gargoyles* (1972—not to be confused with the 1990s' animated series of the same name), which were made specifically for the small screen, garnered very high ratings, resulting in a spinoff series based on the first two movies called *Kolchak: The Night Stalker* (1974–75). Other memorable TV films include *The Norliss Tapes* (1973), *Don't Be Afraid of the Dark* (1973), *Satan's School for Girls* (1973), *The Turn of the Screw* (1974), *Trilogy of Terror* (1975), and *When Michael Calls* (1972), based on a novel by up-and-coming author John Farris, who was one of the breakthrough writers in what became a paperback horror fiction wave that would grow to amazing proportions.

Starting around the time that Ira Levin's book *Rosemary's Baby* (1967) hit *The New York Times* best-seller list, horror began to seep into the mainstream fiction market; conventional publishers reconsidered the genre and opened their doors to submissions. This resulted in a string of best sellers from authors like Farris (*The Fury*, *All Heads Turn When the Hunt Goes By*), Thomas Tryon (*The Other*, *Harvest Home*), William Peter Blatty (*The Exorcist*), Peter Straub (*Ghost Story*, *Shadowland*), Anne Rice (*Interview with the Vampire*), and the best-selling one of all—Stephen King (*Carrie*, *The Shining*, *'Salem's Lot*, *The Stand*).

These books and others like them had a sweeping effect on media consumption in the decade. All but two of the novels mentioned above were adapted for television miniseries or feature films, and all those projects fared well with viewers. As the demand for horror grew with readers, it grew with moviegoers and TV viewers.

In theaters, *The Exorcist* (1973) consistently drew lines around the block, and contributed to setting off what became known as the satanic panic: the creeping fear that Satanism had expanded beyond cult groups in urban enclaves and was spreading to suburbia in a big way. This fear enveloped America, and in the 1970s and '80s thousands of unsubstantiated reports of satanic worship and activity, including ritual abuse, clogged police blotters and newspaper pages. Old Nick became a huge box office draw with films like *The Blood on Satan's Claw* (1971), *Lisa and the Devil* (1973), *The Devil's Rain* (1975), *To the Devil a Daughter* (1976), *The Omen* (1976), and *Damien: Omen II* (1978).

Seeing the big-screen adaptation of Blatty's novel in 1973 was a transformative experience for Lisa Morton, the Bram Stoker Award–winning author of *The Castle of Los Angeles*. "I was fifteen when I saw *The Exorcist,* in its third month of release; it was still selling out every showing. I went into that movie wanting to be an anthropologist and came out knowing I had to be a writer. I'd never imagined that any work of art could have that kind of impact on audiences, and I knew it was what I wanted to do. My parents and school counselors were horrified, but it was unquestionably the right choice for me, and I've never looked back!"

On US radios, musical acts like Alice Cooper and Kiss took the nascent horror flavoring of 1950s voodoo rocker Screamin' Jay Hawkins, "Monster Mash" performer Bobby "Boris" Pickett, and horror movie host Zacherley and applied some marketing elbow grease, competent musicianship, and songwriting skills to great success. The legions of Kiss fans purchased not only millions of dollars' worth of records, but at least the same amount in merchandise featuring the band's likenesses.

In the United Kingdom, rampant unemployment and inflation—combined with a disaffected youth population—worked together to create a massive counterculture clash that gave birth to punk rock. Punk's influence proliferated into fashion, visual art, and film. The movement rapidly spread and was adopted by outsiders worldwide, but as it dispersed it diluted; the emblems and mottos were hijacked by privileged youth to represent their struggle against establishment ideology and punk gave way to the less angry, more sociologically acceptable new wave movement.

Monster master Ray Harryhausen expanded his Dynamation pantheon with a pair of films, *The Golden Voyage of Sinbad* (1973) and *Sinbad and the Eye of the Tiger* (1977), both featuring multiple memorable monster characters, dashing heroes, and lovely heroines.

A series of high-budget, high-concept supernatural films, a few nature-gone-berserk offerings, and a few bold new sci-fi–based concepts bolstered the second half of the decade in theaters, among them *The Food of the Gods*, *Squirm*, *Grizzly*, and Dino De Laurentiis's

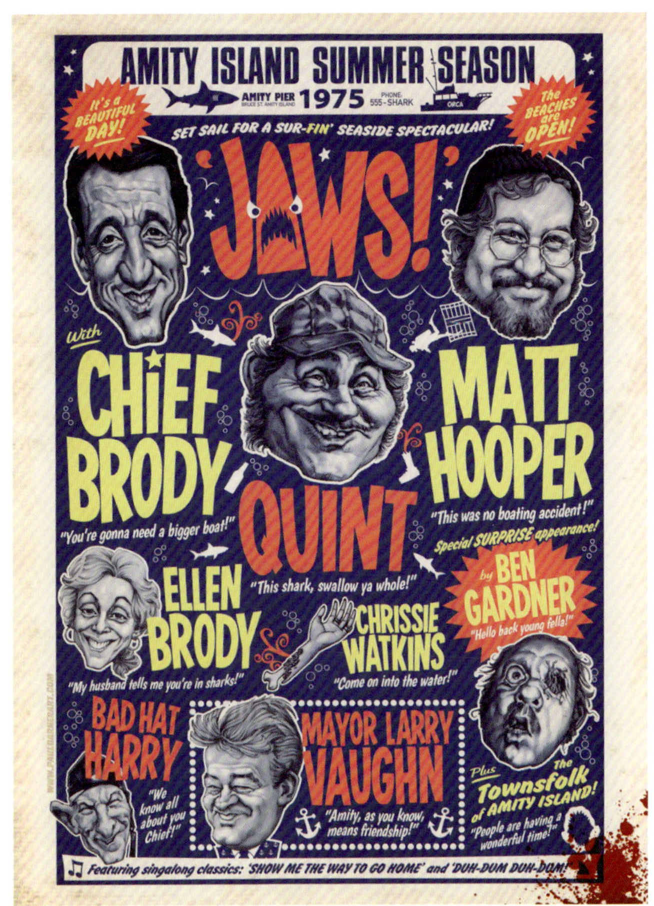

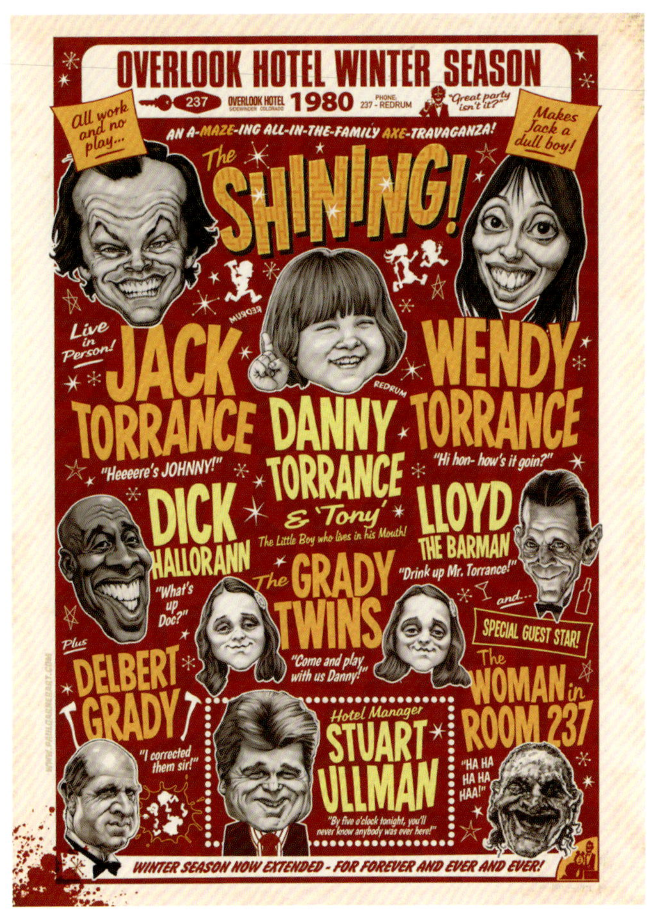

disastrous (but nostalgically remembered) *King Kong* remake (all in 1976), the legitimately batshit-crazy *The Sentinel* (1977), *The Medusa Touch*, *The Manitou*, *The Legacy*, and the superlative Philip Kaufman remake of *Invasion of the Body Snatchers* (all 1978). *Phantasm*, *The Brood*, *The Amityville Horror*, *Prophecy*, John Badham's *Dracula* with Frank Langella, and the instantly iconic *Alien* made 1979 an unforgettable year to eat popcorn and cringe in the dark.

Two films set precedents for subgenres to expand in future decades: Tobe Hooper's *The Texas Chainsaw Massacre* (1974) and George A. Romero's *Dawn of the Dead* (1979). Hooper's film, based loosely on the real-life horror perpetrated by serial killer Ed Gein (as was Hitchcock's 1960 *Psycho*), was the first of a successful string of non-supernatural spree-killing movies that would take full flight with the release of John Carpenter's *Halloween* in 1978 (which does have the slight supernatural twist that the killer never seems to actually die).

"I feel you can make a case that the Manson murders affected the notion of what is a monster," says writer-director Robert Tinnell (*Frankenstein and Me*). "I find it hard to see that the emergence of films like *Texas Chainsaw Massacre* did not owe at least something in their storytelling to the sickening plausibility that the murders injected into the genre. Though I suppose one could say the same of *In Cold Blood*, which predated Manson."

Romero revisited the fertile ground he sowed of zombies versus besieged humans but framed *Dawn of the Dead* as a comment on the cultural shift in America toward rampant consumerism. In this sequel to *Night of the Living Dead*, our heroes are cached inside a suburban shopping mall, holding off an army of the undead as though there were only one gooey sugar roll left at Cinnabon and they weren't about to share it.

The Me Generation were about to take over, as were postpunk and new wave music. Better than any of that was what was to come for horror and monster fans.

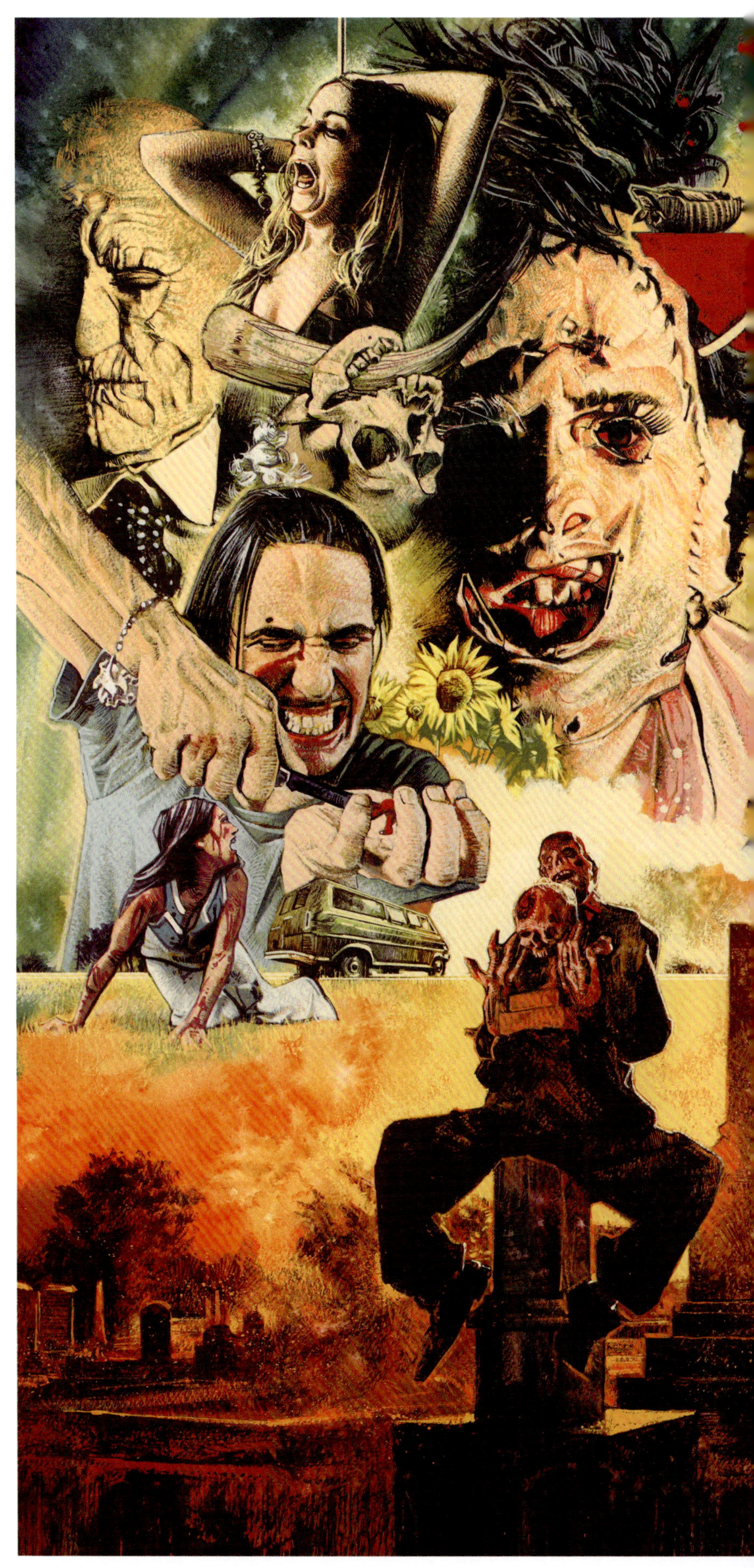

RIGHT *The Texas Chainsaw Massacre* by Graham Humphreys. Poster art for Mondo. Mixed media, 2023.

OPPOSITE *Jessica Harper in "Suspiria"* by Susana "Suspiria" Vilchez. Acrylic on canvas, 2020.

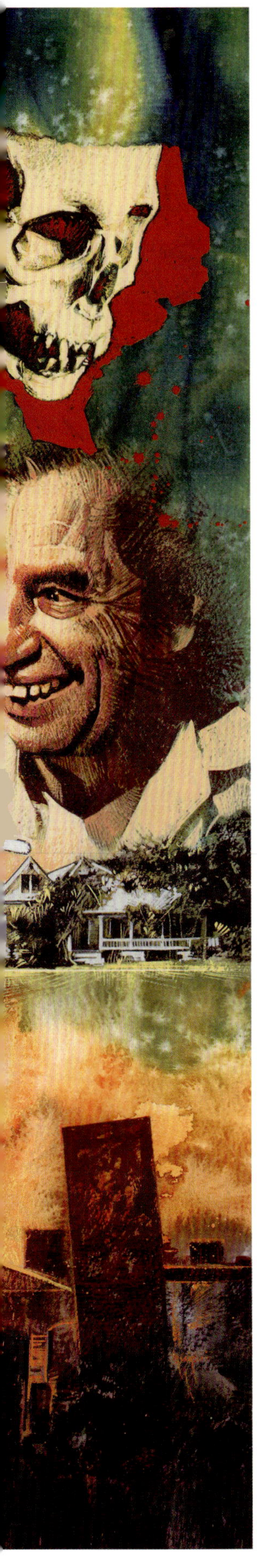

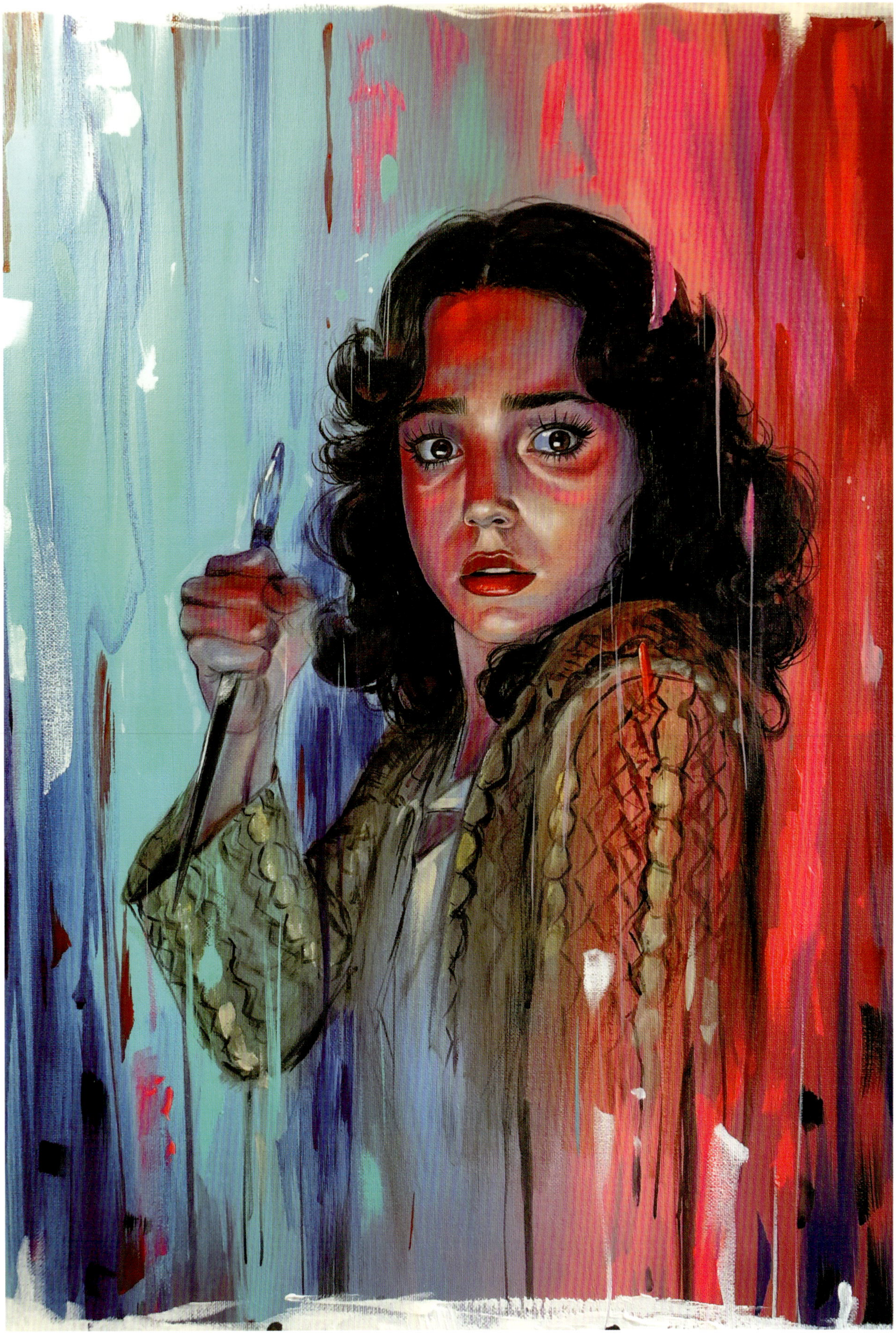

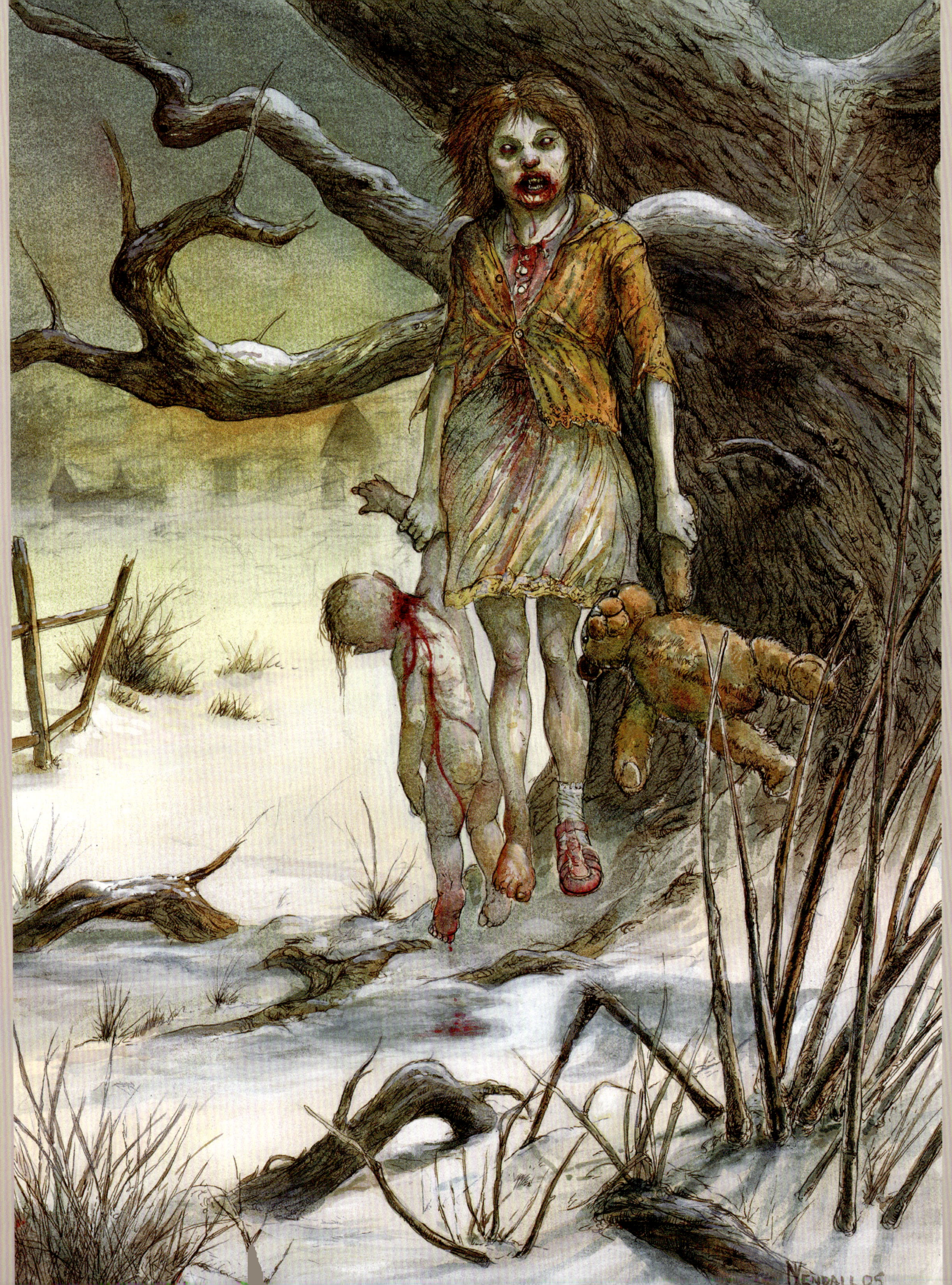

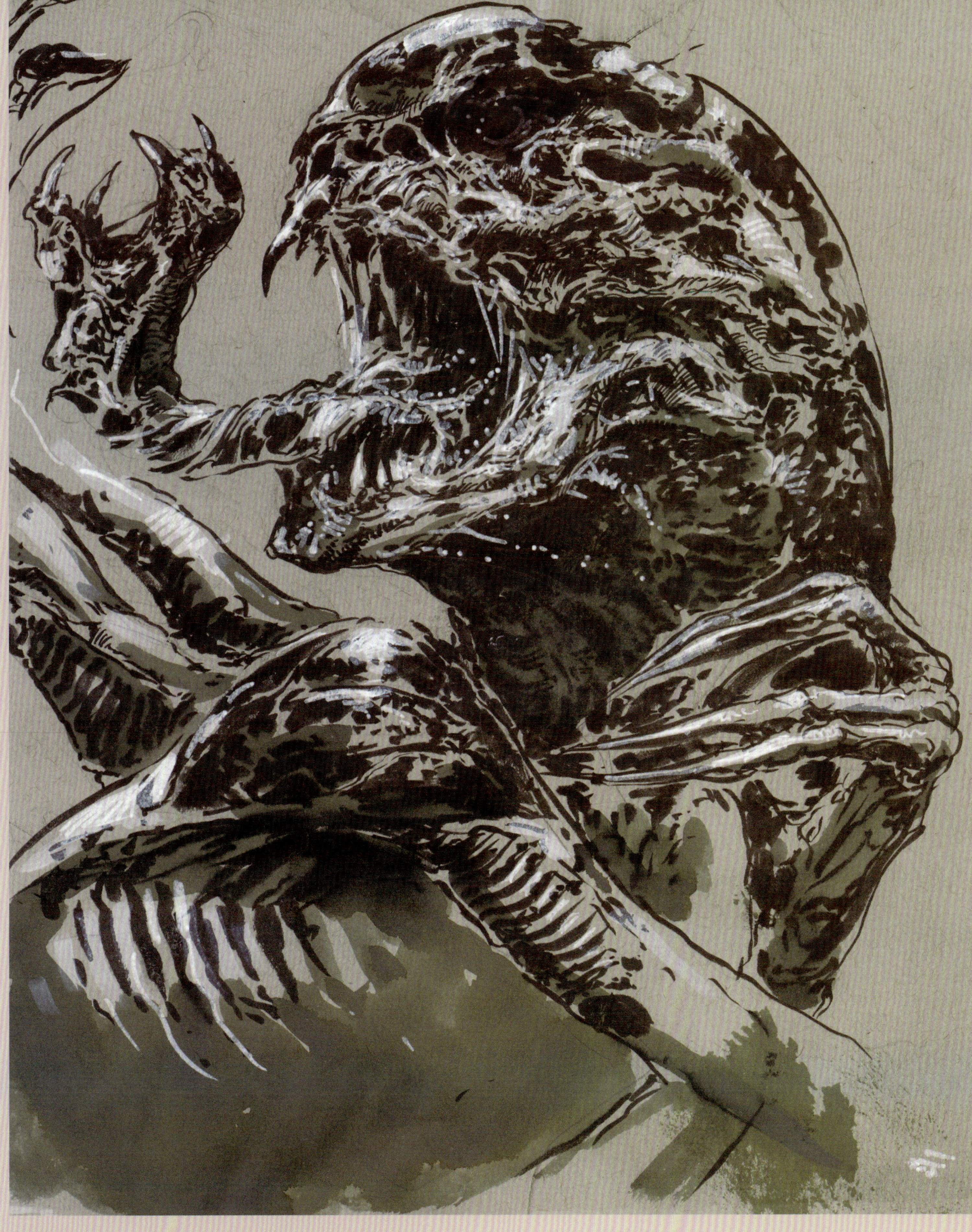

OPPOSITE *One for the Road* by Dave Kendall. Watercolor, 2005.

ABOVE *Alien* sketch by Dave Kendall. Mixed media on toned paper, 2016.

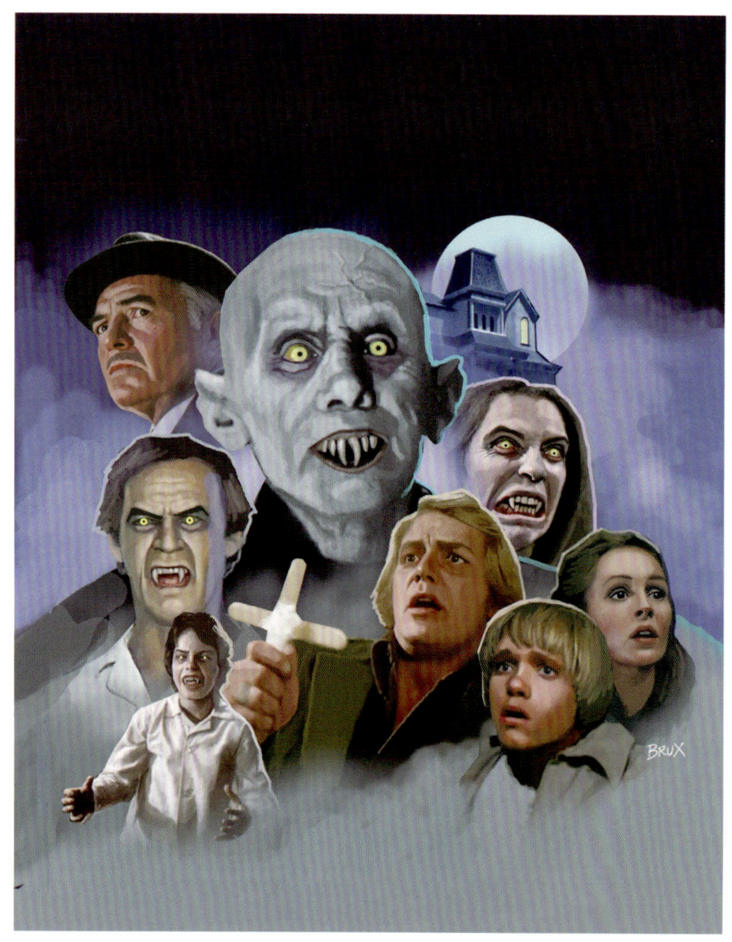

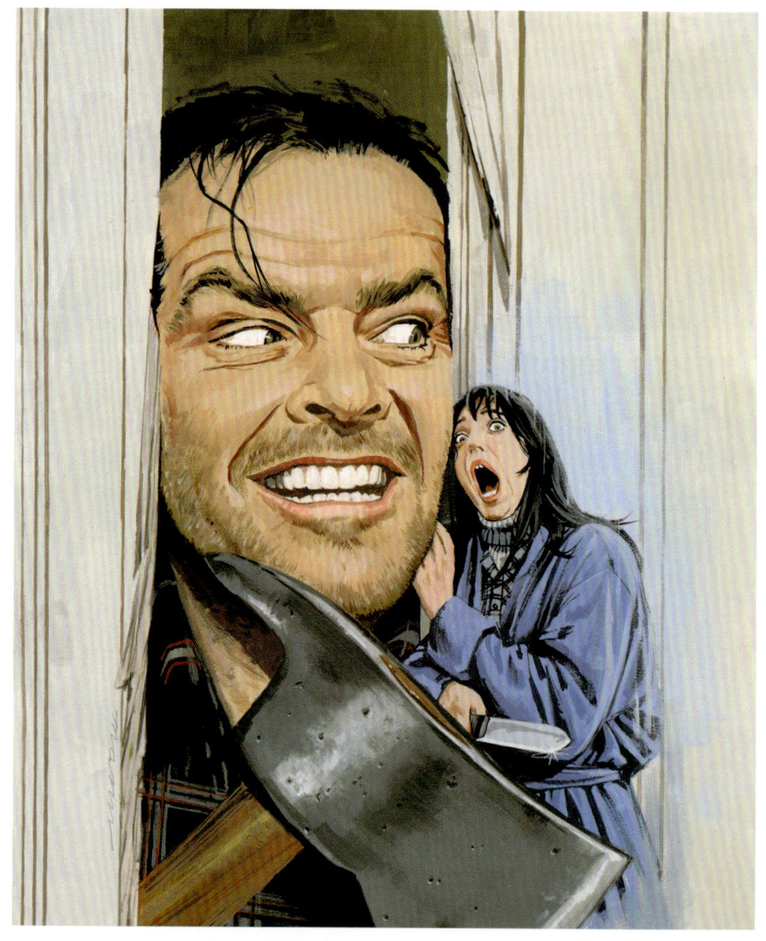

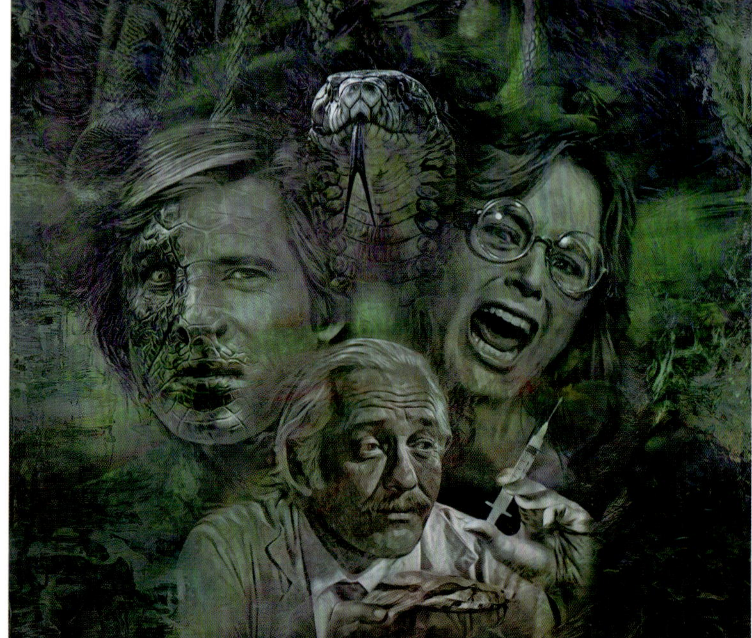

TOP LEFT *'Salem's Lot* by David Brooks (Brux). Cover for *We Belong Dead* magazine #28. Digital, 2023.

TOP RIGHT *Here's Johnny!* by Paul Mann. Acrylic, 2022.

RIGHT *Sssssss* by Frederick Cooper. Blu-ray cover art for Wicked Vision Distribution GmbH. Digital, 2022.

OPPOSITE *Prom Queen* by Joel Robinson. *Carrie* Blu-ray cover art for Scream Factory. Digital, 2016.

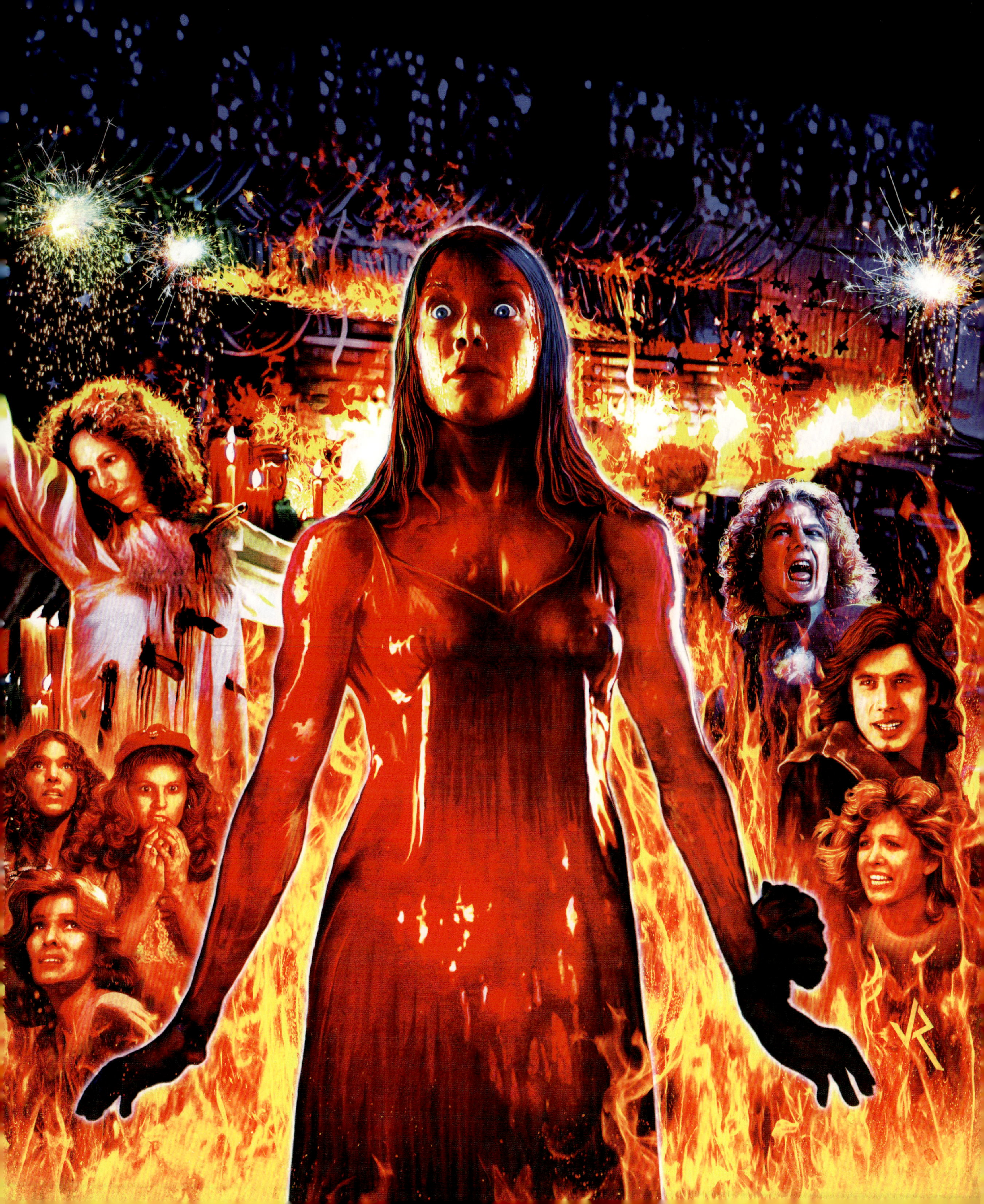

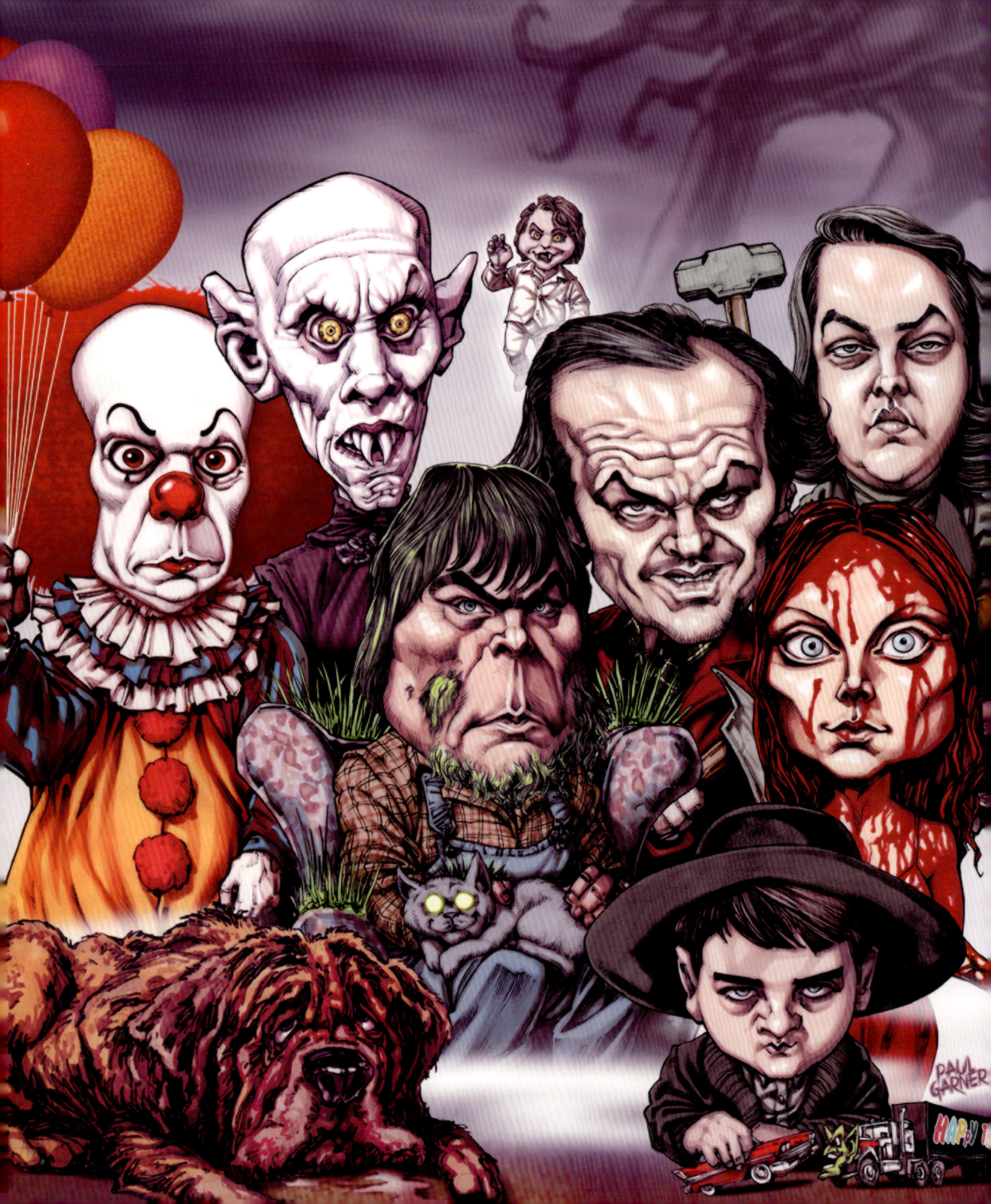
PAUL
GARNER

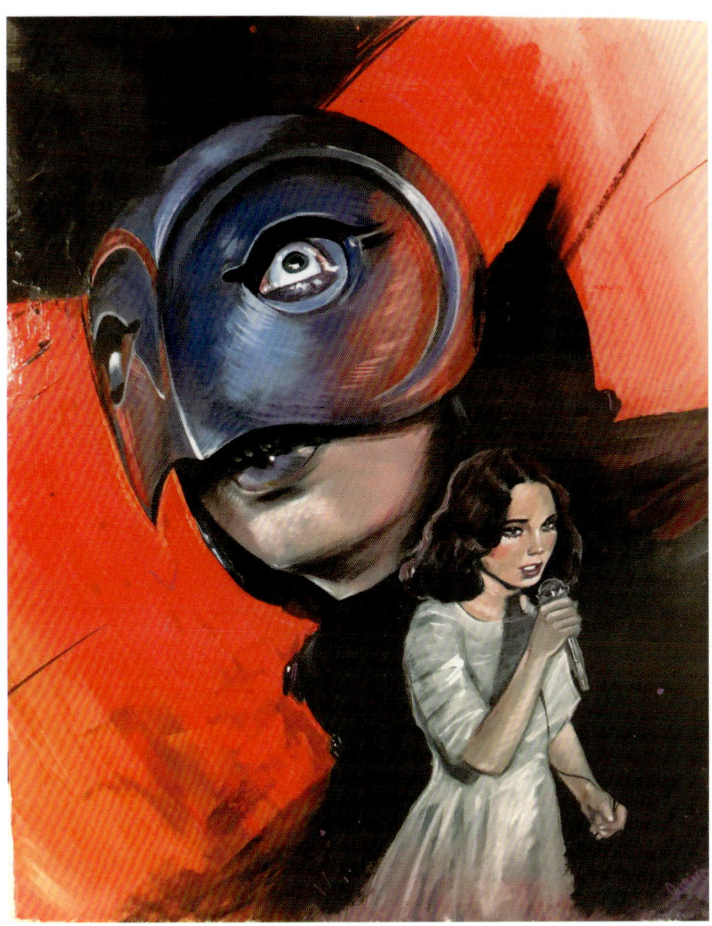

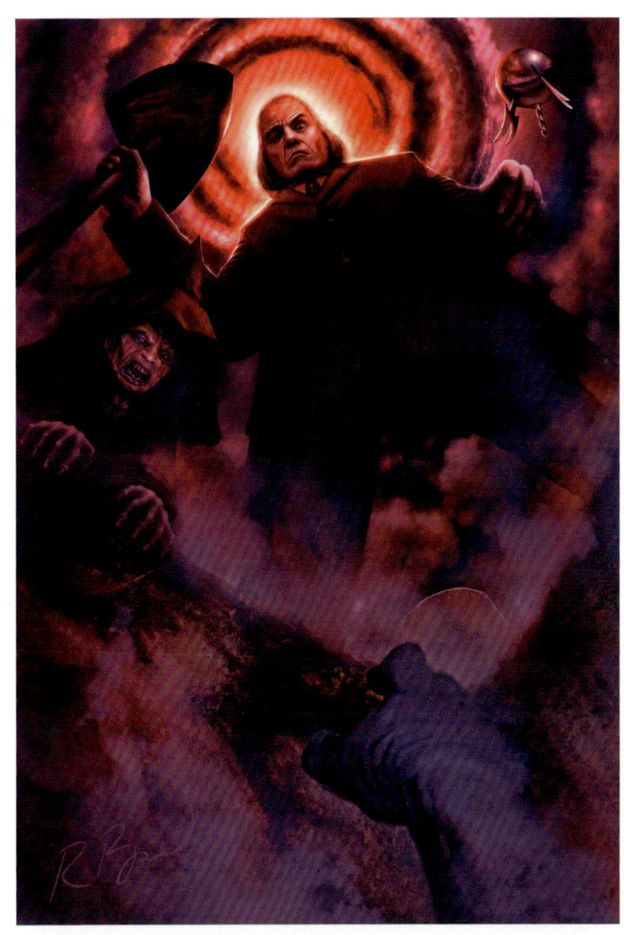

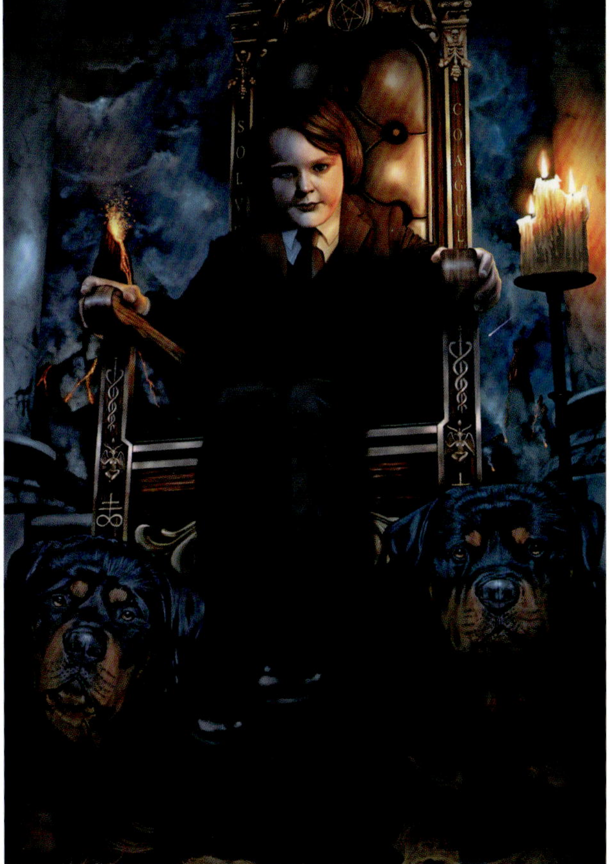

OPPOSITE *Stephen King Film and TV Characters* by Paul Garner. Cover for *HorrorHound* magazine #48. Mixed media, 2014.

TOP LEFT *Phantom of the Paradise* by Susana "Suspiria" Vilchez. Acrylic on wood panel, 2022.

TOP RIGHT *Phantasm* by Rob Birchfield. Acrylic, 2024.

RIGHT *Damien Thorn* by Rob Birchfield. Acrylic, 2022.

John Carpenter's *HALLOWEEN*

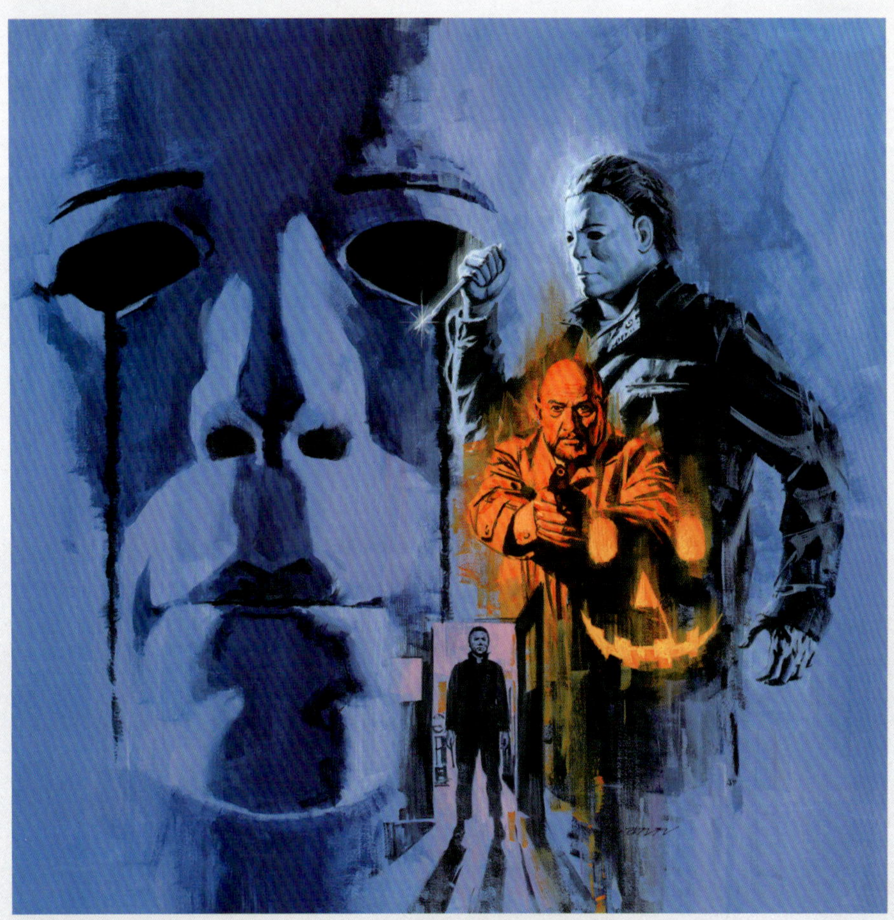

ABOVE *Halloween 2* by Paul Mann. Cover art for Mondo soundtrack LP release. Acrylic, 2019.

OPPOSITE *The Night He Came Home* by Joel Robinson. Mixed media, 2021.

FOLLOWING SPREAD *Halloween 2* by Paul Mann. Gatefold art for Mondo soundtrack LP release. Acrylic, 2019.

Writer John Kenneth Muir's extensive output on horror films in his decade-by-decade survey books has led him to focus on certain fixed points. His book *The Films of John Carpenter* is an essential volume exploring the filmmaker's impact on horror and cinema in general. Here, he provides detail on Carpenter's most well-known work and *Halloween*'s influence on popular culture:

"Following the release of *Assault on Precinct 13* (1976), a young and unemployed John Carpenter met with distributor Irwin Yablans from Compass International Ltd. and listened to a unique pitch for a new horror film. Yablans wanted to make a movie about teenage babysitters under attack from a psycho killer, and he wanted the attacks to occur on a holiday, on Halloween. Carpenter listened with interest and set some ground rules for his participation.

"First, Carpenter sought complete autonomy to direct the film as he pleased. Second, he wanted to compose the film's score himself, and third, the young maverick extracted a promise that no money men would interfere with the final cut of his film—as had happened on *Dark Star* (1975), earlier in Carpenter's career. Yablans agreed to his terms, and with a budget set at $300,000, Carpenter teamed with Debra Hill to write a screenplay in just ten days. The film was shot in a little over three weeks (twenty-two days) under the eye of cinematographer Dean Cundey, and in the process, horror film history was made.

"*Halloween* starred former James Bond villain Donald Pleasence and a relative newcomer to the movie scene, Janet Leigh's daughter: Jamie Lee Curtis. Carpenter's film also highlighted a boogeyman who promptly became a genre icon himself: Michael Myers. Termed the Shape in the film's credits, Michael was presented on-screen in unforgettable fashion, donning a stark, featureless white mask, one modified for the film's production from a William Shatner *Star Trek* mask. This post–Captain Kirk mask was altered not only to remove the flesh coloring but to also feature larger eye holes. The Starfleet officer's trademark sideburns were also trimmed, and the result was visceral. Several times throughout the film, the Shape would appear to materialize out of impenetrable night, his ivory mask the only point of light in the dark.

"Spare and suspenseful, Carpenter's *Halloween* premiered in 1978 and became the highest-grossing independent film of all time, a record it held until 1990, grossing more than $80 million. Carpenter was compared to the master of suspense, Alfred Hitchcock, and the rights to air *Halloween* on TV sold to NBC in 1980 for a whopping $3 million. *Halloween* also ignited the 'slasher movie' trend of the early 1980s. Slasher films set during holiday or other special events included *Friday the 13th*, *Prom Night*, *Mother's Day*, *Christmas Evil*, and *New Year's Evil* (all released in 1980), *Graduation Day* (1981); *My Bloody Valentine* (1981); and so on and so forth. These productions all owed their genesis to Carpenter's original. Over the decades, there have also been six sequels to *Halloween*, two reboots directed by Rob Zombie, and three legacy sequels between 2018 and 2022, starring Jamie Lee Curtis.

"But the *Halloween* mystique—the qualities that render the film relevant and unforgettable over forty-five years later—may result from its unforgettable depiction of two

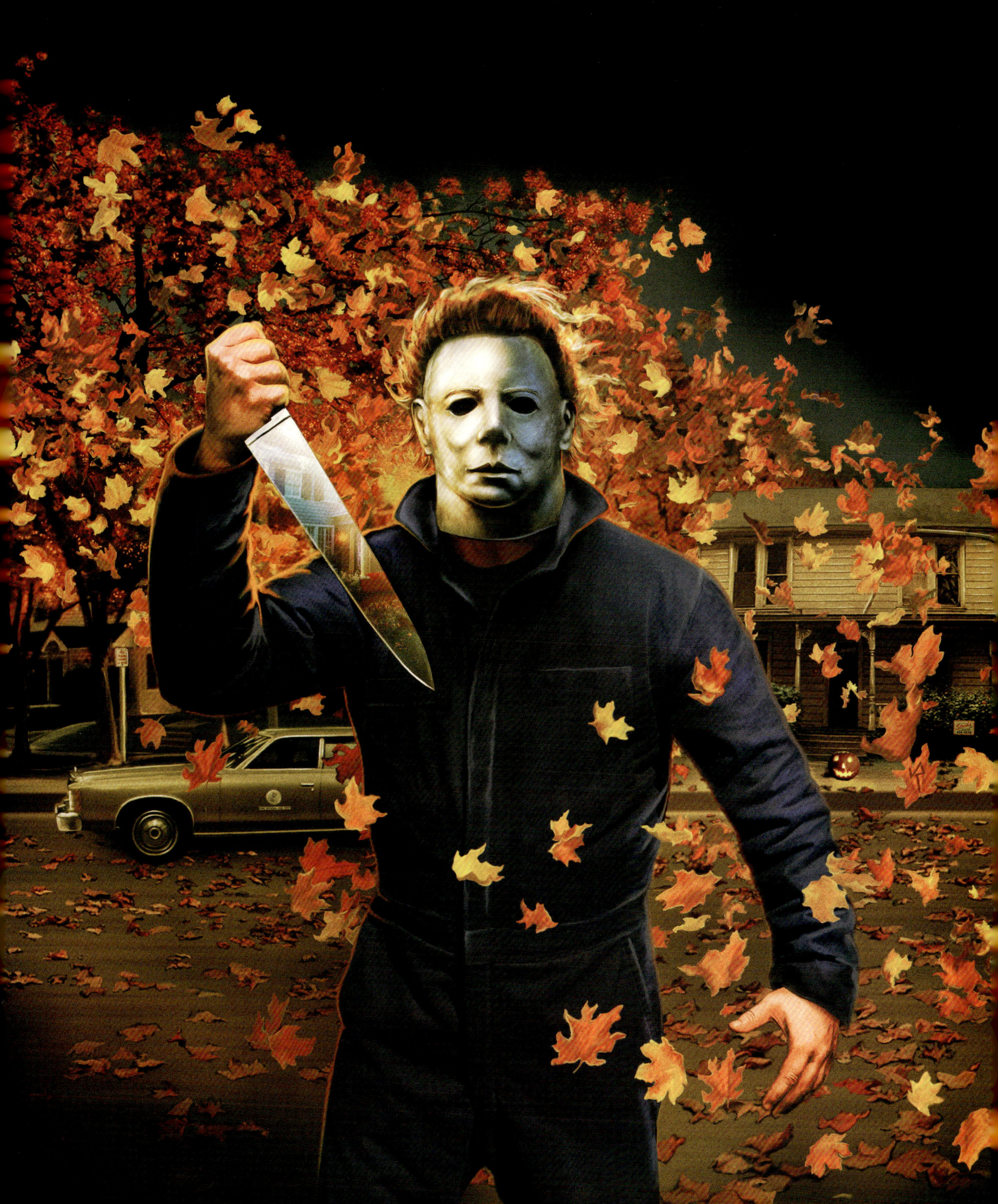

characters in conflict. First, there is Curtis's Laurie Strode, anything but a damsel in distress. Arguably, she is the first 'final girl,' a new genre archetype, and one who projects intelligence and resourcefulness. Jamie Lee Curtis brings the character to life with humanity and empathy, and has revisited the character at various stages of her life (in Laurie's forties and sixties). Laurie is Michael's equal.

"Then there is Carpenter and Hill's the Shape himself. He remains forever an enigma. We don't know why he kills. We don't know what he is, either. He seems more than human in his abilities, and yet, apparently, human in (biological) nature. Myers is thus the ultimate Rorschach test for viewers, since Carpenter cloaks his motivations under that featureless mask. We all see what we want to see. We all understand the Shape as being, simply, the thing that scares us most. As audience members, we gaze intently at the blank, white, visage of the Shape, and recognize that we are missing some crucial aspect of understanding of Michael.

"Michael's true motives—his personality and purpose—seem oddly incomplete, and thus the mask fully reflects our inability to conceptualize the thing that he represents. From this lack of understanding grow the seeds of terror. Why does Michael kill? Is he the boogeyman? What drives him? How does he survive six point-blank bullets? As in life itself, *Halloween* provides no digestible answer to myriad questions about mortality and murder, destiny, choice, and chance. Yet *Halloween* brilliantly provides the attentive viewer intriguing clues about Michael Myers and the things he signifies. Some of these hints seem to conflict, but again, this ambiguity makes the film resonate more powerfully in our minds. *Halloween* permits our imagination to fill in the narrative, explanatory gaps, and terror takes hold. We see reflected in that blank, chilling white mask all the things we fear—all the things we don't understand—about life on this mortal coil.

"Nearly five decades later, we still don't know the real Michael. Is he a physical manifestation of Laurie's id? Is he fate personified, as the famous classroom scene seems to speculate? Is Michael a developmentally arrested kid playing Halloween tricks? Could he be an indictment of our contemporary scientific world and the removal of evil from our discussions of human psychology?

"Pick your poison, or your nightmare, as the case may be, but *Halloween* is immortal because Carpenter created a remarkable boogeyman, a new face of horror. And in nearly fifty years, no one has come close to replicating the terror that the Shape generates."

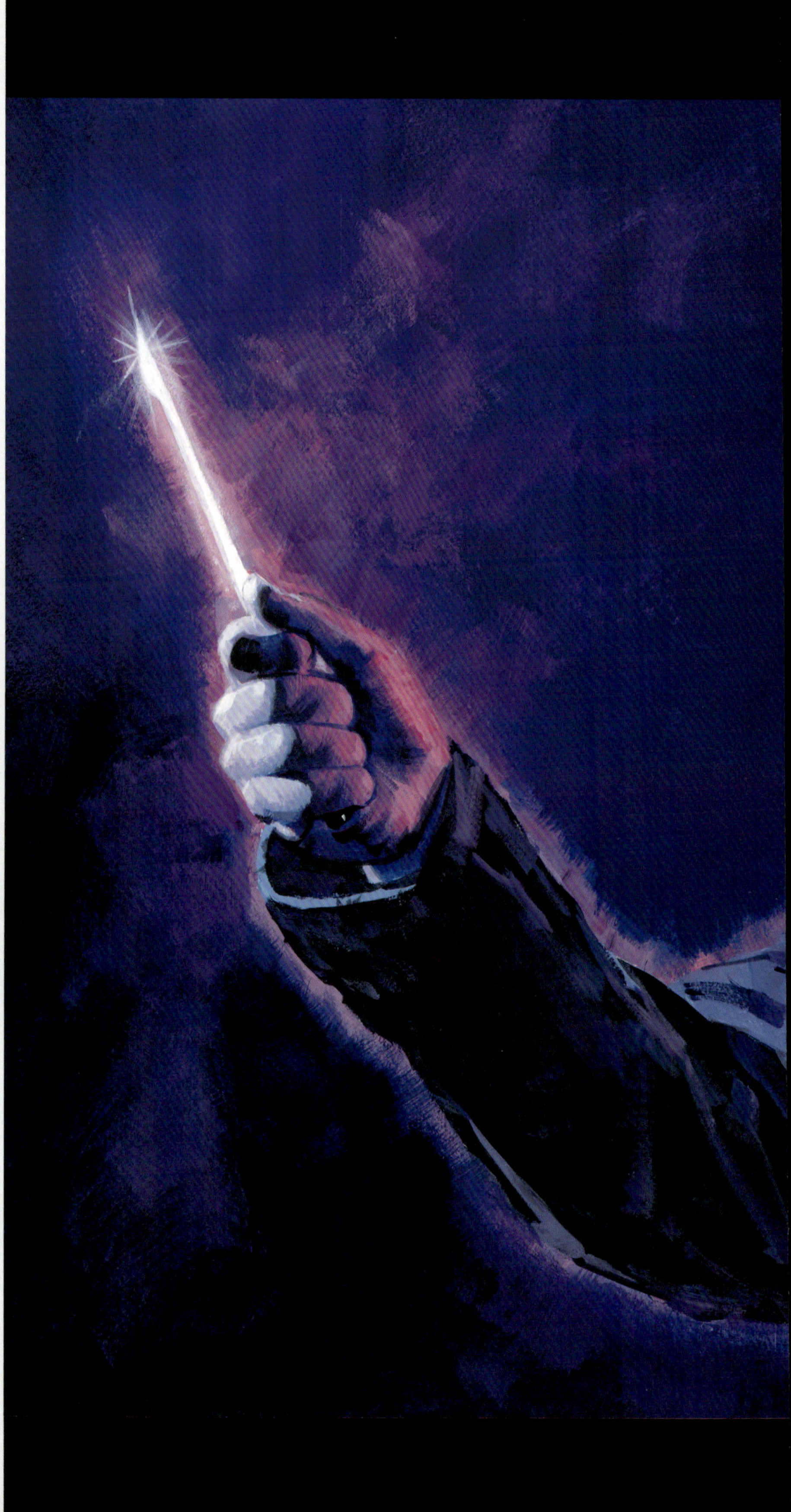

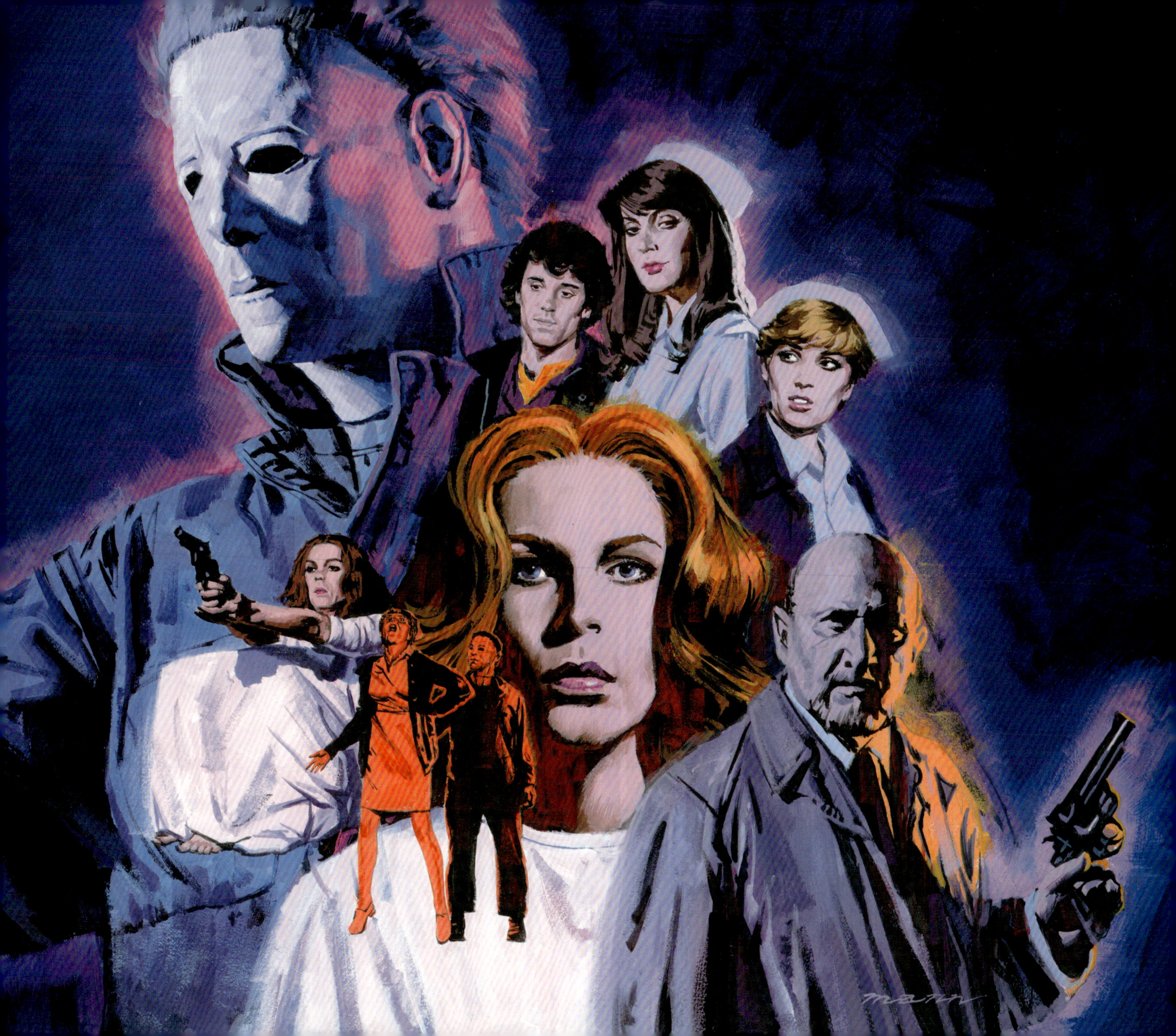

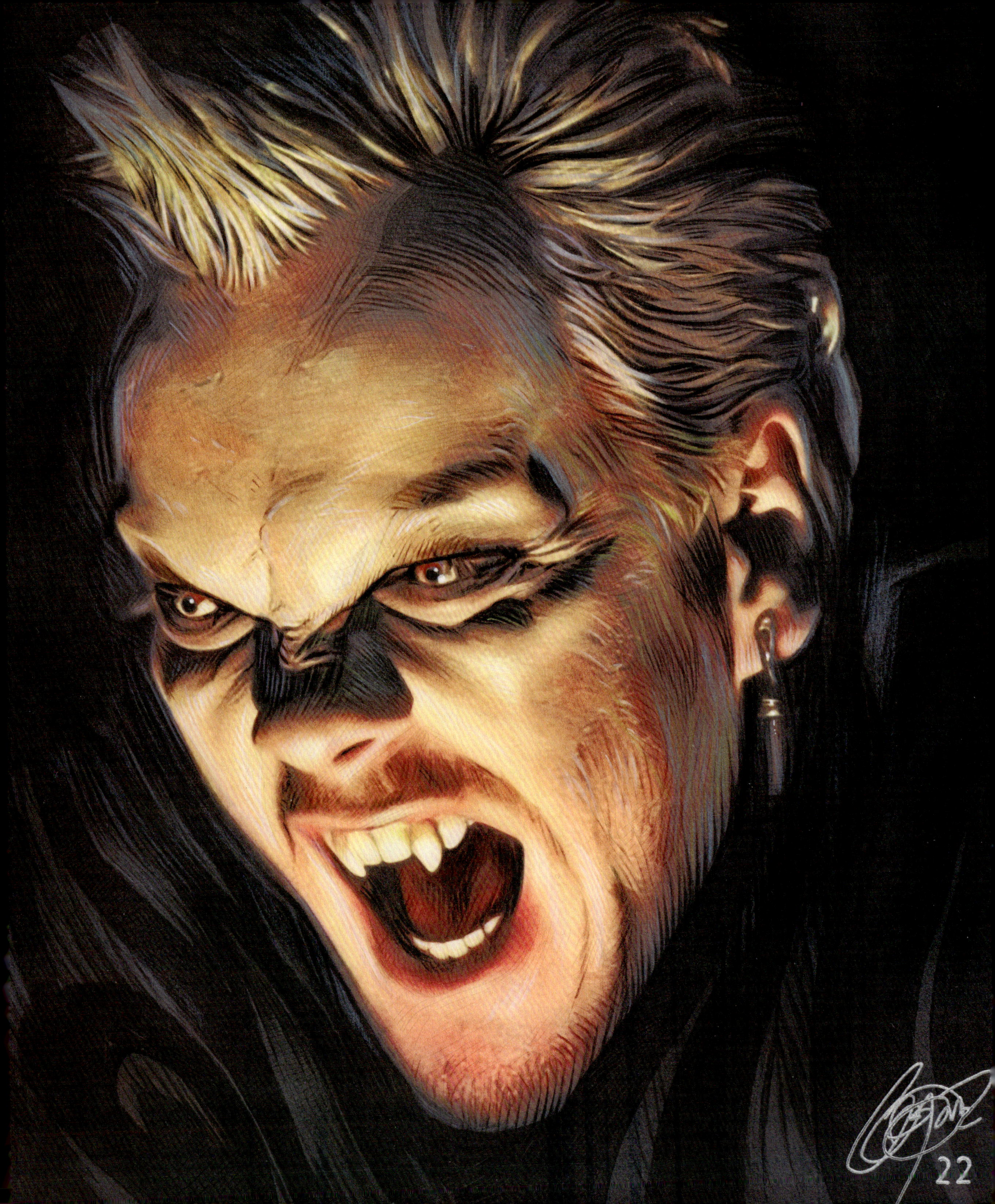
22

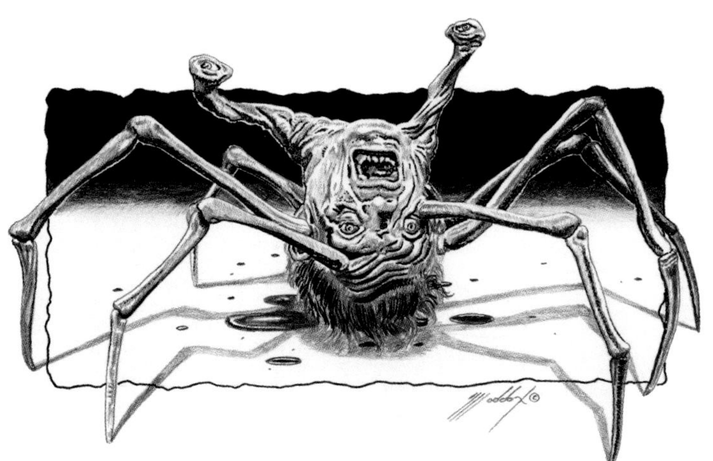

CHAPTER 8

A New Wave of Gods and Monsters (1980–1989)

Text, subtext, and context are present in any creative work, be it visual imagery, literature, theater, film, or music. Text is, of course, the main thrust of any work—the surface vision of the creator that propels the viewer from the beginning of the work to the end. In a work of literature, theater, or film, it's usually described as plot, though plot must contain characterization as well. In music, it would be the melody, and lyrics if there are any. In visual art, text entails composition and subject matter.

Context, as described earlier, is the aggregation of earmarks of the environment into which the work is released—the era, the place, the conterminous developmental events and works upon which it impacts, the cultural temperature surrounding and enveloping it. However, context can also include character and environmental details within the work: In music, it might be harmonic resonance, for instance; in literature or film, it can be character traits, set dressing, or the like. In visual art, it might be color palette, which also plays a part in subtext. In this instance, the work is a metacontext, which can contain its own individual consistent contexts that describe and define the work internally.

Subtext is the part of a work that affects the viewer or listener on a lower level, sometimes a subconscious level. It's that detail that sticks in your mind because you may not fully comprehend the significance or meaning of it without further consideration. In music, a minor key conveys an ominous or melancholy emotional feel, while a major key creates a more normal or exuberant feeling, for instance. Dissonance of rhythm or melody can also create a subtextual message. In theater, film, or literature, subtext can be conveyed via dialogue, imagery, setting, action, or context, and with so many options available, it can float very closely to the surface text if that's the intent of the creator, or it can be buried very deeply.

In visual imagery, subtext can be conveyed by color choice, hidden imagery, or subliminal cues. Sometimes, the creator of a piece is not even aware of subtext that is carried deeply within until it's pointed out by sharp-eyed observers. These secret layers reveal as much about the artist as the work.

Communication via visual imagery can be the most potent way to attract attention. "A good piece of art will grab a new potential fan," says writer and retired *Scarlet Street* and *Famous Monsters of Filmland* editor Jessie Lilley. "A magazine article won't do it—few people read anymore. Blog commentary or podcasts won't do it, unless you happen to read/listen to such things. Music won't do it, because not everyone listens to the same

OPPOSITE *Kiefer Sutherland as David from "The Lost Boys"* by Frederick Cooper. Mixed media, 2022.

ABOVE *Norris–Thing* by Mark Maddox. Colored pencil on coquille board, 2022.

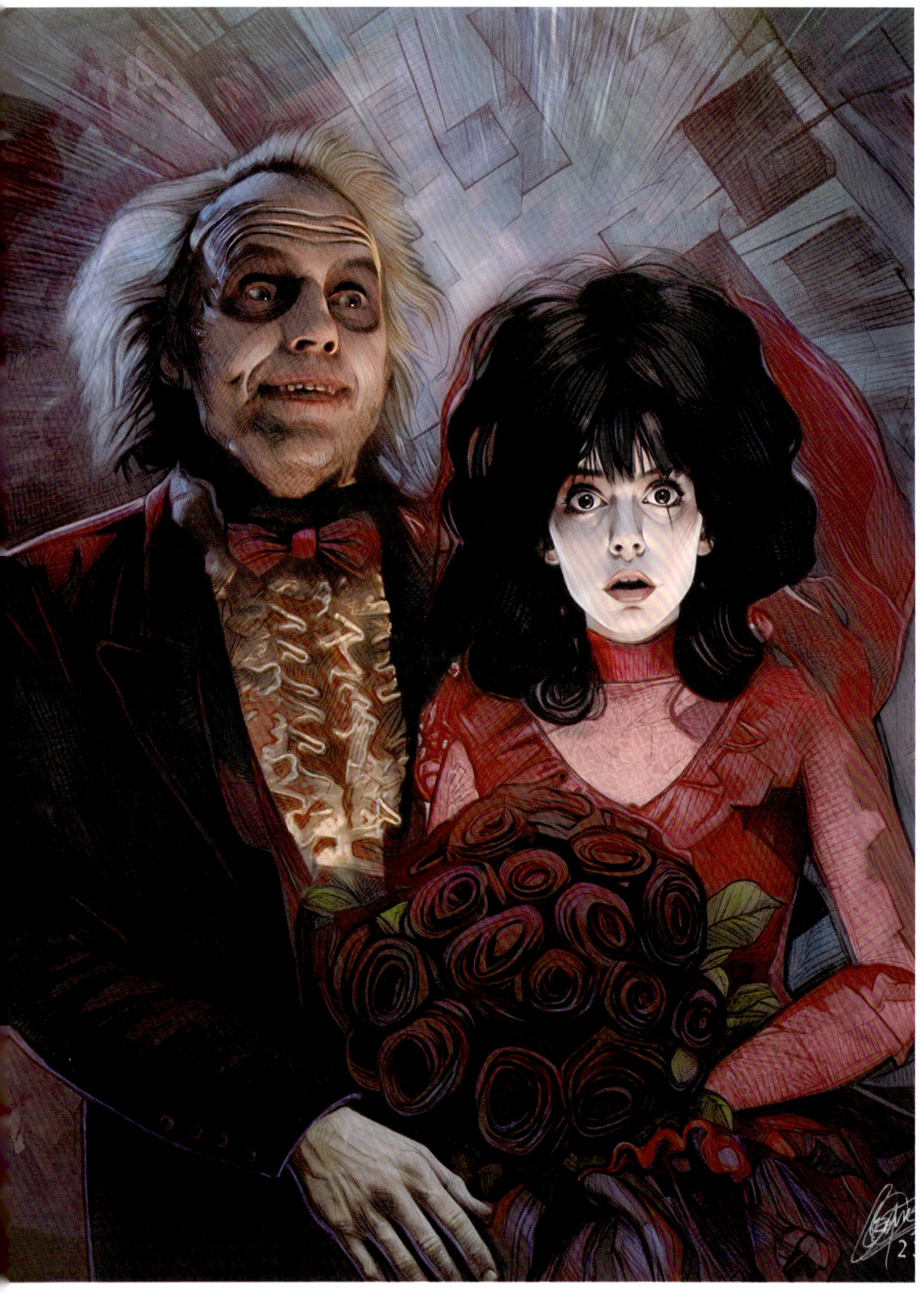

music. But throw a picture out there online somewhere and bang! Instant interest from countless corners. And it must be new, and it must be current, or your target audience won't care. Like the man said, 'A picture is worth a thousand words.'"

As John Carpenter's *Halloween* stayed in theaters racking up unprecedented box office receipts and inspiring a deluge of holiday-themed, spree-killing films, one thing became clear: The 1980s were a bad time to be a horny teenager at camp, prom, on vacation, home alone, babysitting, or, well, anywhere. First, it was Haddonfield on Halloween in 1978. Then, two summers later, it was Camp Crystal Lake, where *Friday the 13th* (1980) kicked off a franchise that continued to spawn sequels until 2009. *Prom Night*, *Mother's Day*, *Christmas Evil*, and *New Year's Evil* followed in 1980, and the trend continued—not that many of the one-off movies were particularly good or entertaining.

Eighties horror films became the predominant media fast food for teenagers once again, and the genre dominated theater marquees. Many classic films—such as Stanley Kubrick's *The Shining;* Ken Russell's *Altered States*; John Carpenter's *The Fog* (all 1980) and *The Thing* (1982), as well as further *Halloween* sequels; David Cronenberg's *Scanners* (1981), *Videodrome*, and *The Dead Zone* (both 1983) and *The Fly* (1986); John Landis's *An American Werewolf in London* (1981); Sam Raimi's *The Evil Dead* (1981) and *Evil Dead II* (1987); and George A. Romero's *Creepshow* (1982) and *Day of the Dead* (1985)—contributed to the growing crowds in neighborhood cineplexes, but one film would reach deep inside and push the horror directly into our dreams: Wes Craven's *A Nightmare on Elm Street* (1984).

Nightmare's monster, dream murderer Freddy Krueger, was the antihero *über alles*—the apex predator of horror film antagonists, targeted directly at teen moviegoers. At first simply menacing, Freddy's demeanor changed into something more cynical, with a pop-culture sensibility, over the life of the franchise that resulted from the success of the first film. He became a mockingbird for the youth culture he set upon to destroy, and eventually a parody of himself in later sequels. The life cycle of Freddy Krueger encapsulates the maturation of a generation of viewers of the original film. He even had his own syndicated television series for two years. Eventually, that generation grew tired of his antics and the films ended, but his impact on the genre lasts.

Bands such as Bauhaus, the Misfits, and the Damned solidified the horror elements of a disparate group of rock acts into what became identified as the goth music scene. The Cult, Siouxsie and the Banshees, and Sisters of Mercy helped fill out the movement's ranks, along with many others.

On the monster scene, Ray Harryhausen's *Clash of the Titans* (1981) would be his final film. The aging animator was forced to hire assistants for the first time in his career to help meet the film's postproduction deadline,

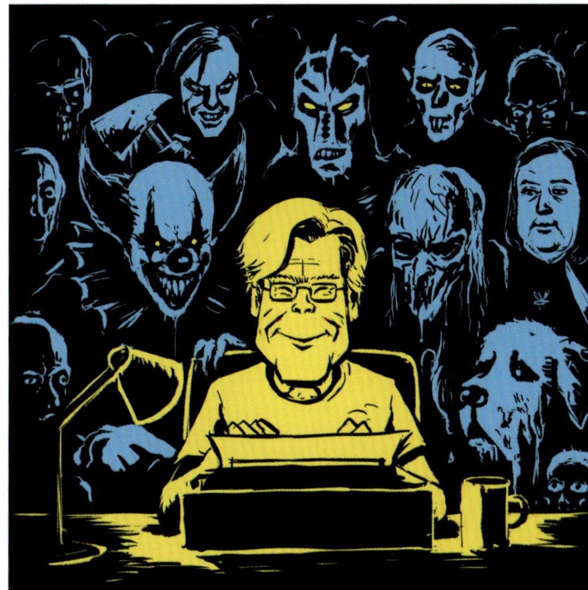

and Ray decided he'd had enough. Jim Henson's *The Dark Crystal* (1982) and Joe Dante's *Gremlins* (1984) set a new high bar for puppetry in creature films, augmented by Henson's *Labyrinth* in 1986.

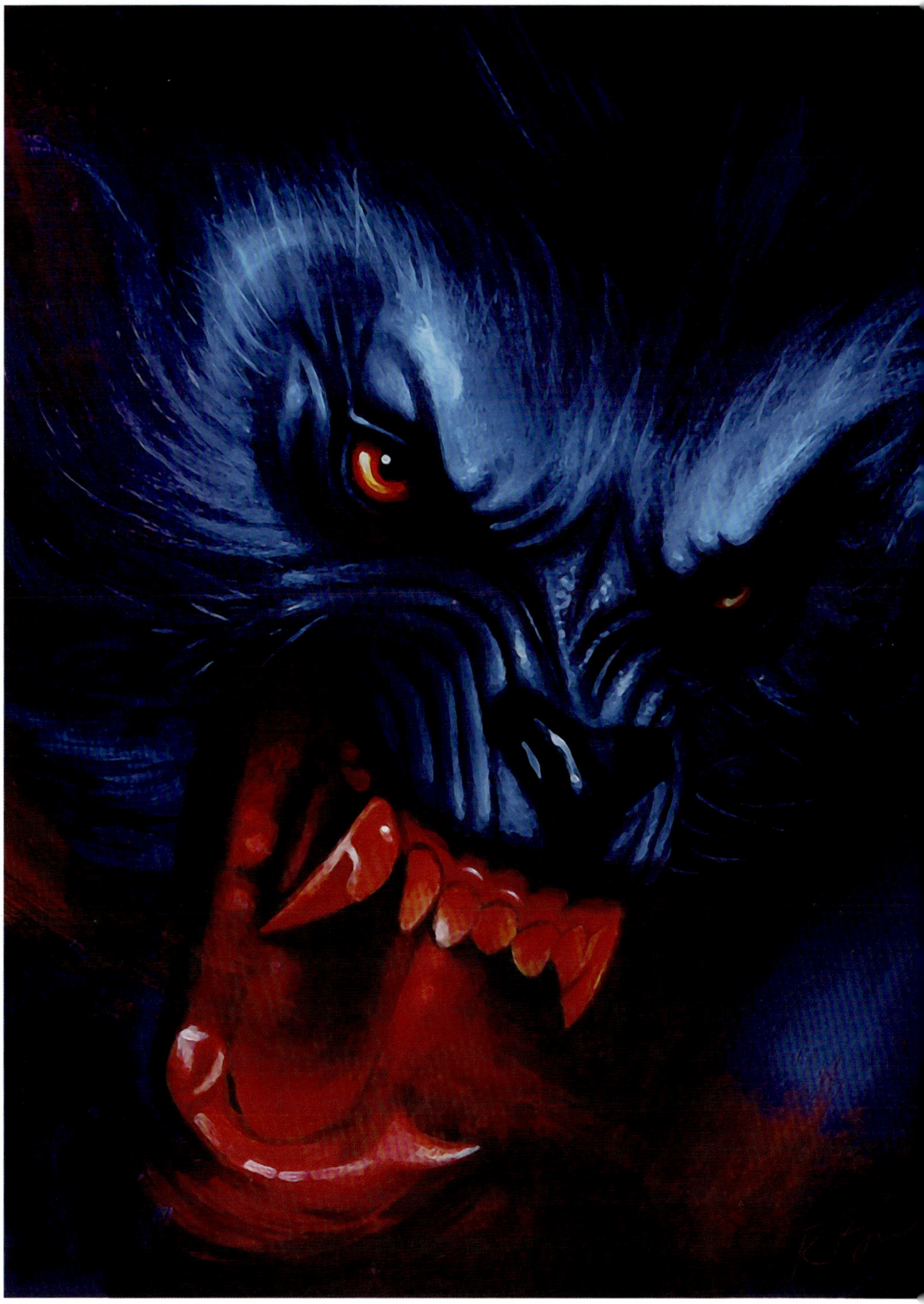

Other monster standouts include Dante's *The Howling* (1981), Toho Studios' *The Return of Godzilla* (aka *Godzilla 1985* in an edited US cut), *Predator* (1987), Fred Dekker's *The Monster Squad* (1987)—aimed right at the heart of the Monster Kid generation—Clive Barker's *Hellraiser* (1987, kicking off another future franchise that would pay sequel dividends for more than a decade), Stan Winston's *Pumpkinhead* (1988), John Carpenter's *They Live* (1988), and *Godzilla vs. Biollante* (1989).

Artist Daryl Joyce has fond memories of seeing David Cronenberg's Academy Award–winning remake of a classic in the theater when it opened. "I saw *The Fly* in '86 at the Odeon Leicester Square, London, and it's the only film I've seen where the audience stood up and applauded as the credits rolled," Joyce recalls. "I love the fact that some of these films are so enduring that artists have made personal interpretations of some scenes that never made the final cut of film, possibly being too graphic for film, but adding a lot as art."

On British television, *Hammer House of Horror* (1980) was the venerable studio's last-gasp grasp for relevancy in a post-gothic horror landscape, and *Darkroom* (1981–82) was a return to the sort of storytelling Roald Dahl's *Tales of the Unexpected* purveyed so well a decade earlier. The '80s also saw stateside revivals of *The Twilight Zone* (1985–89)—very good—and *Alfred Hitchcock Presents* (1985–89)—somewhat less so,

OPPOSITE *Beetlejuice!* by Frederick Cooper. Mixed media, 2023.

TOP LEFT *Stephen King* by Krent Able. Illustration for unpublished book. Mixed media, 2023.

TOP RIGHT *An American Werewolf in London* by Rob Birchfield. Acrylic on illustration board, 2022.

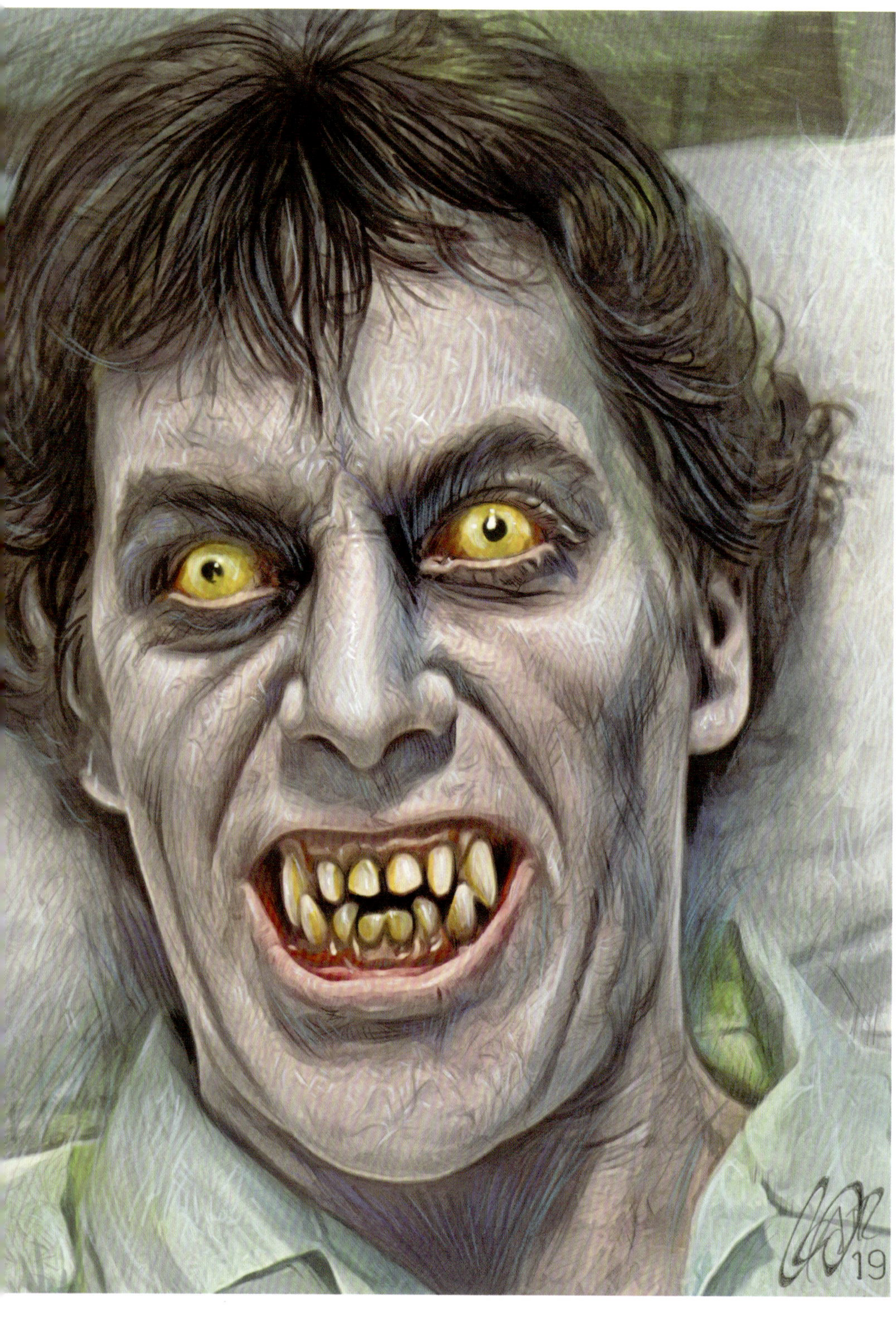

ABOVE *David Kessler, Werewolf* by Frederick Cooper. Mixed media, 2019.

OPPOSITE *Killer Klowns* by Nick Percival. Mixed media, 2000.

but still very watchable. Syndicated anthology series like *Tales from the Darkside* (1983–88) and *Monsters* (1988–91) were a great way to kill a half-hour. On HBO, an adaptation of the old EC comic book *Tales from the Crypt* went the distance from 1989 through 1996. Take that, Senator Kefauver!

Bernie Wrightson's sublime illustrated version of Mary Shelley's *Frankenstein*, with its precise black-and-white line work, was released in hardcover by Marvel Comics in 1983, the culmination of more than a decade of work by the artist. Wrightson explained to Gary Groth in *The Comics Journal* just before release, "I'm kind of aping [early twentieth-century illustrator] Franklin Booth on this thing. I'm trying to do it all with single lines varying in thickness, to kind of imitate an old steel engraving or woodcut. So, there's not a lot of cross-hatching. There's not a lot of that kind of pen texture. So . . . let's call it an engraving technique, with a pen. . . . After you've done twenty or thirty pictures, you really start getting the hang of what a line this thick is going to do when you narrow it down across the space of seven inches to a hairline. And then lay another line exactly like it, next to it. And the next one is a little bit thinner so you can get a gradation." The result is an unbelievably lush brushscape of contrasting imagery that has become a modern classic and the definitive visual interpretation of Shelley's classic tale. Wrightson's illustrations capture the pathos of the monster so effectively that it's impossible to remain unmoved. When the artist died in 2017 after a battle with brain cancer, film director Guillermo del Toro, self-admittedly influenced greatly by Wrightson's work, posted on his Twitter feed that he would be observing twenty-four hours of silence in tribute. "As it comes to all of us, the end came for the greatest that ever lived: Bernie Wrightson. My North dark star of youth. A master."

For screenwriter and producer Mark Protosevich (*I Am Legend* in 2007, and the 2024 series *Sugar*), these were formative times. "In my teens and early twenties, I was greatly influenced by the films of George Romero, Wes Craven, and especially David Cronenberg. I consider them the Three Greats," he says. "I fell in love with horror as a child and I still love it. I'll always love it. Horror gives creative people the opportunity to explore disturbing, challenging, and provocative ideas within a commercially viable framework."

Though quality may have been spotty on the smorgasbord of '80s horror movie offerings, its quantity was lavish and immense. By the end of the decade, over one thousand horror and monster films were released in theaters and on television—a staggering number by any measure. Our psyches needed that comfort food of watching bad people meet good monsters and get their comeuppance.

But as a new century was looming, a new era of uncertainty was on the horizon.

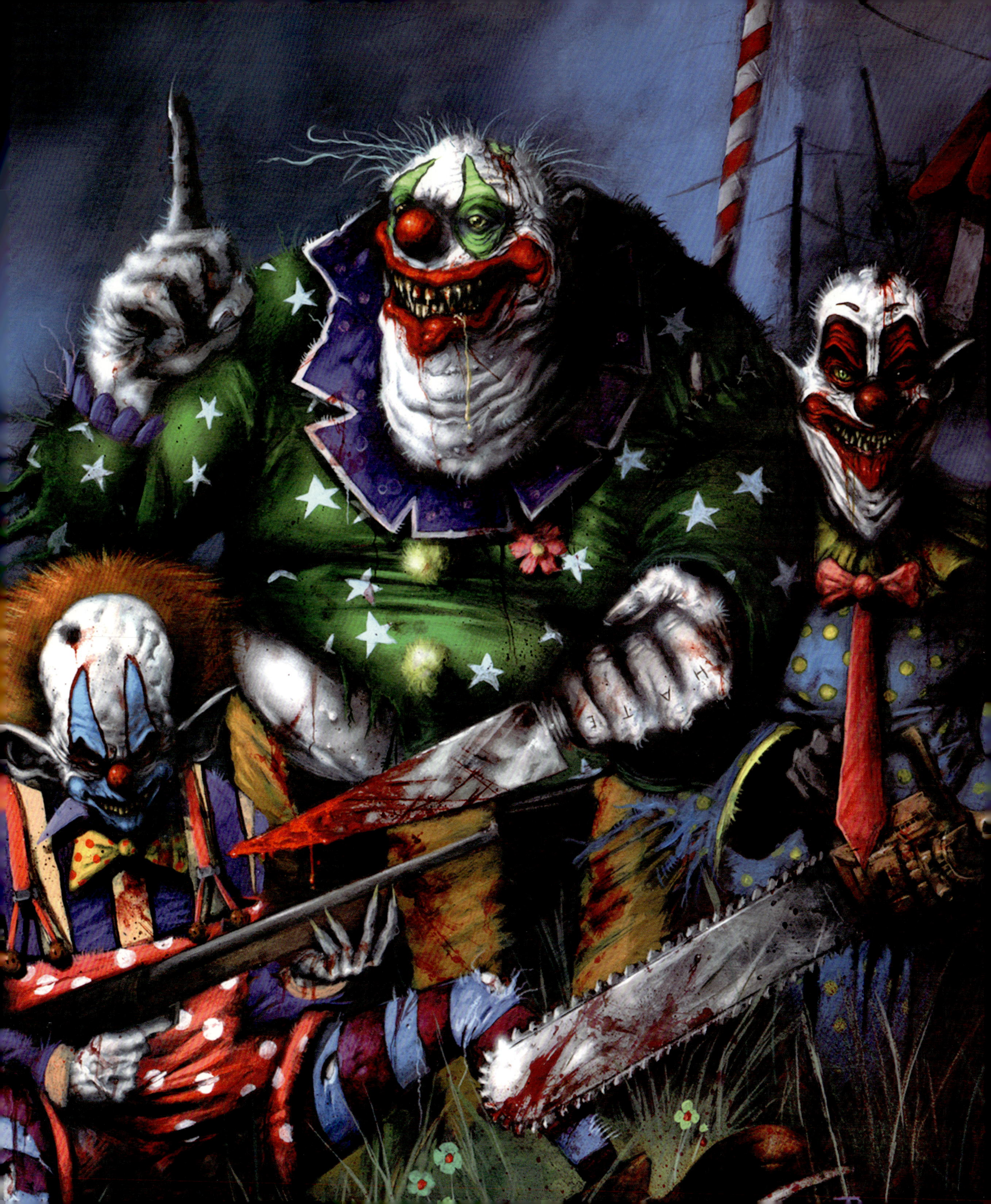
HATE

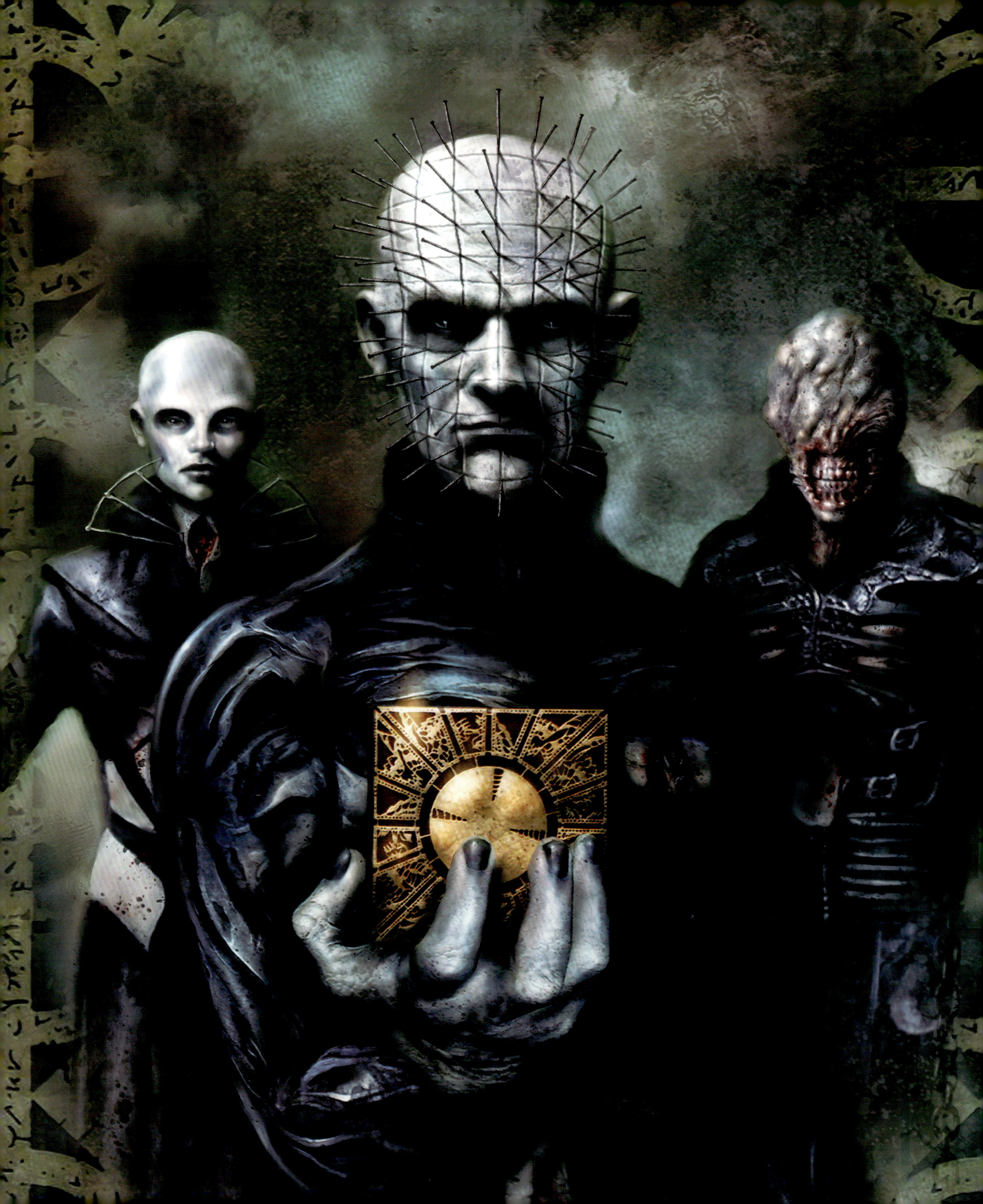

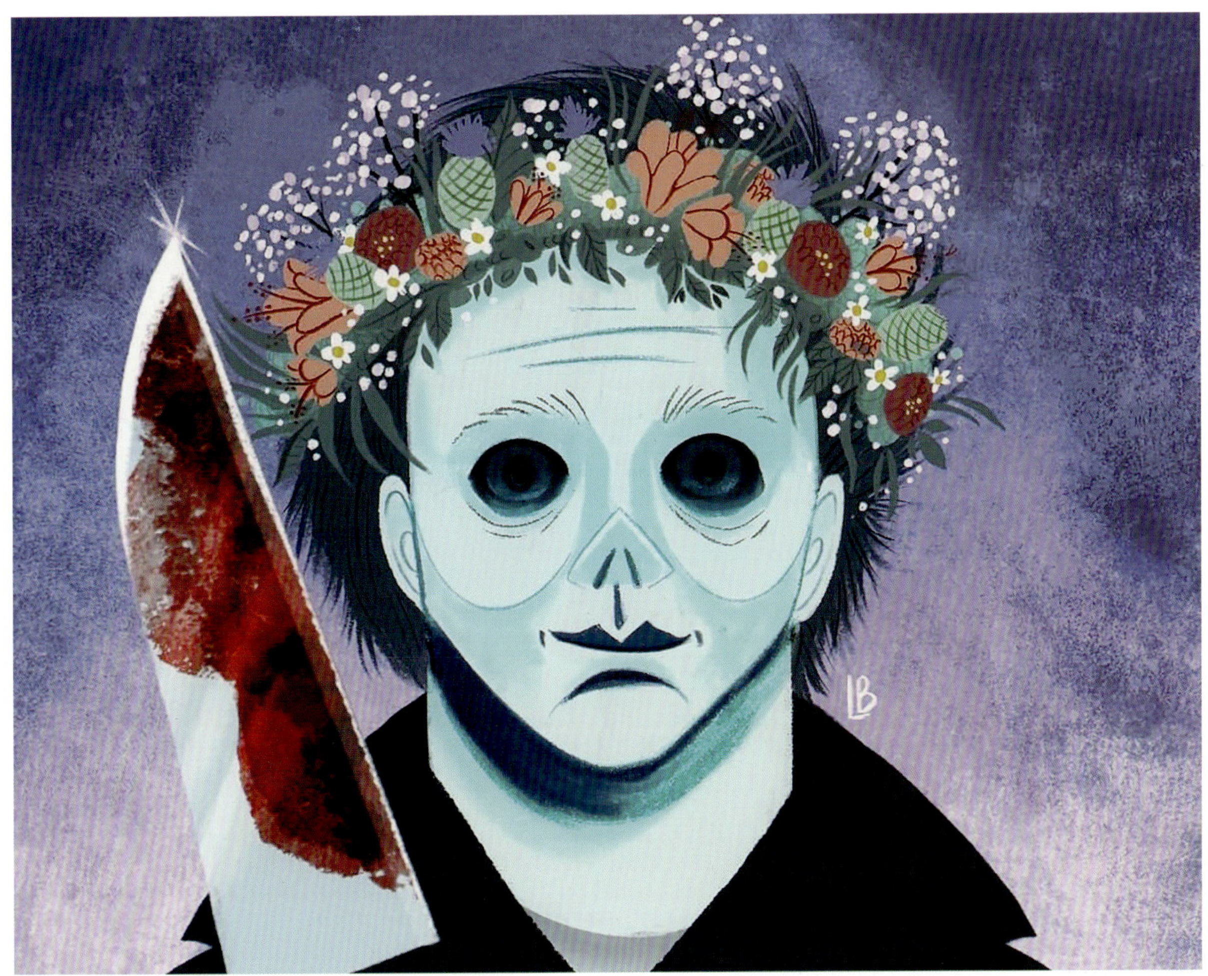

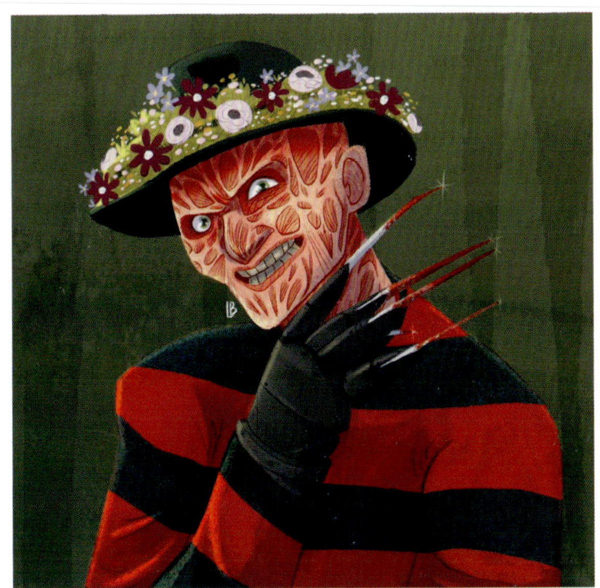

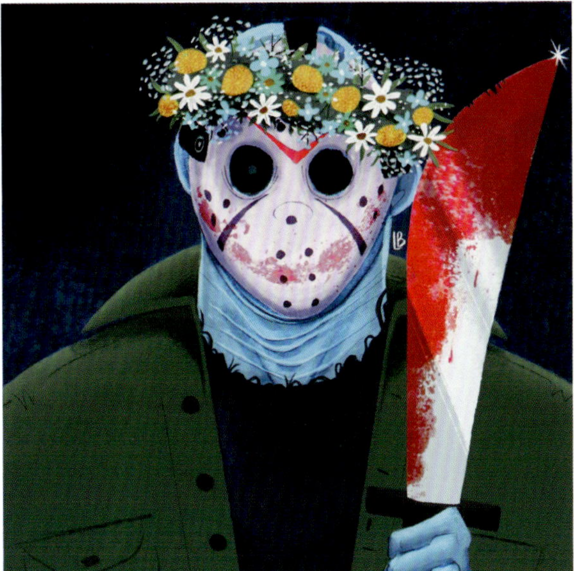

OPPOSITE *Such Sights to Show You* by Nick Percival. Acrylic, 2014.

THIS PAGE A trio of flowery slashers by Lacie Barker. Clockwise: *Michael Myers*, digital, 2020; *Jason Vorhees*, digital, 2021; *Freddie Krueger*, digital, 2020.

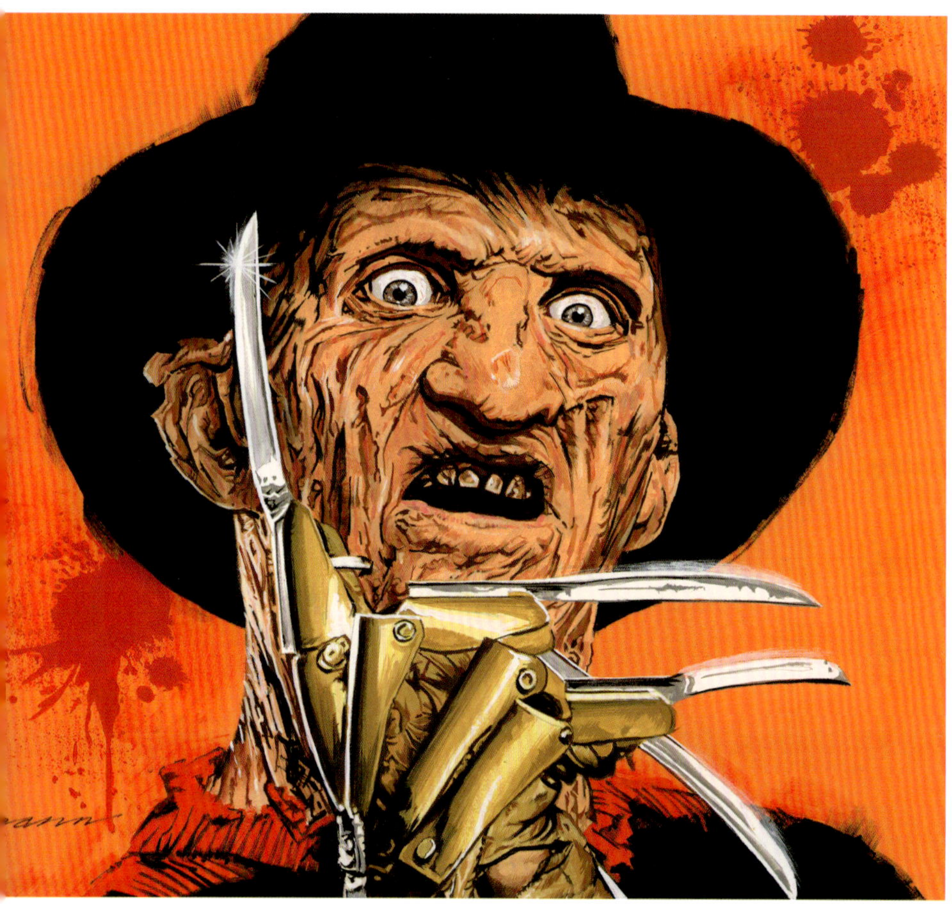

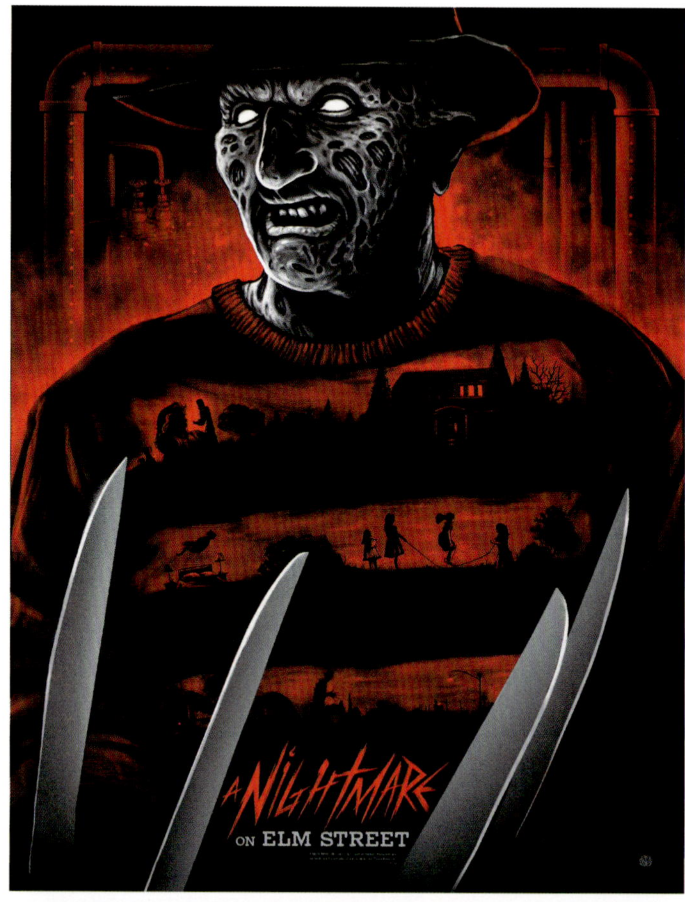

TOP LEFT *Nightmare Man* by Paul Mann. Acrylic, 2022.

TOP RIGHT *A Nightmare on Elm Street* by "Ghoulish" Gary Pullin. Mondo Poster Art. Digital, 2015.

RIGHT *A Nightmare on Elm Street 2: Freddy's Revenge* by Susana "Suspiria" Vilchez. Acrylic, 2023.

OPPOSITE *Freddy Krueger* by Mitch O'Connell. Pen and ink with digital color, 2014.

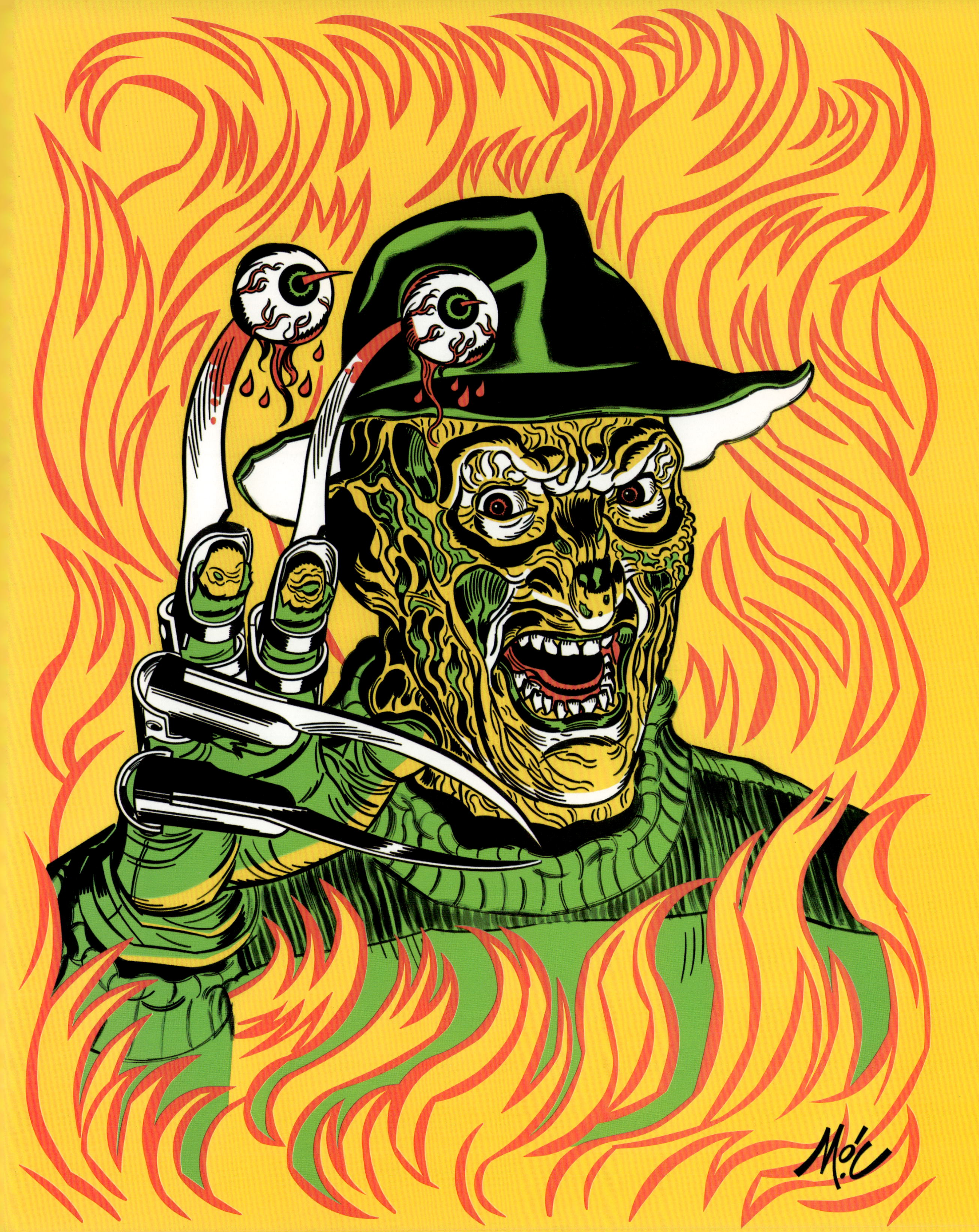

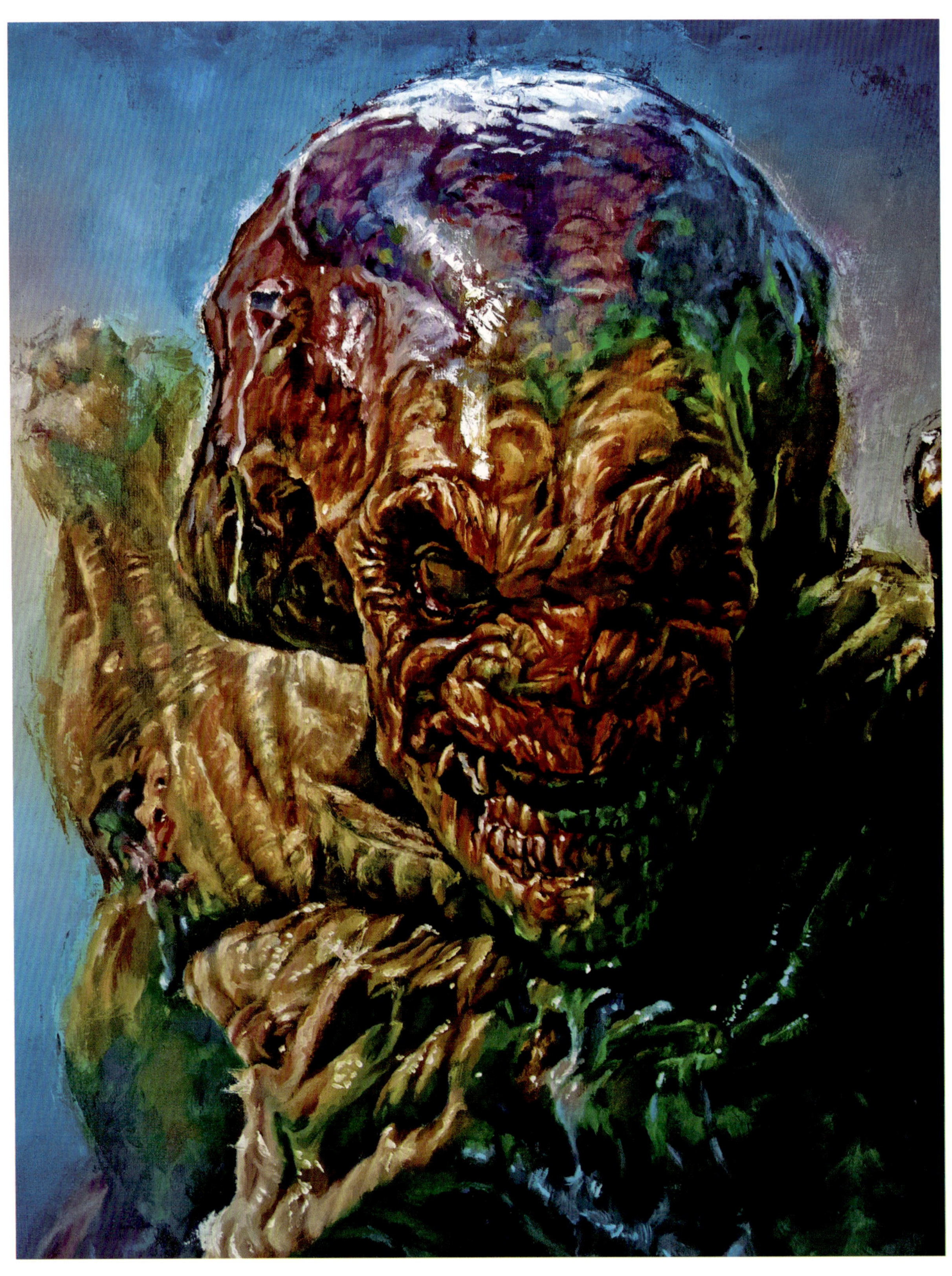

ABOVE *Pumpkinhead* by Cecil Porter. Oil on board, 2024.

OPPOSITE *Godzilla 1984* by Rob Birchfield. Cover art for *Gnarly Magazine* #6. Acrylic, 2018.

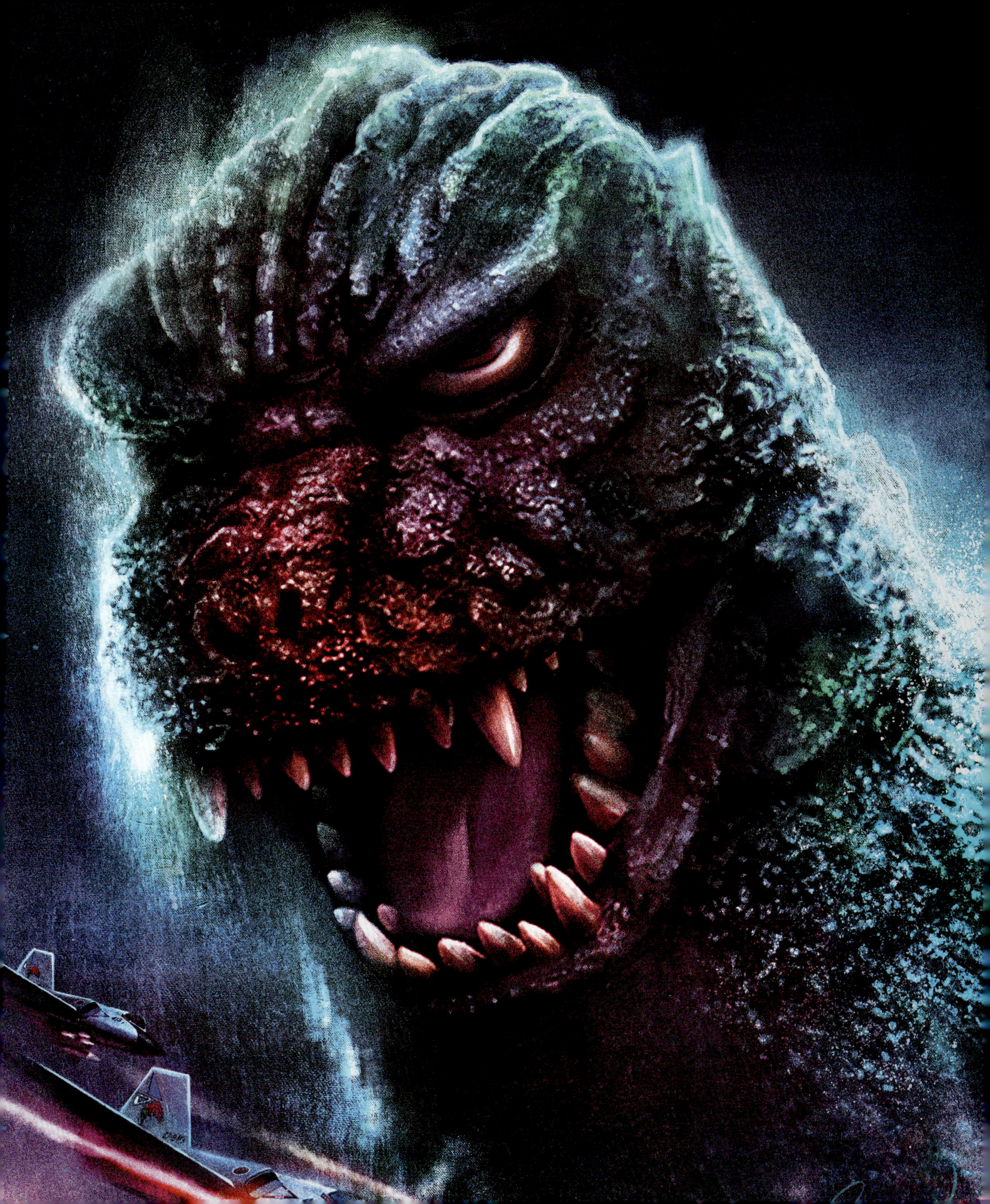

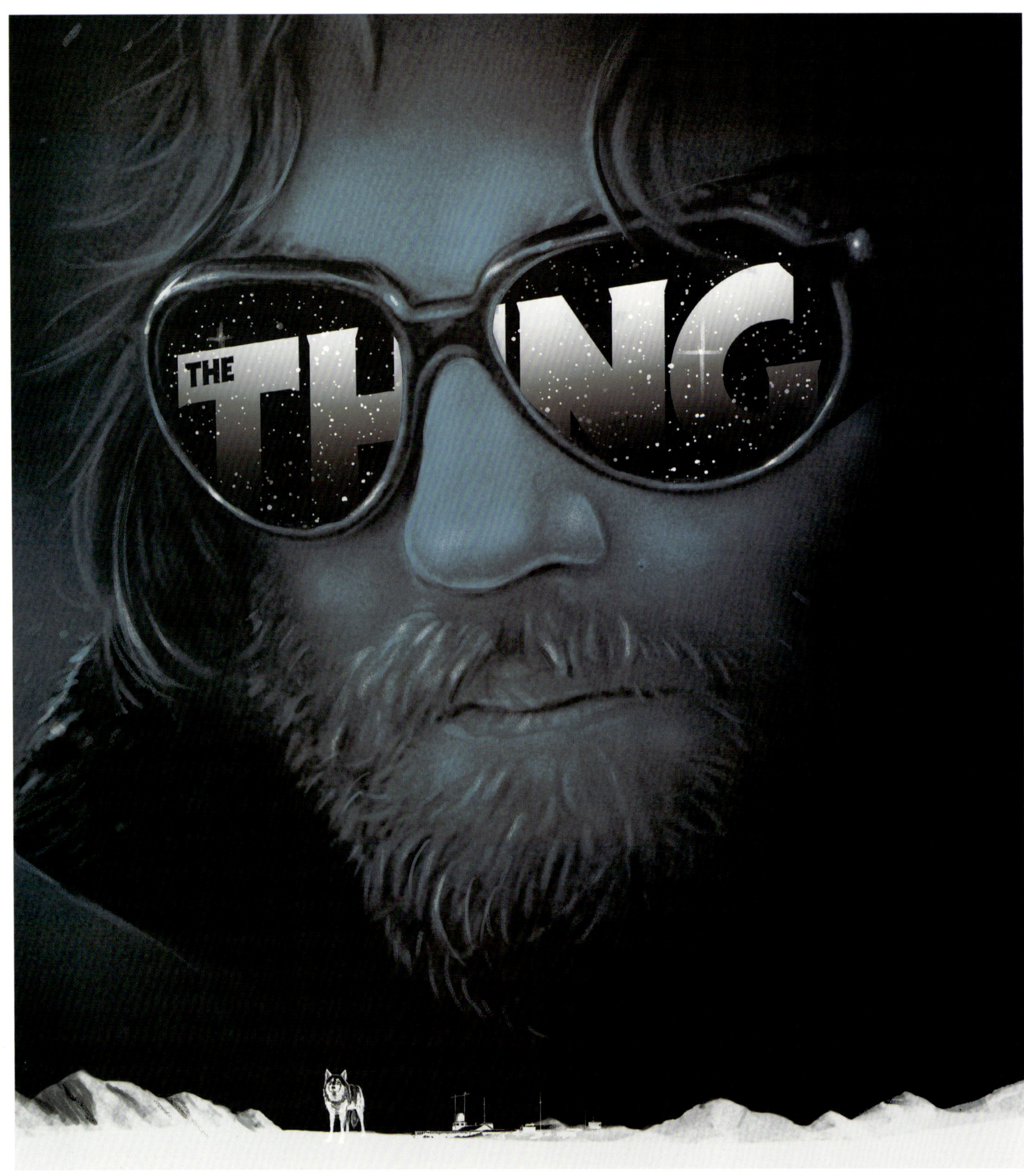

ABOVE *The Thing* by "Ghoulish" Gary Pullin. Arrow Blu-ray booklet cover. Digital, 2017.

OPPOSITE *The Warmest Place to Hide* by Paul Mann. Limited edition screen print for Vandelay Art Collective. Acrylic, 2018.

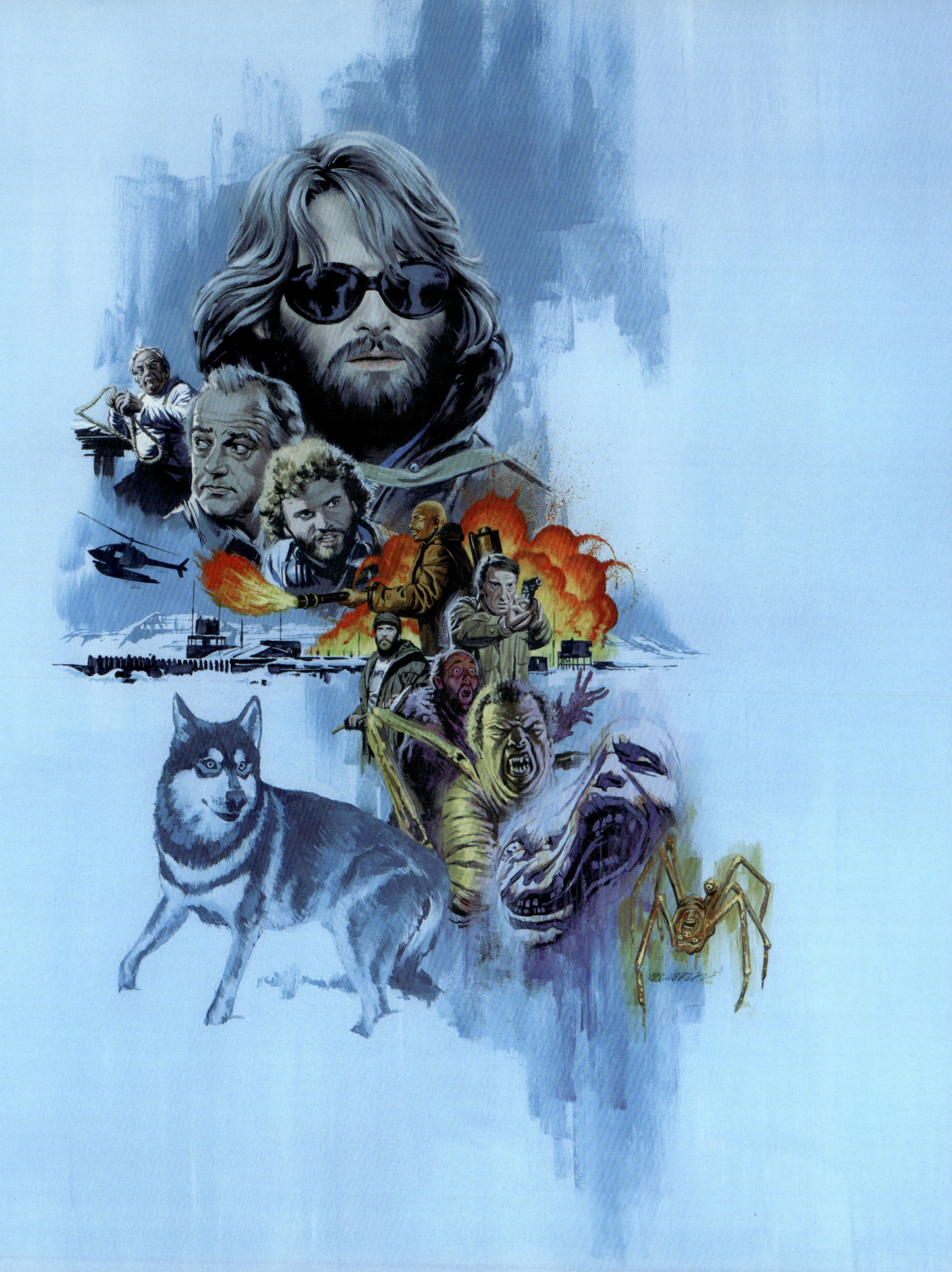

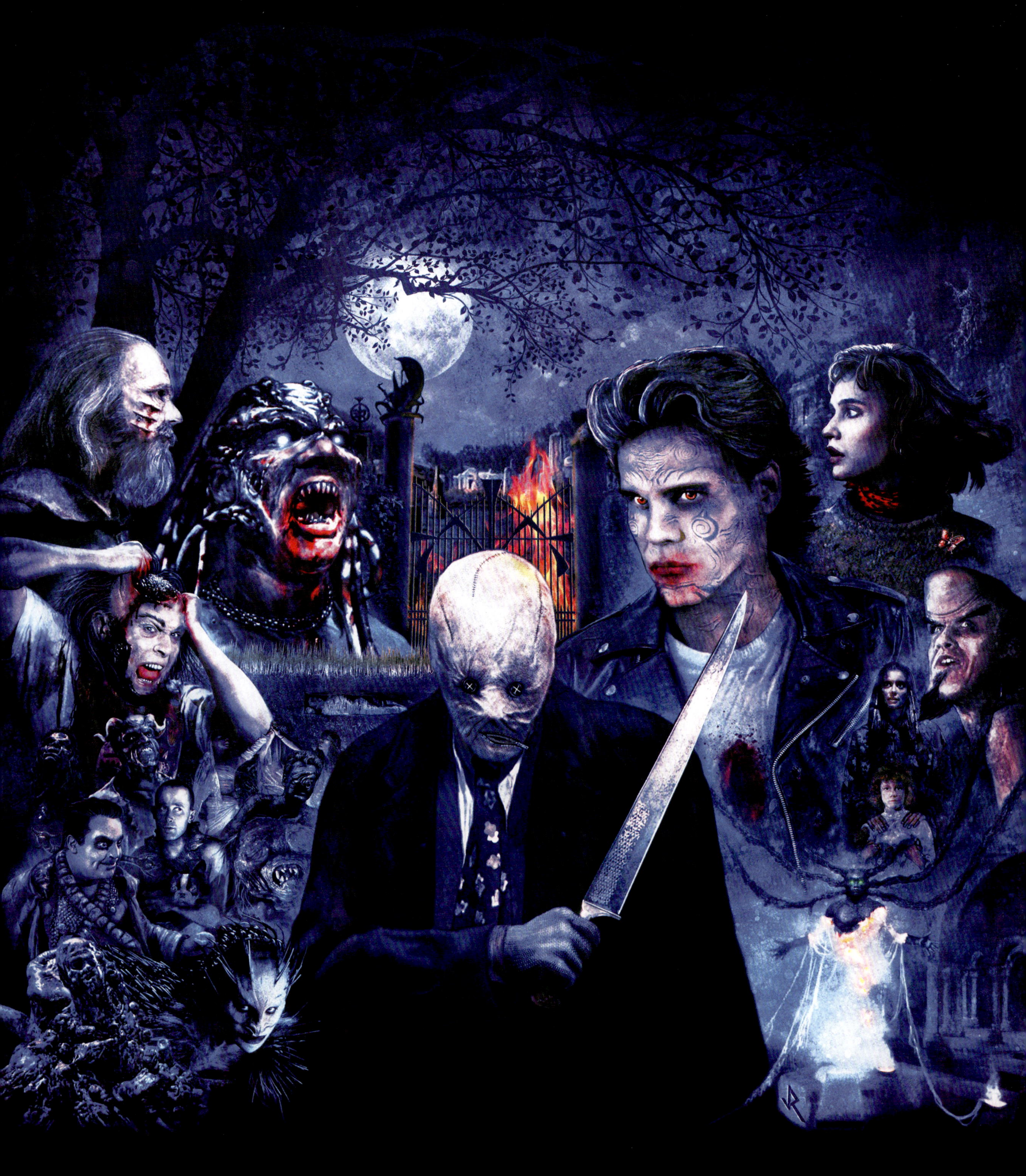

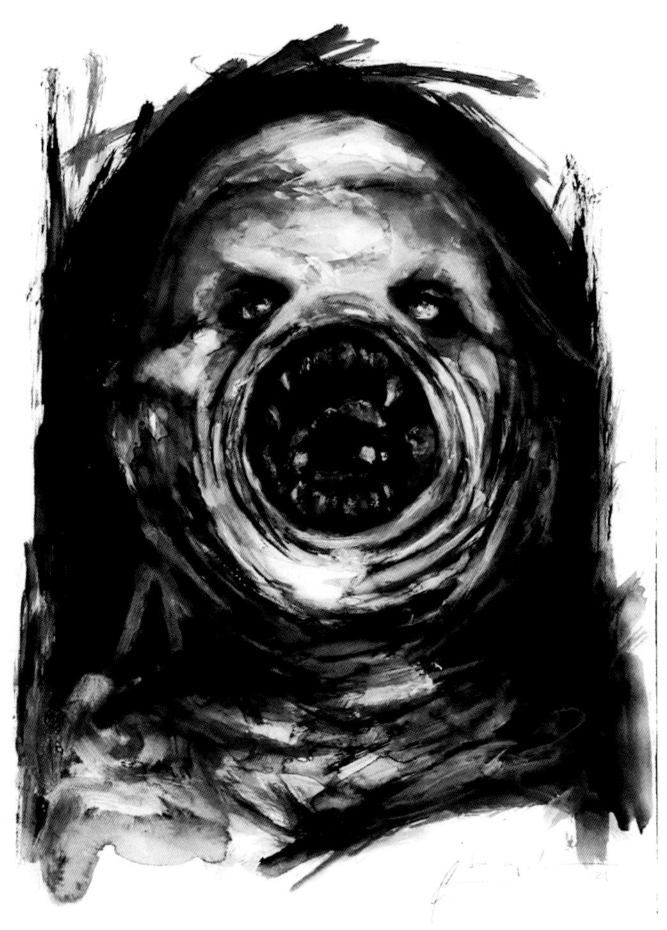

CHAPTER 9

Millennium Bugs (1990–1999)

No discussion of monsters would be complete without pointing out that the most common monster of all is . . . us. We've put masks on to cover our faces while we do terrible things, we've created ciphers and doppelgängers like zombies to do the dirty work for us in fictional narratives and deflect attention away from the fact that humanity is often less than humane. Nowhere were these stand-ins more succinctly and adroitly pointed out with regularity than, of all places, a cartoon television series called *Scooby Doo, Where Are You!* (1969) from Hanna-Barbera Studios. The Scooby gang, four humans and the titular cowardly Great Dane, investigated supernatural mysteries and goings-on that *always* ended with the heroes unmasking the ghost, vampire, monster, or other mysterious villain as a human being in disguise with financial or otherwise profit-based motives.

"Horror has shifted away from demonizing external forces and some 'Other'—be it nature, communists, or teenagers. It has instead been signaling that we, the 'civilized humans,' are the problem, and the 'monsters' are there to not-so-gently encourage us to take responsibility," points out artist Erika Deoudes. "Satan isn't the bad guy in *Rosemary's Baby*, [her husband] Guy is. We are the ones who came from outer space."

John Carpenter has said, "Monsters in movies are us, always us, one way or the other. They're us with hats on. The zombies in George A. Romero's movies are us. They're hungry. Monsters are us, the dangerous parts of us. The part that wants to destroy. The part of us with the reptile brain. The part of us that's vicious and cruel. We express these in our stories as these monsters out there."

We become monsters—and not the sympathetic, good kind we see on-screen—when we refuse to take responsibility for our actions, when we blame others for our own transgressions and decide that we are better than the people around us and deserve more because of our self-inflated egos. When we feel above those who walk next to us every day, we insulate ourselves from humanity and become inhumane. That's the very definition of the word *monstrous*, and something humans have fought against since time immemorial. This is why so many of the sympathetic monster characters resonate with viewers, especially younger ones.

"The characters, even those not in classic Universal films, are classically universal as archetypes. Each—even if inhuman—represents something basic and eternal in the human psyche, and that's made them something like old friends welcomed by generation after

OPPOSITE *Nightbreed* by Joel Robinson. Blu-ray cover art for Shout! Factory. Mixed media, 2014.

ABOVE *"The X-Files" Flukeman* by Gustavo Rapela. Gouache, 2021.

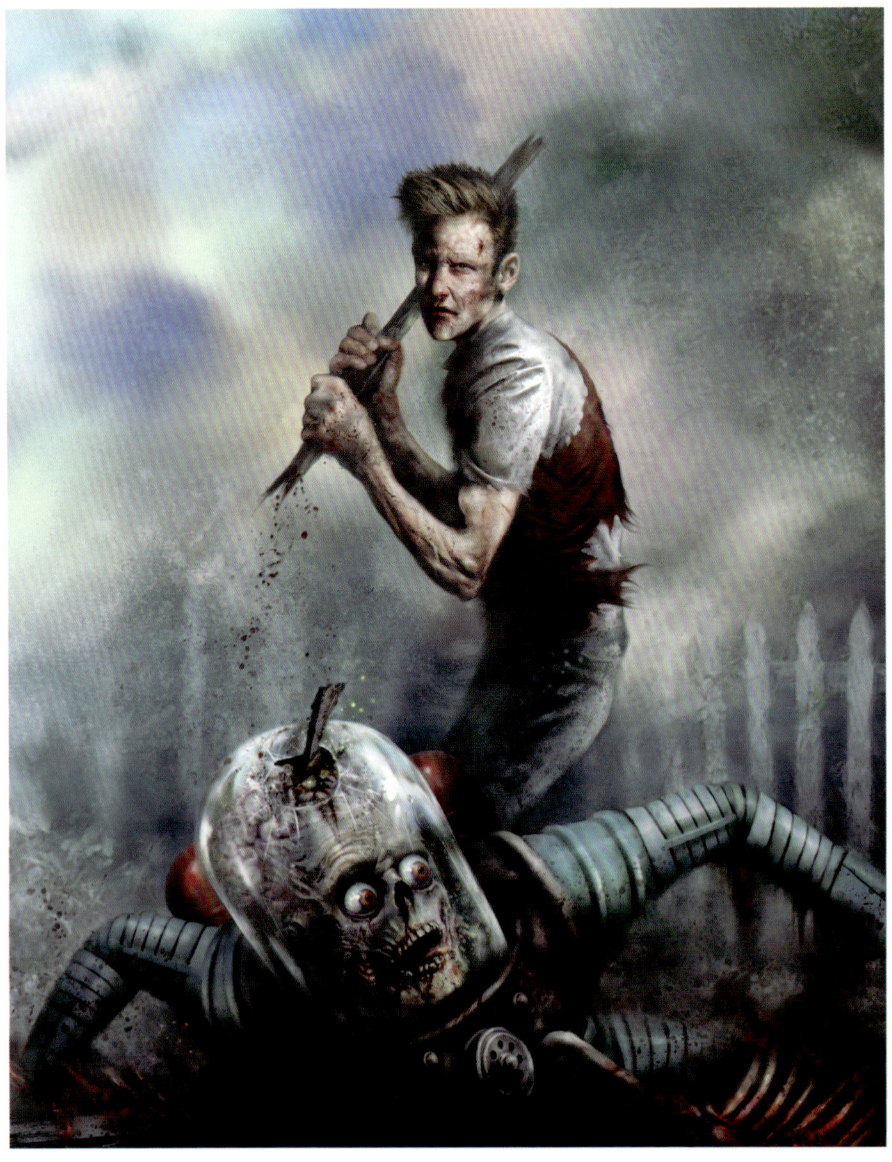

ABOVE *Mars, Attacked* by Nick Percival. Variant cover for IDW Publishing's *Mars Attacks* #9. Digital, 2013.

OPPOSITE *An Ocean of Time* by Susana "Suspiria" Valchez. Acrylic, 2020.

generation," remarks Mark Dawidziak, author of *The Night Stalker Companion* and *Everything I Need to Know I Learned in The Twilight Zone.* "Most are probably first attracted at an early age to such images and characters because they are neat, creepy, powerful, misunderstood, or wonderfully scary. The magic is that they prove to be great friends as you get older and deal with changing bodies and the horrors of adolescence, the fear of not being accepted, and the terror of dating (or mastering geometry). They remain good friends as these terrors are replaced by those of being a young adult in a world where the rules often seem confusing and sometimes downright scary. Human nature doesn't change, so the resonance of these characters and images can't change."

Fear and excitement are often two sides of the same coin, and that was certainly true as the 1990s dawned. Anticipation of the new millennium triggered both feelings, often at the same time. Change was imminent, and no negotiation would stave off what was to come. Out of this emotional environment sprang a new cadre of quirky and quasi-intellectual films and television series, beginning with David Lynch's fever-dream series *Twin Peaks* (1990–91) and a remake of Dan Curtis's *Dark Shadows* for prime time (1991). Thanks to constant interruptions in scheduling for US news coverage of the Iraq War, neither show fared well, but *Twin Peaks* was allowed the benefit of a truncated second season that *Dark Shadows* was denied.

In 1993, Fox created a Friday night lineup of destination viewing with *The Adventures of Brisco County, Jr.*, followed by *The X-Files* (inspired heavily by *Kolchak: The Night Stalker*) and *Picket Fences. The X-Files* was the only true horror/sci-fi show of the trio and was festooned with monsters throughout its original nine-season run, but *Brisco*—whose lead character was played by *The Evil Dead*'s Bruce Campbell—had enough weird science thrown into it to make it an entertaining watch. *Picket Fences* wasn't supernatural at all, but featured an episode with one of the best serial killer stories ever produced for television ("Be My Valentine," episode 17 of season 1).

Shaun Cassidy, the '70s teen-heartthrob musician and actor, created *American Gothic* (1995–96), which provided demonic Midwestern fun for a season or so, and *X-Files* producer Chris Carter's *Millennium* (1996–99) made no effort to hide the angst of Lance Henriksen's character, Frank Black, about what was coming in the new era. Showtime's reboot of the classic series *The Outer Limits* lasted for a whopping 152 episodes between 1995 and 2002, a full 103 episodes more than the original series. Were these as good or iconic as those original forty-nine? Doubtful, though there are standouts—just don't attempt to adjust your television.

The ever-expanding lineup of goth and horror-related musical acts spawned the likes of AFI, London After Midnight, Marilyn Manson, Nick Cave and the Bad Seeds, and White Zombie, and kept the genre vibrant and relevant for the last decade of the century.

In 1996, Motorola released the first flip phone for cellular service, the StarTAC. The name gives it away, but it was absolutely based on the communicators from the original *Star Trek* (1966–69) television series. Although the World Wide Web (as it was then called) first emerged in 1989, it wasn't opened to the public until 1993, and it slowly seeped into the consciousness of later adopters around the middle of the decade. With

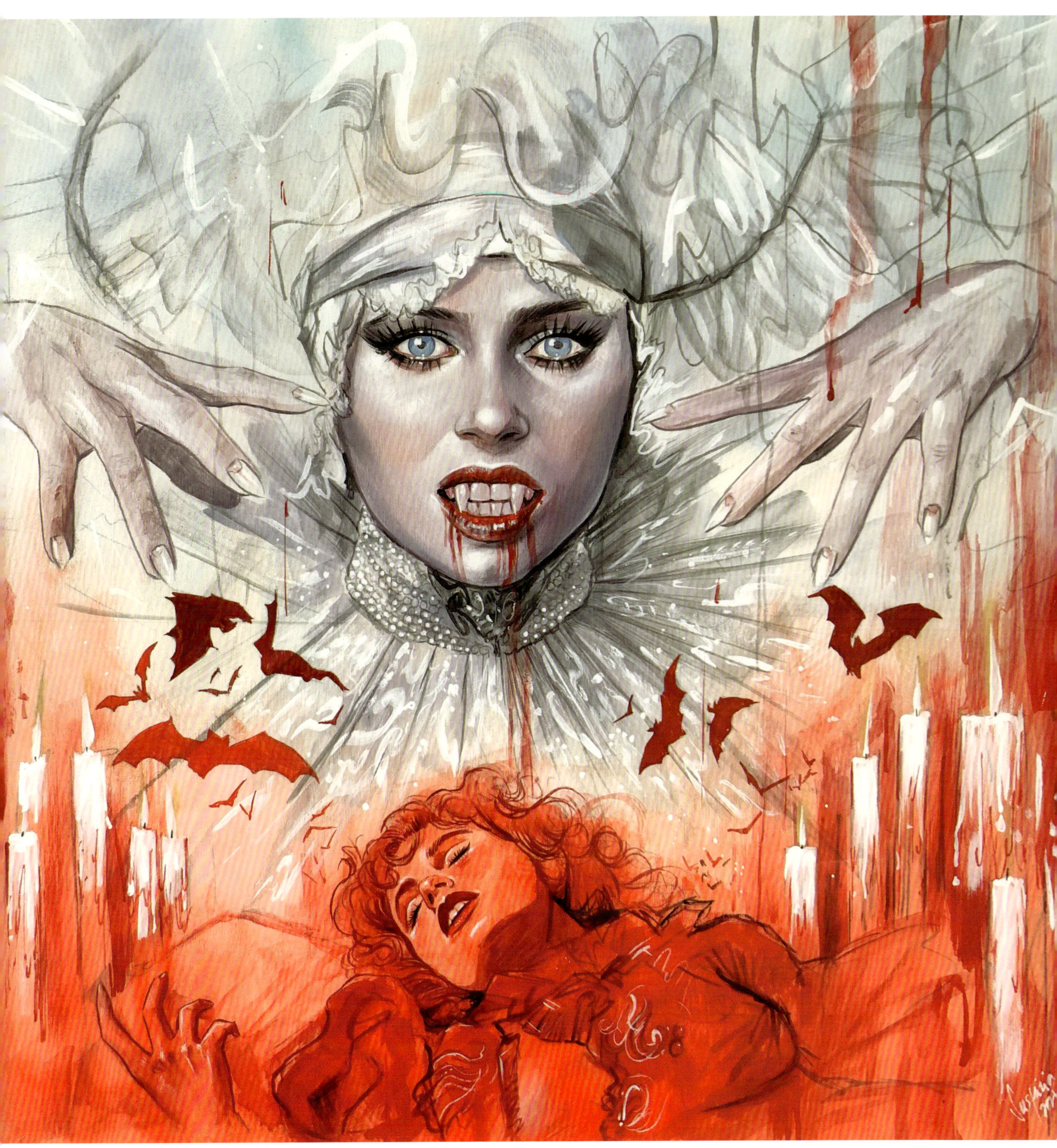

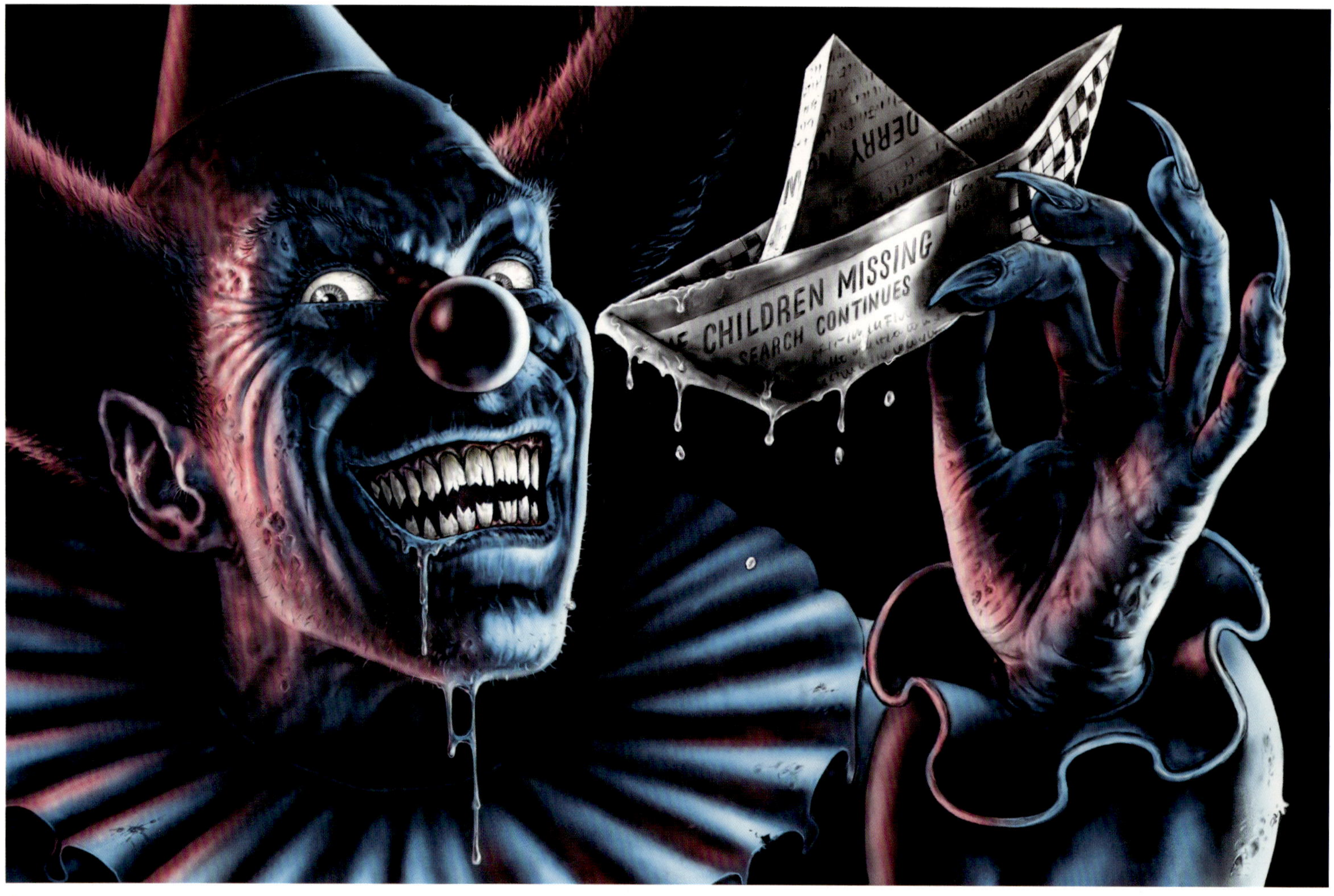

ABOVE *We All Float Down Here* by Krent Able. Illustration for *Pop Icons: Stephen King—A Cinematic Multiverse of Horror*. Airbrush, 2022.

OPPOSITE *Do You Like Flowery Movies?* by Lacie Barker. Digital, 2021.

the proliferation of web services and online communities, the depth of the global pop-culture ocean increased and gave momentum to the creation of fan sites for art, film, music, and literature, including those devoted to beloved monsters. Suddenly, people could communicate and collaborate on a global basis with fellow fans on just about any subject.

In 1995, Pierre Omidyar founded an auction website—AuctionWeb—that would go on to become one of the driving forces in online commerce once it was renamed eBay. Within months of eBay going live, toys, collectibles, books, and movies of all genres began changing hands on the platform. A common base for collectors to exchange goods and meet virtually was born, and it's never slowed down.

"eBay made a huge change in the monster-toy collecting landscape, as did the internet in general," recalls author John "Toyzilla" Marshall (*Collecting Monster Toys*). "Pre-internet, the issue was not just finding a highly coveted toy, but knowing it existed in the first place! eBay made it possible for sellers and buyers, dealers and collectors to interact 24/7 instead of [only] at whatever local events they could attend."

Monsters fared well in theaters, with memorable outings in 1990 such as *Tremors*, *Nightbreed*, and Roger Corman's last picture as a director, *Frankenstein Unbound*. Then, *Godzilla vs. King Ghidorah* (1991), *Bram Stoker's Dracula* (1992), *Godzilla vs. Mechagodzilla II* (1993), *Interview with the Vampire* and *The Crow* (both 1994), *Species* (1995), *Mars Attacks!* (1996), and *Mimic* (1997) led the pack through the rest of the decade.

Horror movies in general were well received, including *Jacob's Ladder* and *The Exorcist III* in 1990; *Candyman* and Peter Jackson's *Dead Alive* (US title: *Braindead*) in 1992; *Needful Things* (1993); *Lord of Illusions* (1995); *Scream*, *From Dusk Till Dawn*, and *The Frighteners* in 1996; *I Know What You Did Last Summer* (1997); *Fallen*, *Dark City*, and *Ringu* in 1998; *The Sixth Sense*, *The Blair Witch Project*, and *Stir of Echoes* in 1999—all memorable examples.

Throughout the decade, a gaggle of sequels to franchises like *Halloween*, *Godzilla*, *Friday the 13th*,

Child's Play, *Hellraiser*, and so many others packed viewers into theater seats as well, although, as with all sequels, quality was spotty at best.

Robert Tinnell, who spent much of the decade in a director's chair making films, has an overarching view of the genre landscape. "From the '90s on, [there] was a combination of nostalgia and self-awareness. Rebooting and retooling the classics, often for the purpose of celebrating the same. Of course, *Scream* is the poster child for self-aware storytelling. We can argue about the original intent of deconstructionism as it applied to literary criticism, but with that film, the concept applies. Then there have been reactions to the swift evolution of technology that were incorporated into stuff like *Blair Witch Project* and *Paranormal Activity* (2007) [with the 'found-footage' subgenre], the medium becoming part of the messaging."

Tinnell also observed how fandom and the social perception of the films changed: "It was unbelievable how Big Media finally figured out there was an audience for all of the horror and monster stuff we grew up with and there was such an explosion of merchandise and media and—maybe most importantly—the convention scene, where so many people could meet their horror heroes in person. Also, during that period, there was a tremendous amount of scholarly work published on the genre, building on the great writing that had been happening in small-press publications like *Midnight Marquee*, *Photon*, *Little Shoppe of Horrors*, and many, many more fanzines and small prozines, that were seriously studying the horror genre as well as exploring the historical foundations of the films. For every mainstream example—like the late, brilliant David J. Skal's books (*The Monster Show*, *Screams of Reason*, *Dark Carnival*)—there were tons of smaller-press works that did a fantastic job of documenting horror films and filmmakers, alongside works that focused on critical analyses. It was a true golden age of scholarship—and it isn't over."

Nineteen ninety-nine became the year of the millennium bug—would computers shut down from a programming glitch when they attempted to turn over to the new date of January 1, 2000? Despite thousands of tests and simulations, the public anxiety refused to be assuaged until the day came, the time was nigh, breaths were held—and nothing whatsoever happened. No digital apocalypse occurred to cleanse the planet of the scourge of information and misinformation on the internet.

A new era began for all, including artists whose main subject matters are monsters, horror, dark fantasy, and weird fiction. Standing on the shoulders of those who came before them, the illustrators of the twenty-first century whose work is contained herein forged into the future by recalling the past and sharing it with a nostalgic bent. Works created for book and magazine covers, interiors, DVDs, toys, collectible packaging, posters, promotional purposes, advertisements, and simply for the joy of creating them, inspired this book.

But how is the relevance of these classic monsters and images maintained for a new generation?

Henson Company puppeteer and fanzine editor–publisher (*Ghastly Phantasms*) Diana Robertson offers insight into the material's continued draw. "Monster/horror media—although reflective of things going on at the time in society—has timeless elements inherent to the human experience that allow for anyone of any age to relate to the characters and images. I wasn't alive in the 1930s, but the character of Frankenstein's creation still resonates with me as a disabled person who was 'othered' in their youth. Because of this, I started a classic horror zine with my other friends who saw themselves in this media even though most of the people involved in that media have passed

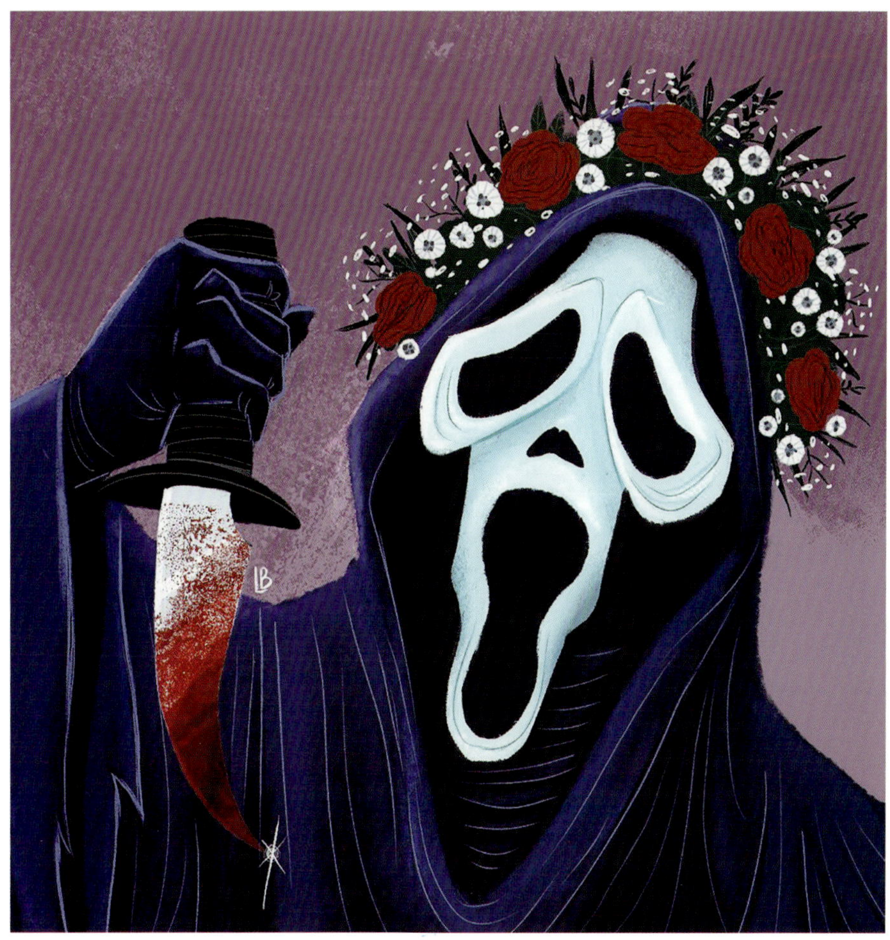

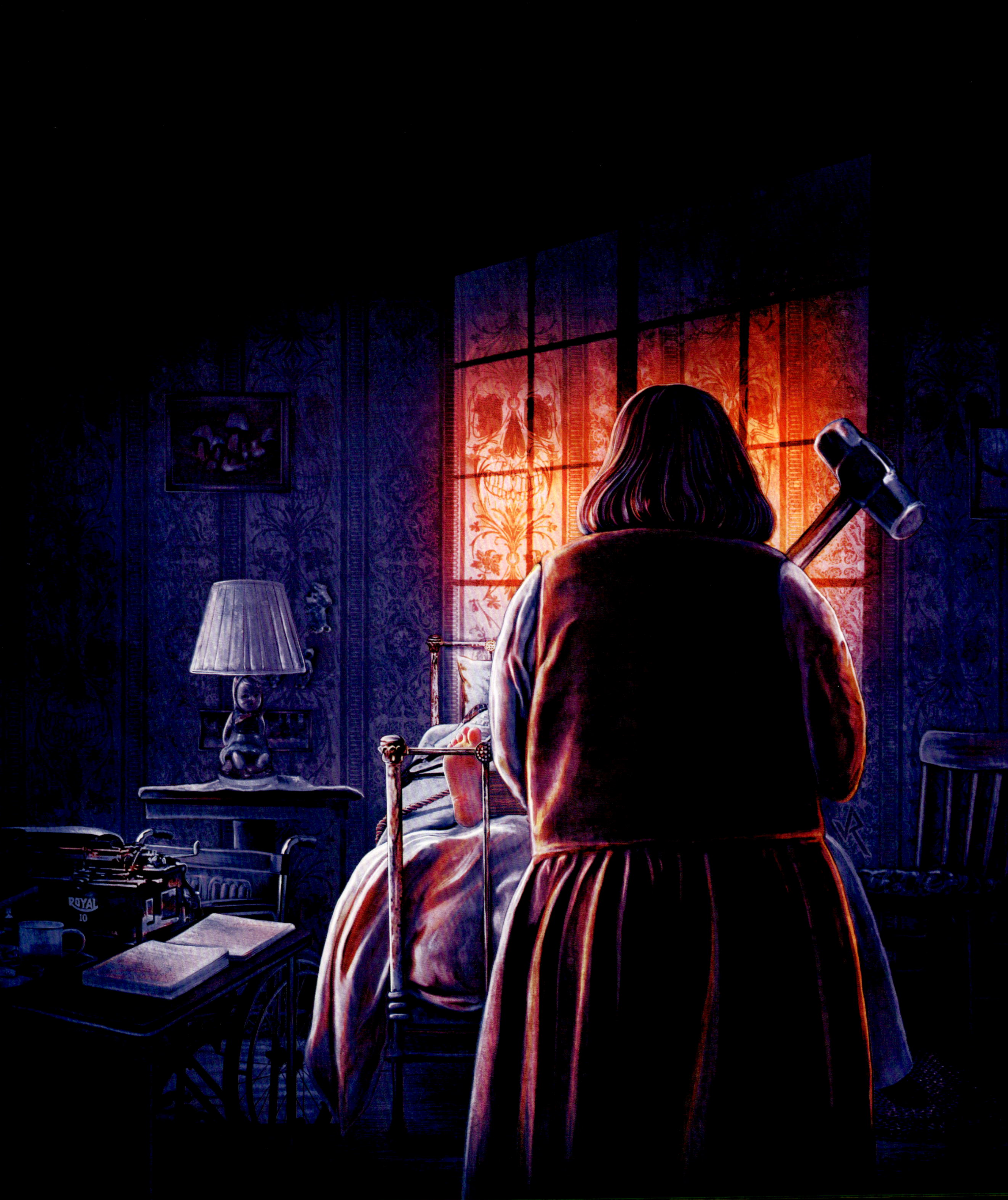
ROYAL
10

on," she says. "Although I've come to horror/monsters of the twenty-first century when those who were a part of the classics are almost all gone, there is still magic in finding community and even purpose with it," Robertson adds. "The friends I have made and the ability to help preserve legacies in various ways are both fulfilling and meaningful."

"Horror has become much more inclusive. It is fantastic to see more people of color and LGBTQ+ characters and themes," reflects painter El Gato Gomez on how relevancy to marginalized viewers can help the genre flourish. "[Jordan Peele's] *Get Out* was called a game changer for Black horror, and the series *Queer for Fear* brought attention to the fact that gay themes were always present in horror, but masked (if thinly), particularly in the work of James Whale. It is exciting to see what more diverse voices will contribute to the genre."

"I think we're seeing a renaissance of classic monster media," says award-winning author James Aquilone, creator of new *Kolchak: The Night Stalker* books and comics. "Image [Comics] has been doing a series of Universal Monsters comics, and director Robert Eggers's *Nosferatu* came out in late 2024. We've already had *The Invisible Man* (2020), *Renfield* (2023), *The Last Voyage of the Demeter* (2023), and *Lisa Frankenstein* (2024) in the movies, and TV shows like *Penny Dreadful*, the BBC's 2020 *Dracula* miniseries, *What We Do in the Shadows*, and *American Horror Story*. Old monsters never die."

"The monsters are actually more accessible today than ever with the new streaming services," states illustrator Ed Repka. "New generations can enjoy and will become imprinted with the love of these classic creatures. We will never see the monster craze like we did in the '60s, but the monsters will live on."

Indeed, there's even a remake of *Creature from the Black Lagoon* underway at Universal Studios. New versions are inevitable, but what of the work of new visual artists?

"New artists bring their own sensibilities to the classic monsters, and I'd include Norman Bates, Michael Myers, Freddy, Chucky, and the rest, along with Frankenstein and the Mummy and such," adds *USA Today* editor emeritus David Colton. "New artistic visions help transform these iconic monsters into symbols of our fears—safer in some ways, but their menace made eternal. You can admire the painter's brushwork, or computerized colors, but no matter the medium, honest artwork always leaves you affected. That's why a young artist drawing their version of the Creature from the Black Lagoon is so important [as director Guillermo del Toro did with 2017's Best Picture Academy Award–winning *The Shape of Water*]. Art keeps the memories and the gentle fears alive."

OPPOSITE *Dirty Birdy* by Joel Robinson. Blu-ray cover for Shout! Factory. Mixed media, 2018.

BELOW *Once More with Feeling* by Paul Mann. Record album art for Mondo. Acrylic on illustration board, 2019.

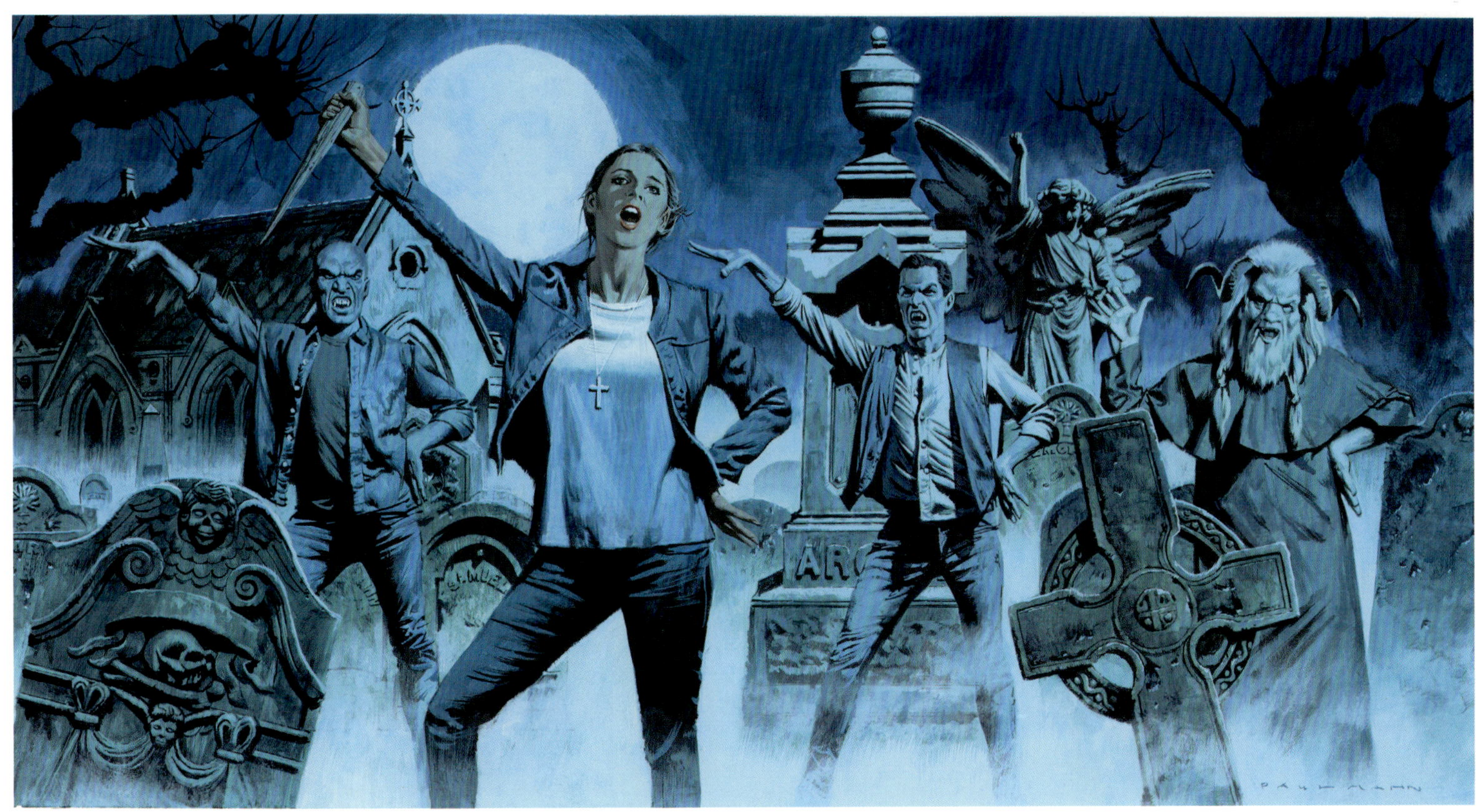

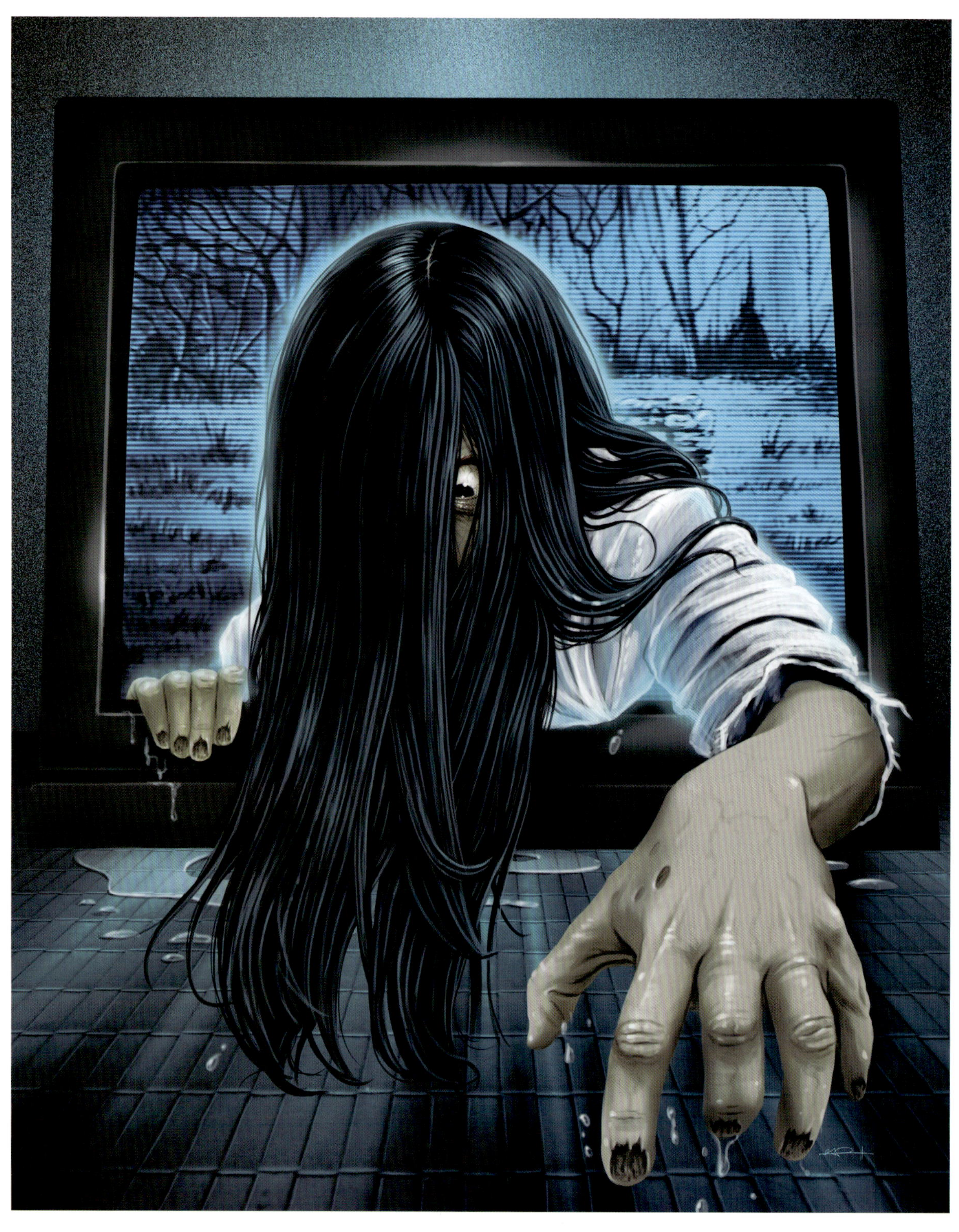

ABOVE *Ringu* by "Ghoulish" Gary Pullin. Cover art for *HorrorHound* magazine #53. Digital, 2016.

OPPOSITE *The Blair Witch* by Dave Kendall. Digital, 2016.

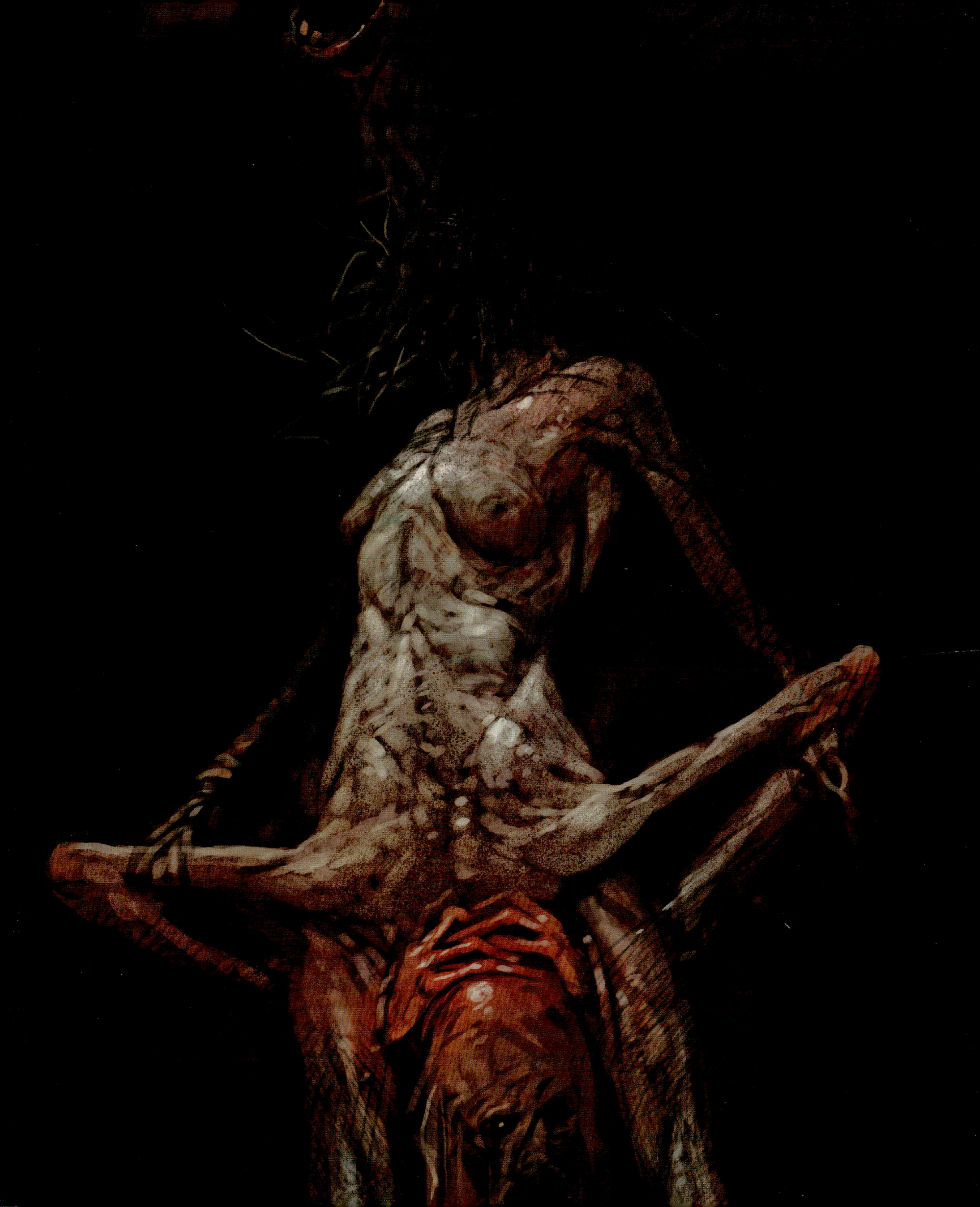

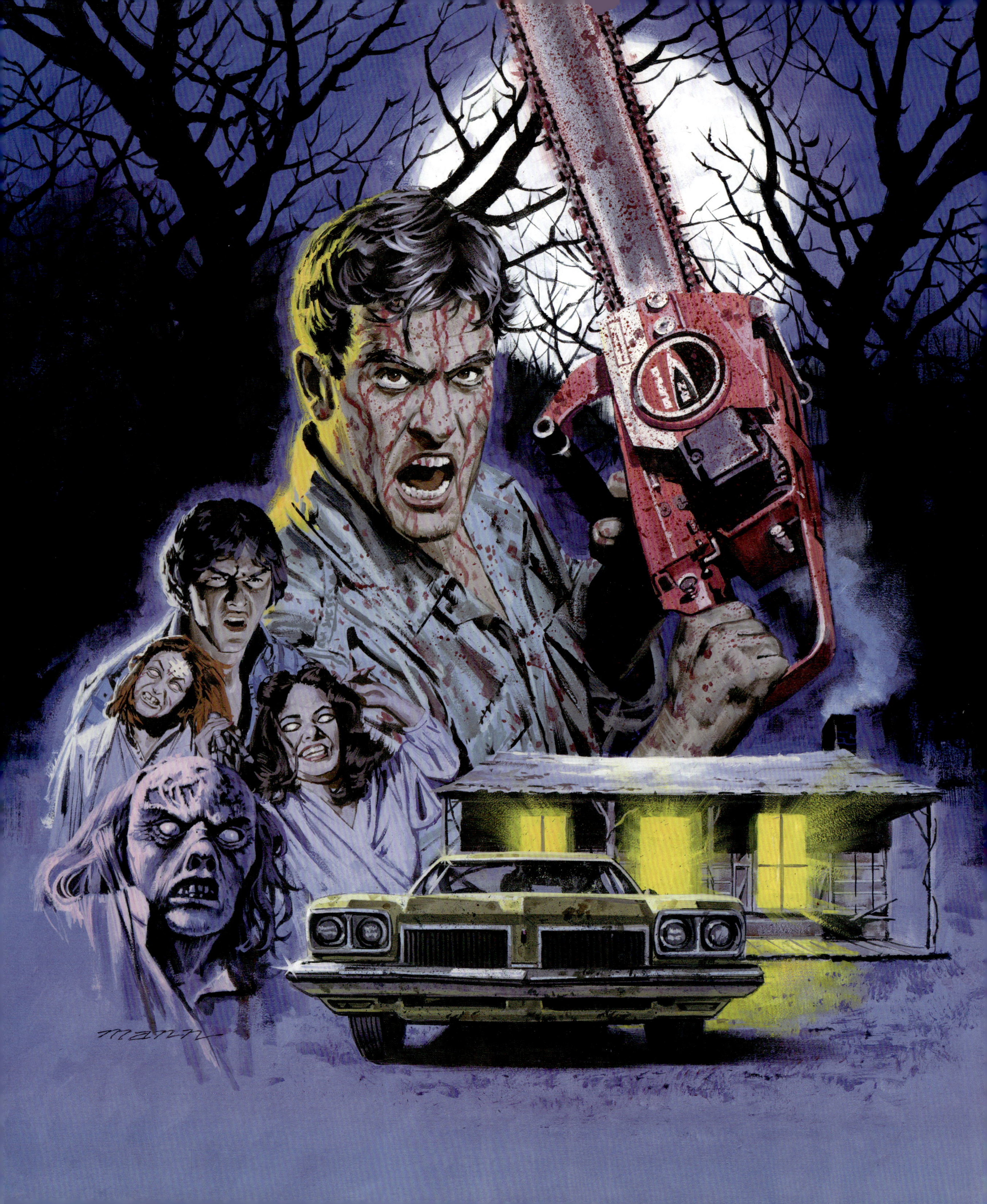

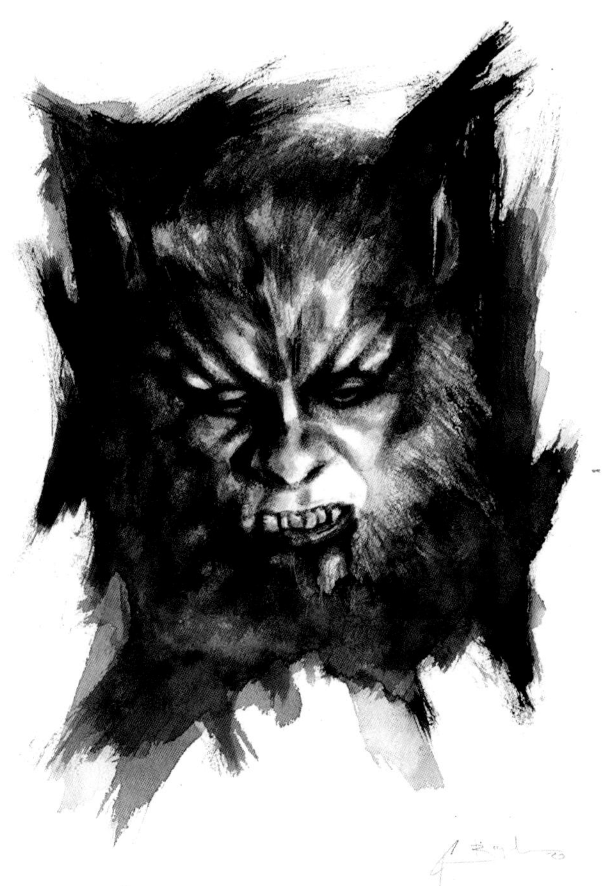

Epilogue

The shadowy flickers on movie and television screens, the words on paper, the paint on canvas, the music—these things matter. But do they have artistic merit? Stephen King believes they do. In his book *Danse Macabre*, he asks, "Is horror art? . . . [T]he work of horror can be nothing else; it achieves the level of art simply because it is looking for something beyond art, something that predates art: It is looking for what I would call phobic pressure points. The good horror tale will dance its way to the center of your life and find the secret door to the room you believed no one but you knew of—as both Albert Camus and Billy Joel have pointed out, 'The Stranger' makes us nervous . . . but we love to try on his face in secret."

These works are sometimes all that keeps someone hanging on; the images we build, the thoughts we share, the songs we sing—the ways that we creatively reveal ourselves—make a difference to people who need hope, who need something to believe in. We share our feelings to clarify and contextualize the works discussed in order to show the value in them to those who might not otherwise perceive it. These works inspire them not only to keep going but also to create something themselves, which in turn inspires others.

"[An illustration or piece of art] allows us to relive the thrills of our favorite films in a single, powerful image," says author Lisa Morton. "If the film or monster is one that we found particularly terrifying, owning an image of that film/monster reminds us that we survived that viewing and learned something about our own limits—like how to overcome them—from that experience." Author Del Howison (*The Survival of Margaret Thomas*), who's also a horror retailer, at Dark Delicacies in Burbank, adds, "Not only new images of classic monsters, but new monsters have to be extensions of the realities and fears people are currently grappling with to be effective. Classic is classic for a reason. There are eternal struggles both mentally and emotionally, but we also need the new terrors as our world changes in every way."

People may look at the images in this book and think that for fans, the great love is horror, monster, and science fiction movies, television shows, art, or books, but we know the truth: The greatest love is *sharing the love* of those things and perpetuating their examination and dissemination.

Share your love of the art in this book with someone you care about.

OPPOSITE *The Evil Dead* by Paul Mann. Mondo poster art. Acrylic, 2018.

ABOVE *The Curse of the Werewolf* by Gustavo Rapela. Gouache, 2020.

Artist Biographies

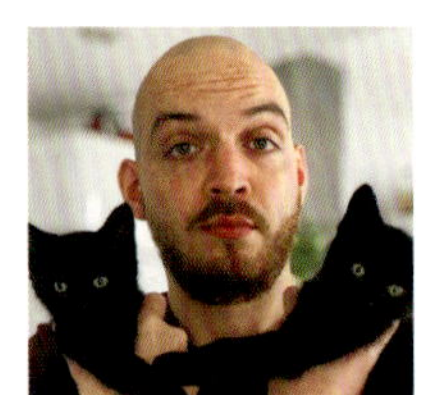

ADAM INSAM (pages 54, 64, 131) is a Londoner living in Yorkshire with his wife, two kids, and four cats. His day job is head of design for a boxing-promotion company, making posters of angry men. For a break, he loves to illustrate angry monsters and horror characters. Website: *AdamInsam.com*

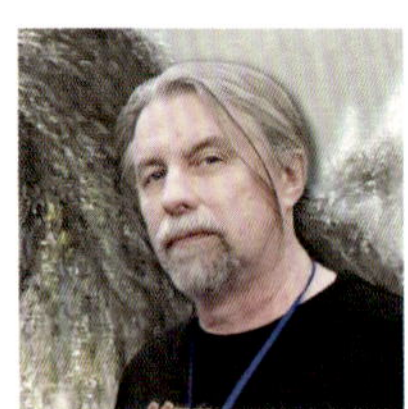

BOB EGGLETON (pages 38, 66–67, 90–91, 93, 118–119, 136–137) is a nine-time Hugo Award–winning artist. He has also been awarded a Rondo, a Mangled Skyscraper Award, twelve Chesleys, and the L. Ron Hubbard Lifetime Achievement Award for the Arts. He has illustrated every major sci-fi author and worked in comics, motion pictures, and animation. Instagram: *@bobeggleton*

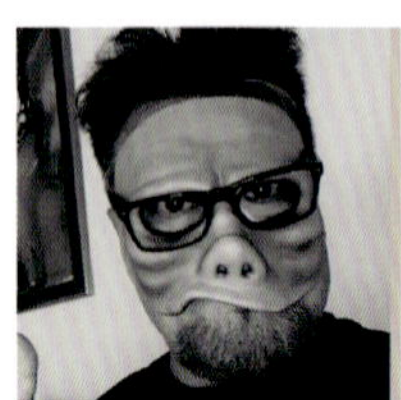

BOB LIZARRAGA (pages 2–3, 17, 92, 99) has developed and designed characters for a variety of animation and CGI productions. His clients include Warner Bros. Animation, *Famous Monsters of Filmland* magazine, Universal Cartoon Studio, Comedy Central, Nickelodeon, *MAD* magazine, and more. Bob creates works combining caricature and surrealism and has exhibited in a number of galleries. Website: *Lizarraga.net*

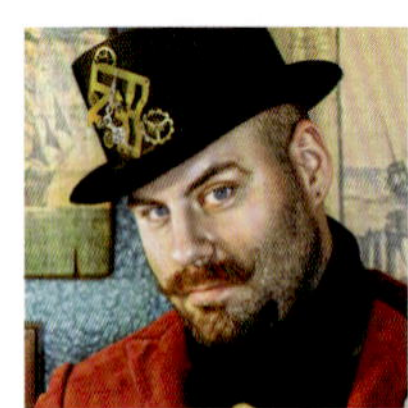

CECIL PORTER (pages 103, 162) is an illustrator and tattoo artist from Portland, Oregon. Attracted to art at an early age, Cecil found refuge in the worlds of comic books, fantasy, and Dungeons & Dragons. He splits his time between every form of art he's come to love—illustration, sculpting, writing, and of course tattooing. Website: *CecilPorterArt.com*

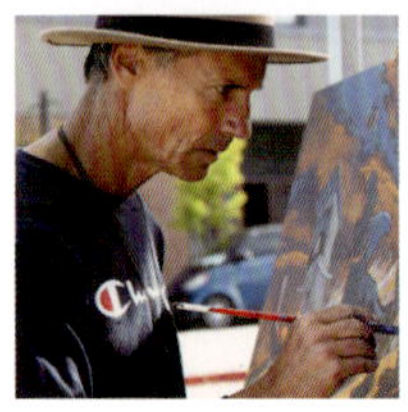

DAMIAN FULTON (pages 58, 96–97) grew up during the '60s watching monster movies and remaking them into Super 8 home movies. Today, Damian directs indie films and paints pop surrealism mash-ups of monsters, surf imagery, and hot rod culture. He's created art for the likes of Disney, Marvel, and Universal Studios. Website: *DamianFultonArt.com*

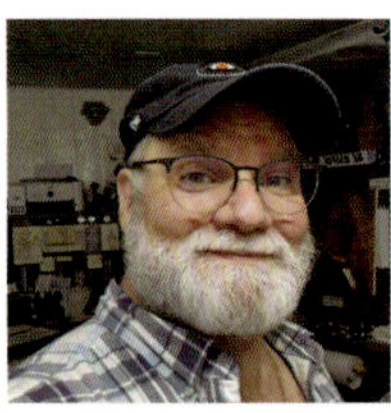

DANIEL HORNE (pages 56, 86, 100) is a celebrated painter and sculptor who has been making art professionally for the past thirty years. His paintings have graced over 400 book and magazine covers throughout that span, including the magazines *Dragon*, *Dungeon*, *Monsters from the Vault*, *Rue Morgue*, and *HorrorHound* and *Spectrum: The Best in Contemporary Fantastic Art*. Instagram: *@oldschooldan*

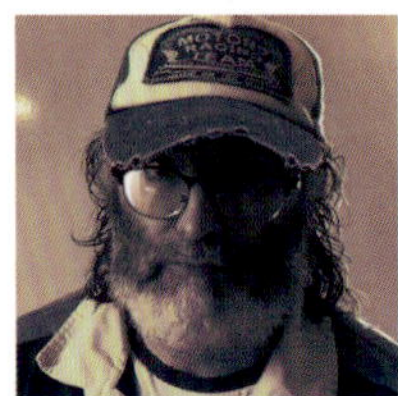

DARYL JOYCE (pages 112, 130) is an English illustrator known for creating physical-media cover art, ebook illustration, and book art. In 2020, he indulged his love of classic horror and set out on a mission to create new art for every Hammer horror movie. Daryl is working on an art book with an emphasis on monsters. Website: *Daryl-Joyce-Illustrator.com*

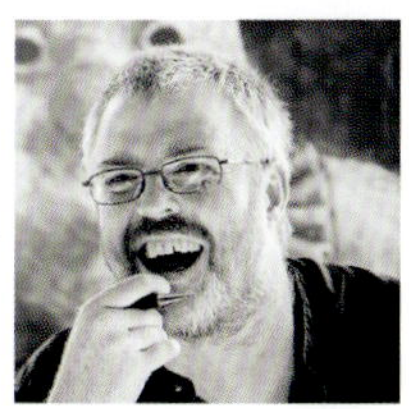

DAVE KENDALL'S (pages 33, 44, 80, 142–143, 175) first professional work was for Pat Mills, the godfather of British comics and creator of the ultraviolent *Action* comic and *2000 AD*. Dave moved on to Brian Lumley's *Necroscope* series, as well as creating comics for the band Metallica. More recently, he's created illustrations for *Magic: The Gathering*, and *World of Warcraft*, as well as collaborating with best-selling author Mike Carey on their series *Houses of the Holy*. Dave is also the co-creator of the *Deadworld* series for *2000 AD*. Website: *RustyBaby.com*

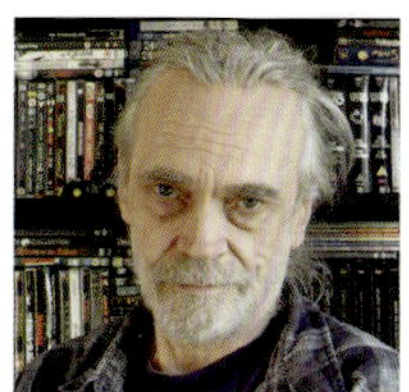

DAVID BROOKS (Brux) (pages 110, 144) has been a regular contributor to *We Belong Dead* magazine since its first issue. His work has also appeared in *Little Shoppe of Horrors* magazine and books, including *'70s Monster Memories*, *Giant Monsters of Filmland*, *Spotlight on Science Fiction*, *A Pictorial History of Hammer Films*, and more. Facebook: *Facebook.com/profile.php?id=100003941927408*

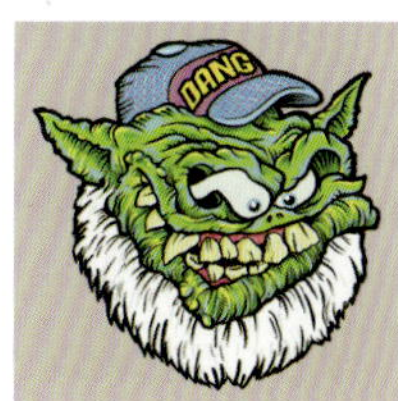

DIRK HAYS's (page 87) artistic sensibility is rooted in the pop-culture iconography of the last half century. The punk rock art scene in Atlanta lured him away from his corporate advertising job to create art full-time, and he has participated in numerous regional group shows as well as several solo shows at various galleries. Website: *DirkHays.com*

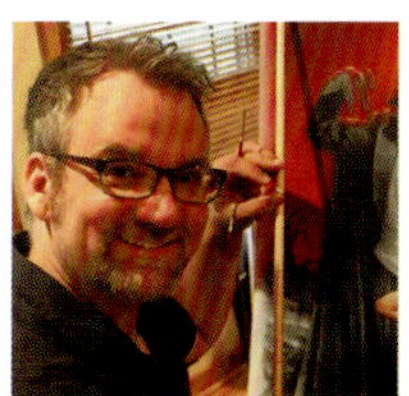

DOUG P'GOSH (pages 20–21, 46, 51, 60–61, 68–69, 81, 107, 122) has more than thirty years of experience creating product designs and illustrations for some of the most popular and well-loved brands and licenses across the world. His paintings have appeared in exhibitions at La Luz De Jesus Gallery, Creature Features Group art shows, Harold Golen Gallery, Van Eaton Gallery, and more. Website: *Pgosh.com*

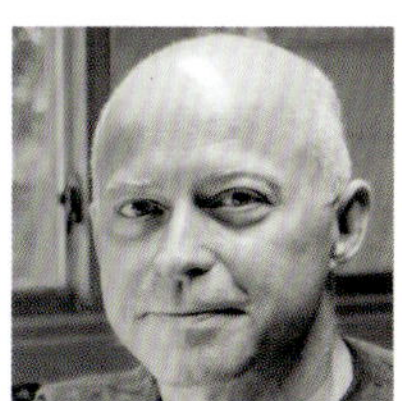

DOUGLAS KLAUBA (pages 34–35, 48, 62, 79) is recognized for his dramatic use of lighting in a heroic-deco style influenced by pulp-magazine art and classic movie poster illustration. His paintings have been in *Spectrum: The Best in Contemporary Fantastic Art*, the *Society of Illustrators Annual*, and *Imagine FX* magazine, as well as *The Art of Horror* and *The Art of Horror Movies* books. Website: *DouglasKlauba.com*

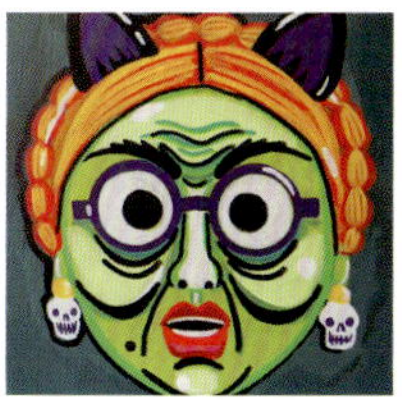

EL GATO GOMEZ (page 106) grew up addicted to monster films and television, including *The Addams Family* and *The Munsters*. All things with retro and creepy imagery are like a magnet to her. Anything mid-century and macabre is her jam, and she calls her personal artistic style mid-century macabre. Website: *ElGatoGomez.BigCartel.com*

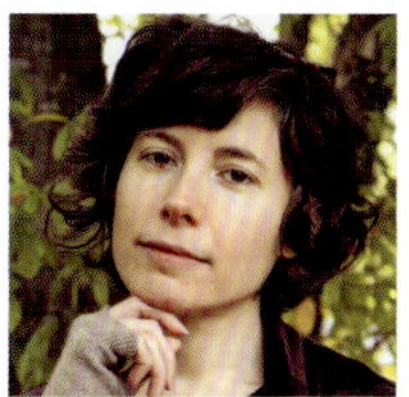

ERIKA DEOUDE's (pages 15, 43) father inspired her love of all things monstery, magical, and cartoony. Drawing from an early age, she's spent time at a multitude of art colleges, as an artist for Trader Joe's, and illustrating sexy monsters since 2012. She's currently a graphic designer in Durham, North Carolina. Website: *ErikaDudes.com*

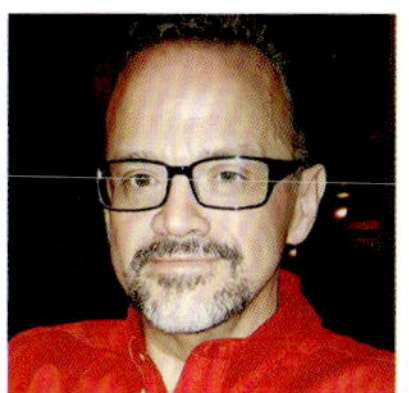

FREDERICK COOPER (pages 43, 47, 49, 75, 84–85, 120–121, 144, 152, 154, 156) has been a successful commercial artist and illustrator for more than forty years. Cooper has lent his talents to some of the most prominent names in the entertainment industry, including Universal Studios, Disney, and many others. His third book, *Creaturae Noctis: The Horror Art of Frederick Cooper*, is now available. Website: *FrederickCooperArts.com*

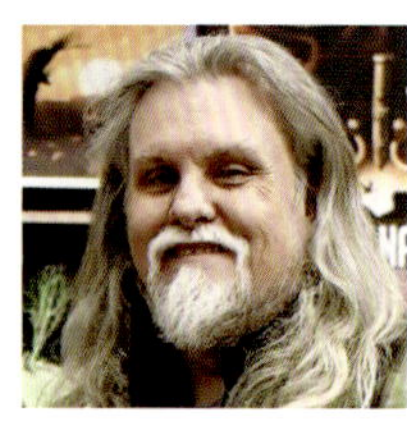

"GHOULISH" GARY PULLIN (pages 25, 89, 160, 164, 174) is a leading designer of alternative movie posters, vinyl record packaging, and pop-culture art. His signature style has graced numerous magazines, including *MAD*, *Fangoria*, and *Rue Morgue*, where he started as its original art director. Gary creates screen prints and his artwork appears on Blu-rays, book covers, soundtracks and in galleries worldwide. Website: *GaryPullin.com*

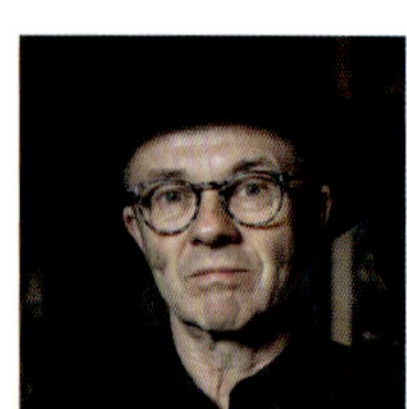

GRAHAM HUMPHREY's (cover, endpapers, and pages 12, 16, 49, 94–95, 134, 140) work has appeared on movie posters, as well as magazine, book, record, and physical-media covers, and more since 1980. Influenced by his love of the horror genre and the music and lyrics of the UK punk scene, he sought a style and approach that encapsulated both. His current efforts include posters, private commissions, and work with some of the UK's premiere horror festivals. Website: *GrahamHumphreys.com*

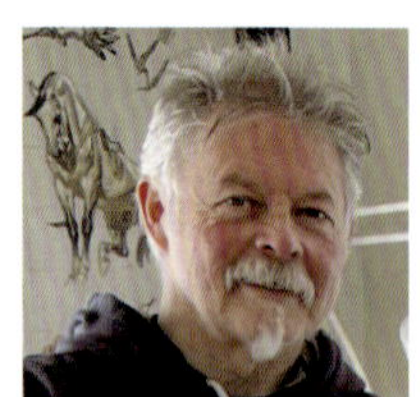

GREGORY MANCHESS (pages 23, 70–71) is a Society of Illustrators Hall of Fame recipient. His clients include the US Postal Service, *National Geographic* magazine, NASA, and he has illustrated the works of Robert E. Howard and L. Frank Baum. His visual novel *Above the Timberline* is in development as a feature film. Website: *Manchess.com*

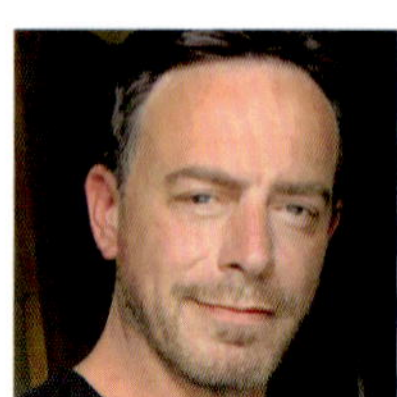

GREG STAPLES (pages 28, 31, 45, 54, 57, 98) is well known for his work on Judge Dredd in *2000 AD*. He's also done concept art for films like *World War Z*, *Doomsday*, *Hellboy*, and *Dredd* as well as numerous video games. Greg is working with Hammer Films on a project. Website: *GregStaples.com*

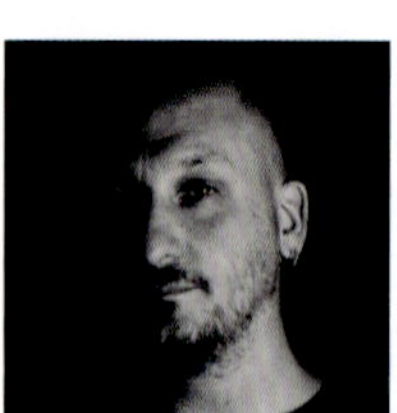

GUSTAVO RAPELA (pages 7, 19, 113–114, 167, 177) is an illustrator known for his skill with ink and his deep passion for horror films. His illustrations, full of detail and with a remarkable use of contrast between darkness and light, have been exhibited in galleries and on books, fanzines, and t-shirts. Instagram: *@gusrapela*

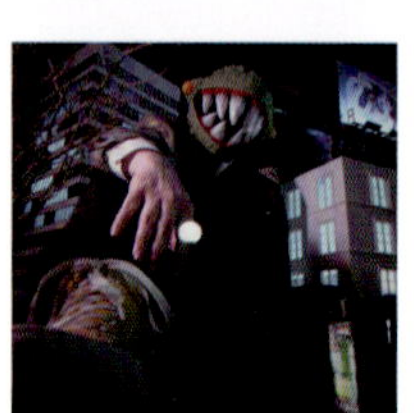

JARED P. FOUST (page 102) is a filmmaker and illustrator from Atlanta, Georgia. All of his illustrative work is non-digital, rendered in traditional paints, inks, and screen tone. Similarly, his principle creative endeavor XENOFAUNA focuses on creating artisanal monster movies utilizing primarily analog special effects. Instagram: *@xenofauna*

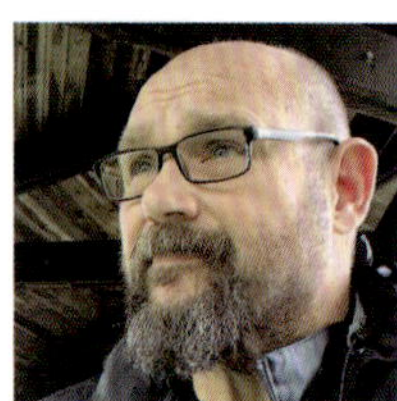

JEFF BUSCH (pages 44, 76, 83) has been an illustrator for more than thirty years. He has created murals for the Field Museum of Natural History in Chicago, was creative director for American Pinball, Inc., and has worked for clients such as Lucasfilm, Capcom, Disney Consumer Products, Enesco, and many more. Website: *JBuschCreative.com*

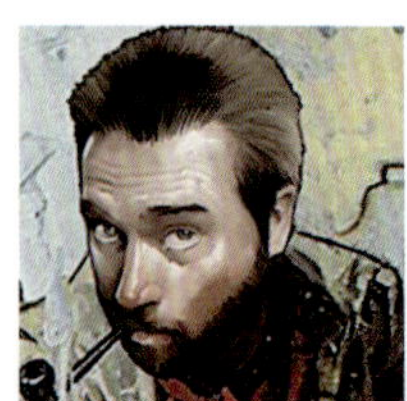

JEFF PRESTON'S (pages 30, 40–41, 52, 73, 128) clients range from *Famous Monsters of Filmland* magazine, to The United Methodist Publishing House, Miller/Coors, Dark Horse Comics, and Cintas the uniform company—his three decades of work have been as diverse as his clientele. He is a member of the Society of Illustrators and a Rondo Award winner. Website: *JeffPreston.net*

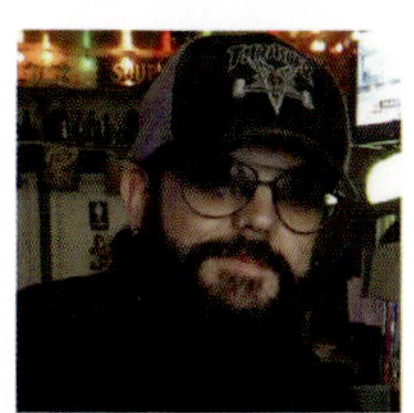

JOEL ROBINSON (pages 145, 149, 166, 172) is an American horror artist specializing in character portraits and movie covers. He has created work for Universal Studios, MGM, Sony, and Scream! Factory. Joel also works with family members of Vincent Price, Bela Lugosi, Lon Chaney Sr. and Jr., and Boris Karloff to create new imagery and help preserve their legacy. Website: *JoelRobinsonArt.com*

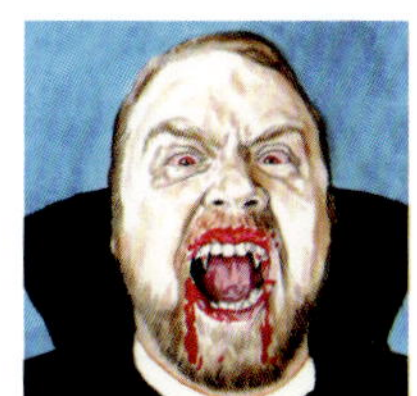

JOSH RYALS (pages 20, 37, 50, 101) has been a monster fan since he was very young. His work has appeared online in a gallery curated by David Lynch, as well as on an episode of *Svengoolie* and in *We Belong Dead*, where he is creating covers for the magazine. Instagram: *@contentabnormal*

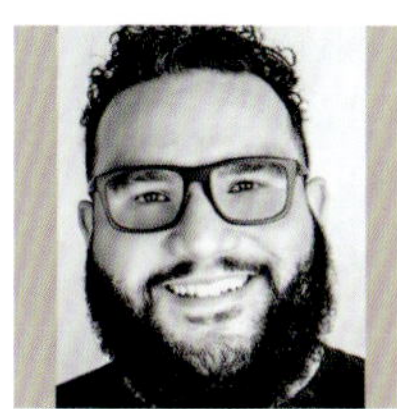

JUAN RAMOS (page 14) has had the honor to work and create art pieces for some of today's biggest companies, such as Disney, Marvel, Amazon Prime, Warner Bros., DC Comics, Lucasfilm, Sideshow Collectibles, and more. He is working on expanding the mediums and channels through which he tells his visual stories. Instagram: *@mrjuandalf*

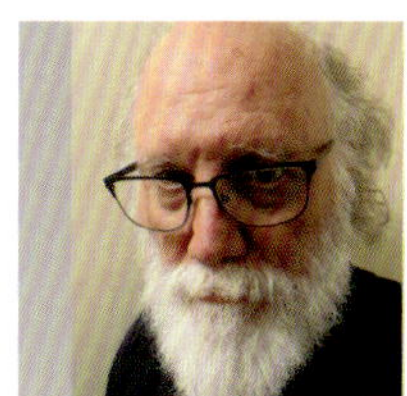

KERRY GAMMILL (page 24) grew up in Ft. Worth, Texas, and became hooked on monster movies at a young age. He began his professional art career at Marvel in 1978, then moved to DC as well before becoming a concept artist for films. He's created many magazine covers and is the co-author of *The Famous Monster Movie Art of Basil Gogos* from Vanguard Press. Instagram: *@kerrygammill*

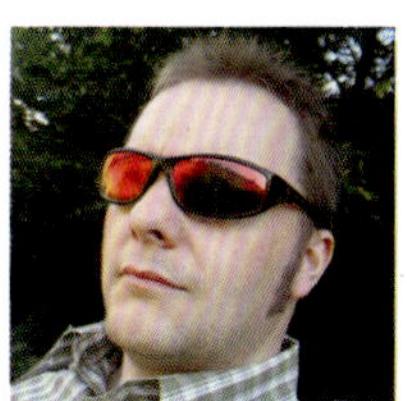

KEV CROSSLEY (page 135) worked as a video game environment and concept artist before becoming a freelance writer and illustrator producing material for graphic novels, gaming manuals, instructional art books, magazines, video games, and TV and film projects for clients such as Ian Livingstone, Ilex, Games Workshop, *Imagine FX*, Ubisoft, and SPIL Games. He illustrated *Find the Xenomorph* for Titan Books and Insight Editions' *Chucky: The Official Coloring Book*. He is producing concept work for various projects as well as color art for an ongoing graphic novel series for the rock group V2A. Website: *KevCrossley.com*

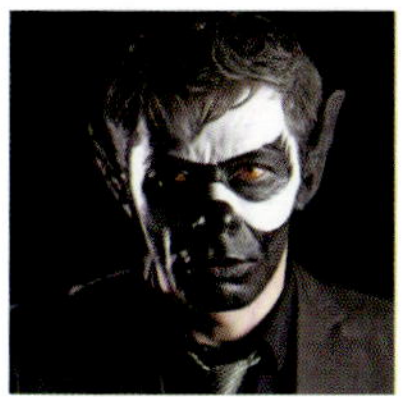

KRENT ABLE (pages 32, 155, 170, 178–183) is a comic artist and illustrator based in London. His books include *Krent Able's Big Book of Mischief* and *The Second Coming of Krent Able* for Knockabout, and *Kane & Able* for Image. He has also edited and contributed to the books *I Feel Machine* and *I Feel Love* for SelfMadeHero. Instagram: *@krentable*

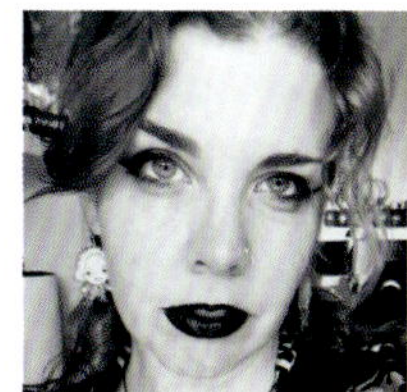

LACIE BARKER (pages 55, 159, 171) has been an illustrator, prop maker, model maker, set designer and dresser, figure painter, costume designer and maker, and scenic artist in her career. Her résumé includes work at Muppet Studios and the Disney Channel, and she resides in Southern California. Website: *TheDarkDoodler.com*

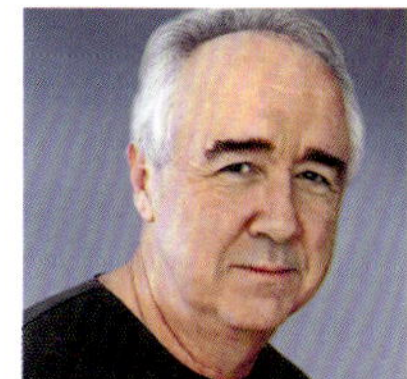

MARK MADDOX (pages 11, 27, 88, 92, 116, 138, 153) has been a professional artist since 1980 but started taking fantasy art seriously in 2007. His work has adorned magazine covers, Blu-ray, toy packaging, and collectibles—such as the *Dark Shadows* lunchbox he designed for MPI Entertainment. He is a multiple Rondo Award winner for Artist of the Year and resides in Florida. Website: *MaddoxPlanet.com*

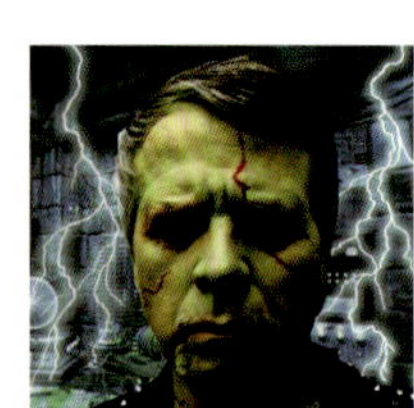

MIKE HOFFMAN (pages 9, 22, 129) is a prolific illustrator, having created thousands of artworks and comics pages, with over one hundred books in print. He's also focusing on teaching art and self-publishing while creating his ongoing bimonthly horror magazine, *Eyrie*. Website: *MikeHoffman.com*

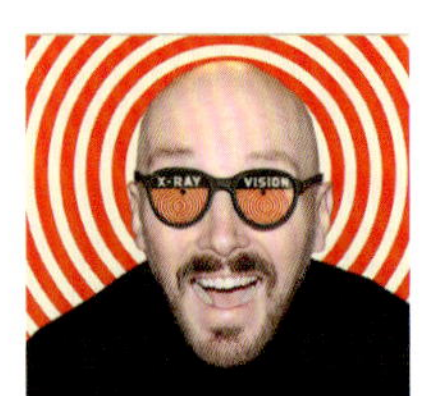

MITCH O'CONNELL (pages 18, 104–105, 161) is a beloved, cherished, and respected leader of the lowbrow art movement! His arty-farty paintings have been in sold-out gallery shows from New York to Berlin, from Tokyo to Miami, and from Hollywood to Mexico City. Catch up with the "World's Best Artist" at his website: *MitchOConnell.com*

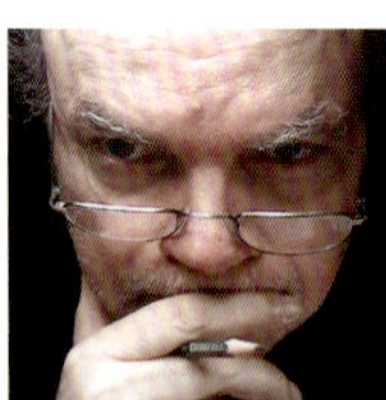

NEIL VOKES (pages 36, 39) began his art career in 1984 at Comico and NOW Comics on titles like *Robotech*, *Speed Racer*, and *Fright Night*. His other horror work includes *Wicked West*, *The Black Forest*, and *Flesh & Blood*, in collaboration with writer Robert Tinnell. He's also a Dracula aficionado extraordinaire. Facebook: *Facebook.com/nvokes*

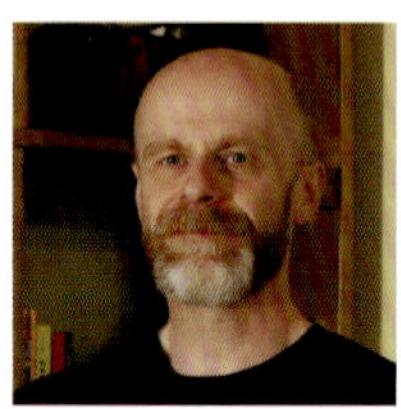

NICK PERCIVAL (pages 157–158, 168) is a multi-award-winning comic book creator best known for Clive Barker's *Hellraiser* comics and his work for director John Carpenter. Other work has covered film, video games, TV, and *2000 AD* for many years (*Judge Dredd*, *Judge Death*, and *Slaine*). He has painted covers for Marvel, BOOM Studios, *Fangoria* magazine, IDW Publishing (*Mars Attacks* and *The X-Files*), and Titan Comics (*Dark Souls*, *Warhammer*, *Bloodborne*, *Penny Dreadful*, *Assassin's Creed*, etc.) and created artwork for *World of Warcraft* and *Magic: The Gathering* card games. His graphic novel, *Legends: The Enchanted*, has been optioned for film. Instagram: *@nickpercivalart*

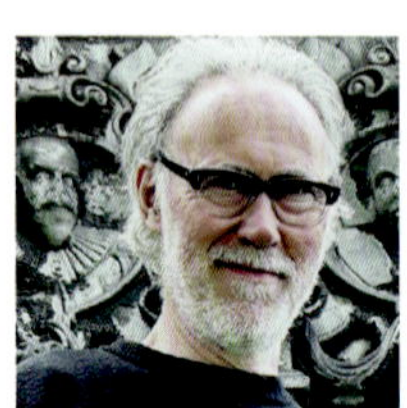

PAUL GARNER (pages 4, 42, 48, 77, 124–125, 139, 146) is a freelance artist based in Brighton, UK. For over thirty years, his cartoon, caricature, and illustration work has appeared in books, magazines, and projects as diverse as tattoo design, gig and theater posters, hot sauce labels, toy designs, T-shirts, CD cover art, sideshow banners, and murals. Website: *PaulGarnerArt.com*

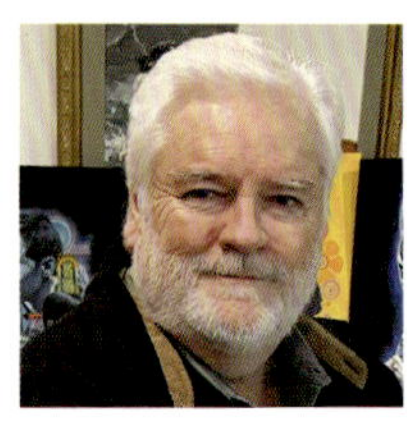

PAUL MANN (pages 72, 74, 114–115, 127, 144, 148, 150–151, 160, 165, 173, 176) is a seasoned illustrator in the Salt Lake City creative scene for over forty years. In 2015, Paul made a significant impact on the poster art scene when he transitioned his classical illustration skills into creating alternative movie posters, swiftly garnering attention and a dedicated following. Website: *PaulMannArtist.com*

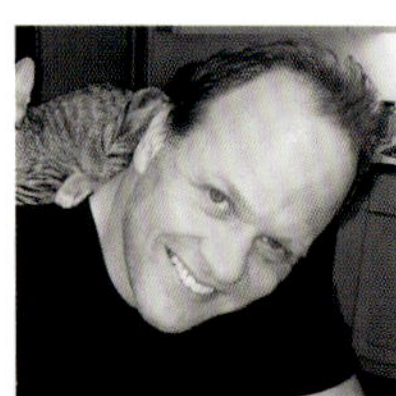

PETE BREGMAN (page 53) is a New York City artist, marketing creative director, animation director, digital-content creator, toy designer, illustrator, and graphic novelist. In addition to co-founding the Monster General Store, a horror-themed toy and novelty company, Pete has designed toys for Nacelle's Robo Force and Legends of Laughter lines. Website: *PeteBregman.com*

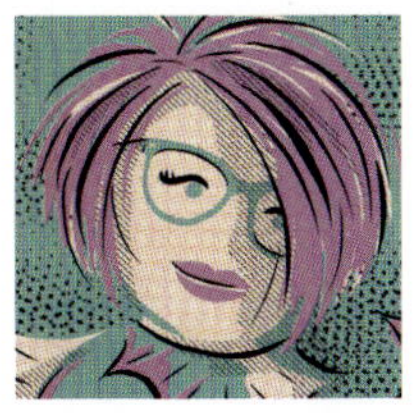

RIDGE ROOMS (page 123) has been a product-development designer for Barnes & Noble, PepsiCo, and her all-time favorite comic strip, *Peanuts*. Retiring from corporate life, Ridge moved to a small Ohio town and opened a nostalgia shop called the Mascot Syndicate to indulge her creative urges. She and the shop can be found online at *TheMascotSyndicate.com*

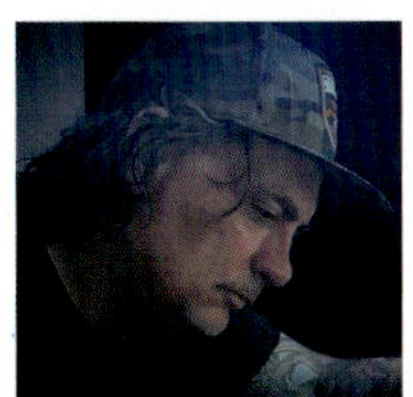

ROB BIRCHFIELD (pages 147, 155, 163) was captivated at a young age by the bright, colorful artwork of Basil Gogos. Proficient in traditional as well as digital art techniques, he's been inspired to follow in Gogos's footsteps, creating highly detailed monster illustrations professionally since 2001. Website: *HorrorMovieArt.com*

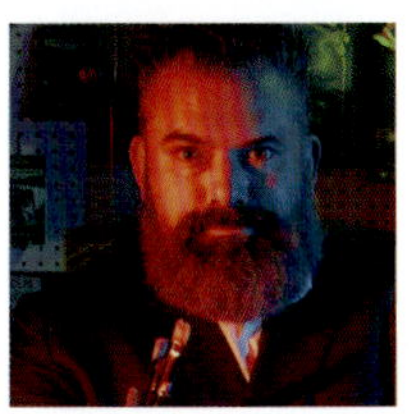

ROBERT LASKEY (pages 48, 59, 63, 65, 82, 132–133) is a freelance illustrator and painter located in Saint Paul, Minnesota. He specializes in fantasy and horror illustration in both traditional and digital media. Robert has spent the last eighteen years creating illustrations for games, books, posters, album covers, and more. Website: *RobertLaskey.com*

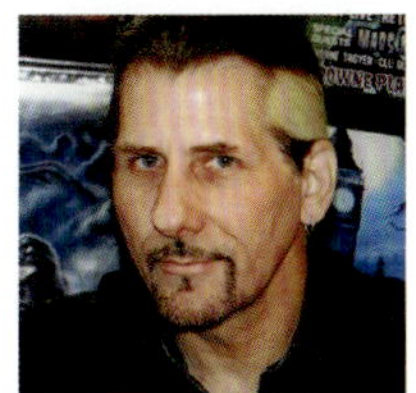

SCOTT JACKSON (page 29) is an illustrator with a penchant for the macabre and hard rock music. Jackson's work has been featured by rock bands Kiss, Pink Floyd, Megadeth, and many others. He is a five-time Rondo Award–winning cover artist for *Scary Monsters* and *Castle of Frankenstein* magazines. Website: *MonstermanGraphic.com*

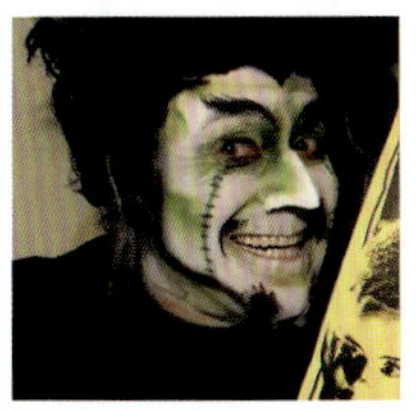

SHANE MORTON (page 26) is the mad scientist behind the Silver Scream FX LAB in Atlanta. In addition to his film and television work, he has designed and built horror attractions all over the country and has designed and fabricated interactive art installations from New York City to Hollywood. He's also the driving force for the Silver Scream Spook Show. Website: *SilverScreamFXLab.com*

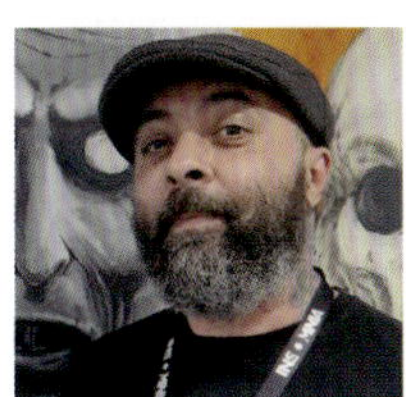

STEPHANE WILLEMY (page 123) is a French illustrator who mainly focuses on horror and sci-fi subjects. His prominent influences are vintage cinema, comic books, pulp magazines, pop surrealism, kaiju movies, and modern sources such as street art and tattoo, with a hint of musical taste from punk-rock to hip-hop. Instagram: *@stef_w_arts*

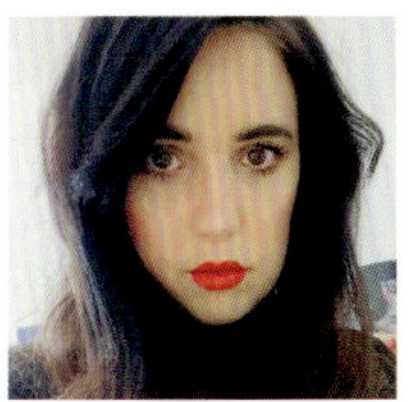

SUSANA "SUSPIRIA" VILCHEZ's (pages 10, 79, 108, 126, 129, 141, 147, 160, 169) work has been exhibited in New York, Los Angeles, Bilbao, Victoria, Barcelona, and Toronto in galleries like Hive, Clutter, Vincon, The Seventh Corner Gallery and at Midsummer Scream in Long Beach, California. She's created covers for *Penthouse Comics*, Boom! Studios, IDW, *Diabolik*, *Delirium* magazine, and many other clients. Website: *SuspiriaLand.com*

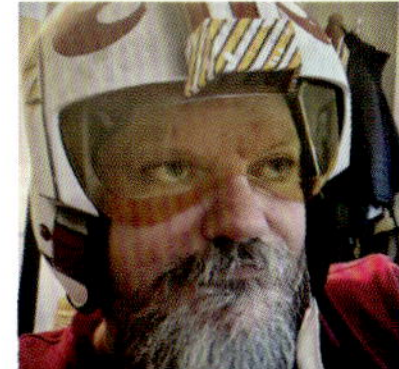

UNLOVELY FRANKENSTEIN aka Wallace McBride (pages 6, 8, 109, 111, 117), is a graphic designer living in Columbia, South Carolina. He's contributed work to *Fangoria*, Joe Bob Briggs, Dark Horse Comics, and the Sleepy Hollow International Film Festival and created numerous show posters for writer, producer, and stand-up comedian Dana Gould's YouTube series *Hanging with Doctor Z*. Website: *UnlovelyFrankenstein.com*

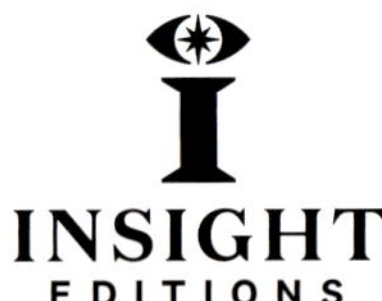

PO Box 3088
San Rafael, CA 94912
www.insighteditions.com

Find us on Facebook: www.facebook.com/InsightEditions
Follow us on Instagram: @insighteditions

All artwork, characters, and films are © and ™ their respective copyright and trademark holders.

Main text ©2026 Anthony Taylor

All rights reserved. Published by Insight Editions, San Rafael, California, in 2026.

No part of this book may be reproduced in any form without written permission from the publisher.

ISBN: 979-8-88663-736-6

Publisher: Raoul Goff
SVP, Group Publisher: Vanessa Lopez
VP, Creative: Chrissy Kwasnik
VP, Manufacturing: Alix Nicholaeff
Art Director: Matt Girard
Designer: John Barnett
Executive Editor: Tim Pilcher
Assistant Editor: Alecsander Zapata
Executive Managing Editor: Maria Spano
Senior Production Manager: Joshua Smith
Strategic Production Planner: Lina s Palma-Temena

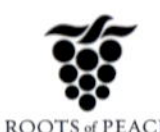

REPLANTED PAPER

Insight Editions, in association with Roots of Peace, will plant two trees for each tree used in the manufacturing of this book. Roots of Peace is an internationally renowned humanitarian organization dedicated to eradicating land mines worldwide and converting war-torn lands into productive farms and wildlife habitats. Roots of Peace will plant two million fruit and nut trees in Afghanistan and provide farmers there with the skills and support necessary for sustainable land use.

Manufactured in China by Insight Editions

10 9 8 7 6 5 4 3 2 1

ACKNOWLEDGMENTS

This book would not exist without the help, inspiration, and encouragement of many people. Most special thanks to Greg Anzalone, who always believes in my ability to tell a story and to part mists to reveal beauty and truth. Also to Kerry Deardorff and Suzanne Najbrt—your constant faith and support enable to me realize the best versions of how to share my passions for art, monsters, and community.

At Insight Editions, my thanks go to my editor, Tim Pilcher, as well as Vanessa Lopez, Raoul Goff, Alexis Colon-Philabaum, Alecsander Zapata, Audrey Salo, and Matt Girard. Many thanks to John Michlig for being my alpha reader and correcting my typos and mistakes.

Thanks to Bob and Marjorie Taylor for buying me monster toys and books when I was young, even if you didn't understand what I saw in them at the time.

This book was inspired by friends like David J. Skal, Bernie Wrightson, John Fasano, David Colton, Mark Maddox, Neil Vokes, Robert Tinnell, Dick Klemensen, Pauline Peart, Steve Smith, Sam Irvin, Richard J. Schellbach, Larry Blamire, Lou Byrne, Tim Lucas, Ted Haycraft, Jim Alexander, Bob Hagerty, Mike Ensley, Lucas Hardwick, Darryl Mayeski, Daniel Roebuck, Rick Stoner, Lou Byrne, Lee Staton, Rocko Jerome, Tami Hamalian, Tim Bradstreet, John-Paul Checkett, Jon Kitley, Joe Jusko, Matt Greenfield, Melinda Angstrom, Chris Herzog, Kal Dwight, Chris Alexander, Lee Stringer, Chris Mills, Sabrina Herman, Mary Forrest, Larry Young, and many, many more. I am wealthy in your influence, and would have no voice without the echoes of your voices.

To every artist who contributed works and words to this book, I salute and praise you—you are the vanguards and keepers of these characters, the look back to the past and the way forward. You inspire the next generation of creators.

Keep making beautiful pictures of ugly protagonists.

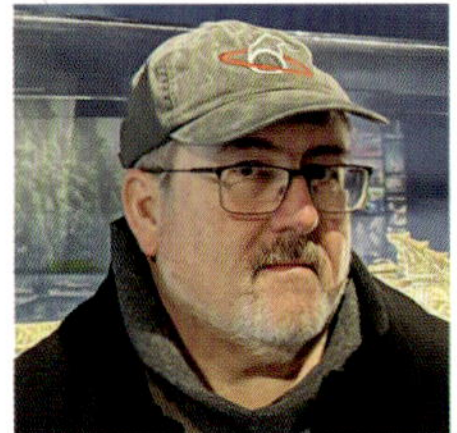

ANTHONY TAYLOR is the author of numerous books, including *The Art of George Wilson*—about the Gold Key and Dell Comics cover artist—and *Aurora Plastic Models Catalogs Volumes 1* and *2*, chronicling the company's history and reprinting their 1960–1977 catalogs. He also wrote *Arctic Adventure!*, an official *Thunderbirds* novel based on the British TV series, and *The Future Was F.A.B.: The Art of Mike Trim*, exploring the artist's career designing models and special effects for Gerry and Sylvia Anderson's TV series like *Captain Scarlet* and *UFO*. Anthony has written for *Retro Fan, Illustrators Quarterly, SFX, Fangoria, SCREEM, Cryptology, HorrorHound, Famous Monsters of Filmland, Filmfax, Video Watchdog, Amazing Figure Modeler*, and many other magazines. He was an editor for *Sci-Fi & Fantasy Models International*, and columnist for *ToyShop Magazine* for twelve years. Anthony is a Rondo Hatton Classic Horror Awards Hall of Fame recipient and a Horror Writers Association member. Website: *GoAnthonyTaylor.com*

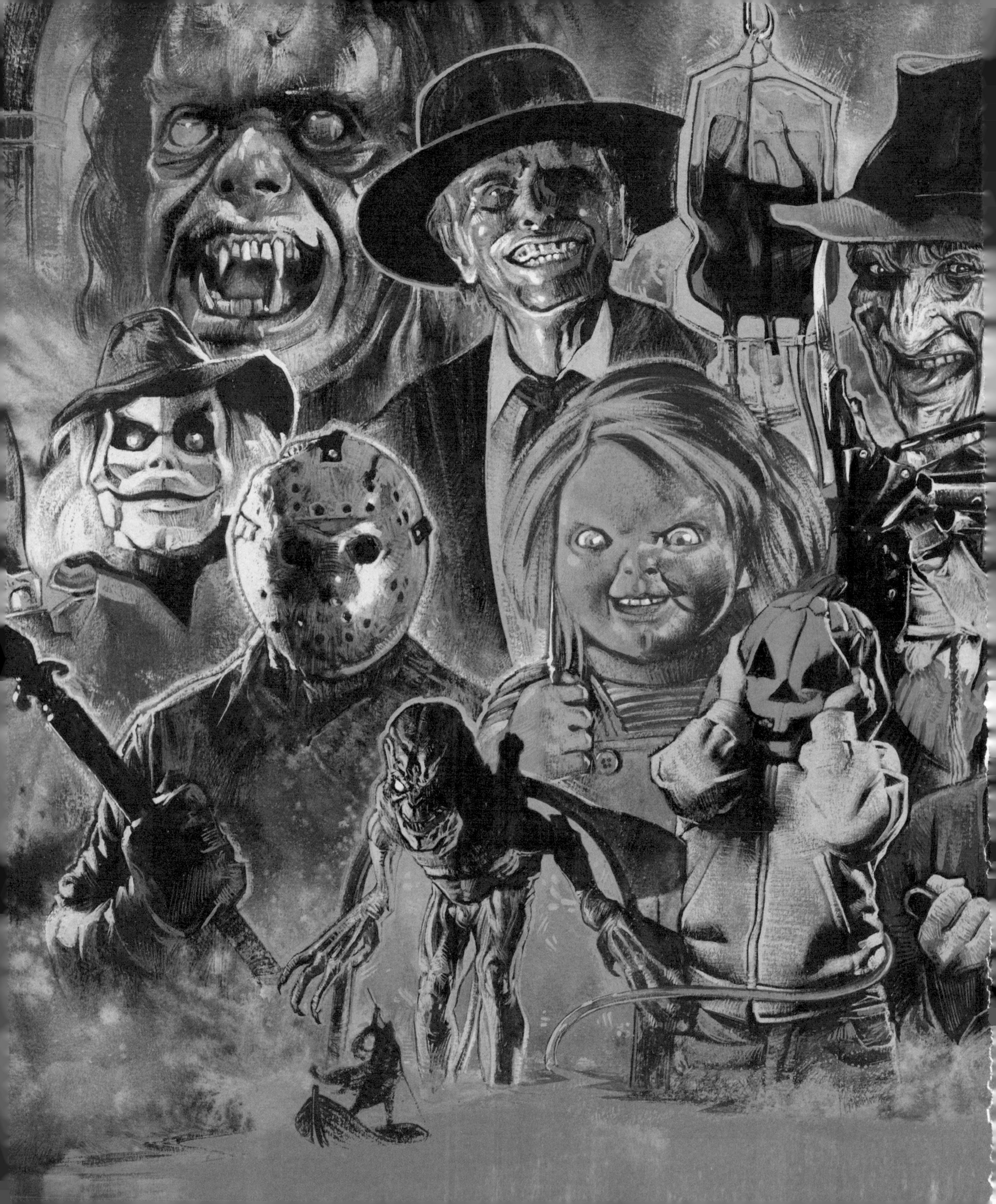